# THE STORY OF WESTERN ARCHITECTURE

Fourth Edition

Bill Risebero

Herbert Press

Copyright © 1979, 1997, 2001, 2011 Bill Risebero
Copyright under the Berne Convention

First published in Great Britain in 1979
by Herbert Press, an imprint of A&C Black Publishers Ltd

Bloomsbury Publishing Plc
50 Bedford Square,
London WC1B 3DP
www.acblack.com

First paperback edition 1985
Second edition 1997
Third edition 2001
Reprinted 2002
Fourth edition 2011

A CIP catalogue record for this book is available
from the British Library.

ISBN  978-1-408-12813-8

Cover design by Sutchinda Rangsi Thompson
Text design by Susan McIntyre

Typeset in 10.5 on 13pt Celeste

Printed and bound in China

# CONTENTS

*For Joshua, Lucas and Rosa*

# INTRODUCTION AND ACKNOWLEDGEMENTS
## Fourth Edition

*The Story of Western Architecture* was one of the first 18 titles David Herbert commissioned for his newly-formed Herbert Press. We discussed a basic history of architecture enabling readers to recognize periods and styles.

I was an architect and city planner, but not an art historian. I respect those with an art-history training, but do not try to emulate their scholarly approach. I am more at home with the practicalities of buildings: their social role, how they are commissioned, designed and constructed, how they are used, and by whom, and for whose benefit.

So we agreed that the book would set periods and styles within a wider view of architectural history. In 1979, this 'historical materialist' approach was not common in architectural criticism. Not all readers have wanted to step outside the world of grand designs and great designers, but to me and indeed to many others, to do so seemed to offer some insights.

The book now appears in many library lists and course bibliographies, has been translated numerous times and has been expanded and updated twice. But, like its author, it has begun to show its age. In 30 years the world has changed, and it is time the book did too. I have had the chance of re-visiting the existing text and of adding new material, including drawings, some of them from the book's various foreign-language editions. I am grateful to MIT Press and A&C Black for giving me the opportunity.

However, it remains the same book, and I am unrepentant about my historical materialist approach. Though even less fashionable now than it was in the Seventies, this still helps me make sense of what I see going on around me. Indeed, given the obscurantism of the postmodern world, it seems to me more necessary than ever.

'The prevailing ideas of any age', as Marx has said, 'have always been the ideas of the ruling class'. Conservative historians often say we study the past 'for its own sake'. That way they disconnect it from common life and make it their own property. Their history, while yet claiming to be neutral and apolitical, presents an elitist interpretation of the past. Architecture is treated as an individual rather than a social activity, and architectural 'history' – to echo Carlyle's famous view of history itself – becomes little more than a succession of monographs on great architects. Cultural and aesthetic analysis predominates, to the virtual exclusion of the social and economic aspects of this most social and economic of the arts. It deals essentially with the great monuments of architectural history, in which the story of the ruling classes alone may be read. Their kind of history is only about the past – and such a past is dead.

My view of history in general, and of architectural history in particular, starts with people and their needs, and how far these can be satisfied through the building process. An analysis which includes social and economic questions as well as aesthetic ones begins to show up the problems of class-society, and the way it treats buildings as saleable commodities rather than as needs. It also helps us see that history is dynamic and dialectical, always changing, always, as Hegel indicates, giving rise to conflict, resolution and further conflict, and always capable of being developed in a more progressive direction by those willing to grasp the opportunities it offers. My view of history is pluralist rather than elitist, concerned with our wider social and physical environment. And above all, it is concerned as much with the present and future as with the past. Our present condition tells us what is historically relevant. If history somehow seems remote and dead, perhaps we are asking it the wrong questions. And our understanding of the past can help us create the future. I would like to think that the building process can help us make a more equitable world.

In the end, though, it is the reader who decides which of these views to accept or reject, and who acts accordingly. I am grateful to all the people who have read my books over the years, including those who have misunderstood them, or understood them only too well. I have learned from them, as well as from my more supportive colleagues, students, reviewers, friends and family.

There are too many for me to mention them all, though I am particularly grateful to Jo Addison, Christine Atha, Mark Beedle, Jonathan Charley, Caroline Dakers, Michael Edwards, Nasser Golzari, Dougie Gordon, Patrick Hannay, Simon Hollington, Aaron McPeake, Malcolm Millais, Lesley Paine, David Pike, Norman Reuter, Michael Rustin, Jane Riches, Chris Seaber and Sam Webb. In previous editions I acknowledged how indebted I was to Ian Boutell, Colin Davis, Gillian Elinor, Brenda Herbert, Diana LeCore, Linda Lambert, Peter Lennard, Scott Melville, Matthew Risebero, Alan Seymour, Nicky Shearman, David Stevenson, Tim Sturgis, Annabel Taylor, Pamela Tudor-Craig and Keith Ward. I gratefully remember David Herbert as the 'onlie begetter' of the original book and for this new edition I am also indebted to my supportive and helpful editors, Linda Lambert and Alison Stace. My love and gratitude, as ever, go to my wife Christine.

# 1 THE URBAN REVOLUTION
## *From prehistory to the birth of Rome*

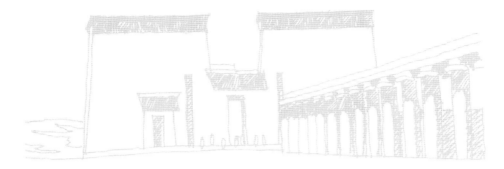

> As men journeyed to the east, they came upon a plain in the land of Shinar and settled
> there. They said to one another, 'Come, let us make bricks and bake them hard'; they used
> bricks for stone and bitumen for mortar.

Since earliest times, like the people of Nimrud described here in the Book of Genesis,
we have tried to adapt our surroundings to our needs, clearing forests, growing crops,
making weapons and tools. Building a shelter against sun, wind or rain is one of the
most fundamental of human needs, essential to our physical and social life. It is also an
act which goes beyond functional necessity: the response to climate and weather, the
finding and shaping of building materials, are a creative partnership with the natural
world, through which we develop our intellect and skills. This process is an act of self-
creation in which man, as Marx says,

> starts, regulates and controls the material reactions between himself and Nature ... by
> thus acting on the external world and changing it, he at the same time changes his own
> nature. He develops his slumbering powers and compels them to act in obedience to his
> sway.

The story told by this book begins in prehistory, a primitive, cruel and superstitious age,
when people's lives were at the mercy of the natural world around them. Yet terrible
and uncertain though life must have been, each advance in weaponry, or tool-making,
or building technique, was a way forward, an act of self-creation through learning to
control one's own environment.

The story stops in the age – for the time being – of capitalism. Ours is an age of
great achievements, both practical and intellectual, and to some it has brought great
wealth and self-fulfilment. Yet it has also brought warfare, famine, poverty and squalor
on a scale never before experienced. In the cities of the capitalist world one sees, in
the words of Marx and Engels, 'wonders far surpassing Egyptian pyramids, Roman
aqueducts, and Gothic cathedrals'. Yet there are also the violent, alienated streets,
the filthy shantytowns and the homelessness. Commodity production for profit, not
human need, now determines what is built and where, how buildings are designed, the

materials they are made of, and who will or will not have access to them. The mass of the people no longer control their own environment.

In one sense it is a story of progress. One building leads to another. Each succeeding generation uses the knowledge of the previous one. As society develops economically, building techniques reflect the fact. But it is also a story of regression. The primitive act of self-creation through building gradually becomes transformed into the sophisticated process of architecture, owned or totally dominated by ruling elites. The story of western architecture is also the story of the growth of class-society.

About seven million years ago, apes began to stand upright, and the first human species evolved. As one species succeeded another, brains and bodies got larger, and so did the ability to adapt the environment. Well over a million years ago, *Homo Erectus* became the first human to use fire, to subsist on hunting, to invent stone tools and, probably, to use language. This primitive Stone Age was inherited by Neanderthal Man who emerged around 600,000 years ago, and developed the ability to make clothing and to do complex carving. *Homo Sapiens* himself emerged in Africa perhaps 200,000 years ago, and by about 50,000 years ago was well-established. He was smaller and physically weaker but cleverer than his Neanderthal predecessor and eventually replaced him.

The first people survived a succession of Ice Ages, in small, unstable groups living on the edges of the habitable world. Their lives depended on hunting and gathering. Their spears, bows and arrows were made with flint or bone. With them, and with the help of dogs, domesticated for the purpose, they competed for game against predators like the sabre-tooth tiger. They sheltered in caves, or built huts of branches or mammoth bones, thatched with reeds or covered with skins, and here developed domestic skills, like weaving or the making of jewellery. Through their culture they came to terms with their surroundings. It included animistic fetishism, whereby the multifarious facets of the natural world were given otherworldly significance. Religious rites included ceremonial burial of the dead, which no doubt gave a sense of continuity in a hostile world. They also included cave painting, examples of which, some as old as 30,000 years, exist all over the world, from Africa to America and Asia to Australia. The famous Palaeolithic examples at Lascaux in France and Altamira in Spain depict bison and deer, emphasising the crucial, magical link between those who live by hunting and their quarry.

Around 8000BC, in possibly the most important environmental change in the history of the planet, the last Ice Age ended and the glaciers melted back. Sea levels rose, separating the continents; forests and grassland began to grow. Many game animals – the musk ox, the great deer, the woolly rhinoceros – were unable to survive the changes, and died out. In the new temperate areas agriculture began to develop, while hunting and nomadism as ways of life were pushed to the more hostile margins. As society became more settled, civilised skills were developed. Around 6000BC the wheel was invented, pottery appeared for the first time and, with copper now being used for weapons and tools, the Stone Age began to give way to the Bronze. The first permanent settlements appeared, as mud-brick villages, some very large, were built in Asia Minor. The Palestinian settlement of Jericho, in today's West Bank, may have existed as early as 8000BC. Certainly by 5000BC people in both Mesopotamia and Egypt were irrigating their fields, associating themselves with the land, its history and its future. In the late

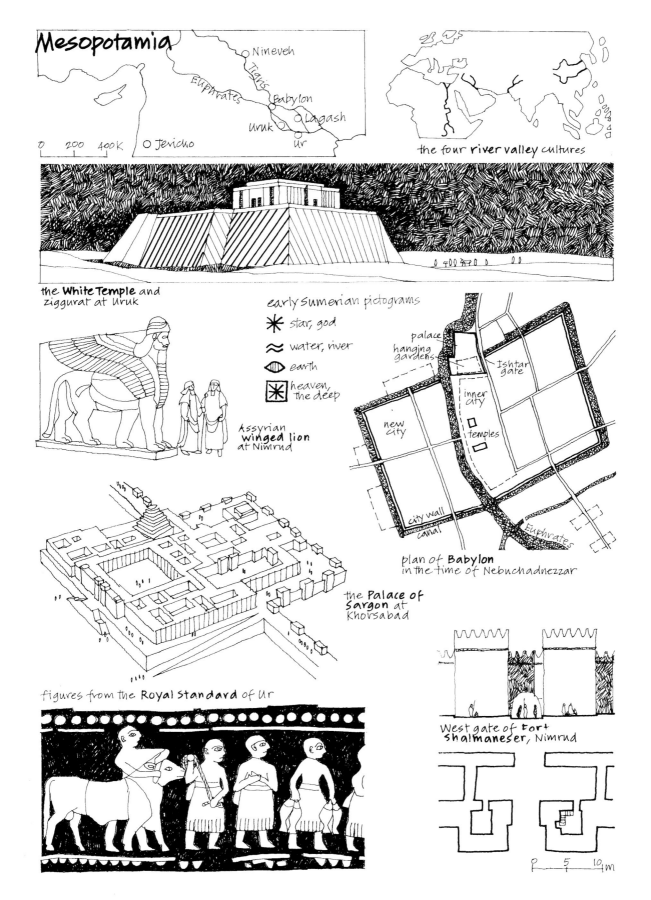

# Mesopotamia

Nineveh

Tigris
Euphrates

Babylon

Lagash
Uruk
Ur

O Jericho

0   200   400K

the four river valley cultures

the **White Temple** and
ziggurat at Uruk

**Assyrian
winged lion**
at Nimrud

early Sumerian pictograms

✳ star, god
≈ water, river
◉ earth
✳ heaven,
   the deep

palace
hanging
gardens

Ishtar
gate

inner
city

new
city

temples

city wall
canal

Euphrates

plan of **Babylon**
in the time of Nebuchadnezzar

the **Palace of
Sargon** at
Khorsabad

figures from the **Royal Standard** of Ur

West gate of **Fort
Shalmaneser**, Nimrud

0   5   10m

Stone Age, from about 4700BC, ritual constructions like the megalithic monuments were built. Often taking the form of dolmens, that is, giant standing stones with capstones placed across as lintels, they seem to have functioned as tombs or temples, a religious mediation between people and their surroundings. Examples exist all over the world, but famous European sites include Carnac in Brittany and Stonehenge in Wiltshire.

Perhaps the biggest social development of ancient times was the Urban Revolution. Around 3500BC, at different places in the world, cities began to appear. With populations of several thousand and covering as many as ten square kilometres, they were bigger than the villages which had existed hitherto. But size was not the main distinction; they were also qualitatively different. Village life was comparatively simple: it was tribal, based on the extended family unit, and most people pursued the same agricultural tasks. But a city had many social layers: a ruling family, its nobles and priests, poets and musicians, bureaucrats and warriors, the citizens, merchants and their families, the artisans, entertainers, workers and slaves. A city was an indication that a new type of social organisation was both possible and necessary. It was possible because agriculture was now developed enough to support such a large group of unproductive consumers. It was necessary because the cohesion of this larger, more productive agricultural community now depended on its being controlled and defended through a political system based on a ruling class.

Ruling classes had emerged over the generations as tribes had begun to come together. The convocations of tribal elders had begun to owe more allegiance to each other than to the tribes they came from, and had established themselves as a permanent elite. Wealth depended on the ownership of land and the disposal of labour. The more land and labour that could be annexed, the greater the wealth. For the ruling class, therefore, problems of control and defence were central. Around 4000BC, the development of writing allowed the emergence of taxation, and of the bureaucracy to administer it. Armies provided both internal security and defence from outside attack. The priesthood and the whole cultural apparatus helped create the hegemony through which the rulers maintained their pre-eminence.

Four great empires emerged, with cities at their heart, two in Asia and two in Asia Minor, all based on fertile river valleys. One was in China, between the Hwang-Ho and Yangtze-Kiang rivers, one in India on the banks of the Indus, and one in Egypt in the Nile valley, which the annual inundation, bringing alluvial mud from the south, made particularly fertile. And the Sumerian civilisation emerged in Mesopotamia – present-day Iraq – in the fertile crescent between the Tigris and the Euphrates, where Ur, Uruk and Lagash, possibly the earliest of all cities, were founded.

The cities were cultural innovators. Animistic religions gave great significance to the natural world: to birth and death, to time and the seasons, to the sun, the moon and the life-giving river. Belief in an afterlife stimulated the art of embalming and helped create a knowledge of anatomy which could also benefit the living; belief in a pleasurable present brought the use of drugs and cosmetics.

In parallel with this, natural science gradually developed, especially in astronomy, mathematics and geometry; the sixty-minute hour, the 365-day year, the 360-degree circle all began in the ancient world. Writing seems to have begun in Sumer, the so-called cuneiform script, made with wedge-shaped sticks on clay tablets. First it took the form of pictographic symbols, representing finite things, a useful tool for clerks to produce inventories of goods or lists of regiments. But as it developed, it became more logographic and was able to represent the sounds of spoken language. This allowed the expression of abstract ideas, and its early administrative role to develop into a cultural one. The written stories which comprise the *Epic of Gilgamesh*, the adventures of a human hero, began to emerge from Sumer from about 3000BC.

For builders in Asia Minor, timber was available, though not abundant. It is likely that palm trunks, and even bundles of reeds tied tightly together, were used for columns or beams. But the most common building material was the mud-brick, dried in the sun – given the shortage of combustible material – rather than fired in a kiln. Mud is a short-lived material, prone to erosion by sun and wind, which in more important buildings might be protected by a skin of fired clay tiles or simply a coat of plaster or limewash – the Egyptian capital city was known as 'Memphis of the white walls'. It is likely that many smaller buildings were roofed in arched vaulting, a system arising naturally from the properties of brick itself and stimulated by the comparative lack of timber for roof-beams. They were mostly single-storey, though as many as four storeys were possible. Of most ancient brick-built buildings we have archaeological evidence only. Most important buildings were built of stone, and it is these which have survived.

The best-known Sumerian building type was the ziggurat, occupying a prominent place in each city and consisting of an artificial mound, often rising in huge steps, surmounted by a temple. The mound was no doubt to elevate the temple to a commanding position in what was otherwise a flat river valley. The great city of Uruk had a number of religious precincts, containing many temples larger and more ambitious than any buildings previously known. In the Pillar Temple free-standing masonry columns were used for the first time, built in brick and decorated in cone-shaped mosaics to resemble the trunks of palm trees. One of the best-preserved examples, dating from before 3000BC, is the so-called White Temple, built of stone, sun-dried brick and fired clay tiles for textural richness, and limewashed for extra protection.

## KINGDOM OF THE NILE

In Egypt, the Pharaonic system was established around 3200BC when Menes, the first named person in history, united upper and lower Egypt, as far south as present-day Aswan, into a single kingdom, locating his capital at Memphis on the Nile Delta. The word 'Pharaoh' means 'great household', and emphasises the enduring link between the ruler, his or her supporters, and the physical location of their rule. Political stability was sought by raising the Pharaoh to the status of a god and organizing society around this fact. From Menes' time to around 2400BC, an unbroken line of royal dynasties constituted the first main phase of Egyptian civilization, known as the Old Kingdom. Politics, culture and religion in general, and burial practices in particular, sought to express the inevitable, incontrovertible continuity of royal power. Pharaonic architecture made a major contribution to this task of persuasion. The brick cities and palaces have all but disappeared, but the stone-built temples, and of course the burial chambers, have remained.

The seat of government remained at Memphis for many centuries, and the earliest tombs were built near there. In Menes' time the typical royal tomb was the mastaba, a long, rectilinear barrow built in brick or stone and containing a number of chambers for the deceased and the possessions he or she would need in the afterlife. Menes himself may have been buried in a simple mastaba at the royal necropolis at Sakkara. After unification and the growth of Egypt's wealth, bigger and higher tombs began to be built, till they eventually took on a pyramidal form and an epic scale. The stepped pyramid of King Zoser at Sakkara (c.2800BC) was the world's first large stone building. Some 60 metres in height, it was organized by Zoser's chief minister Imhotep, who therefore qualifies as the world's first known architect. The burial chamber was underground, beneath the mountain of stone; it was already necessary to try to protect the dead Pharaoh's valuable possessions from tomb-robbers. The pyramid of King Huni at Meidum (c.2700BC) and the 'bent' pyramid of King Seneferu at Dashur (c.2600BC) were even larger, with respective heights of 90 and 102 metres.

Most impressive of all was the group at Gizeh, near present-day Cairo, built around 2500BC and consisting of the colossal figure of a Sphinx and three pyramids, two of which are among the largest buildings ever built. The pyramid of Menkauré was comparatively small, but the Great Pyramid of Khufu (Cheops) was originally 146 metres in height, larger than St Peter's basilica in Rome, while that of Khafra (Chephren) was only slightly smaller. The burial chamber in Khufu's pyramid was at the exact centre, some 70 metres above the ground, a square, solemn room lined in granite, housing the granite sarcophagus.

Apart from the size, a remarkable thing about these buildings is the precision of their construction. They were aligned almost exactly on the cardinal points of the compass, and the base from which they rose was absolutely level. The stone blocks were remarkably accurate, especially so considering that they must have been quarried with copper chisels. The stonework joints were minutely narrow, and contained mortar only as a lubricant to aid the positioning of the blocks. Originally the pyramids were faced all over with smooth limestone, most of which has been removed over the ages and incorporated into other buildings.

If the craftsmanship of the pyramids is remarkable, even more so is the feat of organisation which created them. There was only the simplest of machinery – the lever, the roller and the inclined plane – but there was of course plenty of manpower, which could be pressed into service by an authoritarian regime – though the popular picture of a wretched slave-labour force is not the real truth. The stonemasons were skilled craftsmen, and the labourers were gangs of peasants released from the fields during the inundation. Perhaps as many as 100,000 men worked during the construction period of the biggest pyramids, organised into gangs of a hundred. From the evidence, the gangs were energetic and competitive, giving themselves team names like 'Lovely Khufu' and 'Tipsy Menkauré'.

Authoritarian regimes are, of course, always vulnerable to greater force from outside or decay within. The Sumerian regime in Mesopotamia fell to the Akkadians around 2800BC; a sequence of usurping rulers ended around 2300BC when Sargon the Great re-established an empire whose boundaries extended far beyond the two river valleys. This period saw the construction of Urnammu's ziggurat complex at Ur, and the royal palace at Mari. The latter also included a writing school for administrators and a royal archive, the discovery of which has provided much of our historical knowledge of

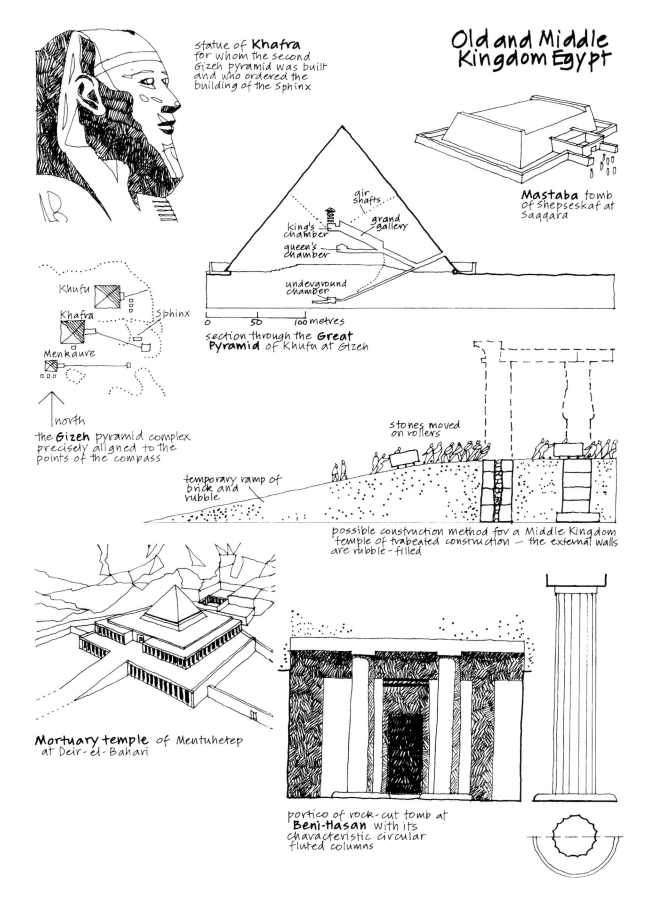

statue of **Khafra** for whom the second Gizeh pyramid was built and who ordered the building of the Sphinx

# Old and Middle Kingdom Egypt

**Mastaba** tomb of Shepseskaf at Saqqara

air shafts

king's chamber

grand gallery

queen's chamber

underground chamber

0    50    100 metres

section through the **Great Pyramid** of Khufu at Gizeh

Khufu

Khafra

Sphinx

Menkaure

north

the **Gizeh** pyramid complex precisely aligned to the points of the compass

stones moved on rollers

temporary ramp of brick and rubble

possible construction method for a Middle Kingdom temple of trabeated construction — the external walls are rubble-filled

**Mortuary temple** of Mentuhetep at Deir-el-Bahari

portico of rock-cut tomb at **Beni-Hasan** with its characteristic circular fluted columns

the region. Wall paintings in the palace establish a link with another emergent urban civilization, that of the Mediterranean island of Crete, which was beginning to form a cultural bridge between the developed Asia Minor and the more primitive Europe.

Egypt too was de-stabilised around 2400BC by a series of invasions from Syria. The Old Kingdom collapsed, and for some three hundred years there was a period of civil warfare which left no lasting monuments. Gradually however, a succession of strong rulers, like Mentuhetep III, began once more to unite the kingdom through conquest. Another period of peace and prosperity, which we now call the Middle Kingdom, began around 2100BC and lasted for three hundred years. A canal was built between the Red Sea and the Mediterranean, stimulating Egypt's overseas trade. The boundaries of Egypt were extended southwards again, this time as far as Nubia, and the seat of government was established nearer the geographical centre, at Thebes on the west bank, across the river from present-day Luxor. It was during the Theban period that the royal necropolis was established at Deir-el-Bahari, just to the south of the city. Its key building was the mortuary temple of Mentuhetep himself, which provided a background to the Pharaoh's funeral rites. It took the extraordinary form of a colonnaded ziggurat surmounted by a pyramid.

For grand buildings Egyptian architects had begun to develop a more sophisticated version of dolmen construction. Known now as 'trabeated' construction, it consisted of flat lintels or beams supported on columns, usually circular in section. Humbler buildings might be more adventurous structurally, making use of the arches and vaults which were possible in brick. The art of using stone for vaulting was not yet developed and indeed unnecessary so long as large blocks of stone were available for beams and the labour available to move them. The weight of the stone blocks in relation to their strength did, however, place a limit on the spans that were possible and large, roofed-over spaces had to have a forest of columns within them. This period saw the construction of another type of tomb; the aristocrats' graves at Beni-Hasan were cut, complete with entrance colonnades, from solid rock. Their columns were circular in section, slightly fluted, and had flat capitals and bases – a form which was to recur many times in western architecture.

Between about 2000 and 1800BC, the whole region was once again in political turmoil. In Mesopotamia the city of Babylon exerted its growing strength. Amid a general conflict, the palace of Mari was destroyed by Hammurabi in about 1757BC. Under him Babylonian power was firmly established and enforced through a strict code of laws, though it was undermined after his death as in turn the Kassites took control of the region. It was probably during this period that the mythical patriarch Abraham moved with his family and followers southwards from his birthplace in Ur, to settle among the Canaanites and the ancient Phoenician trading nation, who occupied the eastern Mediterranean seaboard to the Jordan and beyond. Those who thus 'crossed the river' were known to the Egyptians as 'Hebrews'.

In Egypt too, order was once again breaking down. Armies of Asiatic invaders mounted on horses and using chariots, till then unknown in Asia Minor, swept in and established the rule of the Hyksos, or shepherd kings, for some two hundred years. The construction of great buildings once again came temporarily to a halt.

During this confusion the biggest cultural contribution was that of Crete, then reaching

# the New Empire

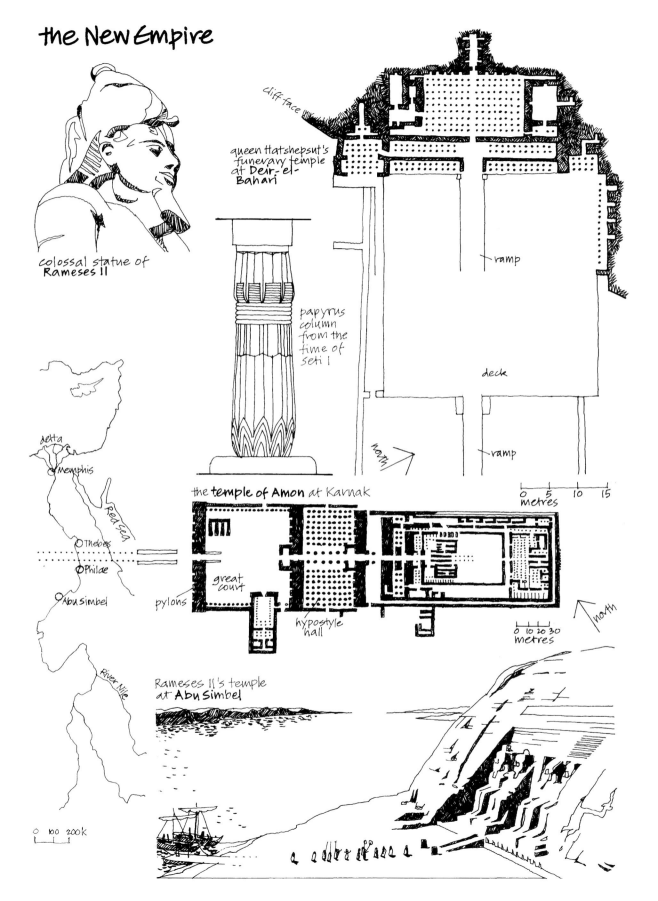

colossal statue of **Rameses II**

queen Hatshepsut's funerary temple at **Deir-el-Bahari**

cliff face

ramp

deck

ramp

papyrus column from the time of **Seti I**

0  5  10  15
metres

the **temple of Amon** at Karnak

pylons

great court

hypostyle hall

0 10 20 30
metres

north

delta

Memphis

Red Sea

Thebes

Philae

Abu Simbel

River Nile

0  100  200k

**Rameses II's temple** at **Abu Simbel**

its political peak. The Aegean area owed much of its early development to its unique land formation, very different from the river valleys. Geologically the Greek mainland consisted of a plate, folded into alps and tipped to the south-east. It provided numerous parallel hills and valleys which emerged into the Aegean as inlets, harbours and islands. In the various valleys and islands separate communities led their independent lives. The Aegean gave them a common interest, developing their seafaring skills and providing a means of communication, trade and cultural exchange. This richness of experience created a livelier, more adaptable way of life than the river valley cultures. The Aegean community was able to inherit the Egyptian experience and develop it further.

Crete's wealth was based on the mining and working of metals, in which it was rich, and on skilful crafting of jewellery and pottery. Under the Minoan dynasty of kings Crete traded with Egypt and Syria, and its political power extended to the Aegean islands and parts of the Greek mainland. Egyptian building forms, particularly the column-and-beam construction of the Middle Kingdom, spread into Greece through Crete. Major Cretan cites grew up at Phaestos and Knossos, the latter incorporating the huge, labyrinthine palace of king Minos, source of the Minotaur legend.

## BELIEF IN ONE GOD

Around 1580BC, the Hyksos were expelled from Egypt and the final and most important phase of ancient Egyptian power, the New Empire, began. This was the period in which the Bronze Age began to give way to the Iron, conferring huge advantages on those who, like Egypt, were able to develop the new weapons and tools. It was the period of the greatest Pharaohs: Tutmose I in the 16th century BC, his daughter Hatshepsut, and Tutmose III in the 15th, and Seti I and Rameses II in the 13th. It was a period of greater interaction with the surrounding peoples and of greater intellectual searching. Religion was moving towards the monotheistic, and Amon-Ra, the sun god, took a predominant place in the pantheon. In the 15th century BC, the Pharaoh Akhenaten moved completely away from polytheism to the worship of the one god Aten, shifting the capital in the process from Thebes to his new city of Amarna.

There are strong parallels between Akhenaten's monotheism and the developing religion of the Egyptian Hebrews. His 'Hymn to the Sun', for example, has often been compared, in style and content, with Psalm 104. Egypt had a variety of religious communities, and it is possible that the one established by Abraham's grandson Jacob, who had moved south from Canaan, was part of a cultural crossover. This small Hebrew group would play a key part in the future development of three great religions.

Akhenaten's experiment, by contrast, was short-lived. Both Thebes and Amon-worship were restored on his death, continuing to have a profound effect on Pharaonic architecture. The archetypal Egyptian temple emerged during this period. This was a long sequence of external and internal spaces, aligned symmetrically about a straight processional route. First might come an avenue of sculptured rams or sphinxes leading to two huge 'pylons', truncated pyramids of stone flanking the main entrance. The first courtyard, surrounded by high walls, would be open to the sky. There might follow a second courtyard surrounded by a roofed colonnade, and then a 'hypostyle' hall, its roof supported on a forest of giant columns and lit through small clerestory windows.

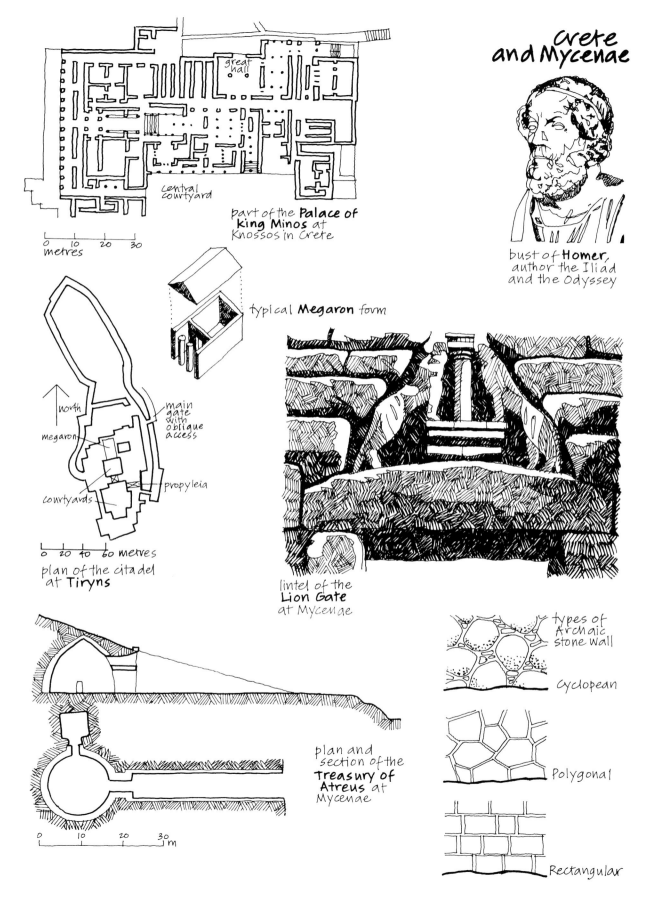

# Crete and Mycenae

part of the **Palace of king Minos** at Knossos in Crete

great hall

central courtyard

0  10  20  30
metres

bust of **Homer**, author the Iliad and the Odyssey

typical **Megaron** form

north

megaron

main gate with oblique access

propyleia

courtyards

0  20  40  60 metres

plan of the citadel at **Tiryns**

lintel of the **Lion Gate** at Mycenae

plan and section of the **Treasury of Atreus** at Mycenae

0  10  20  30 m

types of Archaic Stone Wall

Cyclopean

Polygonal

Rectangular

A succession of chambers would get progressively darker and more mysterious till the holy of holies was reached at the end.

A temple was not a place of collective worship but a meeting place between the god and the Pharaoh, his or her representative on earth. The sequence of spaces, moving from open sunlight to darkness and mystery, housed the ceremony by which this relationship was expressed. The buildings were full of natural symbolism; the pylons were mountains, the roof of the hypostyle hall was the sky; the columns were carved as palms or papyrus plants, and the orientation was such that the sun's rays struck between the pylons, or into certain chambers, at significant times or seasons. Sculptures or reliefs depicted the gods, or Pharaohs in the form of gods: Amon-Ra himself, Horus and Hathor, god and goddess of the sky, Osiris and Isis, god and goddess of fertility, Anubis, the jackal-headed god of death.

The mortuary temple of queen Hatshepsut at Deir-el-Bahari on the west bank near Thebes (c.1520BC) was a magnificent tiered and ramped structure built into the rocky hillside. Its design was based on that of Mentuhetep some 500 years earlier, and incorporated the circular columns with flat capitals typical of the Middle Kingdom. The nearby Ramesseum was the mortuary temple of Rameses II (c.1300BC); it had huge pylons and columns, some of the latter in the form of the god Osiris. Largest of all was the complex of temples on the east bank. The Luxor temple was built over a hundred-year period from about 1400BC. It followed the typical pattern but was grander in scale, with a huge entrance courtyard added in the time of Rameses II. A processional avenue led from there to the temple of Amon at nearby Karnak.

This gigantic building stood in a heavily-walled enclosure 360 by 110 metres in extent. The hypostyle hall contained 134 columns in sixteen rows and was some 24 metres in height, a space of overpowering grandeur. Karnak was begun around 1530BC and, though the main work was done in the time of Seti I and Rameses II, it was added to over a period of 1000 years. The extensive grounds enclosed other smaller temples, a sacred lake, dwellings for the priests and their servants, and a military garrison. The soldiers were needed to guard the priesthood's huge stockpile of treasure, which gradually grew to rival that of the Pharaoh and even to threaten his political ascendancy.

After Rameses II the Pharaonic system, and with it Egypt's political power, did begin a slow decline. Ancient societies were politically rigid, and very slow to innovate. Almost by definition, wealth could not be used to improve society; it fell into the hands of the already wealthy, where it was consumed or displayed or hidden away. At some point this unproductive accumulation reached its limit. It is an irony therefore that great architectural achievements, which seem to proclaim the enduring power of those who create them, often signify the beginning of the end.

The buildings most closely associated today with Rameses II are those which marked the southern extent of his huge kingdom: the two temples of Abu Simbel (c.1300BC) cut into the cliff-face on the banks of the Nile in Nubia. The entrance front of the smaller temple, dedicated to Rameses' wife Nefertari and to the goddess Hathor, incorporated four colossal statues of the queen in the guise of the goddess. The larger had four seated colossi of the deified Rameses himself, each 20 metres in height. A main hall, supported by Osiris columns, led to a sanctuary some 60 metres inside the rock, where three carved deities were illuminated at certain times when the rising sun shone the entire length of the temple. A fourth, representing Ptah, god of the underworld, remained in permanent darkness.

The gradual decline of Egyptian power encouraged population movement out of the area. One such was that of a Hebrew group led, according to the story, by the patriarch Moses. Whether this was in the nature of an escape from slavery, as the Book of Exodus has it, or simply an economic migration, is not clear. Canaan was productive, and attractive to migrants; it had a developed economy, based on its trading cities of Tyre, Sidon and Jerusalem. At first, the Hebrews spent many semi-nomadic years on its desert fringes. Survival here depended on living in harmony with the land. Strict laws, later laid down in the Book of Leviticus, were devised to codify what should be eaten, how animals should be husbanded, and how the land should be maintained in a sustainable way.

Around 1400BC the Minoan kingdom of Crete – why is unclear – came abruptly to an end, and the palace at Knossos was destroyed. But by this time the centre of gravity of Aegean culture was moving to the Cycladic islands and the Peloponnese on the Greek mainland. At Tiryns and Mycenae tribal communities were growing up. It was their war with Troy which later formed the basis of Homer's epic *Iliad* legend. Their architecture was warlike too; their citadels were heavily fortified – more so than the island cities, which relied on their navies – with walls seven metres or more in thickness. The main entrance to Mycenae was through the famous Lion Gate (*c.*1250BC), a narrow opening spanned by an immense stone lintel and surmounted by a pair of carved stone lions. The walls themselves were constructed in huge, random stone blocks now known, in another Homeric reference, as Cyclopean. The Treasury of Atreus in Mycenae (*c.*1325BC) – sometimes called the tomb of Agamemnon – was a beehive-shaped underground chamber some 13 metres high, entered through a dromos, a corridor cut into the hillside and open to the sky. Aegean architecture was less sophisticated than that of Egypt, but in its way equally powerful. Moreover, the primitive stone dome of the Treasury of Atreus was more inventive than the trabeated stone construction of contemporary Egypt.

As Egypt's power began to decline, that of Assyria grew. The Assyrians were the most warlike people in the ancient world. They invented battering rams and siege engines for which sun-dried brick city walls were no match. Within some four hundred years their empire would stretch from the Persian Gulf to the Mediterranean, north almost to the Black Sea and south into Egypt. As in all military regimes, their power depended on good control; a road network and a postal system enabled an army of provincial governors and officers to do their work. Cities like Ashur developed, and later Nimrud, Khorsabad and Nineveh, and were enhanced by temples, palaces and administrative buildings. Ashur was the cultural and religious centre of the Assyrian state; its ziggurat temple (*c.*1250BC) was dedicated to the national god after whom the city was named.

By about 1200BC the economic effects of the Trojan Wars had seriously weakened Mycenae. Northern tribes – mainly Dorians and Ionians – had begun to infiltrate the Greek mainland, and their Iron Age technology proved decisive. The Dorians occupied northern Greece and the Peloponnese; the Ionians Attica, the Aegean islands and the Aegean coast of Anatolia – present-day Turkey. The invaders' main building form, the megaron, was a translation into local materials of timber techniques brought from the northern forests. The megaron was equally suited to house or temple, and consisted of a rectangular pitched-roofed building with a simple, colonnaded porch. It was the antecedent of the classical Greek temple which was to play such a fundamental part in the story of western architecture.

Meanwhile, the Hebrews' strength was growing – enough for them to confront the Canaanites in battle and to succeed in taking over Jerusalem and carving a state of Israel out of Canaan. For some 400 years there followed a golden age, under a succession of strong kings, notably Saul, David and Solomon. During the 10th century BC a truly symbolic act, for a previously nomadic people, was the establishment of Solomon's Temple in Jerusalem, a final resting-place for the travelling Ark of the Covenant. There is little archaeological evidence for this building on the present-day Temple Mount, but the biblical account makes it rich with gold, copper and exotic woods, and describes a form, with its succession of courtyards and chambers, like that of an Egyptian temple.

As Assyria's empire got bigger one great city after another was established. In about 880BC Ashurnasirpal II rebuilt the citadel of Nimrud, making it his capital, and built a huge palace, its numerous buildings set around courtyards, which established the form of Assyrian palaces for years to come. His successor Shalmaneser III built a fort outside Nimrud in 859BC, to which the capital was transferred, and where it remained till about 720BC when Sargon II built the new city of Khorsabad. This covered over 3 square kilometres and was surrounded by a huge wall with numerous towers and gateways. One corner of the site was taken up by a complex of public buildings dominated by Sargon's own palace, itself covering some 10 hectares. Chambers and courtyards alike were decorated with brilliantly-coloured glazed bricks and carved with winged bulls and lions. Finally, early in the 7th century BC, the heavily fortified city of Nineveh was founded by Sargon's son Sennacherib, and in turn became the capital. By 670BC Assyrian power extended through Asia Minor and deep into the weakened Egypt.

But the empire was by now under threat from the warlike Chaldeans from the north. In 612BC Nineveh fell to the invaders, never to rise again. Nebuchadnezzar of Chaldea rebuilt the old city of Babylon, destroyed by Sennacherib, as his capital, and established his power over the whole region, including Israel and Canaan. In 586BC Solomon's Temple was destroyed. This was the time of the so-called Babylonian captivity, a period as penitential to the Israelites as it was splendid to the Babylonians. Babylon itself was given two concentric lines of fortification. The kilometre-square inner city sat on the banks of the Euphrates. It housed the main buildings, a broad processional way and numerous towers, including that of the Ishtar Gate and the spiral 'Tower of Babel' ziggurat. Dominating the whole place was the royal palace whose riverside 'hanging gardens' were among the wonders of the ancient world.

Meanwhile the western Mediterranean was beginning to develop the political and cultural identity which was to play such an important part in the subsequent history of the West. The economy was still mainly agricultural but seaborne trade was helping to establish a number of coastal cities. From the eighth century the small Etruscan nation began to exercise its economic and political power over the neighbouring Latins, and to develop a number of practical urban skills, including the use of stone arches, not only in buildings but also in the construction of drains and sewers.

## THE RISE OF THE POLIS

Greece was developing too. Its fragmented geography and the rich mix of tribal origins ensured that its cities – Athens, Corinth and the rest – grew up politically and culturally separate. The social unit formed by the autonomous city, its agricultural hinterland and its trading links, became known as the *polis*, a term usually translated into English as 'city-state'. The synonymity between city and state distinguished Greece from the huge river valley empires. Large and productive enough to become a political force, yet small and focussed enough to allow all its citizens a measure of political control, the polis was a framework for the development of Greece's two most important political legacies: the democratic system and Platonic thought.

These developments were the result of a change of socio-economic structure. Agriculture and trade had created a new wealthy class. From the 8th century onwards the tribal system, with its petty kings, began to give way to oligarchies of aristocrats and merchants – power based on wealth rather than on birth. The best-known example was the city of Sparta in Laconia, which had been important in Minoan times but which developed its particular character after the Dorian invasion. An inland city, its trade opportunities were limited and it became a self-contained agricultural community held together by strict military discipline. Its rigid social structure had three main tiers: the Spartiate aristocracy, descendants of the Dorians themselves, the indigenous Periceci who were landlords and tradesmen, and the Helots, also indigenous, who as serfs formed the largest class. At the bottom of every ancient society were the slaves, who had no rights at all.

All over Greece, a more stable society and the growth of the city led to the creation of more permanent buildings in stone. The builders could draw on a number of existing sources: the imported timber forms of the north, memories of Tiryns and Mycenae, and the still-living traditions of Egypt. The early masons crudely translated timber building forms into stone, but later, forms were developed which arose more naturally from the special properties of stone itself, typically in the archetypal Greek building, the temple. Temple plans gradually developed from the squarish megaron type into something more refined. They generally had two rooms placed end to end: a naos, or religious chamber, and an adytum, used either as a treasury or as a parthenon – a sanctuary for the temple virgins. The building was elongated further by porches placed at each end. Thus emerged the typical longitudinal temple, whose width could easily be spanned by a timber-framed, pitched roof. Larger and more important temples were designed peripteral, that is to say with a continuous colonnade all round. This simple basic form remained in use for many years, becoming increasingly subtle in execution.

This process of refinement involved what we now know as the 'order', a system of detail and proportion developed for the temple but applicable to all buildings. There were three Greek orders, the Doric, Ionic and Corinthian, identifiable mainly by the characteristic forms of the columns. The earliest of these, the Doric, was typified by its round, fluted column, with a flat capital, and by its general appearance of solidity. In some respects it was reminiscent of columns at the funerary temples of Mentuhetep and Hatshepsut and the tombs at Beni Hasan. As its name suggests, it was associated originally with the Dorian area of Greece, particularly with Corinth and Sparta. Early examples include the temples of Hera at Olympia (*c.*590BC), and of Apollo at Corinth (*c.*540BC) and Delphi (*c.*510BC).

Politically, Sparta never really developed beyond its oligarchical origins, but other city-states did, most notably Athens. Its sea and harbours gave it access, through trade, to grain, olives, wine and honey, and to iron, clay, marble and silver. Its Ionian – rather than Dorian – culture was open to a wider range of influences, including the richer east. During the 7th and 6th centuriesBC, intellectual growth was taking place. This was the age of Ionian philosophers and scientists like Pythagoras, Thales, Heraclitus and Xenophanes, and of growing cultural unity through the Greek language, as developed by Homer, Hesiod, Aesop and Sappho. Vase painting, sculpture, and the Ionic style of architecture – the second of the orders – with its elegant, deeply-fluted columns and voluted capitals, curled like rams' horns, were rich in decorative effects. The best early examples of Ionic building were on the seaboard of Anatolia, and included the temples of Artemis at Ephesus (*c.*560BC) and of Hera on the Aegean island of Samos (*c.*525BC).

Economically, the Aegean provided a community of interest; colonial cities, like Miletos and Priene, were established on the Anatolian coast. Parent cities, grown up over time, often had irregular layouts, whereas colonial cities often showed their origins by their regular grids of streets, laid out quickly by surveyors. Through the ages, right down to 19th-century Chicago, the grid plan became a feature of many newly-established cities. It was easy to divide it into administrative districts, and its rectangular street blocks into building plots. In Greek colonial cities these took the form of low, rectangular houses facing inwards to open courtyards, which provided a focus for household activities and allowed the circulation of cooling breezes.

Its Aegean context gave Athens a freer social system than Sparta: a loose hierarchy of nobles, merchants and artisans, of peasants, of metics – foreign traders attracted to the city – and slaves. All these classes had different political interests, and Athens' main contributions to political theory and practice grew out of a need to reconcile the conflicts.

In the late 7th century BC the aristocrat Draco codified a severe legal system designed to subdue unrest. A generation later Solon, also an aristocrat, reduced land-owners' powers and increased those of the lower classes, creating an upper-class Council of Four Hundred and a popular assembly. From time to time the balance shifted even further, as tyrannies emerged based on popular lower-class support. The tyrant Peristratus, for example, enacted anti-aristocratic laws and held tenuously onto power through conspicuous public works. Late in the 6th century however, the uncertainty came to an end with the political reforms of Kleisthenes, which extended citizenship to all free adult males and allowed all citizens to meet, debate and vote in the popular assembly. This was Democracy, the rule of the *demos* – the people – though 'the people' were only about one-third of the population: women and slaves were excluded.

The Athenian system was put sternly to the test in the first years of the 5th century BC by the Persian Wars. In the mid-6th century BC, Cyrus the Great and his son Cambyses had conquered the Babylonians and come to power in the fertile crescent. Their empire, the biggest yet seen, was extended west to Anatolia and south to Asia Minor and, under Darius I, into Egypt and India. It was divided into 20 provinces, each controlled by a satrap, who exercised an absolute but magnanimous power. In the interests of stability Darius tolerated and even promoted the local cultures. The exiled Israelites were

# Golden Age Greece

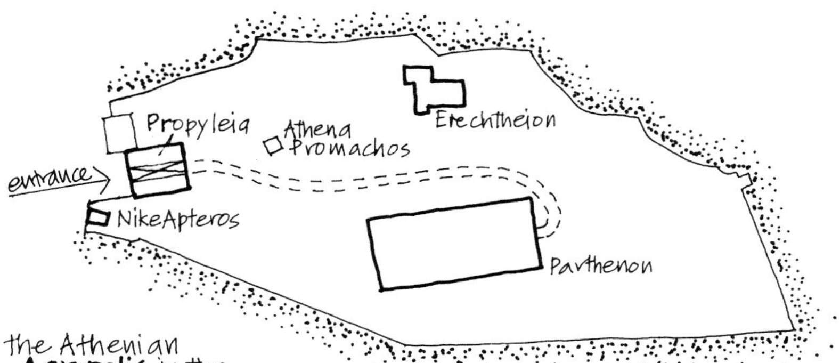

the Athenian **Acropolis** in the 5th century BC

Propyleia
Athena Promachos
Erechtheion
entrance
NikeApteros
Parthenon

**Pericles**, leader of the democratic Athenian state

caryatid from the south porch of the **Erechtheion**

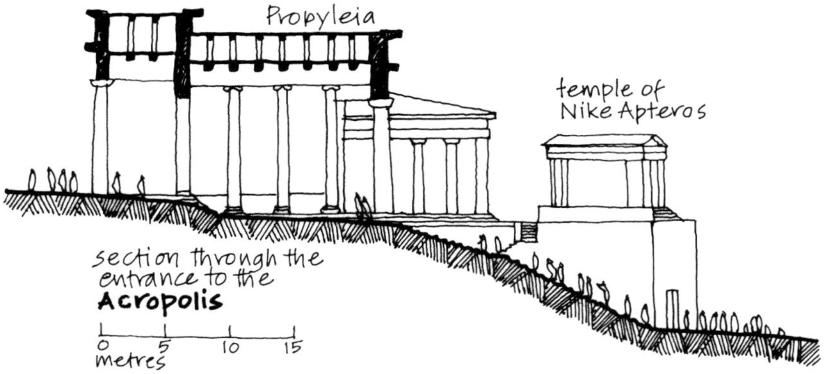

Propyleia

temple of Nike Apteros

section through the entrance to the **Acropolis**

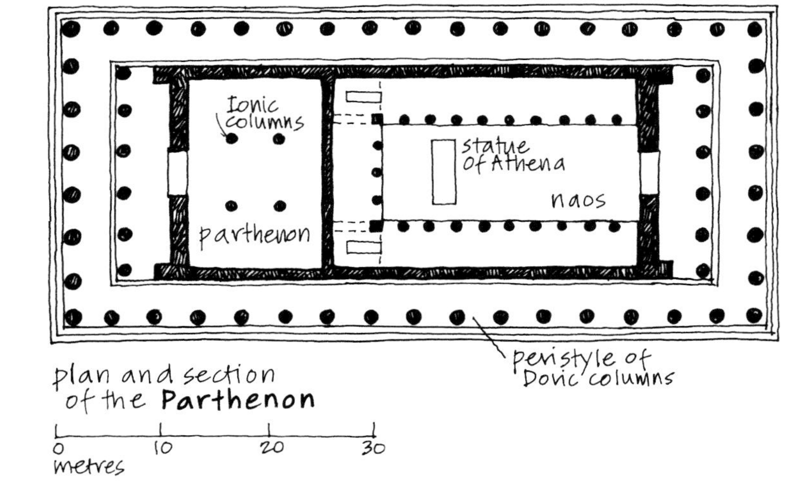

0 5 10 15
metres

Ionic columns

statue of Athena

naos

parthenon

peristyle of Doric columns

plan and section of the **Parthenon**

0 10 20 30
metres

allowed to return, and the economy of occupied Egypt was developed. Persian art and architecture began to reflect this cultural richness. For the new capital of Susa, sited near the Persian Gulf on the ancient city of Elam, Darius imported Assyrian, Egyptian and Greek craftsmen. The brick-makers were Babylonian, and cedar was brought from Lebanon. Here, and at Darius's palace of Persepolis, the distinctive Persian style emerged, grand in scale, as in the Hall of a Hundred Columns, rich in detail, and brilliant with polychrome glazed brickwork.

Conflict with Athens came when Persia took control of the Greek colonial cities in Anatolia. A revolt by the citizens of Miletos was put down, but drew both Athens and Sparta into an intermittent Persian war, during which a Spartan force was annihilated at the pass of Thermopylae in central Greece, and Athens was occupied and destroyed, but which ended in 480–479BC with decisive Greek victories at Salamis, Plataea and Mycale. Post-war recovery, with the threat of invasion now lifted, was rapid. The Spartan economy was self-sufficient, but the growth of Athens involved imperial expansion, from the Black Sea to Sicily – though its power did not extend to the Italian mainland. Here, in 509BC, the Latins had revolted against Etruscan domination and established a new Republic based on the city of Rome.

Athenian power depended first on controlling Greece by dominating the Delian League of city-states and by appropriating the League's funds. On this basis Athens entered its golden age of economic and cultural development. The amazing cultural achievements of the 5th century BC tend to imply a 'perfect' society. We see it through the eyes of those who have left the records, of educated Athenian men – not Spartans nor Scythians, nor Athenian women and still less, those who served them. It was an age of contradictions; on the one hand, democracy, on the other, imperialism; freedom for the citizens, but the subjugation of women and the exploitation of slaves.

After the war Athens needed to be reconstructed both socially and physically. There was considerable social unrest, and leaders like Pericles offered popular power by creating the democratic system. The physical destruction demanded major public works, which provided much-needed employment. The 'long walls' were built, a protective corridor joining the city to the sea. Athens began to take on the archetypal form of the ancient Greek city; it became the physical expression of the philosophical concept of the polis. At its heart lay the Agora, a square surrounded by public buildings which combined the roles of commercial, social and civic centre. Here the state laws were displayed on stone tablets while the noticeboards carried information about political assemblies and court cases. In the mornings the Agora was laid out with merchants' stalls. In the evenings it was visited by people of leisure, or craftsmen after their day's work, looking to be entertained by actors or musicians. It incorporated the gymnasium, where young men were educated in writing, poetry, music, dance and the arts of war. Young women had no such schools, needing to learn only the household arts.

On a hill above the Agora was the Acropolis. Formerly defensive citadel and the core of the ancient city, by the 5th century BC it had become a religious precinct dedicated to Athena, protective goddess of the city. Doric temple building had reached maturity with the temple of Apollo at Delphi (510BC), of Zeus at Olympia (460BC) and the Theseion in Athens (449BC). Now, with the rebuilding of the Athenian Acropolis, the style reached its highest level of perfection.

A processional route led up the steep hillside to the new Propyleia, a tall gateway to the precinct designed by the architect Mnesicles in an imaginative mixture of styles including, for the first time on the mainland, the Ionic. Next to it stood the elegant little Ionic temple of Nike Apteros, or Wingless Victory. Through the Propyleia the route led first to the colossal bronze statue of Athena, probably by the sculptor Pheidias and high enough, it is said, to be seen off Cape Sounion, 50 kilometres down the coast. To the left was the Erechtheion, a curious little free-form temple with some Ionic columns and some in the shape of standing maidens, the so-called caryatids. On the right, at the back of the precinct, was Athena's huge Doric temple, the masterpiece of the architects Ictinus and Kallicrates: the Parthenon. The disposition of these buildings on their rocky outcrop, their form and siting perfectly in key with the landscape, the freedom with which the orders were used and combined, the extraordinary subtlety of detail, the consummate craftsmanship of the marble work, make this group one of the finest achievements of western architecture.

The Parthenon itself was built in only nine years, between 447 and 438BC. It assumed the typical temple form consisting of two chambers, the naos and the parthenon – the latter giving the building its name – placed end to end and surrounded by a peristyle. The scale was large, the footprint of the building on the site measuring some 30 by 70 metres. The peristyle consisted of eight Doric columns across the ends and seventeen down the sides. They rose from a crepidoma, a plinth three steps in height, whose main function was to take up variations of ground level and provide the columns with a level stylobate, or base. The columns supported a structure of horizontal beams faced all round with an entablature, above which the roof rose, its triangular gables appearing at each end in the form of a pediment.

Every proportion and detail was carefully considered: the width of the columns in relation to their height, which in a Doric building was six or seven to one; the column spacing; the number of flutings on the column shafts; the make-up of the entablature, consisting of three distinct elements – the architrave, the frieze and the cornice. The greatest subtlety of all was the system of optical correction, which required that the columns be given entasis, that is to bulge slightly, in order to appear straight; that they be spaced unevenly in order to appear equidistant; and that they lean inwards in order to emphasise their verticality. The four corner columns, which appeared against the sky and were thus visually diminished by the spill of light round their sides, were made slightly fatter than the rest. All the seemingly level surfaces such as the stylobate and the frieze were made convex so that they would look horizontal.

In the naos, which had a greater internal height than the peristyle, Ionic columns were used, their ram's horn volutes contrasting with the flat Doric capitals elsewhere. The Ionic, with its rather less rigid rules of proportion and its more decorative nature, could be used to solve particular design problems, in this case to allow the columns extra height without a corresponding increase in width. The building appealed to more than the intellect. It was Dionysian as well as Apollonian, glowing with colour, rich in decoration and adorned with sculpture – freestanding figures in the two pediments, high-relief sculptures on the metopes at roof level, and the magnificent low-relief frieze, high up inside the peristyle. Most spectacular of all was Pheidias's chryselephantine statue of Athena inside the naos.

The Parthenon amazes by the precision of its craftsmanship. The stone blocks in the naos walls were linked together with iron cramps, caulked with lead. Otherwise, notably in the columns, the stones were held only by gravity. To achieve a seamless appearance the blocks were slightly hollowed on the meeting surfaces, so that only the edges touched, and that tightly. The heavier stones were pulled to the site by oxen and slid or lifted into place by means of ramps or simple cranes. The roof was framed up in timber and covered in loose tiles, held in place by gravity. That something so refined could be produced by such simple means tells us a lot about the intellectual background out of which the building emerged.

In the 5th century BC, Socrates was teaching his pupils to aspire to absolute standards of virtue and, through respect for the 'divine principle', to seek spiritual truth. In the same way, artists aspired to absolute standards of beauty, which were seen to lie in the principles of order. Musicians, in laying the foundations of western music, were developing concepts of scale, harmony and rhythm, and similar ideas of appropriate order applied to other arts. The drama of Aeschylus, Sophocles and Euripedes was organized around the three Unities of time, place and action. For sculptors, absolute beauty was to be found in the proportions of the human figure, which they depicted according to convention – the male nude and the female draped. The idea of universal harmony united all the arts as a means of expressing the 'ethos', the essence which lay above and beyond the material world.

## DEMOCRACY IN DECLINE

Athenian thought was very sophisticated but, as in all ancient societies, it had its limits. Despite its democratic aims, this was still a slave-owning class-society which the state was dedicated to maintaining. Protecting a grossly unequal social structure also meant placing definite limits on intellectual growth. Slaves and free women, two-thirds of the population, were denied both education and the right to participate. And among the educated, innovators or dissenters might face exile or death; Socrates himself was executed for alleged subversion of the polis. Science remained undeveloped; even Democritus, despite brilliant insights, tended to rely on speculation rather than observation. The growth of technology proceeded by custom and practice, trial and error. Science-based technology, capable of improving production and transforming society, was not well-developed in the ancient world.

Architecture was a clear expression of these contradictions. Trabeated construction was simple, even banal, and showed much less inventiveness than the Greeks were capable of in other fields. The builders over-sized the roof timbers of a temple because they had no theory of structures and no conception of the principles of triangulation. They were happier to bring an unadventurous structure to the ultimate degree of refinement than to search for any new structural principles.

The contradiction between the democratic state and its underlying imperialism was brought to a head in 431BC when Corinth and Sparta rebelled against Athenian power. The Peloponnesian War continued till 404BC. Pericles led Athens willingly to war, thinking they would win easily, but it all went wrong. Besieged behind its long walls and ravaged by plague, Athens at last capitulated when its army was destroyed in Sicily.

The democratic experiment gave way to a puppet state run by a Spartiate oligarchy.

The Delian League continued, its leadership passing to Sparta, and trade went on much as before. But during the war social unrest had grown. Much of the land had been laid waste and productivity was down. The increased use of slave labour undercut the prices of the small traders; disaffected artisans and peasants staged frequent revolts or emigrated, to Italy, Russia, Asia Minor or North Africa, incidentally creating an influential diaspora of Greek culture wherever they went.

This was the uncertain background out of which Platonic philosophy grew during the 4th century BC. Both Plato and his follower Aristotle were concerned with a real problem – how best to organise society to attain two perhaps contradictory ends: the stability of the regime and individual self-fulfilment. Plato's main political work was *Politeia*, usually translated into English as *The Republic*, though the modern meaning of this term is narrower than Plato intended; he was not so much concerned with the mere constitution, as with the whole social system. In *The Politics* Aristotle developed the idea of the entire 'organic' state.

According to the Platonists, democracy had failed, and the unsettled aftermath was no better. Till now all politicians, even the great Pericles, had led the people towards wrong, materialistic ends; their goals were power and wealth rather than truth and beauty. Idealism was needed. We believe we live in the real world, but ours is only the shadow of a more real world, outside time and space, that of the ultimately unattainable but still to be striven for, Ideal. Humans are made up of three elements. Desire resides in the abdomen and Courage in the heart; these two belong to ordinary space and time. In the mind lies the third, Reason, which alone has the power to aspire to the Ideal. Politicians, needless to say, remain on the lower plane, which is why the polis fails. Their reason gives way to cunning, courage to violence, and desire becomes excess.

Politically, this can be resolved only through the creation of the ideal state, based on the labour of those who express true desire through their honest work. It would be defended by a specially trained corps of guardians, the men of true courage. It would be ruled by men of true reason, philosopher-kings both bred and trained for the task. Their lives would be strict. They would have no family or home to divert them. Property excites ambition, so they would own none. They would be isolated and mysterious to emphasise that they ruled by divine right.

Platonic thought had a profound effect on later western philosophy, but it was also very much of its time. Its insistence on inequality was a justification of slavery. Its authoritarian, elitist, anti-democratic viewpoint was a response to the complexity and instability which followed the certainties of the Periclean age. The Greeks had been left with only one model of political stability; there is a sense in which Plato's polis is an idealised Spartan state.

In these less certain times, art was becoming less spiritual. The calmness of Golden Age sculpture gave way to humanism and emotionalism. The nude female figure, previously not acceptable, was now depicted. The archetypal sculptor of the 4th century BC was Praxiteles, whose *Hermes* and *Aphrodite* typify the softer, more romantic modelling of the period. During this time too, the Ionic style of architecture reached its highest level. Among the smaller examples, the Nereid Monument on Xanthos (*c.*400BC) was a tomb surmounted by a small temple, the columns widely spaced to alternate with richly-carved statues of Nereids, or water nymphs. Among the largest and most magnificent was the rebuilt temple of Artemis – 'Diana of the Ephesians' – at Ephesus ( 356BC), the fifth successive building on this important colonial site. Measuring about 52 by 112 metres at the base it was designed dipteral, that is with a double row of columns, almost 18 metres in height, encircling the naos, and was noted for the richness of its sculpture.

Ephesus was the site of the Pan-Ionian festival. Greece had many such sites, at which religion and culture periodically brought the surrounding communities together. Olympia, in the western Peloponnese, was the best-known of a number of sites at which religious festivals every four years were accompanied by games in honour of the gods. At first the games were ancillary to the religious rites and probably took the form of running with offerings to the temple, but as the festival grew more popular, attracting groups from all over the Greek world, the games became an end in themselves. A stadium was built, a wrestling school, a hotel for visitors.

Another such site was the Asclepion at Epidavros in Argolis. Here, the festival celebrated Asclepios, the mythical healer from whom Hippocrates derived his inspiration. As at Olympia, the festival involved religious ceremonies and games, but with a special emphasis on dramatic performances. The finest theatre of the ancient world was built for the Asclepion in the 4th century BC. The form had by now been standardized: a horseshoe-shaped bowl of open-air seating, the *cavea*, enclosing a circular space, the *orchestra*, on which the chorus performed, at the back of which was the actors' raised stage, the *skene*. The theatre at Epidavros was huge, with a cavea 118 metres in diameter, seating 14,000 people. Despite this the sightlines were designed with geometrical precision so that everyone had a view, and the acoustics were perfect.

In each of these sites the rugged yet poetic nature of the landscape is beautifully complemented by the organic buildings and layout. This relationship is at its most magical, perhaps, in the spectacular site at Delphi, on the Gulf of Corinth, dedicated to the god Apollo. A broad sacred way wound up the mountainside, first passing a group of shrines and treasury buildings, then the Doric temple of Apollo itself, reaching at the top of the hill the theatre and the stadium of the Pythian games. Delphi's best-known building is the charming Tholos (*c.*400BC), a circular temple some 15 metres across with an outer peristyle of 20 Doric columns. However it was the temple of Apollo which was the main focus of worship and pilgrimage as powerful statesmen or unknown peasants came to consult the Pythian oracle. The Pythia were the temple's women clairvoyants, whose ecstatic predictions were reinterpreted by the priests in suitably ambiguous terms. The powerful king Croesus of Lydia was said by Herodotus to have asked advice on his intended campaign against the Persians. On being told that he would destroy a great kingdom he proceeded readily. The kingdom he destroyed was his own.

Sparta's reign as leading power was brief. It was unsuited to an imperial role and after further conflict, leadership of the League passed to Thebes. In the late 4th century BC, amid a growing weariness with the hegemony of one state after another and with the upheavals they created, the concept of Panhellenism, the unity of the Greek-speaking world, began to take shape. This was pre-empted by the growing power of Philip of Macedonia, who by 338BC had taken over the Athenian colonies in Asia Minor, defeated the armies of the League, and occupied Thebes itself, which was later destroyed as an

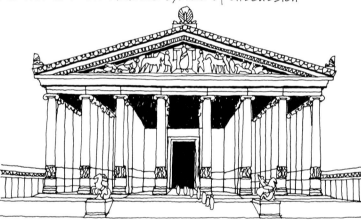

living room

porch

entrance

open court

kitchen

stairs to upper storey

a 2nd-century house on the Cycladic island of **Delos** – the generous communal spaces lent themselves to the Platonic system of discussion

# the rise of Hellenism

the sculptural virtuosity of the **Winged Victory** of Samothraki

the **Temple of Artemis** at Ephesus demonstrated the oriental richness of which the Ionic style was capable

one of the huge and ornate columns of the temple of Artemis

the **Nereid Monument** on Xanthos – another rich Ionic design

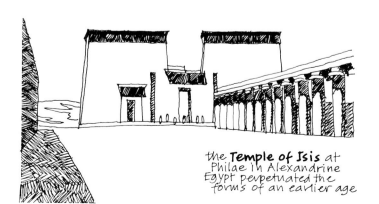

the **Temple of Isis** at Philae in Alexandrine Egypt perpetuated the forms of an earlier age

example to the rest of Greeks. In 336BC his son, Alexander the Great, succeeded to the throne. In five years a brilliant military campaign had destroyed the power of Persia and annexed and extended its empire from the borders of India down into Egypt.

An unexpected kind of Panhellenism was quickly imposed over the whole area. Alexander, who was taught by Aristotle himself, looked to the Greek language and culture to provide an overall unity. These were enriched by oriental influences as the centre of gravity of the empire moved eastwards. This so-called Hellenistic period was notable for the splendid patronage of wealthy rulers and the richness and maturity of its culture. It was an age of scientific discovery, of Euclid's geometric Elements, of Archimedes' mechanics, and of the astronomy of Hipparchus. The human body was dissected and the nervous system identified. The Greek religious tradition was enriched by the importation of mystery cults from the east, like Zoroastrianism. Philosophy moved from the Platonic certainties to the relativism of the Epicureans and Stoics. Schools and libraries were founded, which spread the new ideas throughout the empire.

Hellenistic sculpture, typified by the group *Laocoön*, or the *Dying Gaul*, or the *Winged Victory of Samothraki*, was technically brilliant and complex in form. Architecture too took on an oriental richness as the Corinthian style – the third order – began to dominate. Its typical buildings were in Athens: the Choragic Monument of Lysicrates (334BC), built to commemorate a successful dramatic contest; the large and magnificent temple of Olympian Zeus (174BC); and the so-called Tower of the Winds (48BC), an horologium built to indicate the time and the weather. The richness of the Corinthian style with its elaborately carved acanthus-leaf capitals suited the confident Hellenistic mood.

Hellenism flourished in Egypt too. Alexander had briefly visited Egypt and established the great Greek city which bears his name. His occupation created a dynasty of Greek-speaking rulers, the Ptolemies, who began to make Alexandria an important intellectual centre, particularly for the natural sciences. Ptolemy II founded the museum and the library, with its half-a-million books, which attracted scholars from all over the world. Alexander had promoted Egypt's old religion, and under the Ptolemies a number of Hellenistic temples were built. These included the elegant and decorative temples of Horus at Edfu (237BC), of Sebek and Horus at Kom Ombo (180BC and later), and of Hathor at Dendera (110BC). Most beautiful of all was the little temple of Isis on the island of Philae near present-day Aswan (289BC). All were sophisticated and accomplished revivals, their forms based on the Pharaonic rituals of the long-vanished New Kingdom.

Alexander died prematurely and his empire was divided into three separate states – of Macedonia, Egypt and the Seleucid kingdom of Syria. But Hellenism persisted, developing its own local characteristics wherever it spread. Through continued trade, Greek culture – including its language and architecture – spread to Russia in the north and Africa in the south, and from Asia Minor as far west as Italy. It was about to become the lingua franca not only of the greatest empire the world had yet seen, but also of its most universal religious movement.

# 2 THE COMING OF THE CHRISTIAN ERA

*2nd century BC to 5th century AD*

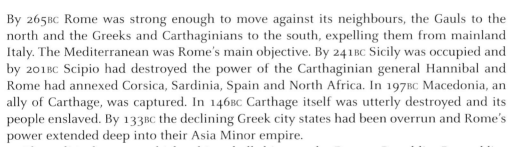

By 265BC Rome was strong enough to move against its neighbours, the Gauls to the north and the Greeks and Carthaginians to the south, expelling them from mainland Italy. The Mediterranean was Rome's main objective. By 241BC Sicily was occupied and by 201BC Scipio had destroyed the power of the Carthaginian general Hannibal and Rome had annexed Corsica, Sardinia, Spain and North Africa. In 197BC Macedonia, an ally of Carthage, was captured. In 146BC Carthage itself was utterly destroyed and its people enslaved. By 133BC the declining Greek city states had been overrun and Rome's power extended deep into their Asia Minor empire.

The political system which achieved all this was the Roman Republic. *Res publica* means 'something belonging to the people' and, like the Greek polis, was represented as being of universal benefit. The protection of free citizens' rights was a major feature of Rome's celebrated legal system. The ideology spoke of freedom and justice yet, also like Greece, Rome could not achieve its external conquests without also exercising strict internal control. Over the years a powerful state machine had emerged. An aristocratic class, the Patricians, dominating the Senate and the Assembly, operated a well-developed military system paid for by heavy taxation.

As Rome grew, and with it the city's wealth, control of the state became a rich prize for which rival politicians were prepared to fight. As time went on Patrician supremacy was challenged by the middle-class Plebeians, but little wealth reached the mass of the people. As the gap between rich and poor widened, more people became disaffected: the rural poor exploited by local governors; urban workers heavily taxed; the army, made up largely of provincials whose allegiance to Rome was often in question; even rebellious slaves. The widespread use of slave labour on the farms dispossessed many peasants, who made their way to the city. There they became a troublesome *lumpenproletariat*, to be placated or exploited by unscrupulous politicians with offers of 'bread and circuses'.

To the state, architecture was a useful ideological weapon. Conspicuous public buildings could be illusory symbols of political unity and provide useful diversions for the discontented. At the centre of Rome lay the Capitol and near it the Forum Romanum, the earliest and most respected of the city's public spaces. Like the Athenian agora, the

Forum began as a market place and entertainment centre, but over the years these uses were moved out and, dignified with temples, ADministrative buildings known as basilicae, victory columns and statues, the Forum became a symbol of Republicanism. Over the years other fora were built, forming a sequence of big public spaces. Around and near them were placed more temples and basilicae, and the theatres, amphitheatres, baths and circuses with which the state held onto the affections of the people.

Rome reproduced itself everywhere. Many colonial towns started as military camps and were laid out with geometric precision. They were usually divided into four quarters by two main roads, the *cardo* and the *decumanus*, meeting at right angles. At the crossing were placed the forum, temple, theatre and basilica and other public buildings which replicated the lifestyle of Rome itself; in the four quadrants were the grids of streets containing the housing; around the perimeter, as in Rome, were a defensive wall and ditch. The characteristic plan of the Roman colonial town could eventually be seen all over the western world, from Chester to Palmyra.

The colonial garrisons helped to hold the system together, on the products of which Rome's wealth was based: raw materials such as iron ore and furs, foodstuffs like wheat, maize and meat, manufactured goods and almost unlimited labour. A two-tier economy existed. At the base was the Celtic peasant, whose territory had been appropriated, producing food by farming small-holdings. Over this were superimposed Roman *villae*, large holdings of rich landowners worked by slaves. Between them they produced most of what the great city needed.

Rome's ruling class also demanded luxuries of all kinds, and merchants ventured ever farther afield to supply them. Transport by sea was quicker and cheaper than by land, and control of the Mediterranean gave Rome the opportunity it needed. To the west lay the unknown Atlantic, still full of terrors for the traveller, so traders turned south to Africa, or east, through the Red Sea and the Persian Gulf, to India and China, bringing back silk, ivory, resins and spices. As a result the staging-posts themselves grew in size and wealth; Byzantium, Antioch and Alexandria began to rival the economic importance of Rome itself

Trade brought more than material goods. As in politics, the Romans also had a pragmatic attitude to culture, taking over anything and everything they thought useful. The Greek empire and its language provided a ready-made ADministrative system. The Greek alphabet was ADapted to Roman use. Greek poetry and drama provided models for Roman writers. The Greek gods and goddesses were ADopted and renamed in Latin.

The Greek architectural styles, ADapted to meet the wider variety of building techniques which Rome appropriated, became Roman styles too. Roman builders were not limited to limestone; they had other building stones, including volcanic tufa, lava and pumice, and made much use of humbler materials like brick, terra-cotta and concrete – the latter a compound of hard-drying earth known as *pozzolana*. While Greek builders had confined themselves to trabeated construction, the Romans developed the semi-circular arch and its derivatives, the barrel-vault, the cross-vault and the dome.

Roman builders laboured under the same social limitations as their Greek counter-parts. Their humble place in an authoritarian society denied them the education and freedom to ADvance by anything other than trial and error. Slavery too, by providing unlimited labour power, acted as a brake on technical innovation. Yet the great wealth of

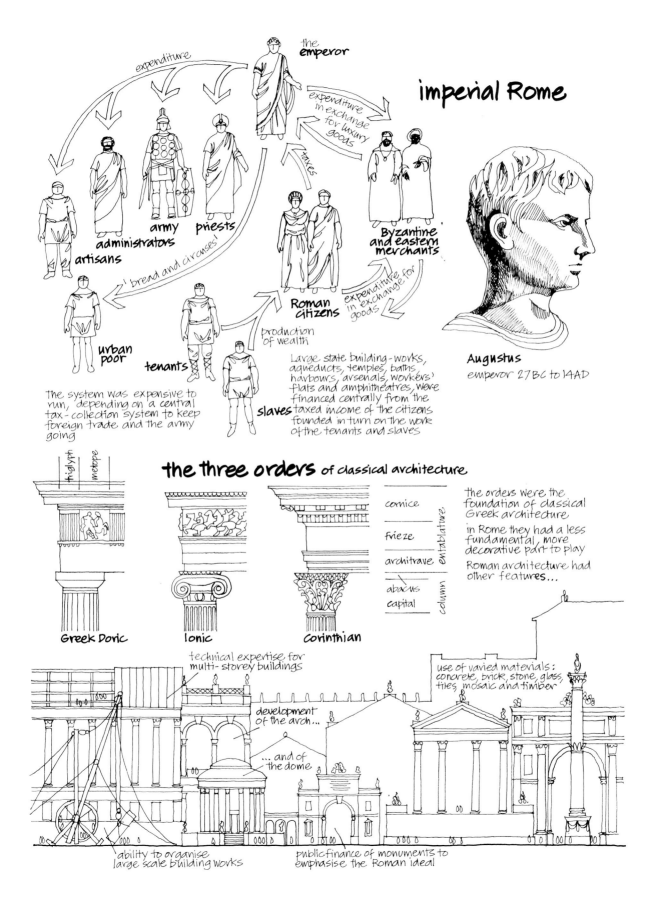

# imperial Rome

expenditure

the emperor

expenditure in exchange for luxury goods

taxes

Byzantine and eastern merchants

administrators

army

priests

artisans

'bread and circuses!'

urban poor

tenants

production of wealth

Roman citizens

expenditure in exchange for goods

slaves

Augustus
emperor 27 BC to 14 AD

The system was expensive to run, depending on a central tax-collection system to keep foreign trade and the army going

Large state building-works, aqueducts, temples, baths, harbours, arsenals, workers' flats and amphitheatres, were financed centrally from the taxed income of the citizens founded in turn on the work of the tenants and slaves

## the three orders of classical architecture

triglyph  metope

Greek Doric

Ionic

Corinthian

cornice

frieze

architrave

abacus

capital

entablature

column

the orders were the foundation of classical Greek architecture

in Rome they had a less fundamental, more decorative part to play

Roman architecture had other features...

technical expertise for multi-storey buildings

use of varied materials: concrete, brick, stone, glass, tiles, mosaic and timber

development of the arch...

...and of the dome

ability to organise large scale building works

public finance of monuments to emphasise the Roman ideal

Rome created a huge demand for major building works, which in turn brought together all the building techniques available in the conquered provinces. This alone meant that technical progress, though still empiric, could come at a faster rate.

In 133BC the ill-fated attempts of Tiberius and Gracchus to make the Republic more egalitarian led only to chaos. Amid slave revolts, barbarian incursions and civil wars, Rome began to slide into dictatorship. Paradoxically it was the city's most cultured period. It was dominated by the sophisticated Epicureanism of Lucretius and by an outpouring of great poetry: Virgil's *Aeneid*, the lyric verse of Catullus, and the wit and satire of Ovid and Horace.

In 60BC the Senate was replaced by a triumvirate, which in turn dissolved into a power struggle between two of its three members, Julius Caesar and Pompey. Caesar, the great general, had already conquered Gaul. He now marched on Rome and pursued Pompey first to Greece, then to Egypt, defeating him and enlarging the empire at the same time. Now an emperor in all but name, Caesar sought an enlightened role for himself. During his short reign he began to improve the city with buildings, including the Forum of the Emperors and the Circus Maximus. He attempted social reforms too, cut short by his assassination in 44BC. A second Triumvirate of Antony, Octavius and Lepidus itself descended into a power struggle from which Octavius emerged the victor, putting an end to the Republic and instituting the Roman Empire. In 30BC he became the Emperor Augustus, appointing himself Consul for life, Tribune, Princeps, or first citizen, Imperator, or general, and Pontifex Maximus, or chief priest. He could create laws at will or veto those of the Senate.

With Augustus, Rome reached its peak of power and influence. The Empire extended from Egypt in the east to Britain in the west, and from the banks of the Rhine and Danube down to north Africa. A so-called *Pax Romana* was instituted, and for some two hundred years the whole European region was stabilized by Rome's legal and tax systems, its business practices, its roads and its armies. Wealth flowed into the city as never before. Prose writers like Seneca, Pliny, Plutarch and Tacitus chronicled or criticized the times, and poets like Martial and Juvenal celebrated or satirized them.

Augustus is said to have found Rome a city of brick and left it a city of marble; under him a huge building programme took place, in both city and colonies. On the Palatine Hill in Rome the Palaces of the Emperors were begun. Theatres, like that of Marcellus (23BC) and numerous temples were built, including that of Mars Ultor (14BC) and those of Concord and of Castor and Pollux (7BC). Temple-building was going on all over the empire from Nîmes, where the so-called Maison Carrée was built in 16BC, to Baalbek, where the temple of Jupiter was built in AD 10. Greek temples were places apart, free-standing buildings in holy precincts. Roman temples were often sited in busy public places; frequently they presented only a facade to the street, the side walls, against which other buildings clustered, were often left blank.

## THE EARLY CHURCH

The boom in temple building belied the fact that the old polytheistic religions, after many centuries of survival, were now almost a spent force. It was during Augustus's reign that Jesus was born in the eastern part of the empire, at Bethlehem in Judaea.

Christianity was qualitatively different from all that had gone before. It was universalist rather than exclusivist in its appeal; it spoke to the poor more eloquently than to the rich, thereby challenging many existing social and political norms. Jesus died a martyr's death in about AD 30, but his teachings survived, through small groups of disciples, meeting clandestinely, and through the writings of followers like Paul of Tarsus.

As Christianity began to diverge from Judaism and to spread to Rome itself, it was seen as dangerous. From time to time Christians were persecuted as alleged subversives or as scapegoats for other social ills, but their religion continued to spread. The Jews too were seen as dangerous, though their aspirations for independence had been kept under control by Herod the Great, who sought co-existence with Rome. His re-building of the Temple in Jerusalem was a conspicuous gesture of continuity and stability. Then, when a Jewish revolt erupted in AD 66, the Romans replied by destroying Herod's Temple and most of Jerusalem with it. By 73 Jewish resistance was eliminated, after making its final stand at the Judean desert citadel of Masada.

After Augustus, absolute imperial power became ever more arbitrary and wilful. The Roman state was inherently brutal but rulers like Caligula and Nero, Vespasian and Titus made brutality even more commonplace than before. Political unrest of any kind was savagely dealt with. Nero's persecution of the 'deadly superstition' of Christianity was later recorded by Tacitus. Fine buildings like the Arch of Titus (AD 82), or the temple of Vespasian (AD 94) celebrated those who crushed the Jewish revolt and destroyed Jerusalem.

The city's consumption grew. To satisfy its needs, northern forests and southern cornfields were laid bare. Paved roads and arched aqueducts brought goods and supplies from ever further afield. The appetite for luxury goods grew, as did the demand for diversion. Numerous theatres were built, though here again the contrast with the Greek custom was significant. Roman theatres were not quasi-religious buildings sited in remote, sanctified valleys; they were unashamed places of entertainment presenting mainly comedy and spectacle, like the plays of Plautus or Terence, to an urban population.

Even more popular were the Circus – where chariot-racing took place – and the arena. The most representative building of the period was the Flavian Amphitheatre, built during the reign of Vespasian in AD 70 and known also as the Colosseum. Some 200 metres long, an ellipse on plan, it was enclosed by a sheer external wall on which Doric, Ionic and Corinthian columns were superimposed in three tiers. Inside, continuous rows of seats raked down to the oval amphitheatre in which the displays took place. Beneath the seats a complex of vaults on three levels contained accommodation for the gladiators, the beasts' cages and the cells of the victims. The audacity of the structure and the use of varied materials according to their constructional role – lava for strength in the foundations, tufa and brick for the walls and pumice to reduce the weight of the vaulting made the building both monumental and ingenious.

Vespasian and Titus were followed by a succession of emperors often known as 'good' – including Trajan, Hadrian and Marcus Aurelius – though given the character of the Roman state the term is perhaps relative. All three, even Marcus Aurelius, the great Stoic philosopher, were persecutors of the Christians. Trajan and his victories were celebrated by the laying-out of a Forum in his name, by the raising of his famous

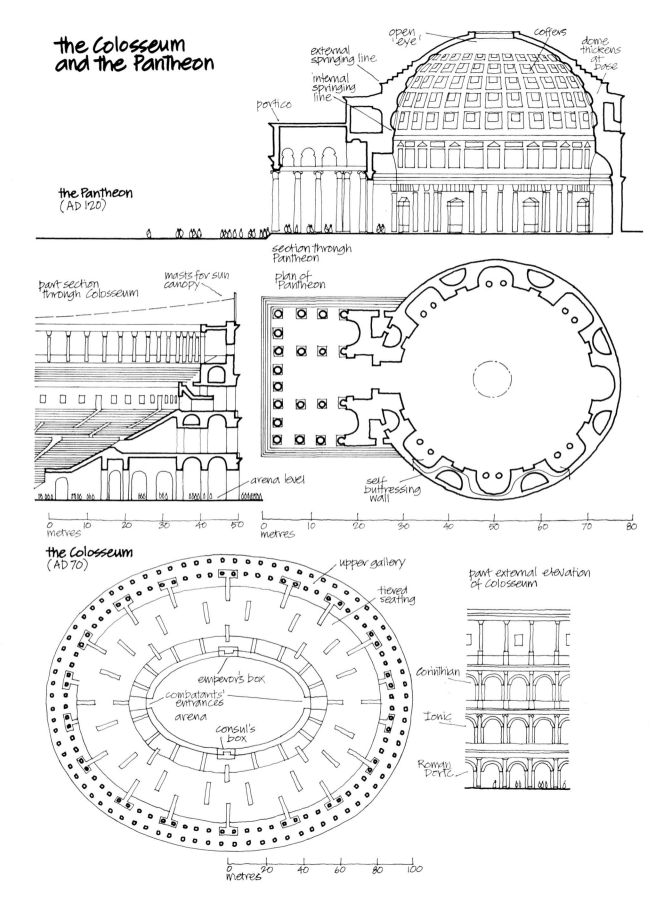

# the Colosseum and the Pantheon

**the Pantheon** (AD 120)

open 'eye'

coffers

dome thickens at base

external springing line

internal springing line

portico

section through Pantheon

part section through Colosseum

masts for sun canopy

plan of Pantheon

arena level

self buttressing wall

0 10 20 30 40 50
metres

0 10 20 30 40 50 60 70 80
metres

**the Colosseum** (AD 70)

upper gallery

tiered seating

emperor's box

combatants' entrances

arena

consul's box

part external elevation of Colosseum

Corinthian

Ionic

Roman Doric

0 20 40 60 80 100
metres

Column (AD 113) and by the construction of another basilica (AD 98). A basilica was a hall for public administration and business transactions. Typically a long, straight nave spanned with a barrel vault or cross-vaults, or more often a timber pitched roof, was flanked by lower aisles above which clerestories let light into the centre part of the building. One or both ends terminated in an apse containing the votive altar – for every important decision was accompanied by a sacrifice – the seats of the assessors and the throne of the praetor. The basilica was a fairly utilitarian building and its simple construction was an economical way of roofing a large rectangular space.

Hadrian's reign is typified by one of the most celebrated Roman buildings, the so-called Villa built for his use at Tivoli (AD 124). This was in effect a private park, of some 18 square kilometres, in which an interlinked sequence of buildings and spaces provided the most luxurious possible country retreat. Its close integration into the hilly landscape made it architecturally similar to Olympia or Delphi – an environment offered to an autocrat which in earlier centuries would have been offered only to the gods.

Tivoli included a hall roofed by a dome. The greatest contemporary example of this form of construction was the temple in Rome known as the Pantheon. Built in AD 120 during Hadrian's reign, on the site of an earlier temple for Agrippa, Augustus' son-in-law, it used some features of the existing building but adapted them in an individual way. The rectangular foundations of the old temple formed the basis of a massive portico, built with salvaged material and re-using the entablature with Agrippa's inscription. The new portico was reduced in width but the height of the pediment was retained so that, with a fine disregard for Greek proportions, it appeared unusually steep.

The main body of the temple was a domed rotunda, its width of 43 metres exactly corresponding with its internal height. Walls and roof were of structural concrete, faced with a variety of materials including brick and marble. From inside, the supports were apparently eight huge piers, alternating with eight large *exedrae*, or niches, but as the piers were hollowed out behind they formed in effect a wall, serpentine on plan, the shape of which was self-buttressing. The drum of the rotunda was three tiers high on the outside but only two inside, since the dome sprang from the top of the second tier. The structure between the second and third tiers was therefore thicker and helped contain the thrust of the dome, the surface of which was coffered to reduce weight. The circular opening or 'eye' in the roof was, and still is, the only means of lighting the interior, adding to the drama of one of the most impressive buildings in Rome.

Gradually the *Pax Romana* began to break down. Rome's great buildings, like its army, its administrators, its luxury goods from the East and its handouts to the urban mob, were paid for by the taxes on its farmers and traders. The economy depended on safeguarding a large enough area of productive land and to meet the demands placed upon it; this was the main role of the legions, whose elaborate system of camps defended the boundary formed by the Black Sea coast, the Danube and the Rhine. The cost to the taxpayer of permanently defending 5000 kilometres of frontier began to tell, and during the 3rd century AD towns throughout the empire were hit by inflation, higher death rates, decreasing fertility and the migration to the country of citizens trying to escape the punitive taxes. The massing of enemy armies on the borders reduced trade and hastened the decline.

The emperors of the 3rd century AD attempted to hold the edifice together. Some of their grander projects are ironical, coming as they did at a time of social decay. The *thermae*, or baths, built for the emperor Caracalla in AD 211 are a case in point: one of the ancient world's greatest buildings, built for one of its more desperate rulers. This huge building, occupying a site some 300 metres square, incorporated a public park and stadium, as well as the baths themselves. These, the open-air *frigidarium* and the domed *caldarium*, were placed on either side of a main meeting hall with an audacious, cross-vaulted roof of concrete. This alone was 56 by 24 metres in extent, and 33 metres high. The interior was rich in marble and mosaic, and contained many of the ancient world's finest sculptures, some of them appropriated from Greece.

Between AD 284 and 305, the emperor Diocletian slowed the political disintegration by ruling as an oriental despot, complete with crown and throne. The thermae built for him in Rome (AD 302) were only slightly less opulent than Caracalla's, but in fact Rome was no longer his main concern. To improve control of the empire he divided it into eastern and western halves, each presided over by an emperor, with each emperor assisted by a 'caesar'. For himself he chose the eastern half, building himself a spectacular palace at Spalato on the Dalmatian coast. About 3.2 hectares in extent, it was rectangular on plan, surrounded by a great wall with defensive towers at the four corners. Two roads crossed it at right angles, giving it the character of a Roman colonial city, which in effect it was. Two of the quadrants held accommodation for guests and officials; the other two, directly facing the ADriatic, were the imperial palace.

The cities of the eastern Mediterranean, stronger economically, were more capable than Rome of surviving. In the 4th century AD the Emperor Constantine moved the capital of the Roman empire to Byzantium, which he renamed Constantinople, leaving Rome a political backwater as well as the economic backwater it had now become. The Roman system had outgrown its strength; decline was now inevitable.

However growing within it were the seeds of a new order founded on the Celtic tribal society which had survived the superimposed Roman system. The arrival of Germanic tribes from north of the Rhine acted as a catalyst. Since the second century AD, infiltrations of Germans into the empire had been assimilated without conflict because the land was not intensively farmed. When in the 4th century AD the Huns from the eastern steppes pushed west to the Caspian Sea, the Germanic tribes themselves migrated south and west in a movement the demoralised Legions could no longer resist.

During the 4th and 5th centuries AD the Ostrogoths and Lombards moved south to Italy, the Visigoths, Vandals and Suevi into Iberia, and the Franks and Burgundians into France. Germany itself became active with tribe movements, one of which involved the Angles and Saxons invading Britain. Everywhere Romans and Celts were displaced or assimilated. Traditionally these barbarians 'destroyed' the western empire, but it had collapsed already; all they did was to occupy and defend the land and develop its agriculture according to a simpler, older system of local production for local needs. Trade declined and money went out of use.

The barbarians were generally tolerant of local customs and laws, and many of them not only tolerated but also professed Rome's religion. Christianity, after its humble beginnings and difficult early years, had gradually grown in influence and authority until astute emperors saw it as a means to political unity. In AD 337 Constantine converted.

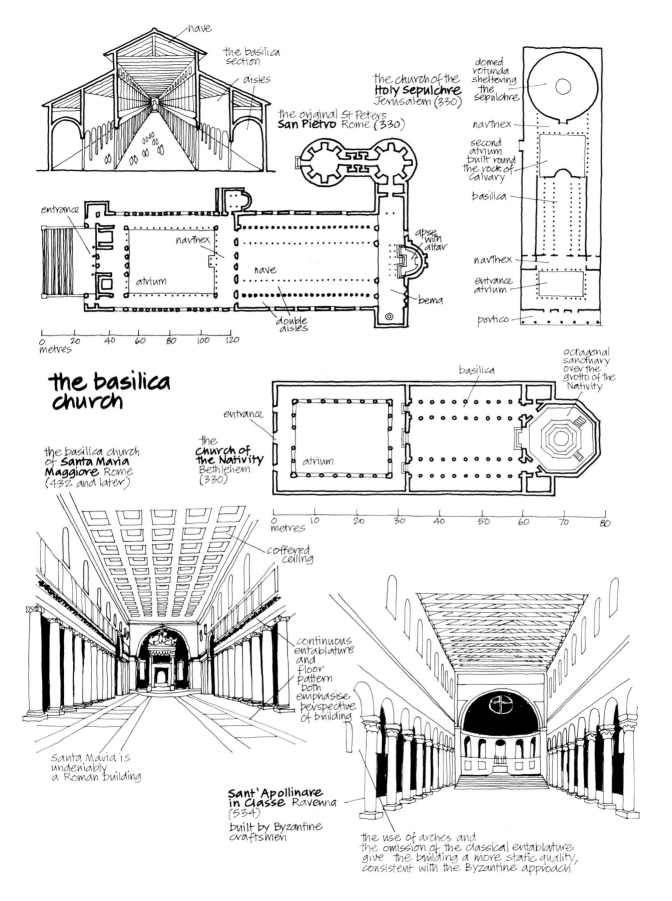

nave

the basilica section

aisles

the church of the **Holy Sepulchre** Jerusalem (330)

the original St Peters **San Pietro** Rome (330)

domed rotunda sheltering the sepulchre

narthex

second atrium built round the rock of Calvary

basilica

narthex

entrance atrium

portico

entrance

narthex

atrium

nave

double aisles

apse with altar

bema

0 20 40 60 80 100 120
metres

# the basilica church

basilica

octagonal sanctuary over the grotto of the Nativity

the basilica church of **Santa Maria Maggiore** Rome (432 and later)

entrance

the **Church of the Nativity** Bethlehem (330)

atrium

0 10 20 30 40 50 60 70 80
metres

coffered ceiling

continuous entablature and floor pattern both emphasise perspective of building

Santa Maria is undeniably a Roman building

**Sant'Apollinare in Classe** Ravenna (534)

built by Byzantine craftsmen

the use of arches and the omission of the classical entablature give the building a more static quality, consistent with the Byzantine approach

His successor Theodosius ADopted Christianity as the Empire's official religion, and its ADherents were able to end their semi-clandestine existence.

The first Christians had met in secret in houses, or buildings ADapted from other purposes. The first actual church is thought to have been built at Dura Europos, on the Euphrates, in AD 232. But the establishment of Christianity now called for a more intensive period of church-building, in the Holy Land and in Rome itself. In AD 330 Constantine founded both the Church of the Nativity, Bethlehem, and the Church of the Holy Sepulchre, Jerusalem, and in Rome the original church of San Pietro and the church of San Giovanni in Laterano.

Pagan temples were shrines to their gods, and worshippers had gathered outside. A church, however, had to house the congregation inside, so a new architectural form was needed. From the beginning, the form ADopted by western Christians was that of the Roman basilica; the long straight nave, flanked by aisles and leading to an end altar, became a pattern for future church-planning. The form was second nature to the Roman craftsmen who built the early examples, sometimes with columns salvaged from the ruins of pagan temples.

Other basilica churches were built in Rome. San Paulo fuori le Mura (AD 380), was one of the largest and finest, and Santa Maria Maggiore (AD 423), among the most beautiful. In both the rows of columns lining the nave supported a classical entablature. Nearby Ravenna was the capital of the Ostrogoth Theodoric the Great during his short but powerful kingship of Italy. In the churches of Sant'Apollinare Nuovo (AD 493), elegant, spacious and rich with Byzantine mosaic, and its sister Sant'Apollinare in Classe (AD 534), the columns supported a row of semi-circular arches.

The Roman Empire did not die; many of its institutions declined but others lived on in forms ADapted to the new circumstances. Its legal system was incorporated into the various codes of the Germans. Its road system fell into disrepair – the barbarians' self-sufficient rural communities had less need for trade and travel – to be rediscovered, at least in part, several centuries later. Many towns began to decay, some surviving as farmsteads, monasteries, bishops' palaces or castles, others disappearing completely. Economically, Byzantium became the inheritor of the empire, providing a degree of continuity, preserving the use of money, and keeping alive the Roman traditions of craftsmanship and building. The Church became Rome's cultural inheritor, the repository of what classical learning and literature still remained. Above all, the Celts and barbarians were there to develop a new economic system out of which feudalism, the basis of medieval society, was to emerge.

# 3 FEUDAL EUROPE
## 6th to 10th centuries

During the Roman empire, western Europe was essentially Celtic. This indigenous culture had gradually been growing since prehistoric times, and particularly during the last few hundred years BC, with its Druidic religion and a developed code of civil and moral law. The Celtic people were warriors, but also weavers, jewellers and smiths, sculptors and musicians.

Agriculture was the economic base of Celtic society and the extended family its main social unit. Society was based on local production for local needs but also had a system of exchange, of both goods and ideas. Its buildings were therefore produced locally, but to common traditions of construction which existed all over Europe. Communities had a two-tier social structure, with the local ruler, his warriors and priests, bards and advisers, dominating a class of peasants. All over the Celtic world, but particularly in Britain, Ireland and western Gaul, these communities lived together as complete social units. Their farmsteads consisted of small groups of dwellings, byres and store-houses protected by ditch, stockade and gatehouse.

In western Gaul, the most common form for all types of building was circular. A typical store-building or small dwelling would consist of a ring of wooden rafters, the ends embedded in the ground, meeting at the top to form a cone and carrying a covering of heather-thatch or turf. In small buildings, headroom was naturally restricted, so often the floor would be lowered, the excavated earth being placed round the outside to help stabilise the feet of the rafters and to form rudimentary walls. A single fireplace in the centre provided heating and cooking; the smoke escaped through a central hole in the roof. The size of a building was limited by the length of timber available for rafters, but when the owner's status required a larger building a composite structure would be used, with two tiers of rafters. A lower set spanned from the ground to a ring-beam supported on a circle of short timber posts, and an upper set from the ring-beam to the apex. This produced a building large enough to house a local chieftain's family and retainers. Typically, a series of cubicles round the edge would each house a family group, the centre being reserved for meetings, entertainments and meals.

Mainland Europe's Celtic population had been declining over the last centuries of the Roman empire, leaving sparsely inhabited areas into which the Germanic tribes migrating from the north were fairly easily assimilated. The Angles and Saxons, displaced westwards, had to fight rather harder for a foothold in Britain, and it took them almost 400 years from about the mid-5th century to the early 9th century to achieve dominance. Like the Celts, the Germans were by tradition subsistence farmers. Most of the migrants were young men, interested less in military conquest than in establishing new homelands for themselves and their families. The settlements of their northern homelands provided the pattern for the new ones they established farther south.

Julius Caesar in his Commentaries draws a sharp distinction between the culture and civilisation of the Germans and the Celts, greatly to the disadvantage of the former whom he calls *feri* or 'savages'. There is certainly little evidence that the Germans had the poetical and musical skills of the Celts, but in other respects there was in fact much cultural overlap. Continued contact between the races over the centuries gave the barbarians many of the Celtic skills in weaving, weapon-making and jewellery, and in one respect the barbarians were more skilful: their life on Europe's northern coasts had given them an affinity with the sea and a shipbuilding tradition. From this would develop, in later centuries, great masterpieces of Viking ship construction and Scandinavian and Anglo-Saxon timber building.

Germanic society had a social pattern similar to the Celtic one: an agricultural base and a hierarchical structure in which local rulers, their warriors, priests and peasants played a part. However, both their settlement patterns and their building types were more varied. Isolated homesteads, rectangular villages surrounded by palisades, circular villages planned with buildings radiating from a central space, and fortified hill-top refuges were all built at various times and places during the first few centuries AD. Most striking were the *Terpen*, loosely-planned villages built in the low-lying coastal areas of northern Friesland and Lower Saxony, often on high artificial mounds to raise them above flood level. The best-known is the 1st century village of Feddersen Wierde, on the north Saxon coast.

Common to German society was the conical timber hut with a hollowed-out floor, similar to the Celtic dwellings and known as the *Grubenhaus*. In Friesland, the more sophisticated 'aisled' or 'long' house was used. This was a rectangular building of great length, more spacious than a circular one. Extant foundations vary from 10 to 30 metres in length and up to 10 metres in width. Composite structures were needed to support the large thatched roofs. Rafters spanned between a long ridge-pole and similar poles at eaves level. The latter were supported on stout columns embedded in the ground, from which hung the wattle hurdles that served as walls. A large span would require very long rafters so these might be laid in sections, carried at mid-span on intermediate beams, or purlins, themselves supported on posts from the ground. A large building resulted, capable by its modular construction of subdivision into different uses. A likely division would be between people and animals, with a hearth and home at one end and rows of stalls at the other. Feddersen Wierde consisted of 20 or more such long houses, with ancillary buildings, grouped loosely in a radial pattern around a big central space.

The northern invaders brought their Germanic languages to Europe, creating a

# the tribal system:
## the structure of Celtic society

reconstructed Celtic village at
**Castell Henllys**
in Wales

Local king
and queen

Warrior

Priest

Bard
and
adviser

A small elite class
dominated...

...a large group of peasants...

... but apart from the power structure,
life in barbarian Europe was in other ways
egalitarian. The quality of housing, clothing
and food did not vary greatly from one
section of society to another. Each local
group produced buildings for its own needs.
The lack of a central authority meant there
was no major concentration of wealth.

heather thatch
or turf, stabilised
with mud

excavated
earth and stone

Simple circular hut with hollowed floor

## Celtic dwellings
## late BC, early AD

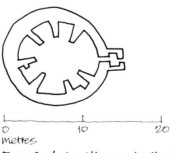

Plan of a 'wheel' house in Shetland:
stone and earth walls divide it into
compartments for different families
or uses

The composite structure
of a large communal
house

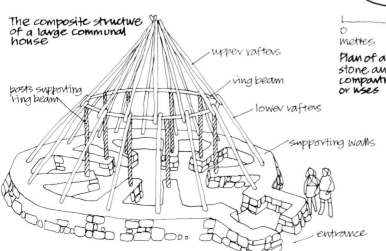

upper rafters

ring beam

lower rafters

supporting walls

posts supporting
ring beam

entrance

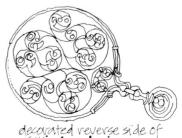

decorated reverse side of
Celtic **hand mirror**

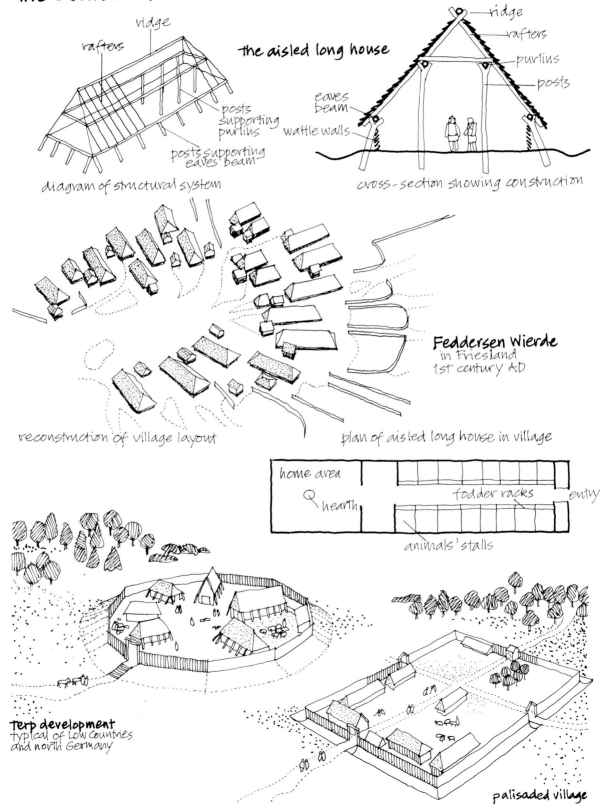

# buildings of the Germanic tribes

## the aisled long house

### diagram of structural system

rafters

vidge

posts supporting purlins

posts supporting eaves beam

### cross-section showing construction

ridge

rafters

purlins

posts

eaves beam

wattle walls

### reconstruction of village layout

**Feddersen Wierde**
in Friesland
1st century AD

### plan of aisled long house in village

home area

hearth

fodder racks

entry

animals' stalls

**terp development**
typical of Low Countries
and north Germany

**palisaded village**

linguistic diversity which still remains today. In other respects, barbarian and Romano-Celtic culture gradually merged. German building and craft techniques were assimilated by the Celts. As Christianity spread, co-existence flourished, intermarriage became more common and the birthrate rose. The greater social responsibility taught by Christianity meant better care for the underprivileged, and the death-rate fell. Between 600 and 800 Europe's population began gradually to increase.

The Romans had grown most of their crops on the Mediterranean littoral where light soils demanded no more than a lightweight 'scratch' plough and production was kept up by intensive cultivation and plot rotation. These farming methods died out in Europe with the collapse of the Roman system, but the increase of population in western Europe as a whole demanded new methods, which came from the north. For the heavier, wetter soils a heavy, wheeled plough drawn by a large team of oxen was developed. Its appearance as early as the 7th century implies a degree of co-operation already existing in the north, since no single farmer would have owned the number of oxen required. This is consistent with a general inventiveness among the northern population who in the next 300 years or so were to introduce into their agriculture the marling of top-soil, water-mills for grinding, the harrow and the flail, and a number of new cereal crops. Forests were cleared and strip-farming of large open fields, tended communally, became the pattern.

Political and economic uncertainty lay ahead, however. Central government was limited and farmers needed protection from local anarchy. The custom begun in the last years of the Empire, that of surrendering certain freedoms to gain the protection of local landlords, resulted in the gradual replacement of the tribal system by that of the feudal manor. Throughout the troubled times of the next four centuries feudalism was the unifying economic force of western Europe and Christianity provided the cultural continuity. This is not to say that the church spoke with one voice, nor that it was uninvolved in politics. The political history of the early Middle Ages is that of the church, and many of its early leaders, Constantine, Theodosius, Justinian, Gregory, were men of temporal as well as spiritual power. It was soon discovered, and repeatedly exploited, that religious unity helped to create national or imperial identity; the building of churches could also be used to demonstrate both spiritual and political power.

## CHRISTIAN BYZANTIUM

From the 5th to the 9th centuries, the uncertainties in western Europe brought major building projects almost to a standstill. Byzantium however remained economically advanced and had, from its trade with the Orient, a plentiful supply of commodities – silk, spice, jewellery, grain – which western rulers wanted to buy. Its economic stability encouraged building in general and constructional innovation in particular. Byzantine architecture developed as a remarkable synthesis of imperial Roman and middle-eastern techniques. From Rome came brick and concrete construction; from the east the use of the dome.

The dome of the Pantheon in Rome was over a circular space, a shape which has a limited number of architectural applications. Byzantine builders devised a means of putting domes over square and rectangular spaces thus giving themselves greater

St Sergius and St Bacchus, Constantinople (525)

narthex

dome area

0 10 20 30 40
metres

# the Byzantine church 1

As in the Pantheon, the springing line of the dome is lower inside than outside. This gives structural thickness where needed and results in the typical flat, Byzantine saucer outline

external springing line

internal springing line

San Vitale, Ravenna (526)

detail of clay pots within dome construction

clay bells

hollow pot dome, protected by wooden roof

amphora

60 cm

dome

pendentive

nave

exedra

exedra

ambulatory

sanctuary

nave

atrium

The eight exedrae have the structural job of buttressing the high dome..

0 10 20 30 40
metres

.. and spatially their effect is to blur the distinction between nave and ambulatory and add to the lightness and insubstantiality

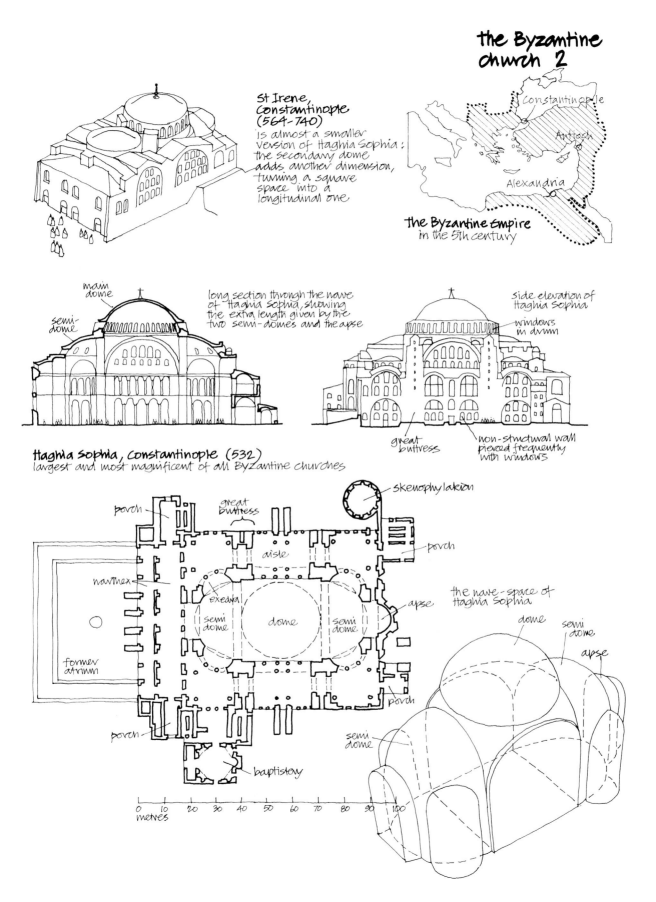

St Irene, Constantinople (564-740) is almost a smaller version of Haghia Sophia: the secondary dome adds another dimension, turning a square space into a longitudinal one.

the Byzantine Empire in the 5th century

Constantinople

Antioch

Alexandria

main dome

semi-dome

long section through the nave of Haghia Sophia, showing the extra length given by the two semi-domes and the apse

side elevation of Haghia Sophia

windows in drum

great buttress

non-structural wall pierced frequently with windows

Haghia Sophia, Constantinople (532)
largest and most magnificent of all Byzantine churches

skenophylakion

porch

great buttress

aisle

porch

narthex

apse

exedra

semi dome

dome

semi dome

former atrium

the nave-space of Haghia Sophia

dome

semi dome

apse

semi dome

porch

porch

baptistery

0   10   20   30   40   50   60   70   80   90   100
metres

freedom to create varied and complex plan forms. Brickwork, which can be shaped in innumerable ways, was one of the keys to this. The Byzantine builders developed a variety of geometric forms, the most ingenious of which was the 'pendentive', a concave triangular shape which took up the space between the bottom of a dome and the four corners of the square space on which it sat. Inside the buildings, the brickwork was rarely left plain. Faced with plaster, marble or mosaic, the pendentives, walls and ceilings provided opportunities for fresco painting and decorative mosaic, and church buildings began to glow with religious iconography.

Constantinople itself produced the chief architectural glories of early Christendom, east or west. The church of St Sergius and St Bacchus (525) is an early example of a dome on eight piers over a square building. San Vitale, Ravenna (526), built by Byzantine craftsmen during the Ostrogothic domination of Italy, has a dome on eight piers within a basic octagon. A lightweight dome of clay pots allows the columns and walls themselves to be light and elegant in appearance. The church of St Irene, Constantinople (564 and later), has two domes of different sizes over the nave of a basilica plan, the larger of which is the earliest example of a dome raised on a drum pierced with windows. The longitudinal plan contrasts with the symmetrical, centralised ones at St Sergius and San Vitale.

The supreme example of a dome placed over a longitudinal plan form is at Haghia Sophia, the great church built for Justinian in Constantinople in 532. Architectural ingenuity gives the building an effect of great simplicity. Four huge stone piers stand at the corners of a square some 30 metres across, and are linked by semi-circular arches which in turn support a huge hemispherical dome. This central space is extended to east and west by the addition of semi-domes supported on further piers. Together, dome and semi-domes form a vast oval-shaped nave some 70 metres long, beyond which lie the lower structures of the entrance narthex, aisles and apse. The semi-domes and their supports buttress the main dome to the east and west, and four massive buttresses over the aisles give support to the north and south sides. The interior is lit by windows in the dome and surrounding walls, and is alive with the colour of varied marbles and mosaics. The richness of decorative detail is in admirable contrast to the majestic simplicity of the overall design. This was Byzantine architecture in its most developed form. The Byzantine domed churches of the 6th century are to eastern Christendom what the basilica is to the west: they crystallised the form which was to be the basis of eastern Christian architecture for the next 1000 years.

But not all Christendom expressed itself by building great churches: there were those who felt that the Christian life could only be one of poverty and hardship. As early as the 3rd century, Christians had gone into the Egyptian desert as hermits, and now, in disenchantment with the established church, a monastic movement grew up, based on a search for spiritual fulfilment through poverty, abstinence and solitude.

The first European monastery is thought to have been at Lérins near Marseille early in the 5th century, and the movement reached Ireland, with St Patrick, in 461. The first English monastery was probably Tintagel in 470. In Scotland, St Columba established his at Iona in 563. These early monasteries, on their remote rocky outcrops, were rough and primitive by comparison with the sophisticated Byzantine churches, owing as much to the denial of worldliness as to the backwardness of local building methods. But

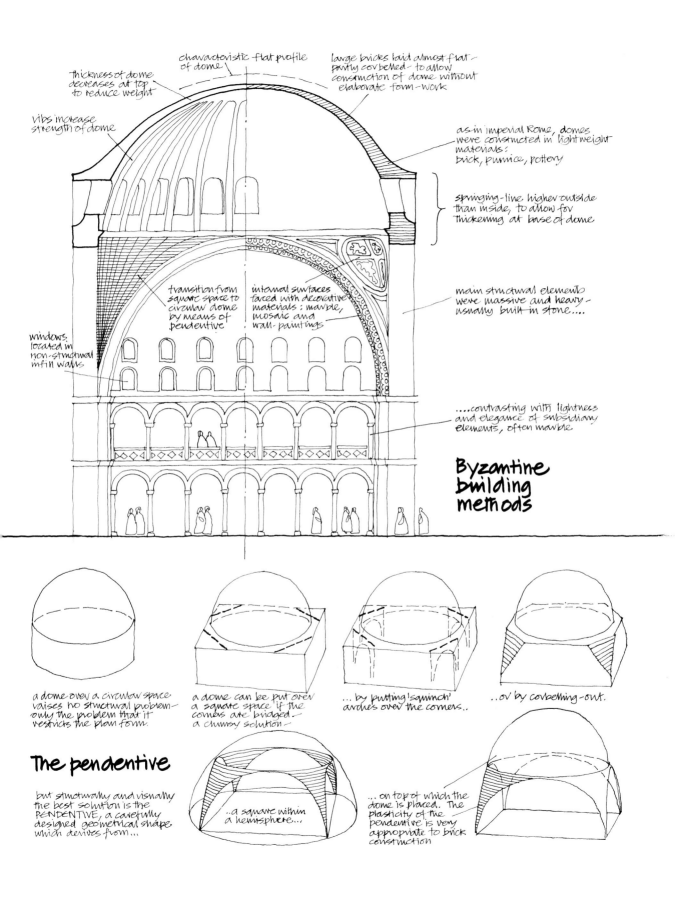

thickness of dome decreases at top to reduce weight

characteristic flat profile of dome

large bricks laid almost flat - partly corbelled - to allow construction of dome without elaborate form-work

ribs increase strength of dome

as in imperial Rome, domes were constructed in lightweight materials: brick, pumice, pottery

springing-line higher outside than inside, to allow for thickening at base of dome

transition from square space to circular dome by means of pendentive

internal surfaces faced with decorative materials: marble, mosaic and wall-paintings

main structural elements were massive and heavy - usually built in stone.....

windows located in non-structural infill walls

....contrasting with lightness and elegance of subsidiary elements, often marble.

## Byzantine building methods

## The pendentive

a dome over a circular space raises no structural problem - only the problem that it restricts the plan form.

a dome can be put over a square space if the corners are bridged - a clumsy solution -

... by putting 'squinch' arches over the corners..

..or by corbelling-out.

but structurally and visually the best solution is the PENDENTIVE, a carefully designed geometrical shape, which derives from...

..a square within a hemisphere...

... on top of which the dome is placed. The plasticity of the pendentive is very appropriate to brick construction

there is nothing unsophisticated about the magnificently appropriate siting of some of these simple buildings, such as Tintagel on its coastal promontory in Cornwall, or Sceilg Mhichíl, some 15 kilometres off the coast of Kerry, clinging to the side of the Great Skellig Rock.

Though originating as a search for truth through poverty and solitude, the movement attracted also the rich and self-indulgent who sought a quiet, romantic life or wished to acquire spiritual merit by excesses of abstinence. Observing this, St Benedict of Nursia (d. 543) established a 'Rule' at his monastery of Monte Cassino in central Italy, prescribing poverty, celibacy, obedience to the abbot, a disciplined prayer-life and fellowship through communal manual labour. The Rule transformed monastic life throughout Europe and helped it develop into a powerful spiritual force. Under the influence of writers like the philosopher Boethius and Theodoric's minister Cassiodorus, learning and scholarship also became the monks' responsibilities and for hundreds of years the monastic movement was a major cultural influence in western Europe.

St Benedict's Rule did not require a church. Before communal monastic worship was fully developed, small cells or oratories for individual monks to pray in were sufficient. The early communal hermitages on the rocky outposts of Europe were often groups of beehive-like stone huts, some of them living-quarters and some oratories, enclosed within defensive stone walls.

But gradually, as communal worship became more common, church buildings became necessary. In a localised and fragmented society which practised its own local building methods, the early monks represented the nearest thing there was to a pan-European culture. Essentially they had two architectural models for a church: some form of longitudinal plan deriving more or less from the basilica of the Romano-Christian tradition, or a centralised plan deriving from the domed churches of Byzantium.

The Celtic church of Ireland and Northumbria, deriving its traditions direct from Rome, built churches whose plan-forms have a distinct longitudinal emphasis. At the same time, a continental tradition was developing among the newly-Christianised barbarians of mainland Europe for whom the cultural leader was still Byzantium, guardian of the only living tradition of masonry building on which the Germans and Anglo-Saxons could draw. The church of San Juan de Bautista (661), built by the Visigoths at Baños in Spain, has a square, centralised plan. The early 8th-century Anglo-Saxon church of Bradford-on-Avon in Wiltshire, though basically Roman in form, has a cruciform plan of Byzantine origin. Most typically Byzantine of small European churches is Germigny-des-Prés near Orléans (806), with its square plan and central dome.

Almost all the survivals of the period are in stone. It is likely however that most church buildings of the time were of combustible timber and failed to survive the political turmoil of the 9th century. This was the most commonly available material and the most easily worked by the local craftsmen with their ship-building traditions. Though there are no direct survivals, contemporary descriptions of wooden Anglo-Saxon churches built on 'four great posts' suggest a Byzantine plan with a central tower. The later 'stave' churches of Norway, combining both Roman and Byzantine influences with mastery of timber techniques, show the heights to which north European timber craftsmanship may have aspired in these early centuries.

Out of the ruins of the old Roman empire a new local culture was gaining stability.

# the early development of the church plan

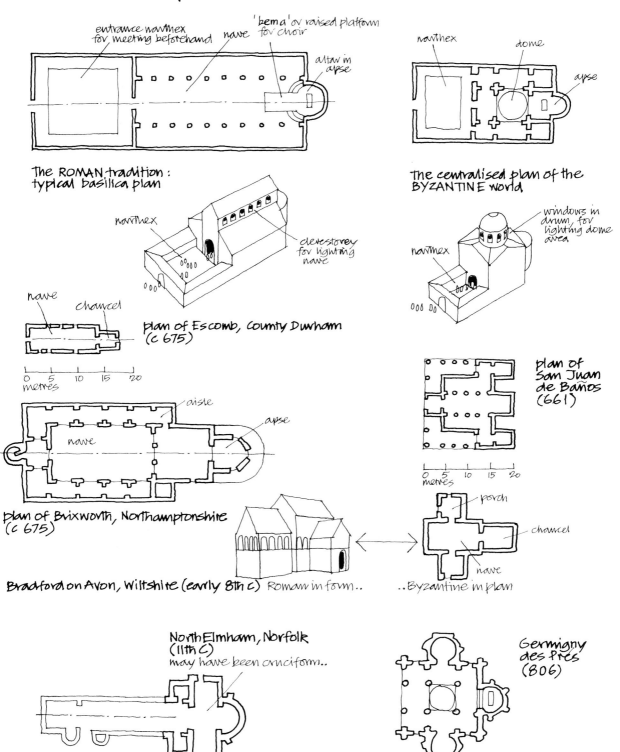

entrance narthex for meeting beforehand

nave

'bema' or raised platform for choir

altar in apse

The ROMAN tradition: typical basilica plan

narthex

dome

apse

The centralised plan of the BYZANTINE world

narthex

clerestorey for lighting nave

narthex

windows in drum, for lighting dome area

nave    chancel

plan of Escomb, County Durham (c 675)

0  5  10  15  20
metres

plan of San Juan de Baños (661)

0  5  10  15  20
metres

aisle

nave

apse

plan of Brixworth, Northamptonshire (c 675)

Bradford on Avon, Wiltshire (early 8th c) Roman in form..

porch

chancel

nave

..Byzantine in plan

North Elmham, Norfolk (11th C)
may have been cruciform..

0  5  10
metres

..till the addition of a later nave gave it a longitudinal plan

Germigny des Pres (806)

0  5  10  15
metres

But meanwhile, away in Asia Minor, in place of the old Persian empire, a religious, cultural and political movement was growing which would once more throw Europe into turmoil. In 569 Muhammad was born in Mecca. His new religion, described in his great work the Qur'ān, was being spread by devoted followers among the Arabian tribes. Motivated by economic forces as well as religious zeal, Muslim armies embarked in the mid-7th century on a journey of conquest. The middle east, India and north Africa fell. Byzantium was barely able to hold out, Spain collapsed and western Europe was threatened.

Of the barbarian tribes, only the Franks, in present-day France and Germany, were organised enough to show resistance. First united under Clovis in 481, the kingdom was taken over and greatly strengthened by Pepin of Heristal in 687. His son Charles Martel (714-41) was able to defeat the Islamic forces at Tours and Poitiers and drive them back into Spain. Western Europe became more united and confident politically, though cultural development was still held back by Islam's control of the Mediterranean, which limited European trade and hence the interchange of ideas. Nevertheless, there were isolated intellectual contributions, mainly by the monasteries. This was the age of the archbishop Isidore of Seville (d. 636) and his scientific researches, of the Lindisfarne Gospels (late 7th century), and of Bede's (d. 735) *Ecclesiastical History of the English People*.

While western Europe looked inwards, the power of Islam expressed itself in marvellous architectural works. Islam was a complete way of life, religious, political and social, carrying its search for religious truth into a striving for excellence in all aspects of life. The followers of Muhammad were generally tolerant of other religions, seeing themselves as the inheritors of the old Judaeo-Christian tradition. Nor did they despise the architectural traditions which they had inherited. They drew inspiration from Hellenistic, Syrian, Roman and Byzantine sources, and re-interpreted them in terms of the local craft techniques of the many regions of the world which their empire eventually covered. They brought the use of brick and stone to a fine art and with them perfected the use of the barrel-vault and the cross-vault, semi-circular and pointed arches, often in colonnades, and above all the dome, which first appears in Islamic architecture at the Kubbet-es-Sakhra, the Dome of the Rock, in Jerusalem (688). This appears to have been designed as a direct counterpart to Constantine's domed Church of the Holy Sepulchre. Nevertheless, it displays characteristically Islamic features which made it influential for centuries to come. In particular, it has a high dome of distinctly oriental rather than western profile, and the interior, clad in marble and glass mosaic, anticipates the rich geometric decoration which was to become such a feature of Islamic architecture.

In 785 Islamic architects built what was probably the most brilliant and sophisticated building yet seen in western Europe, the Great Mosque in Córdova, constructed by Syrian builders in a style inherited from Damascus. The main part of the building was built off the tops of a forest of salvaged classical marble columns. As the columns nowhere matched the height of interior required, the arches they supported were raised on 'stilts', and still more height was gained by making the crown of the arches in one direction into the springing-line of arches in the transverse direction. This simple functional approach provided a great fluidity and variety of form which is further enriched by the introduction of domes at certain points and by the variety of surface decoration.

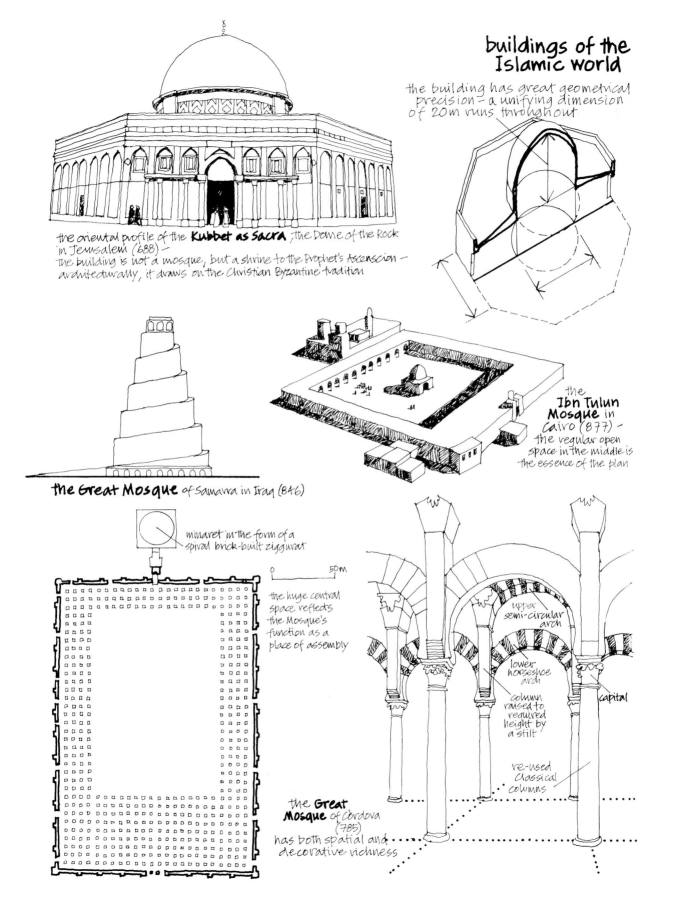

# buildings of the Islamic world

the building has great geometrical precision — a unifying dimension of 20m runs throughout

the oriental profile of the **Kubbet as Sacra**, the Dome of the Rock in Jerusalem (688) —
the building is not a mosque, but a shrine to the Prophet's Ascension — architecturally, it draws on the Christian Byzantine tradition

**the Great Mosque** of Samarra in Iraq (846)

the **Ibn Tulun Mosque** in Cairo (877) —
the regular open space in the middle is the essence of the plan

minaret in the form of a spiral brick-built ziggurat

0    50M

the huge central space reflects the Mosque's function as a place of assembly

upper semi-circular arch

lower horseshoe arch

column raised to required height by a stilt

capital

re-used classical columns

the **Great Mosque** of Cordova (785) has both spatial and decorative richness

All over the Islamic world, the approach to architecture was more consistent than that of Christendom, largely due to the universal acceptance of the Qur'ān as a guide to all the questions of life, including those of building design. As a result, certain basic features emerged: an essential similarity between both religious and secular buildings, for there was no sharp distinction between spiritual and everyday life; and a rejection of monumentality in favour of a small, human scale, resulting in buildings which were essentially low and horizontal in conception.

In one basic respect Islamic architecture had great influence on western building. The Qur'an forbade representational art in a religious context. Painting and sculpture on the western pattern were rare, but abstract applied art became well-developed, especially in the surface decoration of buildings, using abstractions developed from natural forms or from Arabic calligraphy. The Arabs were accomplished mathematicians, and their designs were carried out in a stylised, mathematical way which enhanced their perception of building geometry. The accuracy and geometrical ingenuity of Islamic building became a permanent lesson to architects in the west.

## CAROLINGIAN EUROPE

In 800, Charlemagne (768–814) was crowned Holy Roman Emperor by Pope Leo III. Energetic, brutal and a brilliant politician, he turned the Frankish kingdom into the strongest political unit in western Europe since the fall of Rome. He established sensible, defensible boundaries to the kingdom, and developed Europe's trade both with the eastern Empire and with Caliph Haroun al Raschid in Baghdad. His delicate relationship with Leo, also a powerful figure, gave rise to a continuing conflict between emperor and Pope. Significantly, Charlemagne chose Aachen for his capital, not Rome. Here he could establish his own institutions, free from Roman influences. For a time there was a return to strong central government. An uneducated man himself, he presided, with the help of the scholars he gathered round him, prominent among whom was Alcuin of York, over a revival of arts and learning. During his brief, brilliant reign came the establishment of the 'Carolingian minuscule' as the standard medieval script, the establishment of the secular Palace Schools of grammar, rhetoric and logic alongside those of the church, the production of beautiful books and psalters, a golden age in the development of Gregorian chant, and new achievements in the crafting of jewellery and metalwork.

In Carolingian Europe the feudal system reached maturity. Social relationships were no longer those of kinship, as in the tribal 'extended family', but were now based on a complex set of reciprocal obligations between different classes of society. Tribalism had not encouraged the division of labour: the man who had tilled the field had also, when necessary, taken up arms to defend it. But now agricultural production and military power belonged to different classes, and the relationship between them, their rights and mutual obligations, were strictly defined.

The basis of the system was the manor, a large estate owned by a lord and tended by the tenants who lived on it. The tenants enjoyed the lord's protection in times of trouble and in return owed him their labour. For his part, the lord owned the estate by authority of the king or emperor and owed him military service in return. Estates were usually in three sections, the 'demesne' belonging exclusively to the lord, the 'mansi' or holdings of the tenants, and the common land over which everyone had certain defined rights. Tenants were usually obliged to work on the demesne for three days a week, and might also owe the lord extra obligations. Possibly the most significant feature of the feudal system was its lack of mobility: a tenant was not only imprisoned within his class but also tied to the land. Attempts to escape from the system incurred severe punishment. Feudal landlords might be abbots or bishops, knights or barons. The emergence of this powerful class to challenge the supremacy of kings and emperors was to be one of the main political issues of the early Middle Ages.

Carolingian Europe was not wealthy: it still had an agricultural economy and a relatively decentralised administrative system. It could not produce buildings to match those of Byzantium and Córdova, but nevertheless an upsurge in building activity did take place. Charlemagne's wealth, like that of his Roman predecessors, depended on taxation, and his government was just strong enough to finance his cultural ambitions: setting up the Palace Schools, developing music and art, and commissioning fine buildings.

The palace complex at Aachen was developed largely by Charlemagne's architect, the monk and scholar Eginhardt. The original Palatine Chapel (792) still survives, a small polygonal building with a central dome, originally intended as Charlemagne's mausoleum and destined to become the scene of the coronation of successive Holy Roman emperors. The building clearly derives from the Byzantine church of San Vitale of Ostrogothic Ravenna: it has the same double-storey colonnade supporting the dome, outside which lies a surrounding aisle. If less subtle than San Vitale, it is nevertheless a remarkably elegant building for its time, and though small by Byzantine standards, its construction was a considerable technical achievement. Its architecture, while belonging to the Byzantine tradition, also shows something of the vigour and inventiveness from which later medieval architecture was to develop. An original feature of the building is the ceremonial west end forming a strong architectural counterpoint to the sanctuary at the east end. Containing the emperor's throne, the west end was intended to show Charlemagne as the representative of Christ on earth. Wherever he travelled, his abbeys and cathedrals were provided with a 'palace chapel' in which the emperor could sit at the west end in opposition to God at the east. Examples include the church of St Riquier at Abbeville in Picardy (790), which has a fully-fledged tower, crossing and transepts at each end of a squarish nave, and the abbey church of Fulda in Hesse (802) which has an apse at each end of a basilican plan.

The Carolingian building that had the most lasting influence was the Benedictine monastery of St Gallen in eastern Switzerland (820). It is notable less for what was built than for the complete plan prepared by Eginhardt, which crystallised the Benedictine design theories of the time and became the prototype for other monasteries for centuries to come. The plan shows a typical Carolingian double-ended church, of the type that was to remain popular, particularly in Germany, into the 11th and 12th centuries. More interestingly it shows a preferred layout for the numerous supporting facilities of which a monastery then consisted, giving some idea of its importance as a social centre: school, infirmary, guest-house, farm, mill, barn and threshing floor in addition to the religious apartments.

The Carolingian renaissance ended with Charlemagne's death. In 843, the Treaty

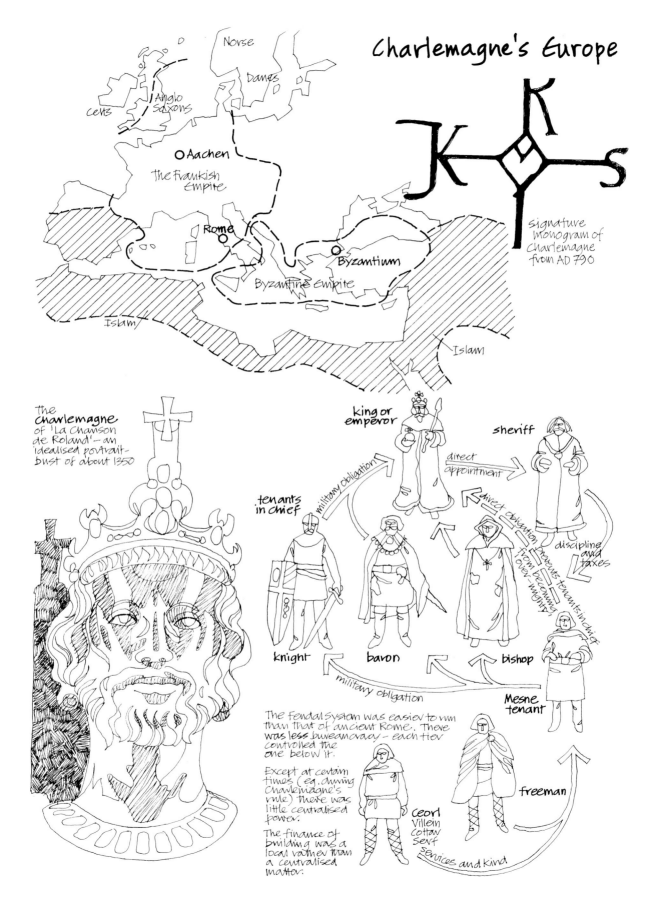

# Charlemagne's Europe

Celts
Anglo Saxons
Norse
Danes

O Aachen

The Frankish Empire

Rome

Byzantium

Byzantine Empire

Islam

Islam

signature monogram of Charlemagne from AD 790

The Charlemagne of 'La Chanson de Roland' — an 'idealised' portrait-bust of about 1350

king or emperor

sheriff

tenants in chief

military obligation

direct appointment

direct obligation prevents tenants in chief from becoming 'over-mighty'

discipline and taxes

knight

baron

bishop

military obligation

Mesne tenant

The Feudal System was easier to run than that of ancient Rome. There was less bureaucracy – each tier controlled the one below it.

Except at certain times (eg. during Charlemagne's rule) there was little centralised power.

The finance of building was a local rather than a centralised matter.

ceorl Villein Cottar Serf

freeman

services and kind

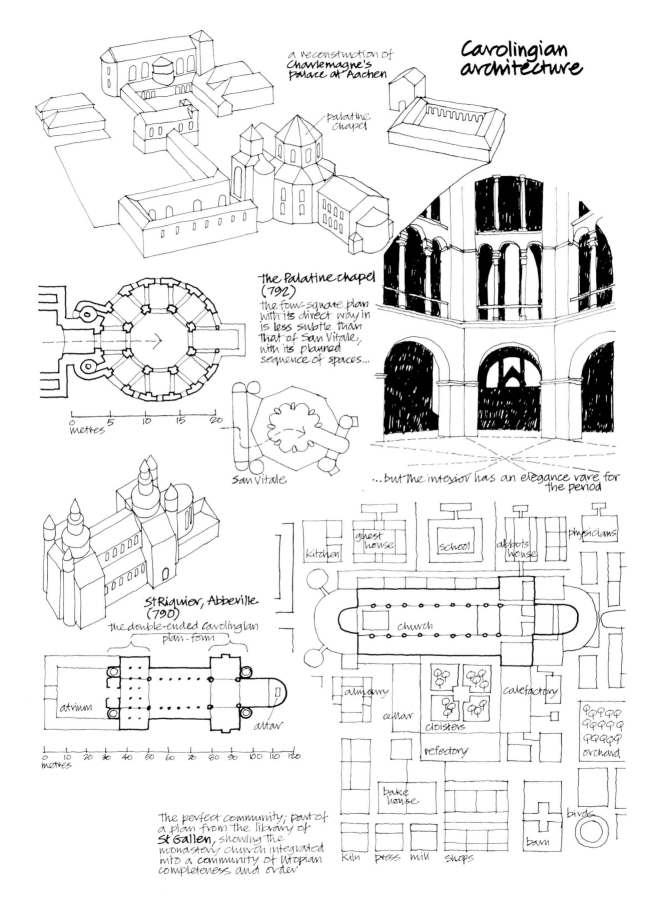

a reconstruction of **Charlemagne's Palace at Aachen**

# Carolingian architecture

Palatine chapel

**the Palatine chapel (792)**
the four-square plan with its direct way in is less subtle than that of San Vitale, with its planned sequence of spaces...

San Vitale

...but the interior has an elegance rare for the period

**St Riquier, Abbeville (790)**
the double-ended Carolingian plan-form

atrium

altar

metres  0 10 20 30 40 50 60 70 80 90 100 110 120

kitchen

guest house

school

abbots house

physicians

church

almonry

cellar

cloisters

refectory

calefactory

orchard

bake house

kiln   press   mill   shops

barn

birds

the perfect community; part of a plan from the library of **St Gallen**, showing the monastery church integrated into a community of utopian completeness and order

of Verdun divided the great empire, according to Frankish custom, among the three sons of his successor Louis, and Europe descended once more into political uncertainty. Magyar incursions from the east and Viking raids all along the northern seaboard from Ireland to Russia broke the fragile peace; trade between western Europe and the eastern Mediterranean ceased almost completely. The Vikings spread into Russia and Poland, into France, Normandy and Britain, and dominated northern Europe. Only Spain, most remote from the invaders in the north and east, seems to have produced significant buildings. The churches of Santa Maria de Naranco, Oviedo (848), Santa Cristina de Lena (c.900) and San Miguel de Escalada, León (913), all show a development of a barrel-vaulted Romanesque style, with, at León, particularly strong Islamic features reminiscent of Córdova. The quality of Spanish workmanship at this time, even in small buildings, surpassed that generally found in northern Europe. Moslem domination had left behind trained craftsmen capable of setting out buildings squarely and of producing a fair brick wall or a geometric arch.

In the rest of Europe, during the late 9th century, with trade at a standstill and society torn either by invasion or by the political struggles of local barons, creative cultural activity might have seemed a thing of the past. Yet out of this situation came a development which set the scene for a cultural renaissance to dwarf that of Charlemagne and to rival imperial Rome. The stringent economic situation in the 9th century had forced a number of trading cities in southern Europe to forge trade links with Byzantium and Islam in order to survive. During the 9th and 10th centuries Naples, Ravenna, Milan, Amalfi, Pisa, Pavia and above all Venice, began to experience a revival of trade and hence of wealth. At the same time, Viking domination of the northern coasts had brought increased trade to northern Europe, from Britain in the west to Russia in the east. From these two developments would eventually emerge the two main trading systems of medieval Europe: in the south the Lombardic league of Italian trading towns and in the north the Hanse.

With the gradual expansion of agriculture, it became possible to support more people. Towns, which had been in a state of decline since the late Roman empire, began to grow in size. During the heyday of feudalism, few western towns had survived as trading centres of any importance. Some had been converted into tribal homesteads; others had been chosen as the seats of bishops or as sites for abbeys, retaining the outward appearance of urban communities but with no economic significance. Many old buildings had been used as quarries for building stone, and large areas of cultivated land now lay within the old city boundaries. But now the migration of people from the countryside into the cities changed their character. From the start, escape to the city conferred independence from feudal ties, so towns became centres of freedom of thought and action, of progress and radicalism, the spearheads of an eventual revolution in the social order.

The feudal system, when not firmly controlled at the top, had resulted in ambitious, 'over-mighty' barons, with consequent political instability. After a succession of weak rulers, strong central government was re-established in Germany by Otto the Great (936-73) and in France by Hugh Capet (987–96). Similar anarchy had prevailed in the church. For many rich land-owning bishops and abbots, corrupt practices such as simony – the buying and selling of religious benefice – had become a way of life. So the Cluniac

# the growth of the city, 400-1200

**The Roman city** lost its economic raison d'être when the barbarians came. The economy had become an agricultural one

portus or harbour

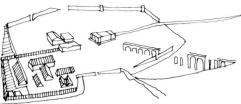

**A barbarian settlement** might be built within the walls, but the rest of the city would fall into ruin

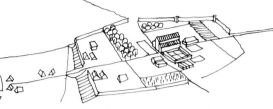

Eventually, it might form the basis of a **medieval abbey or see,** with a church at its centre. Thus, it did not completely disintegrate, though it lost much population.

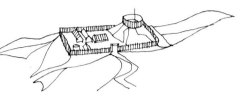

The 9th century saw the establishment of **burgs** in strategic places, fortified strongholds of military rather than economic origin.

As yet, neither **bishopric** nor **burg** was a real city: neither had an independent economic life and neither engaged in commerce or industry except to provide its own immediate needs. Both were based on the feudal system and lived off the surrounding countryside.

portus or commercial centre

When cities revived in the 11th and 12th centuries, they expanded. Much of the land inside the old walls might be owned by the church, so a **portus** of commerce might grow up outside.

faubourg

A burg at the centre of a similar commercial growth might develop a business area or **faubourg** outside the fortified centre

At first, neither **portus** nor **faubourg** was fortified. As competition for wealth grew, fear of attack increased. It was also important to protect the 'free' citizens inside the city from the feudal world outside. So where the citizens could afford it, massive outer lines of defence were built.

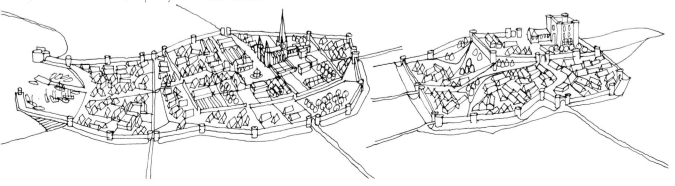

# the emergence of Romanesque

**Cluny II (981)** the archetype of the 'parallel-chapel' plan-forms

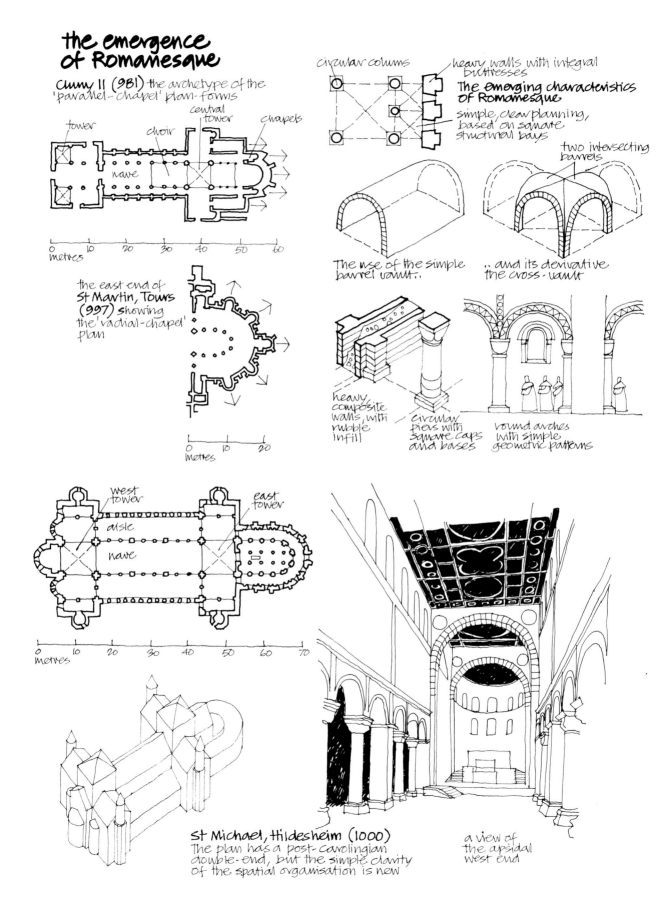

tower

choir

central tower

chapels

nave

0 10 20 30 40 50 60
metres

the east end of **St Martin, Tours (997)** showing the 'radial-chapel' plan

0 10 20
metres

circular columns

heavy walls with integral buttresses

## The emerging characteristics of Romanesque

simple, clean planning, based on square structural bays

two intersecting barrels

The use of the simple barrel vault...

... and its derivative the cross-vault

heavy, composite walls with rubble infill

circular piers with square caps and bases

round arches with simple geometric patterns

west tower

east tower

aisle

nave

0 10 20 30 40 50 60 70
metres

**St Michael, Hildesheim (1000)**
The plan has a post-Carolingian double-end, but the simple clarity of the spatial organisation is new

a view of the apsidal west end

movement now sought to purify the church by the strict application of Benedict's Rule. The emperor Otto III (d.1002) saw Cluny as a force to help unify the empire; his support for it established a new era of co-operation between the empire and the church.

The centre of the reform was Cluny in Burgundy, where the abbot Majeul authorised the rebuilding of the abbey church. 'Cluny II' as it is known, consecrated in 981, represented not only monastic reform but also a new architectural era – in fact, the birth of the romanesque style. Not only at Cluny but also at St Martin, Tours, on the Loire (997), and at St Michael's, Hildesheim, in Lower Saxony (1000), the rigorous spirit of Cluniac reform was interpreted in architecture of increasing ambition and of great quality. The builders were masons and carpenters, but the designers were evidently churchmen seeking to express their religious ideals. Most remarkable in the French churches were the many chapels which the liturgy now required, for the many priests to say mass or prayers for the souls of the departed. These chapels, parallel at Cluny and radial at St Martin's, opened off an ambulatory – a wide, curving corridor which ran round the east end behind the high altar. The plan of St Michael's is based on the double-ended east-west opposition of the Carolingian churches. These buildings are no longer reworkings of half-remembered styles of the past. They are large, simple, functional, and above all have a completeness of conception, an ordered relationship between one part and another, which represents a new approach.

The 'millennial' theory of medieval history – that intellectual effort in the 10th century was stifled because so many people thought the world would end in the year 1000 – does not fit the facts. The papacy and the empire were emerging as great political powers, population was increasing, towns were growing, a new religious spirit was in the air and a social and cultural movement had begun which within 200 years would culminate in the greatest achievements of European architecture.

# 4 REBUILDING THE FAITH
## The 11th and 12th centuries

> Therefore, after the above-mentioned year of the millennium, now about three years past, there occurred, throughout the world, especially in Italy and Gaul, a rebuilding of church basilicas … each Christian people strove against the others to erect nobler ones. It was as if the whole earth, having cast off the old by shaking itself, were clothing itself everywhere in the white robe of the Church.

Raoul Glaber, a Cluniac chronicler, wrote this enthusiastic passage in 1003. We are so used to thinking of architecture as one style succeeding another that it is easy to overlook changes of a more basic kind. Just as remarkable as the development of the romanesque style itself, with its new-found clarity of thought, was the number of buildings and, above all, their great size. During the 11th century, all over western Europe new buildings were appearing whose ambition, for the first time in eight centuries, rivalled that of ancient Rome.

The surge of activity reflects growing wealth and political stability, but the great size of the buildings suggests something more: the ability to organise, plan and budget for large-scale works, to transport materials and to bring together teams of workers. The early Middle Ages had seen the emergence of an ordered feudal society, which by the 11th century had reached a plateau of development. In control were two wealthy social groups: on the one hand a hierarchy of emperors, kings and barons, and on the other the Church. Both were well established and had developed that degree of internal organisation which makes them recognisable as classes – classes, moreover, with an increasingly European rather than merely local outlook, and their buildings, as expressions of class strength, were developing identifiable European characteristics.

The Normans were typical of this new spirit. 'Norman' means 'north-man', and three or four generations earlier they had been Viking invaders. Now Normandy was a small, dynamic feudal state which the kings of France, technically their overlords, had great difficulty in controlling. During the 11th century their influence spread through Europe: to England in 1066, thenceforth linking its cultural development to that of mainland Europe, to Italy and Sicily in 1071, and in 1084 to Rome itself. The story of the conquest

# the Norman castle

## The Motte and Bailey castle

: AT · HESTENGA · CEASTRA : HIC · N · WILLEM

A motte and bailey castle under construction at Hastings, depicted on the Bayeux Tapestry. The horizontal bands on the motte may represent layers of different materials, to give strength. The tower may be built of prefabricated sections

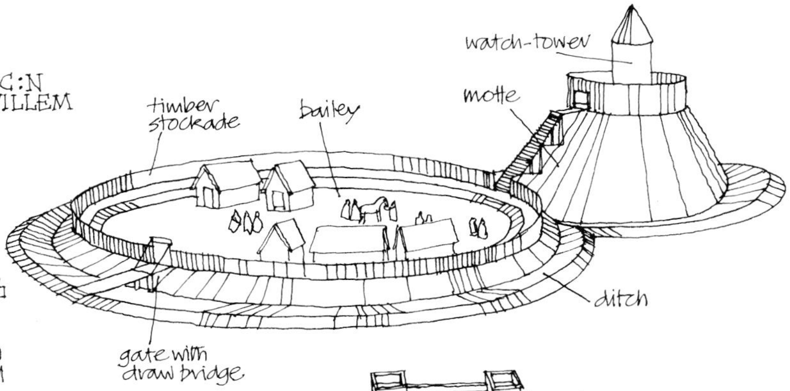

watch-tower
motte
bailey
timber stockade
ditch
gate with draw bridge

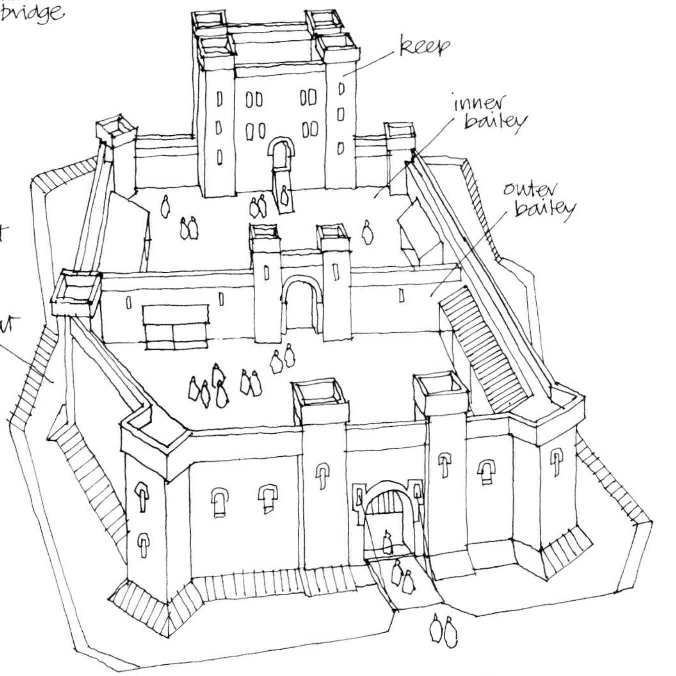

## Stone-built castle with tower-keep or donjon

In a Norman castle, the keep is the strongest point, the last line of defence when all others have fallen

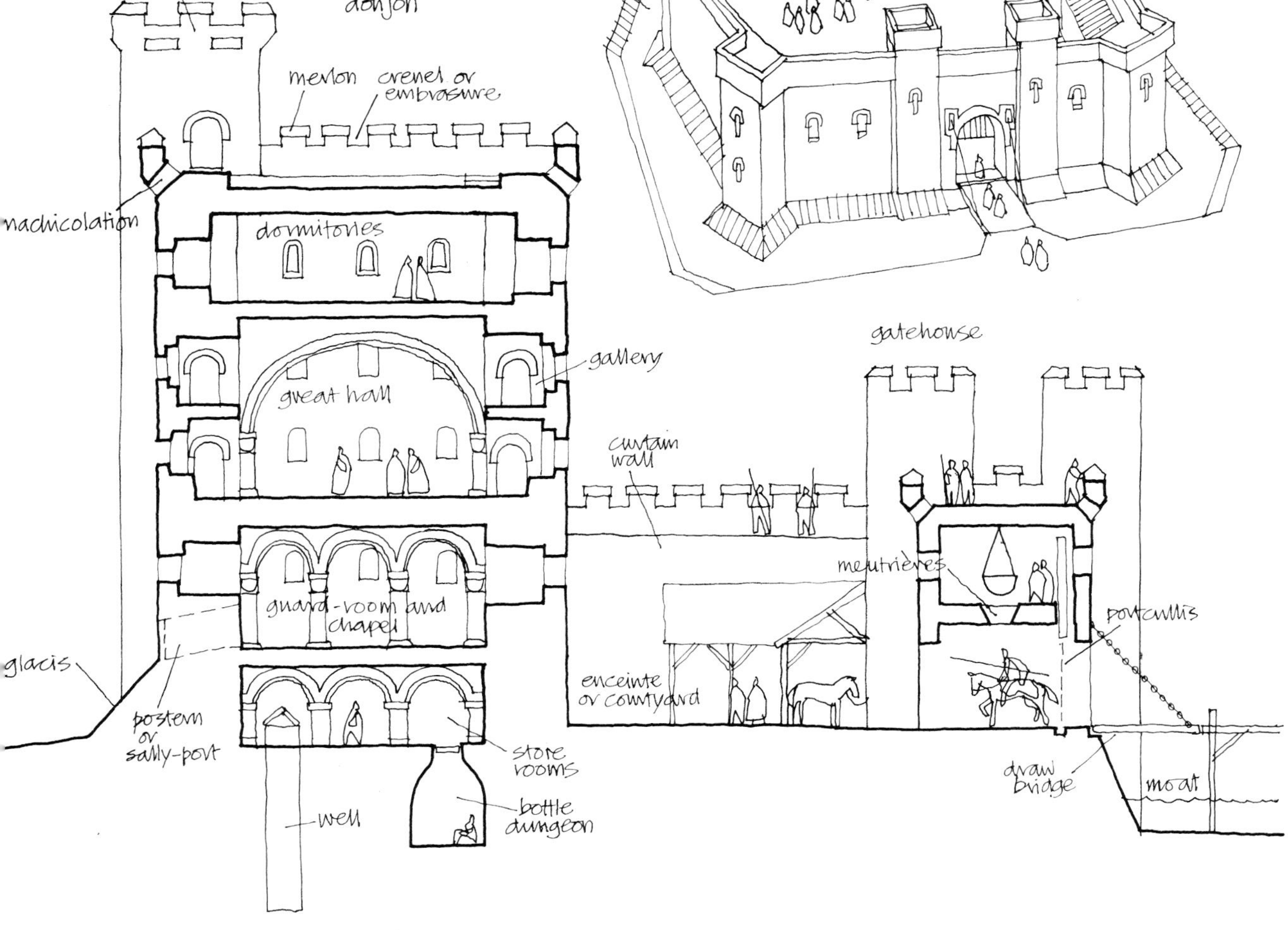

keep
inner bailey
outer bailey
moat

staircase tower
donjon
merlon
crenel or embrasure
machicolation
dormitories
gallery
great hall
glacis
postern or sally-port
guard-room and chapel
well
store rooms
bottle dungeon

gatehouse
curtain wall
meurtrières
portcullis
enceinte or courtyard
draw bridge
moat

of England is related visually in the famous Bayeux 'tapestry', probably made by Anglo-Saxon artists working for Bishop Odo of Bayeux, and completed around 1077. There is also the *Roman de Rou*, a written account by Wace, a 12th century Canon of Bayeux. As soon as the invaders landed,

> ... they consulted together and sought for a good spot to place a strong fort upon. Then they cast out of the ships the materials and drew them to land, all shaped, framed and pierced to receive the pins which they had brought, cut and ready in long barrels; so that before evening had well set in, they had finished a fort.

A similar fort is shown in the tapestry itself, a version of what we know as the 'motte and bailey' castle. The bailey was a compound, with ditch and stockade, sheltering a group of dwellings and storehouses. The motte was the strong-point of the castle, an artificial mound, also protected by a ditch and surmounted by a palisade or a wooden tower. Castles began in Europe in the 9th century, when both Charlemagne and the emperor Charles the Bald defended key border points by building block-houses in strategic places. King Edward the Confessor introduced the castle to England in the early 11th century, but the Normans established the motte and bailey form. There are many surviving examples: Thetford in Norfolk has one of the largest, 25 metres in height, and Dromore in Northern Ireland (1180) one of the most intact.

Guillaume of Normandy (d. 1087) became William I of England. He ruled efficiently, and his exhaustive survey of the country's economic resources, the Domesday Book (1081), was part of his plan to control the country through universal taxation. This depended on local control by his barons, so he built castles to provide them with bases for tax gathering and from which to mount punitive raids on the restless Anglo-Saxon people. During his 21-year reign, 50 baronial castles were built. William kept large tracts of land for himself, and built himself no less than 49 castles all over the country from which he and his sheriffs could oversee the barons' activities.

During the first years, castles were built in wood for speed and convenience, but a permanent site demanded, for greater safety, a castle of stone. The motte and bailey principle was used, but the defensive stockade around the bailey soon became a stone wall and, where feasible, the palisade on the motte became a squat circular defensive tower of stone known as a 'shell keep'. Often though, a hastily thrown-up motte might not be consolidated enough to carry a shell keep of any size, and so to replace both motte and keep, the 'donjon' was developed, This was a large, square tower, several storeys high, containing guardrooms, a living-floor, sleeping quarters for the lord's family, and possibly cells for prisoners. At the base there was often a 'glacis', an angled surface which kept sappers at a distance from the walls and caused offensive missiles dropped from above to ricochet among the attackers. An entrance high up in the wall discouraged the use of battering rams.

At intervals along the outer bailey, projecting towers were built to allow defenders to cover the walls with flanking arrow-fire, and the main entrance to the bailey, easier to storm than the donjon, often had a gatehouse with a portcullis, and sometimes a separate forward defensive tower, known as a barbican, for extra protection. Besiegers reaching the portcullis would find themselves under attack from *meurtrières*, 'murder holes', in the stonework above.

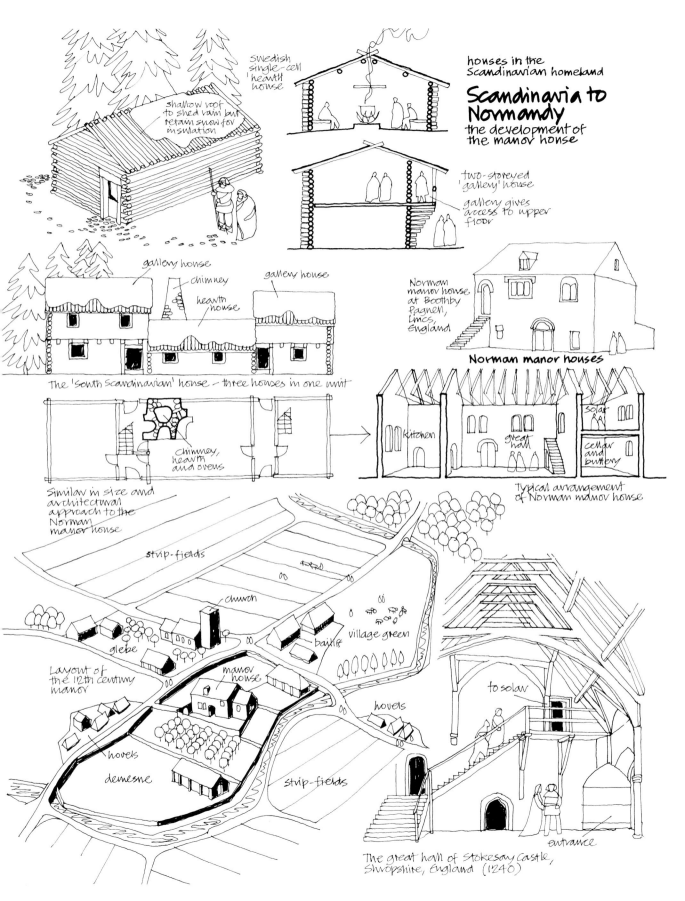

houses in the Scandinavian homeland

# Scandinavia to Normandy
the development of the manor house

swedish single-cell 'hearth' house

shallow roof to shed rain but retain snow for insulation

two-storeyed 'gallery' house

gallery gives access to upper floor

gallery house

chimney

hearth house

gallery house

The 'South Scandinavian' house – three houses in one unit

chimney, hearth and ovens

Similar in size and architectural approach to the Norman manor house

Norman manor house at Boothby Pagnell, Lincs, England

## Norman manor houses

kitchen

great hall

solar

cellar and buttery

Typical arrangement of Norman manor house

strip-fields

church

glebe

bailiff

village green

Layout of the 12th century manor

manor house

hovels

hovels

demesne

strip-fields

to solar

entrance

The great hall of Stokesay Castle, Shropshire, England (1240)

Shell keeps still exist at Carisbrooke on the Isle of Wight (1140) and Windsor Castle near London (1170), but the greatest castles of the period were of the donjon type. Finest of all were the White Tower in London, begun in 1086, and the Château Gaillard in France (1196). The former is a square building, 30 metres in height with a tower at each corner, one of which is enlarged to accommodate the uniquely beautiful little romanesque chapel of St John. The latter, built for Richard I of England on a strategic site at Les Andelys in Normandy, was a massive construction protected by three successive lines of earthworks and towers.

Like the Roman camp, the castle enabled a strong central authority to defend its borders from an outside enemy. Though used as a dwelling-place by its lord and often the centre of a large feudal manor, it was primarily a military installation, belonging to a specialist military elite. Just as membership of that elite was in the gift of the king, so was the construction of a castle, which required a royal 'license to crenellate'.

Castles continued to be built to defend borders and mountain passes from outsiders, but they also had an internal political role, that of controlling the local populace. The immense strength of the great castles of the 11th and 12th centuries meant they could be defended by very small garrisons, often of only 20 or 30 men. But no doubt this strength also had a deliberately intimidating effect on the local people. Ironically, the castles were often built by the serfs themselves. Royal licences also gave the power arbitrarily to impress workers into service, often many miles from home.

Below the baronial class was a larger group of minor lords, the tenants on whom the day-to-day workings of the feudal system depended. Their typical dwelling was the manor-house, a group of buildings consisting of dwelling, byres and store houses, usually round a fortified courtyard. The main building was the lord's house, consisting of a large central hall for meals and daily living, nearby kitchens, butteries and pantries, and an upper retiring chamber, the solar or 'sun-room', for sleeping.

The origins of the manor-house can be seen in the houses of the Normans' Scandinavian homeland. Here, for centuries, ordinary houses had been single-cell buildings with pitched roofs. The walls consisted of long, straight baulks of softwood laid horizontally, notched together at the corners in 'log-cabin' style. As living standards improved in the early Middle Ages, two-storeyed and multi-roomed houses were built, which set the pattern for the manor-houses of France and England. These too were usually of timber, but the best surviving examples are of stone, built in a simple, straightforward style like that of contemporary churches. None survive from the 11th century, but the 12th-century English houses at Boothby Pagnell, Lincolnshire, at St Mary's Guild in Lincoln, and at Christchurch, Dorset, are typical of the style.

## THE SPIRIT OF CLUNY

Europe's growing political order re-energised the feudal system, to the benefit of the land-owners – not only the barons, but also the Church, which by this time also owned large estates. Among the richest were the monasteries, which gained from the generosity of kings seeking their moral support and of rich laymen in search of spiritual justification. If a rich man entered monastic life, the Rule forbade him his personal wealth, which came to the monastery. By the 11th century, the monasteries owned money and property equivalent, it is estimated, to one-sixth of the entire wealth of Europe.

Their economic power was matched by their spiritual influence. Founded as they were in protest against the church establishment, the monastic or 'religious' orders, stood apart from the Pope, his bishops and priests, or 'secular' clergy. Concentrating on spiritual and social matters, they remained largely untainted by the political intrigues and corruption which over the centuries had so reduced papal authority. They gave Europe a spiritual leadership in which the example of Cluny was dominant: the great Cluniac abbots like St Odilo (994-1049) or St Hugh (1049–1109) spoke with more spiritual authority than the Pope himself. The movement grew. During the 11th century more orders were founded: the Carthusians at Grenoble in southeast France in 1086 and the Cistercians at Cîteaux and Clairvaux in eastern France in 1098.

In church building, monastic influence was strong. Designing a complex building required education, a commodity of which the monasteries still had a monopoly. The masons and carpenters were often serfs – though the more fortunate might have gained their freedom and received some sort of education. The masters who designed the buildings would all have been educated men, usually monks, but sometimes – increasingly so from the 10th century – tutored laymen.

The Papacy itself was subjected to a Cluniac reformation in 1046. This increased the standing of the secular church, as did the growth, all over Europe, of the parochial system. Parishes had three main features: a geographical boundary, often based on the boundaries of the feudal estates, a parish priest, appointed as a 'cure of souls' to the local population, and a church building.

Parish churches and monastic churches had certain differences of function and hence of form. In a monastic church the main space was the 'choir', where the monks worshipped. Lay worshippers, if any, had little or no dedicated space. A parish church however needed to house its secular congregation. From the 9th century onwards identifiably secular churches, with large naves, began to appear. Pre-conquest parish churches in Britain include St Nicholas at Worth in Sussex (c.950), with a simple cellular plan in which the nave undoubtedly dominates, and All Saints at Earls Barton in Northamptonshire (c.970) whose nave took the form of a large tower, famous for its Anglo-Saxon 'long-and-short' decoration.

Increasingly, parish churches were purpose-built, but sometimes monastic churches were adapted, often using monastic finance and the monks' building skills. Designing churches had for so long been a monastic prerogative that the secular Church was only beginning to learn the art. In France, the church of St Philibert Tournus in Burgundy (950 and later) began as the church of a Benedictine abbey but was extended with a nave spanned by fine diaphragm arches. The beautiful church of San Miniato al Monte, Florence (1018), appears from the outside to be a basilica in the Roman tradition, but the interior shows some romanesque innovations, in particular the division of the long straight nave by piers and transverse semi-circular diaphragm arches into three basic compartments, showing an increased interest in spatial organisation.

Throughout western Europe great church buildings, both monastic and secular, began to display identifiable romanesque features. In southern and eastern Europe,

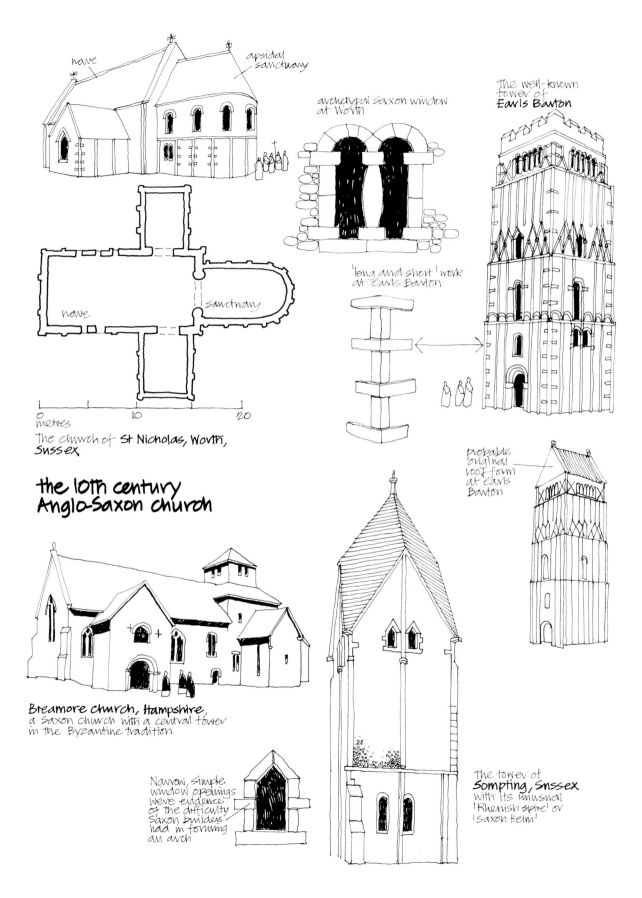

nave

apsidal sanctuary

archetypal Saxon window at Worth

the well-known tower of **Earls Barton**

nave

sanctuary

'long and short' work at Earls Barton

0 metres    10    20

The church of St Nicholas, Worth, Sussex

probable original roof form at Earls Barton

# the 10th century Anglo-Saxon church

Breamore church, Hampshire, a Saxon church with a central tower in the Byzantine tradition

Narrow, simple window openings were evidence of the difficulty Saxon builders had in forming an arch

the tower of **Sompting, Sussex** with its unusual 'Rhenish spire' or 'Saxon Helm'

however, the Byzantine influence was still strong. The church of San Marco in Venice (1063), is a *tour-de-force* which owes much less to western than to eastern Europe. Built to replace an earlier basilican church burnt down in 976, it has a Greek-cross plan with a main central dome on pendentives, carried on four great piers, and smaller domes over the entrance narthex, the transepts and the sanctuary. Its unique urban location, and the rich symbolism of its mosaics, frescoes and statuary, extolling the city's rise to power, make it a building *sui generis*.

In Byzantine Greece, by contrast, the finest contemporary buildings were remote and monastic. The monastery of Hosios Loukas in the Peloponnese, was begun in the early 10th century, with the church dedicated to Mary, the *Theotokos*. It had a simple cross-in-a-square plan. In the early 11th century there followed the cathedral church or *Katholikon*, with its hemispherical dome over an octagonal space. On the remote island of Chios, the 11th century Nea Moni monastery contained several churches, also devoted to the Theotokos. And in a forest near Athens, the monastery of Dafni was centred on the church of the Dormition, and also planned as a cross in a square. All three monasteries were built in a beautifully simple 'mixed' style of brick and stone, and all were decorated internally with fine 11th century frescoes and mosaics. Those at Dafni are exemplary, representing as they do an entire Byzantine cosmology of God and Man, dominated by a magnificent *Christos Pantocrator* in the dome.

The Christianity of Byzantium had spread to Russia in the year 998, when Prince Vladimir of Kiev had converted, and adopted it as the state religion. Kiev and Novgorod, in the Dniepr valley, had been growing since the mid-9th century, situated as they were on the trade route from the Baltic in the north to the Black Sea and Byzantium in the south. Churches dedicated to Santa Sophia, the Divine Wisdom, were built in Kiev in 1036 and Novgorod in 1045. Both were huge, built like the Greek churches in 'mixed' construction, and roofed with multiple domes raised on drums. They provided the reference point for all subsequent Russian church architecture.

Around 1130, another great symbol of medieval Russia, the icon of the Virgin of Vladimir, was brought to Kiev from Byzantium, providing a model and setting the standard for all subsequent religious painting. As Christianity spread, more religious centres were founded. Eastwards, towards the Volga, lay the cities of Suzdal and Vladimir, the former founded in 1024 and the latter in 1108, its celebrated Golden Gate being built in 1158 and the beautiful little church of the Intercession, the 'church on the River Nerl' in 1166. It was to Vladimir that the icon of the Virgin was transferred, and displayed in the Dimitriyevsky cathedral of 1197. In the central Kremlin of nearby Suzdal, the Vladimir Monomakh's cathedral of 1096 was the first of many churches on the site. The churches of Vladimir-Suzdal were built in the white limestone of the Volga region, which allowed for carved decoration in intricate detail. Many of the characteristic features of Russian churches – the decorative 'column belts' around the façades, the numerous ogee-shaped gables or '*zakomaras*', the high drums for the domes, the onion shapes of the domes themselves, and the compact Greek-cross plans – derive from these buildings.

During the 11th century, as western church-builders grew more ambitious, this centralised Greek-cross plan of Byzantium became synthesised with the basilican plan of the Roman tradition. Designers began to enlarge the volume of their buildings

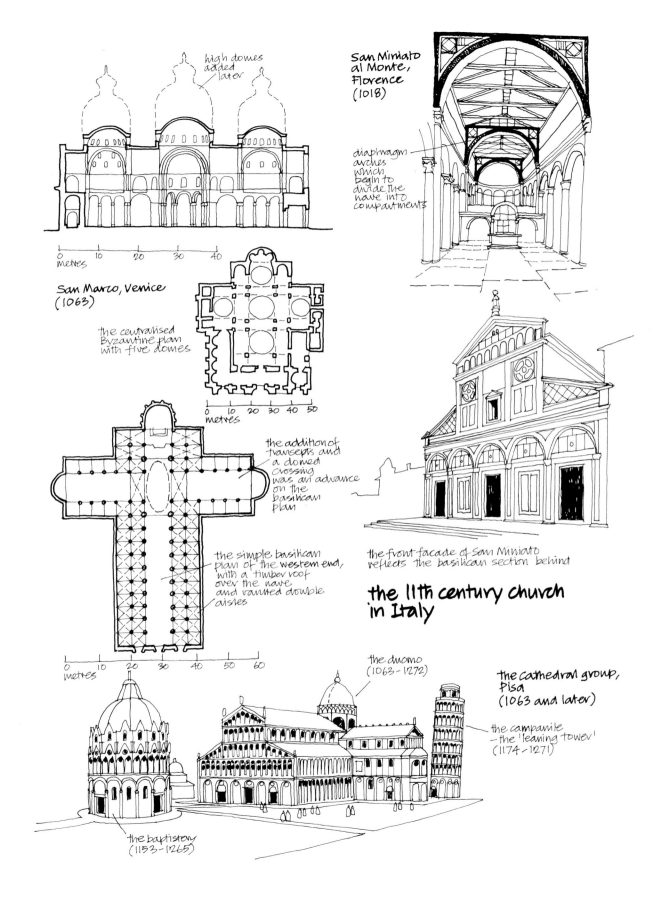

high domes added later

San Miniato al Monte, Florence (1018)

diaphragm arches which begin to divide the nave into compartments

0  10  20  30  40
metres

San Marco, Venice (1063)

the centralised Byzantine plan with five domes

0  10  20  30  40  50
metres

the addition of transepts and a domed crossing was an advance on the basilican plan

the simple basilican plan of the western end, with a timber roof over the nave and vaulted double aisles

the front facade of San Miniato reflects the basilican section behind

**the 11th century church in Italy**

0  10  20  30  40  50  60
metres

the duomo (1063–1272)

the cathedral group, Pisa (1063 and later)

the campanile – the 'leaning tower' (1174–1271)

the baptistery (1153–1265)

**Kiev Rus**
in the Middle Ages

# the Church in Russia

Gulf of Finland

Novgorod

Yaroslavl

Zagovsk

Vladimir Suzdal

the Golden River

Kiev

Dniepr

Black Sea

Byzantium

0          500 K

reconstruction of **Santa Sophia** Kiev (1057) built for Yaroslav the Wise in emulation of the earlier cathedral of Novgorod

0   5   10   15m

**Santa Sophia** Novgorod (1045) one of the earliest stone churches in Russia

the 'white stone' **Dmitrievsky** church at Vladimir (1194) typical of the 12th century Suzdal style

the **Virgin of Vladimir** the archetypal 'Eleusa', or 'tenderness' icon, brought from Constantinople to Vladimir via Kiev, and destined to become a symbol of medieval Russia

the **Golden Gate** Vladimir (1164) was originally the main entrance to the fortified city

the Virgin

Christ in Majesty

Virgin and Child

John the Baptist

prophets

'deesis' tier of icons

church holy days

Virgin and Child

tsar doors

name saint of church

'veneration' tier of icons which the worshippers could touch

the **iconostasis** separated the sanctuary from the nave of the church

by intersecting the long nave of the basilica with another nave-shaped space running across at right angles, known as the 'transepts'. Where they intersected, the four huge piers at the corners of the large square space known as the 'crossing' might provide the support for a central tower, spire or dome. Interpreted in the rigorous romanesque idiom, the result was the Latin-cross plan, the first truly indigenous church plan of north-west Europe, and the basis for the planning of almost all later medieval cathedrals.

The cathedral of Pisa (1063) forms the centrepiece of the celebrated group which also contains the later Baptistery and Campanile. Like San Miniato, it is basically a basilican building. Its nave has rows of columns supporting semi-circular arches from which rises a clerestorey, and at the sides, double aisles provide a wide ground-floor space. But the formation of a crossing by the addition of transepts relates the plan-form to contemporary buildings in north-western Europe.

Church-building in Normandy provided the models. La Trinité in Caen (1062), the Abbaye-aux-Dames, is one of the earliest of the great Norman churches with nave, transepts and square crossing-tower establishing the basic formal arrangement used time and again in succeeding centuries. The roof is vaulted, with early and slightly crude 'sexpartite' vaulting. The sister-church of St Etienne in Caen (1068), the Abbaye-aux-Hommes, originally featured the characteristic *chevet* east end of Cluny II. The sexpartite vaults of La Trinité are developed in a more confident way and two other features used in later centuries were introduced: the west end with twin towers surmounted by spires is an early prototype for later, gothic façades, and the outward thrust of the nave vault is contained on each side by a continuous, half barrel-vault built against it – a concept anticipating the flying buttress.

Norman architectural influence had been felt in Britain some years before the Conquest, the most celebrated example being Edward the Confessor's original Westminster Abbey (1055), then a continental monastery in the Cluniac tradition. But the style reached its peak in the great churches built by the Normans themselves. Like Westminster, most English cathedrals had a monastic origin. Many retain their cloisters and ancillary buildings, now adapted to other uses. The ruins of the great abbeys of Rievaulx (1132), Fountains (1135) and Kirkstall (1152) give a clearer picture of what a Norman abbey was like in its day. Fountains is dominated by the ruins of a late medieval tower, but its cruciform church, with its unusual 'chapel of the nine altars', was mid-12th century. On the south side was a cloister garth, flanked on one side by the 90-metre-long block which housed the refectory and dormitory of the lay brethren. Nearby were the monks' dormitory and refectory, chapter-house, kitchens, infirmary, abbot's house and stores.

Seventeen English and Welsh cathedrals still retain substantial examples of Norman work, including the naves of Ely, Chichester, St Albans and St Davids, the choirs of Gloucester and Winchester, and the twin transept-towers of Exeter. The most complete examples, however, are Peterborough (1117) with its fine interior and original decorative timber roof, Norwich (1096) with its long nave and *chevet*-type choir with radial chapels and, above all, Durham.

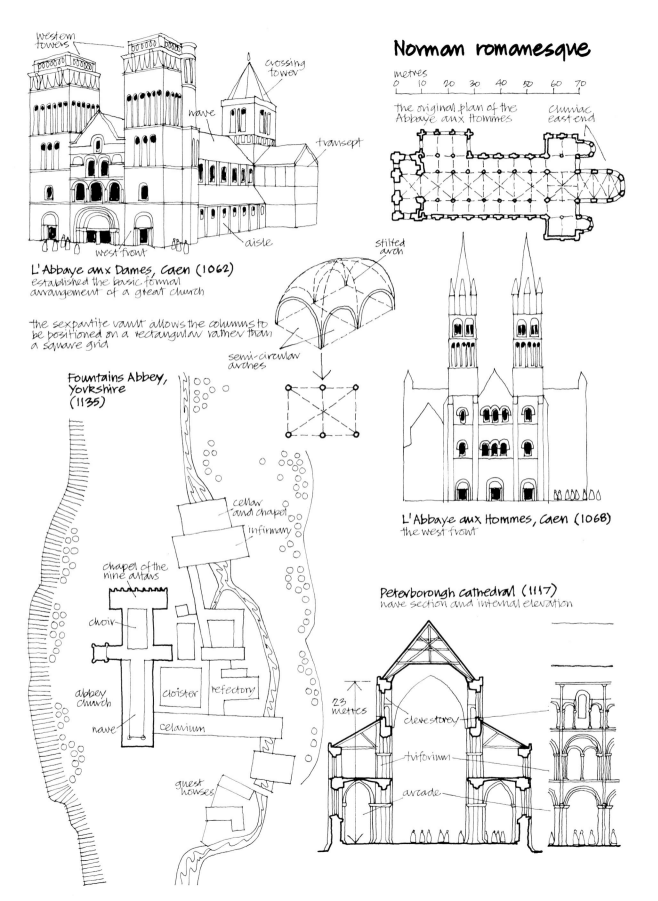

western towers

crossing tower

nave

transept

west front

aisle

**L'Abbaye aux Dames, Caen (1062)**
established the basic formal
arrangement of a great church

the sexpartite vault allows the columns to
be positioned on a rectangular rather than
a square grid

stilted arch

semi-circular arches

# Norman romanesque

metres
0  10  20  30  40  50  60  70

the original plan of the
Abbaye aux Hommes

Cluniac east end

**L'Abbaye aux Hommes, Caen (1068)**
the west front

**Fountains Abbey,
Yorkshire
(1135)**

cellar and chapel

infirmary

chapel of the nine altars

choir

abbey church

cloister

refectory

nave

cellarium

guest houses

**Peterborough cathedral (1117)**
nave section and internal elevation

23 metres

clerestorey

triforium

arcade

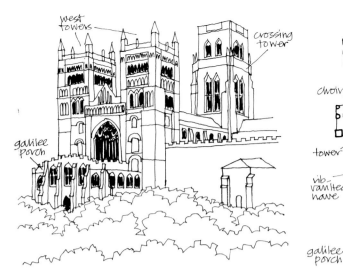

west towers

crossing tower

galilee porch

chapel of the nine altars

altar

choir

tower

rib-vaulted nave

galilee porch

cloister garth

monastic buildings

0 20 40 60 80 100
metres

# Durham and the rib-vault

the Romans had used simple barrel vaults, coffered to reduce their weight...

repetitive bay or compartment

... and had also developed the groined or cross-vault which introduced the concept of vaulting in compartments

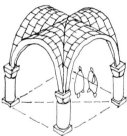

The Normans were able to use heavy, stone groined vaults, mainly in undercrofts and crypts

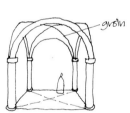

groin

One of the weakest aspects of the groined vault was the groin itself, liable to failure. Another problem was the continuous, all-over support which the groined vault needed during construction.

ribs

this changed with the 12thC development of the rib-vault. Only the ribs themselves required support during construction, and...

light weight infill panels

...the panels in between could be filled afterwards with light-weight stone, allowing the size of the supports to be reduced

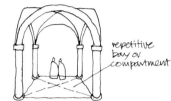

pointed arch

pointed arch

ribs

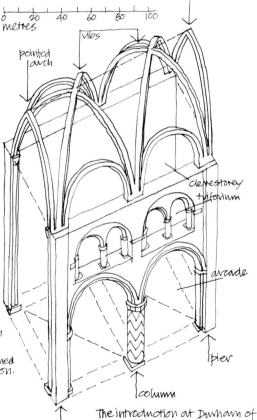

clerestorey

triforium

arcade

pier

column

pier

The introduction at Durham of the pointed arch allows its apex to be brought in line with that of a round arch of greater span

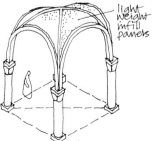

end arch

diagonal arch

## THE ROMANESQUE WORLD

Durham Cathedral (1093 and later) is built on a great rock above the River Wear. It is a dramatic location, suitable for a castle, and the building has an appropriate masculine quality. The long, tall nave has massive circular piers with round arches supporting a second-tier 'triforium' and a third-tier clerestory. Their effect, though sober, is airy rather than oppressive, lightened by simple but delicately carved abstract decoration, flutings and zig-zags. The choir, finished in 1104, has probably the earliest example of rib-vaulting known in Europe, a feature of great importance in the subsequent development of stone-built roofing. The nave vaulting, finished in 1130, is taken even further, for here the pointed arch is introduced in order to allow its apex to be brought in line with the top of rounded arches of greater span, a feature which would be brought to its logical conclusion in gothic buildings two and three centuries later.

One of the impulses behind the architecture of the 11th century was the search for roofs capable of spanning larger spaces. These could, of course, be of timber, but the use of candles and rushes for lighting made the risk of fire ever-present. The Romans had used barrel-vaults and groined-vaults over wide spans, but the 11th century did not have Roman concrete; a barrel-vault in stone alone has a high weight-to-strength ratio which limits its span. This was changed by the development of the rib-vault: here the ribs alone were structural, and could be infilled with relatively lightweight panels of stone, allowing wider spans. Furthermore, the ribs concentrated the stresses onto localised points where they could be carried on columns, rather than on the continuous wall implied by the barrel-vault. The rib-vaulting at Durham, clearly demonstrating the lines of stress, gave the interior a tense, lively appearance and presaged the great gothic interiors of the 12th and 13th centuries.

Though seldom as structurally dynamic as Durham, church designs all over Europe were beginning to show a similar concern for articulation, for the clear expression of structural elements and the division of internal space into bays and compartments. The church of Sant' Ambrogio in Milan (1080 and later) was an ancient foundation, begun by St Ambrose himself in the 4th century and still retaining archaic features such as an entrance atrium and an eastern apse, but its rebuilding in the late 11th and early 12th centuries incorporated new ideas. The severe and majestic nave is divided by diaphragm arches into bays, each vaulted with round-arched rib-vaults. Like those at Durham, the rib-vaults are among the earliest in Europe and the pattern for subsequent imitations, notably at San Michele, Pavia (1100).

Contemporary churches in north Germany still retained Carolingian elements but here, too, new ideas appeared. Maria Laach abbey (1093), south of Cologne, has an apse at the west end, recalling Charlemagne's Palace Chapels, but the three eastern apses and the many towers are more reminiscent of Cluny. The 11th-century cathedral of Worms, a major monument of the period, also has a western apse but also transepts and a crossing-tower, two eastern towers, and a further pair of flanking towers at the west end. Nave and aisles are roofed by stone cross-vaults on square compartments. The later Church of the Apostles, Cologne (1190), has an eastern transept with apsidal ends over which is an octagonal crossing-tower. The west end is given prominence by a single tall tower on the axis of the nave.

Sant'Ambrogio, Milan (1080)

depressed diaphragm arch

semi-circular diagonal ribs

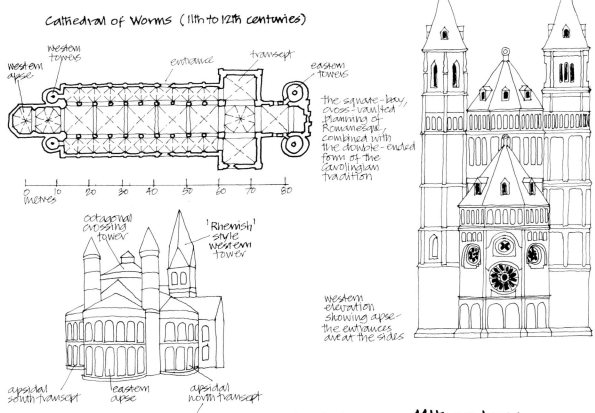

Cathedral of Worms (11th to 12th centuries)

western apse
western towers
entrance
transept
eastern towers

0 10 20 30 40 50 60 70 80
metres

the square-bay, cross-vaulted planning of Romanesque, combined with the double-ended form of the Carolingian tradition

octagonal crossing tower

'Rhenish' style western tower

apsidal south transept
eastern apse
apsidal north transept

western elevation showing apse- the entrances are at the sides

west tower
eastern apse
crossing tower

Church of the Apostles, Cologne (1190 and later)

0 20 40 60 80
metres

# 11th century Italy and Germany

Ste Madeleine at Vézelay in Burgundy (1104) presents a different aspect of romanesque architecture. Like Durham, it is a large building on a commanding hill-top site. It has an aisled nave, transepts, double towers at the west end and a *chevet* at the east. Its structure is less adventurous than that of Durham, consisting basically of a series of semi-circular groined vaults, the vaulting compartments articulated by great transverse arches. It is remarkable, however, for less tangible reasons: the elegance of its proportions, the rightness of its balance between structural simplicity and decorative richness, and above all, the contrast between the subdued lighting of the nave with its high clerestories and the transparent luminosity of the east end.

Farther south in France, Byzantine influences were still felt. The cathedral of Angoulême (1105), though undoubtedly a romanesque building in the clarity of its Latin-cross plan and the multiplicity of its eastern chapels, both radial and parallel, is roofed with a series of shallow domes on pendentives. The great church of St Front at Périgueux (1120) also has a mixed parentage. It has almost exactly the layout of San Marco, Venice, with its Greek-cross plan and five domes, but whereas San Marco glows with Byzantine mosaic, St Front has a severe stone interior, a model of romanesque sobriety.

Islamic occupation had made Spain the subject of Europe's ambition, so for political as well as religious reasons much interest was shown in the shrine of St James at Compostela and the pilgrimage route to it. St Martin at Tours became a great pilgrimage church, and others were built along the route at Limoges, Conques and Toulouse. The symbolic importance of Compostela itself demanded a major building (1075 and later) at the shrine of Santiago. It has a cruciform plan with a crossing-tower and barrel-vaulted nave and transepts. At the sides are aisles with galleries above; the gallery roofs are a half-barrel-vaults, as at St Etienne, buttressing the nave vault. The east end has an ambulatory with radiating chapels on the pattern already seen at St Martin, Tours. The whole building is enlivened by its rich detail, of which the Portico de la Gloria (1168) is the supreme example.

The various pilgrimage churches, if not directly inspired by Cluny II, certainly show a Cluniac influence. In 1088, the abbey church of Cluny itself was rebuilt again, and with its length of nearly 140 metres became the largest and most splendid building in France. Most of this building, Cluny III, has been destroyed, which has tended to obscure its importance in the history of architecture. It was a complex building with a long double-aisled nave, two transepts, each with towers over the crossing, and a multiplicity of chapels at the east end. Its great size presented a structural problem, and for the first time rows of fully-developed flying buttresses were used, above the aisles, to contain the outward thrust of the nave roof. This device was to become a major structural feature of churches for the next three centuries. At Cluny, in the late 11th century, it was a celebration of virtuosity, of the growing confidence of its builders. The new knowledge and skills were part of a general re-awakening, not only in the arts but in all branches of knowledge.

Cultural progress is not necessarily a reflection of general social progress; greater knowledge provides the opportunity for social improvement, but does not guarantee it. The fine achievements of the 11th century did not, for example, improve the conditions of the serf. Indeed, cultural development depended partly on inequality and

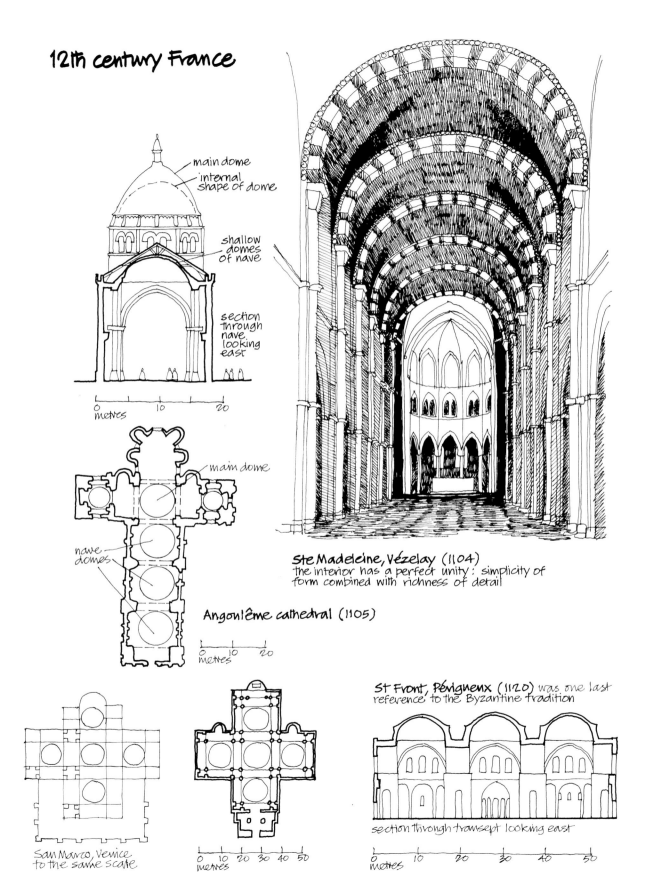

# 12th century France

main dome

internal shape of dome

shallow domes of nave

section through nave, looking east

0 — 10 — 20 metres

main dome

nave domes

Angoulême cathedral (1105)

0 — 10 — 20 metres

Ste Madeleine, Vézelay (1104)
the interior has a perfect unity: simplicity of form combined with richness of detail

San Marco, Venice to the same scale.

0 10 20 30 40 50 metres

St Front, Périgueux (1120) was one last reference to the Byzantine tradition

section through transept looking east

0 — 10 — 20 — 30 — 40 — 50 metres

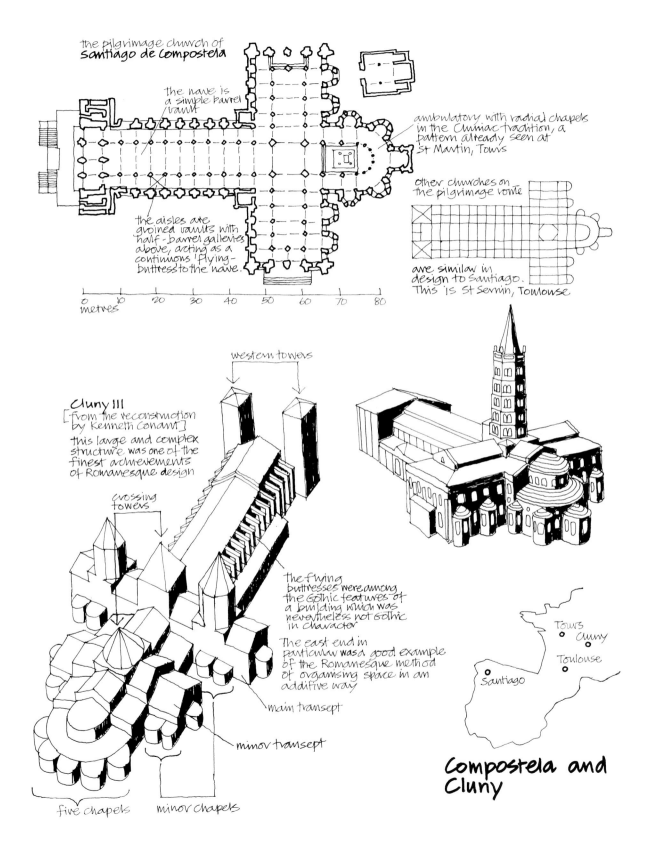

the pilgrimage church of
**Santiago de Compostela**

the nave is a simple barrel vault

ambulatory with radial chapels in the Cluniac tradition, a pattern already seen at St Martin, Tours

the aisles are groined vaults with half-barrel galleries above, acting as a continuous 'flying-buttress' to the nave.

other churches on the pilgrimage route

are similar in design to Santiago. This is St Sernin, Toulouse

0  10  20  30  40  50  60  70  80
metres

western towers

**Cluny III**
[from the reconstruction by Kenneth Conant]

this large and complex structure was one of the finest achievements of Romanesque design

crossing towers

the flying buttresses were among the Gothic features of a building which was nevertheless not Gothic in character

The east end in particular was a good example of the Romanesque method of organising space in an additive way

main transept

minor transept

five chapels

minor chapels

Tours
Cluny
Toulouse
Santiago

# Compostela and Cluny

exploitation; a cultural elite could develop only if society relieved it of the responsibility of supporting itself by primary labour. The building of a great church depended on the existence of wealth and power in the hands of a few. Though possibly conceived, and certainly presented, as a symbol of unity and fellowship, its very existence indicated a divided society.

Most people in 11th-century Europe still lived in primitive huts, similar to those of the 5th-century barbarian. Except in barren, rocky districts where stone rubble was more common, timber was the most typical structural material. Roofs were still covered in heather or reed thatch or turf, with low walls of wattle or mud. The homes of the peasants, and of the poorest townspeople, were mainly single-room dwellings, with a central hearth from which smoke filtered out through cracks in the roof. A second space under the same roof might provide shelter for the animals. One or two 'wind-eyes', unglazed openings in the outside walls, provided some light and ventilation.

Hovels like these, probably built by the owner for a generation's occupation, were not made to last long. The few medieval houses which remain today are those of the rural freeman or richer urban merchant, built in more enduring materials. Characteristic of the Anglo-Saxon world was the use of heavy hardwood framing for walls and roof, often in the form of 'crucks', opposed pairs of curved timbers spanning from ground to ridge forming a basic frame onto which subsidiary timbers, walls and rafters, were fixed. Crucks were used in better-class houses, both single- and double-storey, until about 1600. Occasionally, the house of a very rich owner might be built in dressed stone. Not many remain today, but the 'Jew's House' (c.1160) of Aaron of Lincoln, the wealthiest man in the city and benefactor of many abbeys, is a simple but very fine two-storey building with round-headed romanesque windows and doorway.

The expansion of the European economy was given great impetus by the First Crusade. By the late 11th century, Byzantine military power had declined, and the eastern emperor Alexis became vulnerable to attack from the Seljuk Turks who then dominated the Islamic world. It was in the interests of the west to keep Byzantium as a buffer-state: so western rulers readily agreed to a joint attack on Turkish holdings in the Holy Land. Pope Urban II, in his famous call to arms at Clermont in 1095, represented it as a religious mission:

> Go forth and fight boldly for the Cause of God. Christ himself will be your leader as, more valiant than the Israelites of old, you fight for *your* Jerusalem ... let the words *Deus vult* resound from every side.

Coming during an especially productive phase in Islamic arts and sciences, the age of the Persian scholar Nizam-al-Mulk and the poet Omar Khayyám, the Crusade brought many thousands of westerners into direct contact with an advanced civilisation. Though the Crusade was initiated for political and religious reasons, there is no doubt that the gains to the west were economic and cultural. The Crusaders, in a campaign notable for both chivalry and brutality, captured Jerusalem in 1099 and established a western feudal state in Palestine. An early task was rebuilding the church of the Holy Sepulchre, destroyed at the beginning of the 11th century.

The military Orders, like that of the Knights Templar, were set up to protect pilgrimage routes to Jerusalem, and European trade began to dominate the eastern Mediterranean

the house of **Aaron of Lincoln** stone-built for both comfort and security - it is likely that there were no windows on the ground storey - the living apartments were above

typical 12th century window - a central mullion in a dense load-bearing stone was a simple way of doubling the width

## the cruck house

crucks were cut from suitable trees..

..and erected in opposed pairs..

... forming the structural framework from which the other timbers were hung

vertical posts for walls

separate floor structure inside

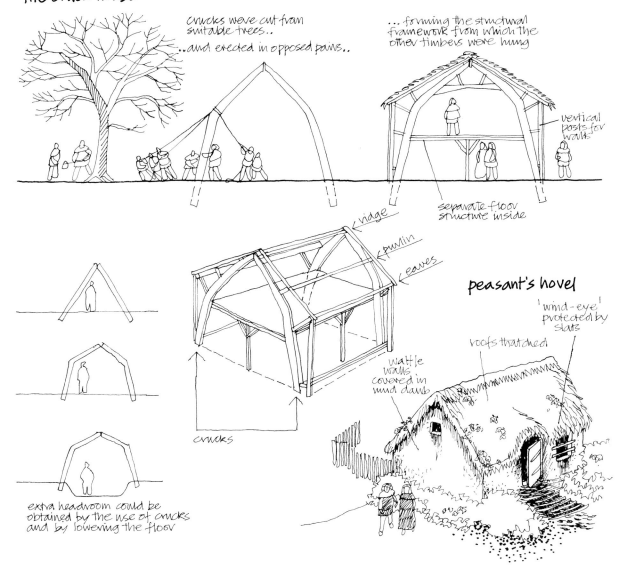

ridge

purlin

eaves

crucks

extra headroom could be obtained by the use of crucks and by lowering the floor

## peasant's hovel

'wind-eye' protected by slats

roofs thatched

wattle walls covered in mud daub

# the concentric castle

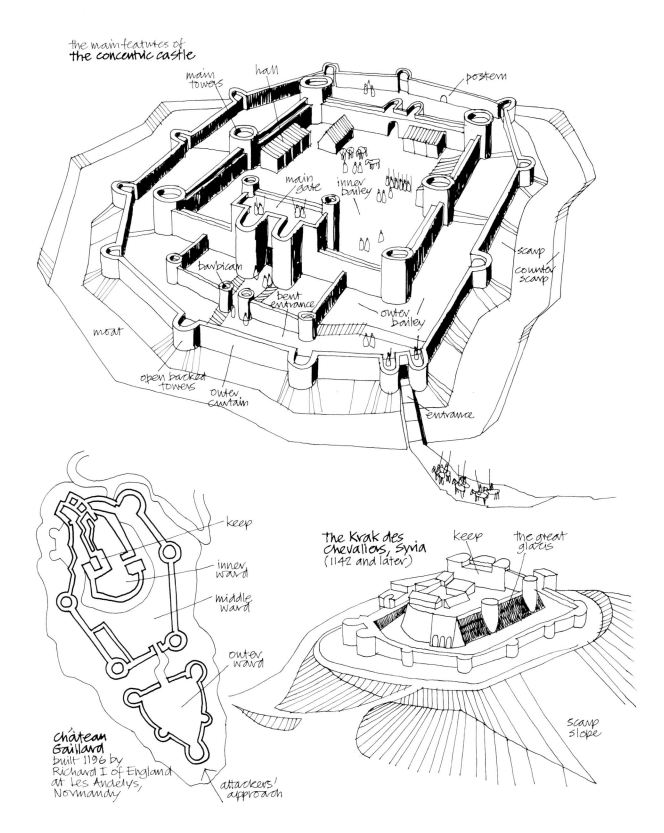

the main features of
**the concentric castle**

main towers

hall

postern

main gate

inner bailey

scarp

counter scarp

barbican

bent entrance

outer bailey

moat

open backed towers

outer curtain

entrance

keep

inner ward

middle ward

outer ward

**the Krak des chevaliers, Syria**
(1142 and later)

keep

the great glacis

**château Gaillard**
built 1196 by
Richard I of England
at Les Andelys,
Normandy

attackers'
approach

scarp
slope

and to open routes into Asia Minor. Captured Moslem craftsmen brought their superior skills into Europe, looted artefacts provided patterns for western craftsmen to copy, and acquired books, some of them surviving from Greek and Roman times, helped to spread Arabic ideas and knowledge: Thus, as the Arabs' political power was arrested, their cultural influence grew. Eastern textiles, cutlery and glassware, agricultural and banking methods, geometrical, mathematical and medical knowledge, and building techniques began to travel west.

Among the first beneficiaries were the Crusaders themselves, and their accompanying builders, who saw Islamic military architecture at first hand. In Spain, the castle of Loarre (1070) with its curtain wall and defensive towers, and the town fortifications of Ávila in Castile (1088), a remarkable 2.5-kilometre wall with 86 towers and ten gates, already showed some influences of the Islamic occupation. However, when the engineers of the Templars, the Hospitallers and the Teutonic Knights came to build defences for the newly-won territory and pilgrim-routes in the east, they adopted Saracenic ideas wholesale, changing the pattern of western castle-building.

Crusader castles were immensely strong, suitable for a war of attrition, and proof against all but the most persistent of sieges. They were also large, for though many were built within sight of each other and able to exchange signals for help, each had to hold a big garrison consisting largely of mercenaries and enough stores for a long siege. Many castles were built with inner strong-points for defence, not only from the enemy outside the walls, but also from internal mutiny.

The castles were concentric in form: the inner strong-point was defended by one or more complete circles of curtain-walls punctuated by towers, which were usually cylindrical to provide more resistance to damage. Most castles, as well as the natural advantages of a well-chosen site, had wide moats, cuttings or earth-works for extra protection. After a long history, the Château de Saône in western Syria was rebuilt by the Crusaders from about 1120. It sits on a triangular rocky outcrop, protected on two sides by natural slopes and on the third by a monumental rock-cut ditch 20 metres wide. It has a square keep in the European style but also some of the first circular towers to be built by the Crusaders. It fell to the forces of the warrior Sultan Salāh ad-Dīn in 1188, since when it became known as Saladin's Castle.

Further south, the famous Krak des Chevaliers, built by the Hospitallers from 1142 onwards, is the most redoubtable fortress in the region, possibly in the world. It has a commanding hill-top position, protected on three sides by steeply sloping terrain. A keep of three clustered towers stands in an inner bailey whose curtain-wall is protected by a gigantic glacis. An outer ward is encircled by a curtain-wall topped with offensive machicolations and punctuated with cylindrical towers. The main gatehouse is reached from a characteristic 'bent entrance', adopted from Moslem town fortifications and consisting of a sloping, twisting and confined route designed to restrict the movements and split up the forces of the enemy. The Krak was attacked or besieged twelve times without success; but on the thirteenth, in 1271, it fell to the Moslems, in whose hands it remained, one of the finest monuments to the terrible beauty of medieval warfare.

# 5 THE CITY REBORN
## *The 12th and 13th centuries*

In 1100, serfs were still the largest class numerically, but enough were escaping feudal obligations by moving to the towns that they created a labour shortage in the country. The sole source of wealth was the ownership of land, which had no market value and did not, as it does today, form a basis for credit. With the merchant class now demanding building-sites, thus placing a commercial value on urban land, there was at first no accepted way of transferring ownership from feudal barons or bishops. Tensions grew, the greatest resistance to change coming from the Church, whose long-standing legal authority seemed threatened and to whom many aspects of commerce – notably usury, the lending of money for profit – were morally unacceptable.

The new bourgeoisie, seeing the Church as a barrier to commercial freedom, proclaimed communes or negotiated self-government. The rigid social layers of feudalism, supported by ethical codes claiming Christian virtue and knightly chivalry, began to collapse before a world in which commercial success was the sole distinction. The merchants, to protect themselves, set up local governments, levied taxes – in particular for the upkeep of the city walls on which security depended – enforced the keeping of the peace, controlled entry into the city, and negotiated trade routes through the countryside. Towns formed trade associations with each other, like the Lombardic League in southern Europe and the Hanse in the north. Within each town, protective craft-guilds – for weavers, dyers, butchers, bakers, chandlers – were set up to control the quality of goods and to fix prices.

For builders, craft-guilds were not appropriate. Between the 12th and 15th centuries, they relied instead on another system of protection known as the 'lodge'. Before then the designers of the great abbeys were usually monks, while the craftsmen who built them were lowly serfs. While this created a feeling of community, and the sense of continuity which came from the handing down of skills from father to son, it nevertheless allowed for little contact or exchange of ideas with outsiders. In the more open urban society of the 12th century there could be much more interchange of ideas – but commercial life was also more precarious. It was logical that building workers, like the other craftsmen, should seek protection.

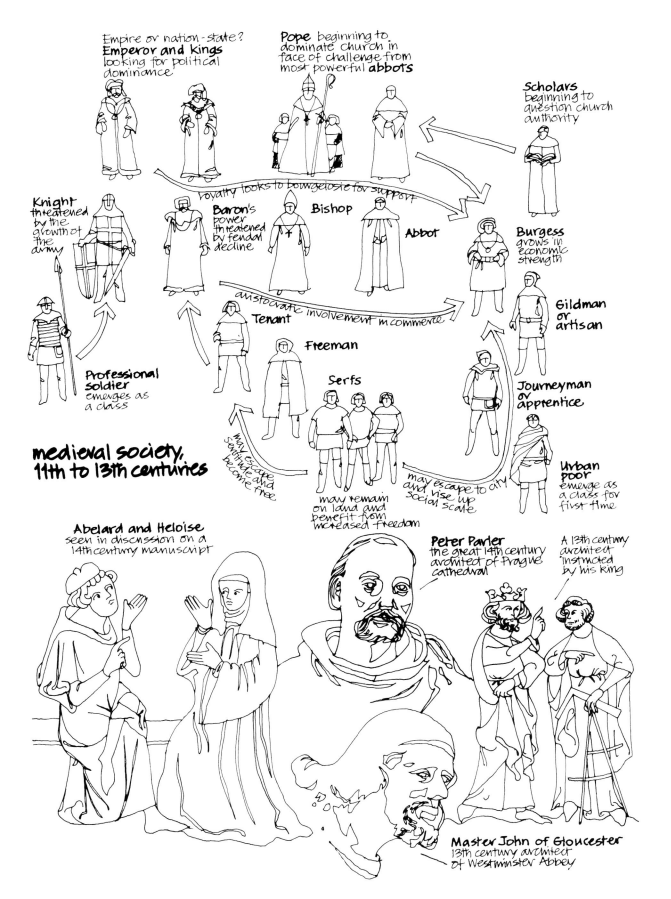

Empire or nation-state?
**Emperor and kings** looking for political dominance

**Pope** beginning to dominate church in face of challenge from most powerful **abbots**

Scholars beginning to question church authority

royalty looks to bourgeoisie for support

**Knight** threatened by the growth of the army

**Baron's** power threatened by feudal decline

**Bishop**

**Abbot**

**Burgess** grows in economic strength

**Professional soldier** emerges as a class

aristocratic involvement in commerce

**Tenant**

**Freeman**

**Gildman or artisan**

**Serfs**

**Journeyman or apprentice**

**medieval society, 11th to 13th centuries**

may escape servitude and become free

may remain on land and benefit from increased freedom

may escape to city and rise up social scale

**Urban poor** emerge as a class for first time

**Abelard and Heloise** seen in discussion on a 14th century manuscript

**Peter Parler** the great 14th century architect of Prague cathedral

A 13th century architect instructed by his king

**Master John of Gloucester** 13th century architect of Westminster Abbey

But building was different: instead of a number of craftsmen following the same trade it involved a team made up of diverse trades. So lodges were formed, hierarchical groups of designers, masons, carpenters, carvers, glaziers, painters and their journeymen and apprentices. A lodge existed for a specific building project; when the work was finished its members would disperse and re-form elsewhere. By its nature it was marked out as different from the rest of the town: the masons' carefully guarded freedom of movement brought independence and allowed new opportunities for exchanging ideas and techniques, but maybe also the mistrust of the townspeople. The lodges developed a self-sufficient attitude, building up a tradition of hospitality to new masons in the face of the hostility of the town.

In Britain, 120 new towns were established between the mid-11th and late 13th centuries, including Ludlow, Windsor, Bury St Edmunds, Portsmouth, Liverpool and Harwich. In France 300 were established in the century or so before 1350, and in Germany even more, including Lübeck, Berlin and Prague. Their distinguishing feature was their regular layout, often a rectangular grid. Most were fortified with walls and ditches, and the fortifications of the great French *bastides* of Aigues-Mortes, Carcassonne and Avignon still remain today.

Generally, medieval towns were built for people on foot, their narrow streets and overhanging buildings making few concessions to wheeled traffic. Towns depended for their livelihood on craft-work and small-scale industry, and most houses were built for or by the craftsmen themselves, with work-places on the ground floor and living-space and storage above. The Shambles district in York and the Fuggerei in Augsburg give a good idea of this intimate medieval building pattern, though often there was also a market-place in the centre, for buying and selling the agricultural produce of the surrounding area and the manufactured goods of the town. Medieval towns were not large by modern standards; as late as the 14th century a typical big town such as Milan, Venice, Ghent, Bruges or London had between 40,000 and 50,000 inhabitants. Only exceptional towns were larger, such as Avignon which, on becoming a papal seat in 1309, grew to 120,000.

The main building material of medieval towns, especially in the north, was still timber. Simple framed houses of the cruck type remained in use but were superseded. By about 1500 the 'box-frame' building had become usual for all except the poorest houses. A plinth of brick or rubble supported a framework of vertical posts or studs on which horizontal beams were fixed, to carry the walls and roof. Studs set closely together – as they were while oak was plentiful – were infilled with plastered hurdle, giving the external walls the characteristic black-and-white appearance known popularly in England as half-timbering. The studs were discontinuous from one storey to another; often the upper floors were projected out over the lower ones in the form of 'jetties'. Roofs were thatched or covered in wooden shingles. Windows, at first without glass, were protected by wooden lattices with shutters, which could be closed for extra protection.

Gradually jettied construction was overtaken by a simpler kind of box-frame known as the 'balloon-frame'. Here the studs were continuous from ground floor to roof, avoiding the over-hang of the jetty. Though the studding became more widely-spaced as timber became scarcer, the continuity of structure increased the stability of the buildings. Infill

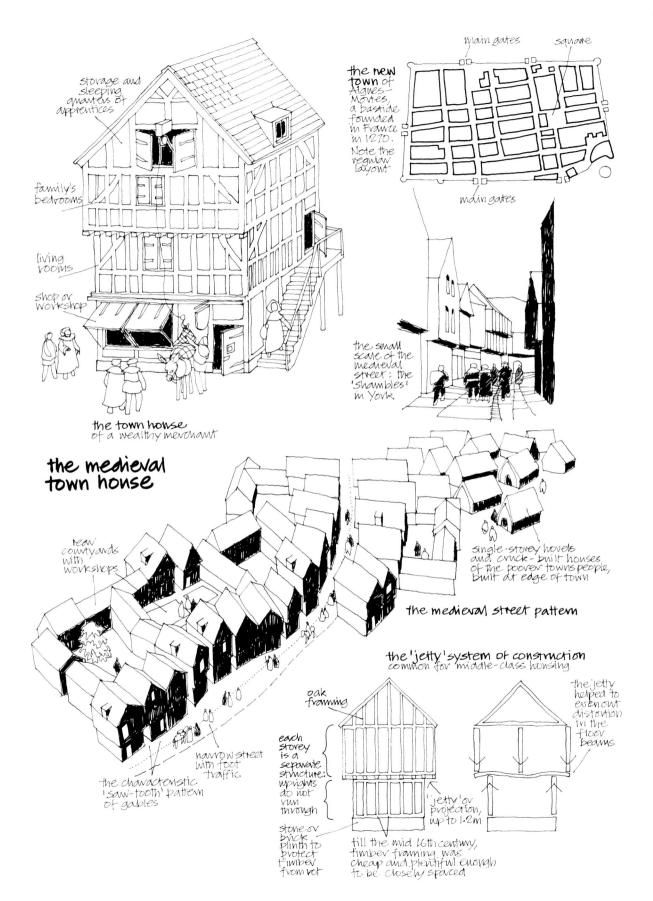

storage and sleeping quarters of apprentices

family's bedrooms

living rooms

shop or workshop

the town house
of a wealthy merchant

the new town of Aigues-Mortes, a bastide founded in France in 1270. Note the regular layout

main gates

square

main gates

the small scale of the medieval street: the 'shambles' in York.

# the medieval town house

rear courtyards with workshops

single-storey hovels and cruck-built houses of the poorer towns people, built at edge of town

the medieval street pattern

the 'jetty' system of construction
common for 'middle-class housing'

oak framing

the jetty helped to even out distortion in the floor beams

each storey is a separate structure: uprights do not run through

'jetty' or projection, up to 1.2m

the characteristic 'saw-tooth' pattern of gables

narrow street with foot traffic.

stone or brick plinth to protect timber from rot

till the mid 16th century, timber framing was cheap and plentiful enough to be closely spaced

panels were still wattle hurdles fixed in place and plastered over; sometimes the whole wall, oak frame and all, would be covered.

Local variations in building style depended on materials. In rocky areas, stone rubble might be used instead of timber-framing. Timber buildings were relatively easy to extend by the addition of another storey, but stone buildings would usually be extended sideways, resulting in the characteristic 'long-house' of the more rugged parts of Europe. In particularly poor areas, the only viable material might be mud. The 'cob' of southern England consisted of mud, chalk and a binding agent such as reed or straw and was reasonably long-lasting if protected by a good thickness of lime-wash.

As towns grew physically, so did their economies. Stronger central government assisted this process. The powerful and shrewd Frederick Barbarossa (1152–90), king of both Germany and Italy and Holy Roman Emperor, challenged the authority of barons and bishops through his 'Magdeburg Law', administered by a central bureaucracy of *ministeriales*. This allowed European towns self-government and encouraged the rise of the merchants. Henry II of England (1154–89), established 'scutage' or money payments as an alternative to feudal services, enriching the central treasury and striking a further blow at feudalism. In France, a bureaucratic system similar to Germany's was set up under the direction of Louis VI (1108–37) and his powerful minister Suger (1081–1151). As towns grew, so did the ambition to rebuild.

Suger was an ecclesiastic as well as a politician. In 1140 he organised the rebuilding of the choir of the abbey of St Denis, near Paris, the kings' historic burial-place, in which religious and political significance were combined. This building marks the appearance of the gothic style, not only because it contains recognisably 'gothic' features – rib-vaults had already appeared at Durham and elsewhere, flying buttresses at Cluny, and pointed arches had many precedents, not least in the middle east – nor merely because they were for the first time combined into a unified design, though that is striking enough; but rather because their unique combination allowed the opportunity for a qualitative change in the ordering of spaces.

While romanesque designers had divided spaces into ordered compartments, the designers of the 12th century and onwards increasingly blurred spatial divisions. The heavy rubble walls of romanesque architecture were dispensed with, succeeded by the more precise and efficient 'ashlar' construction of dressed stone. Columns could become lighter, dividing walls less substantial, roofs freer in shape, allowing space to flow from one area into another. This is all seen at the east end of St Denis, with its curving ambulatory, its *chevet* of chapels and, above all, its use of light as an aid to worship – a feature which derived from Suger's strongly-held theology.

The point had been reached at which great buildings needed a specialist designer; St Denis is not the work of an amateur, in any sense, and Abbot Suger's two 'little books', which describe in glowing terms the improvements to the building without once mentioning the name of an architect, should not be taken to mean that such a man did not exist. They suggest, instead, a man whose humble status and lay origin made his name not worth mentioning, at least, not to the Abbot. The credit for historical achievements always goes to those who write the histories – and in the 12th century the monks did the writing.

The building itself indicates a man of intellect and capability, and points to a growing feature of the 12th century: the educated and cultured but secular mind playing an

# St Denis and Canterbury
## The birth of the Gothic style

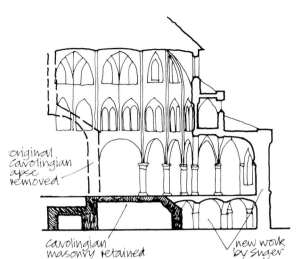

original Carolingian apse removed

Carolingian masonry retained

new work by Suger

**St Denis** section through east end by Suger and his unknown architect (1140)

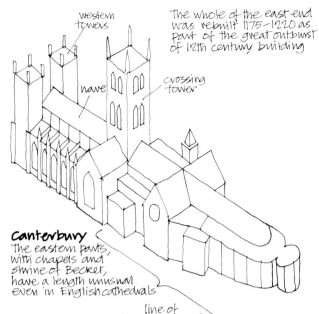

western towers

nave

crossing tower

The whole of the east end was rebuilt 1175-1220 as part of the great outburst of 12th century building

**Canterbury**
The eastern parts, with chapels and shrine of Becket, have a length unusual even in English cathedrals

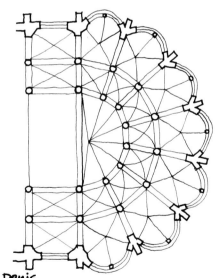

**St Denis**
Plan of the east end
The freedom of plan-form allowed by the pointed arch results in a fluidity of space not seen since San Vitale

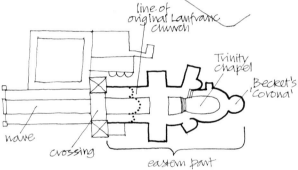

line of original Lanfranc church

Trinity chapel

Becket's 'Corona'

nave

crossing

eastern part

**Canterbury**
the Trinity chapel with its 'Early English' lancet windows

# medieval building

## An ordinary house..

...could be financed and even built by the owner himself...

..helped perhaps by a local carpenter and roofer using their own simple tools.

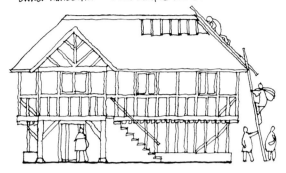

## A building like a great church was more complex

The church provided the finance...

assisted by the burgesses of the city

The Dean might act as building manager..

..on behalf of the chapter

 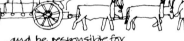

He would own the machinery and tools, hiring smiths to maintain them..

..and be responsible for quarrying the stone, cutting the timber and getting them to the site

In this he had the help and advice of his most important appointee, the master mason

It was the master's job to draw plans for the work, set out the building and hire masons to build it

The masons were craftsmen, mostly from outside the city

During construction they built a lodge where they lived and where they laid out a tracing floor on which to draw templates for the work

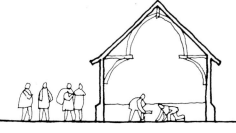

Masons worked long hours, usually those of daylight

They therefore earned more, in summer than in winter

A building with complex timber works would justify the appointment of a master carpenter to oversee the work of the craftsmen carpenters

unskilled labour would be got locally

There were two types of mason

The setters and wallers were skilled in heavy ashlar work..

As outsiders they were suspected by the townspeople

and the freemasons were decorative carvers

they were therefore hospitable to new masons

close-knit and powerful, they were capable of taking up tools and leaving the job

increasingly dominant part in intellectual life. Western philosophy owed a great deal to its contacts with the east. The Second and Third Crusades in 1149 and 1190 ended in military failure, but at least continued the traffic in ideas. Under the influence of Arab scholars and those Greek and Latin classics – including, significantly, the geometry of Euclid – which had been translated from Arabic versions, reason became a major element in philosophy. Open-minded inquiry began to replace blind faith.

## THE MASTER MASON

The intellectual tension of the day is epitomised by the disputations between the orthodox St Bernard of Clairvaux (1091–1153) and the progressive scholar Peter Abelard (1079–1142), author of the inquiring treatise *Sic et Non*. We tend to think of 'the Renaissance' as a phenomenon of 15th-century Italy, yet many of its ideas and attitudes, as expressed by men like Aquinas, Bacon, Dante and Giotto, were already alive in the 12th and 13th centuries, not only in Italy but all over Europe. Universities were being founded, Magna Carta (1215) had guaranteed key constitutional rights, and with the gothic cathedrals, western architecture was entering its finest historical phase.

> Who has ever seen! Who has ever heard tell ... that nobles, men and women have bent their proud and haughty necks to the harness of carts and ... have dragged to the abode of Christ these wagons, loaded with wines, grains, oil, stone, wood, and all that is necessary for the wants of life or for the construction of the church?

Confronted today by the sheer power of gothic architecture, we tend to argue a *posteriori* that it must have been the product of a uniquely religious society. The great size of the buildings themselves leads us further to imagine that only the collective efforts of the whole community could have been capable of such achievements. Yet we misunderstand gothic architecture if we fail to see it as the product of an increasingly secular society, and of a small section of society, at that. A great cathedral was without doubt built to the glory of God by religious men, yet paradoxically its construction depended on the money of the bourgeoisie, a class in moral conflict with the church, on non-Christian mathematical and building knowledge and on the talents of a master-mason whose education and experience now lay outside the confines of the church. The enthusiastic description above, written by Abbot Haimon in 1145, of the people of Chartres banding together to rebuild their cathedral, has helped spread the myth that a gothic building was the outpouring of medieval society's collective unconscious and, moreover, that it was an expression of universal religious faith. It may be that on occasions the voluntary efforts of townsfolk were needed to lift and carry. Yet the fact is that design and construction now lay in the hands of a highly skilled team of secular architects and craftsmen who approached their work in a newly analytical way.

Gothic buildings stand at a crucial transition-point in history, between the church-dominated early Middle Ages and the free, secular world of the Renaissance. It is perhaps this very fact which makes them arguably the finest achievements in the history of western architecture. They are the perfect expression of the dialectical tension between two worlds: between religious faith and analytical reason, between the serene, closed monastic society of the old order and the dynamic expansionism of the new.

Master-masons begin to be mentioned in the chronicles. An early glimpse of one of them is given by the monk Gervase, writing in about 1200 of the destruction by fire, twenty-six years earlier, of the choir of Canterbury cathedral. Among the eminent French and English masons called in, offering a babel of contradictory advice, there was

> ... a certain William of Sens, a man active and ready, and ... a workman most skilful in both wood and stone. Him, therefore, they retained, on account of his lively genius and good reputation, and dismissed the others. And to him, and to the providence of God, was the execution of the work committed.

William emerges as both resourceful and inventive, dedicated to his work and independent of spirit. He brings stone over from France by ship, devising ingenious machines for loading and unloading it. He provides his sculptors with drawings and templates to guide their carving, and directs their work himself. And when after four years, with the work well advanced, he falls from a high scaffold and is badly injured, he continues supervision from a stretcher.

At length, Gervase tells us, 'the master, perceiving that he derived no benefit from the physicians, gave up the work and crossing the sea, returned to his home in France', leaving behind, on the foundations of the ruined Norman choir, a new, bigger choir which, with its pointed arches and rib-vaults, was Britain's first gothic building, as significant there as St Denis in France.

During the remainder of the 12th century and for most of the 13th, Europe was an open society with few political barriers to travel and trade. The easy passage of master-masons from one place to another encouraged the spread of architectural ideas and expertise, and from its beginnings on the Île-de-France the gothic style spread rapidly. A common vocabulary was evolved, of both form and content; a basic pattern which allowed many local variations. Central to gothic cathedral building was the latin-cross plan, which formed a spatial sequence from the nave at the west, through the crossing, to the choir and sanctuary in the east.

Also typical were the great stone rib-vaulted roofs, their outward thrust counter-balanced by flying buttresses. As rib-vaults permitted the concentration of forces onto localised points along the wall, larger and larger openings could be made in the spaces between, and during the 12th century this allowed the phenomenal development of the art of stained glass. Today, we tend to think of medieval churches as essays in grey, functional stonework, but in the Middle Ages their interiors were covered with symbolic wall-paintings and carvings and lit by the glorious colours of windows telling the stories of prophets and martyrs to the illiterate poor.

The pointed arch allowed greater freedom in planning. If all the arches in a bay are to be the same height, a semi-circular arch demands a square structural bay. This limited romanesque planning to square compartments. But since pointed arches of the same height can easily be adjusted to varying spans, gothic planning had much greater freedom. Rectangular or triangular structural bays became common, resulting in planning flexibility, structural economy and more subtle spatial effects.

In France, the great gothic cathedral emerged fully-formed. With money available and ambitions high, construction proceeded rapidly. Many were completed as a single

# features of the gothic style 1

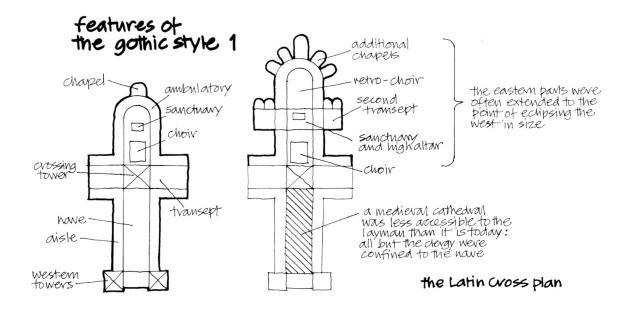

chapel

ambulatory

sanctuary

choir

crossing tower

transept

nave

aisle

western towers

additional chapels

retro-choir

second transept

sanctuary and high altar

choir

the eastern parts were often extended to the point of eclipsing the west in size

a medieval cathedral was less accessible to the layman than it is today: all but the clergy were confined to the nave

**the Latin cross plan**

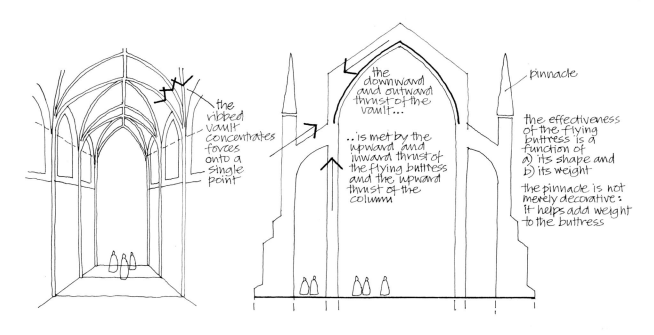

the ribbed vault concentrates forces onto a single point

the downward and outward thrust of the vault...

..is met by the upward and inward thrust of the flying buttress and the upward thrust of the column

pinnacle

the effectiveness of the flying buttress is a function of a) its shape and b) its weight

the pinnacle is not merely decorative: it helps add weight to the buttress

the ribbed vault and flying buttress

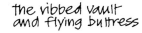

a barrel vault required continuous edge support

window-sizes were therefore kept small

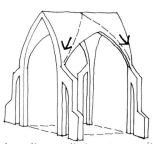

the rib-vault together with the flying buttress allowed the concentration of forces and the walls to be opened up

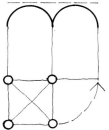

## the pointed arch

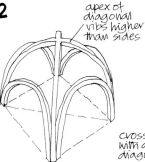

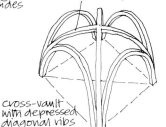

apex of diagonal ribs higher than sides

diagonal ribs same height as sides but structurally unsound

cross-vault with semi-circular arches on sides and diagonals

the pointed arch offered the freedom to depart from the square bay

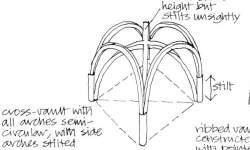

cross-vault with depressed diagonal ribs

all ribs same height but stilts unsightly

stilt

cross-vault with all arches semi-circular, with side arches stilted

ribbed vault constructed with pointed arches: structurally sound, consonant in height and visually satisfactory

## the development of the timber roof

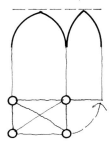

rafters

small simple roof consists entirely of rafters

collars

pairs of rafters linked with collars for extra strength

trusses

purlins

collared rafters acting as trusses to support rafters on purlins

timber roofs were often used above stone vaults to carry the weathering

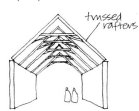

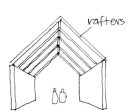

trussed rafters

in smaller buildings, trussed roofs were often used for their own decorative effect

an alternative treatment was the cladding of the trusses with a decorative wood ceiling: known as a barrel roof

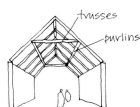

tie beam

a collar lowered to eaves-level became a tie-beam, structurally very sound

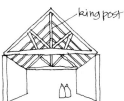

king post

like the tie-beam roof, the king-post truss obscured the roof-shape

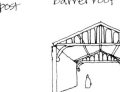

the tie-beam roof, often highly decorated, was appropriate to a low-pitched roof

the arch-braced roof-truss was a step towards the construction of...

...the wide-span hammer-beam roof truss, probably the highest form of medieval roof design

continuous project – Chartres took only 27 years to build – and show a remarkable unity of design.

The essential model was Notre Dame de Paris (1163). It is very high; its rib-vaulted nave is 32 metres to the top of the arches. The nave extends sideways into double aisles, which threaten to engulf the short transepts. The transepts themselves occur about half-way along the building; the eastern parts with their *chevet*-end and numerous chapels are almost as large as the western. The great height demands three levels of flying buttresses all round, the lowest contained within the aisle roofs. The west end has twin towers flanking a central entrance with a great wheel window above. The crossing has no tower but a single tall *flèche* – the building itself is already so high that the extra height of a big central tower would be neither necessary nor structurally feasible. The interior and exterior are both sober and majestic, enlivened at key points with intricate and humanistic carvings.

In perfect counterpoint to Notre Dame, the Sainte Chapelle in Paris (1243), though smaller and simpler, still uses the full gothic vocabulary. Apart from an entrance porch it consists of a single rectangular space with an apsidal east end. The roof is carried entirely on a series of deep buttresses, turned at right angles to the outside wall, and hardly noticeable from inside. The outer wall consists largely of jewel-like coloured glass, giving the interior a dramatic appearance of insubstantiality.

Other great churches throughout the Île de France closely followed the pattern of Notre Dame, with western towers, high nave, flying buttresses spanning over side aisles, vaulted roof and *chevet* east end. This is all seen, with numerous variations, at Rouen, both in the cathedral (1200) and in the nearby abbey church of St Ouen (1318), at Laon (1170), Bourges (1192), Chartres (1195), Reims (1211), Amiens (1220) and Beauvais (1247).

Laon is notable for the magnificent west front, with entrance-porches which emphasise their function by projecting boldly. The twin towers have a new plasticity of form, changing in plan from square at the bottom to octagonal above, and are enriched by fantastic corner-turrets in the form of carved oxen. The plan of Bourges is very similar to that of Notre Dame, but the complete absence of transepts gives both interior and exterior an impressively single-minded uniformity. The west front, with projecting buttresses at every junction, is equally strong and monumental.

Chartres is perhaps the most appealing of French gothic cathedrals, both in the profusion and richness of its decorative sculpture and in the unsurpassed beauty of its copper-red and cobalt-blue glass. Spires are unusual in France, but Chartres has two, above its two western towers. The southern one is earlier, lower and simpler; the northern, an early 16th-century rebuild, is higher and magnificently decorative. Together they give the building a unique skyline which dominates the town and the countryside around but is nevertheless informal and humane.

It is likely that the designers of Chartres also worked at Rouen. The same high nave, with similar vaulting, and the same cobalt-blue glass, make the connection. The main departure is a spectacularly large crossing-tower, which made it for a while the tallest building in the world. The intricately decorated west front was celebrated much later in the paintings of Monet.

The plan of Reims cathedral resembles Notre Dame, though Reims, the setting for the crowning of several French kings, has wider and deeper transepts to accommodate a coronation theatre. The impressive interior is very high – 38 metres to the top of the roof-vault. Amiens is perhaps the culmination of the pattern set by Notre Dame, with its powerful western towers framing a central entrance, its soaring nave – 42 metres in height – and its repetitive columns leading relentlessly to a dramatic *chevet* of chapels at the east end.

Higher still is Beauvais, an amazing 48 metres to the apex of its roof-vault, the highest cathedral in Europe and the most ambitious of all gothic buildings. What we see today, vast though it is, is no more than the choir and transept of a building that was never completed. The proposed nave was not even begun, and an enormously high crossing-tower, 150 metres to the top, collapsed in the 16th century. What remains is held together by tie-rods and a double row of gigantic flying buttresses. The Middle Ages had no theory of structures; the stability of a building could not be predicted beforehand but only tested in practice, testimony to the faith, or daring, or *hubris*, of the builders. At Beauvais the striving for extreme height overstepped the bounds of medieval technology.

For three centuries or more the gothic style dominated northern and western Europe, north to the Low Countries and Germany, south to Spain and northern Italy. In southern Italy the influence of Rome persisted and in the Balkans and Russia, the Byzantine.

## GOTHIC IN ENGLAND

In England, this French invention was pursued with particular vigour. The choir of Canterbury was a distinctly French building, but English Gothic soon began to develop a character of its own. The great English cathedrals were often built slowly, over the centuries, and display a greater variety of design. Many originated as monasteries, complete with cloisters, refectories and dorters, some of which remain today. In monastic churches only the monks worshipped in the choir area, with its various associated chapels, so a larger nave was often provided to accommodate the laity, giving English cathedrals much greater length. Possibly as a result of this, they were often narrower and lower than their French counterparts with less need for big flying buttresses – though the lack of height in the nave was often offset by the construction of towers and spires. A high tower over the crossing, with two lower ones flanking the western entrance, was a common pattern.

The largest English cathedral is York Minster, impressive in scale, simple and powerful in design, but livened by the intricate decoration of its later west front and medieval glass. In the north transept, the tall, simple outlines of the 'lancet' windows, reminiscent of knife-blades, are typical of the early phase of English Gothic, known as 'Early English'.

The longest cathedral is Winchester, where the completion of a retro-choir in 1235 gave a total length of 170 metres, more than any other medieval cathedral in Europe. The nave at Winchester, a beautiful combination of early and late medieval styles, occupies about half the length of the building. The nave of Norwich cathedral is even longer. Here the horizontality of a long, low church was offset by a high crossing tower, with a later spire, visible across the flat countryside for miles around.

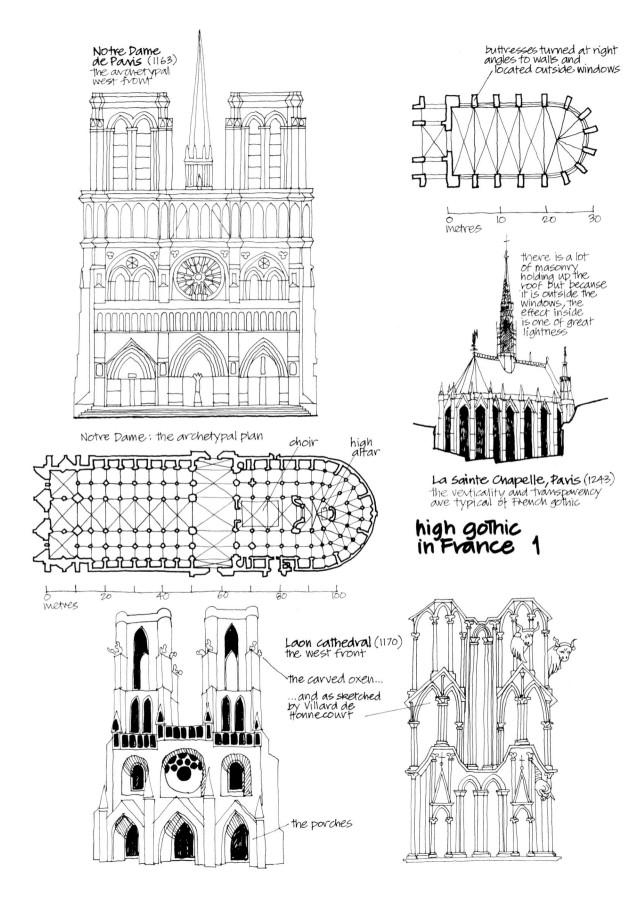

Notre Dame
de Paris (1163)
the archetypal
west front

buttresses turned at right
angles to walls and
located outside windows

there is a lot
of masonry
holding up the
roof. But because
it is outside the
windows, the
effect inside
is one of great
lightness

Notre Dame: the archetypal plan

choir

high
altar

0    20    40    60    80    100
metres

La Sainte Chapelle, Paris (1243)
the verticality and transparency
are typical of French gothic

high gothic
in France 1

Laon cathedral (1170)
the west front

the carved oxen...

...and as sketched
by Villard de
Honnecourt

the porches

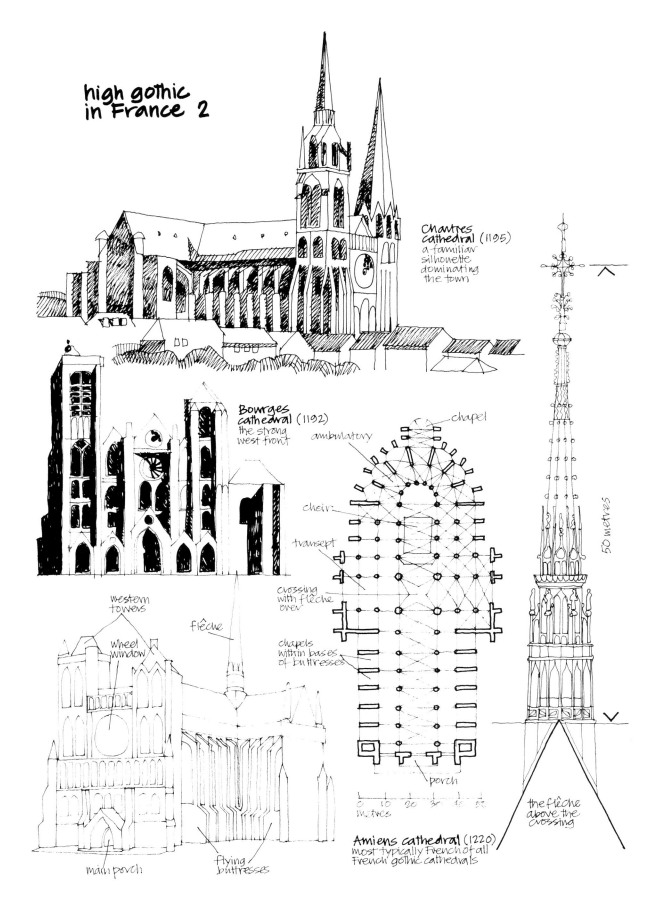

**high gothic in France 2**

Chartres cathedral (1195)
a familiar silhouette dominating the town

Bourges cathedral (1192)
the strong west front

chapel

ambulatory

choir

transept

crossing with flèche over

chapels within bases of buttresses

porch

western towers

wheel window

flèche

main porch

flying buttresses

0 10 20 30 40 50
metres

Amiens cathedral (1220)
most typically French of all French gothic cathedrals

50 metres

the flèche above the crossing

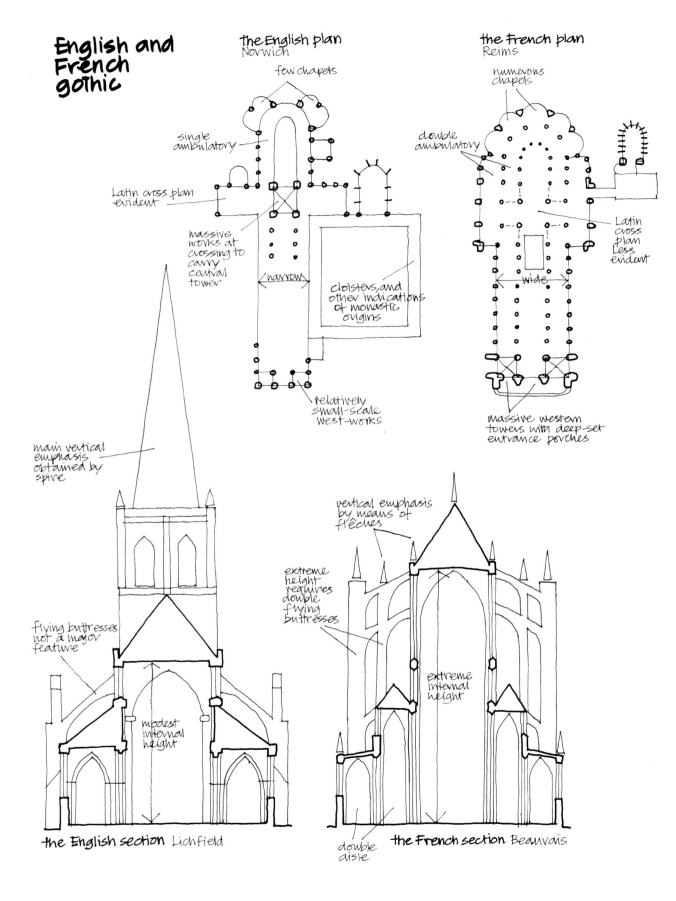

# English and French gothic

**the English plan** Norwich

few chapels

single ambulatory

Latin cross plan evident

massive works at crossing to carry central tower

← narrow →

cloisters, and other indications of monastic origins

relatively small-scale west-works

**the French plan** Reims

numerous chapels

double ambulatory

Latin cross plan less evident

← wide →

massive western towers with deep-set entrance porches

main vertical emphasis obtained by spire

vertical emphasis by means of flèches

extreme height requires double flying buttresses

flying buttresses not a major feature

modest internal height

extreme internal height

**the English section** Lichfield

double aisle

**the French section** Beauvais

The spire of Salisbury, the highest in Britain, is also a prominent feature in the landscape. This, the most characteristic of Early English cathedrals, begun in 1220 by the master Nicholas of Ely and largely completed by 1258, displays great consistency of style. It has a long though not very high nave, double transepts with a crossing-tower over the larger, and monastic cloisters and chapter-house adjoining the south aisle. The plan-form is simple and rectangular, including that of the extensive eastern parts which contrast strongly with the fluidity of the typical French equivalent at, say, Amiens.

Ely cathedral also had a significantly large, simply designed east end, within a rectilinear latin-cross plan. Perhaps the most spectacular east end was that of Canterbury, where double transepts, an ambulatory and numerous chapels in the French style, all made necessary by the cathedral's role as a pilgrimage shrine to Thomas à Becket, greatly outweigh the later English-style nave.

The monastic origin of Lincoln, too, is reflected in the size of its eastern section. Here, on a prominent hill in the city, is the first Early English building known to us, begun in the late 12th century by the master Alexander. The choir and lesser transept date from 1192, and the style was continued in the larger transept, the crossing-tower, the entrance-porch and chapter-house of 1209. The overall length was further increased in 1256 by the addition of a retro-choir. On the west front, a curious external screen wall conceals much of the building behind.

The treatment of the west front, fairly consistent in the great French cathedrals, was seen by English designers as an opportunity to experiment, and there are many different forms. Durham, has no west entrance at all, its place being taken by a gothic 'Galilee chapel'. Wells, with its taut unified interior, has a spectacular west front dating from 1206–42, with fine decoration by the architect Thomas Norreys and his sculptor master Simon. Peterborough, basically a romanesque building, has an Early English west front consisting of three gigantic lancet-arched recesses which reflect the presence of nave and aisles behind them.

The most important medieval site in England, the centre of English political life for almost 1000 years, was Westminster. Like Charlemagne's Aachen, it combined the seats of both temporal and spiritual power: the king's Palace of Westminster sat next to the great abbey, an indicator of the unity of monarchy and church. Founded in 960 by St Dunstan on the site of a 7th-century church, the abbey was largely rebuilt in 1055 during the reign of Edward the Confessor, and again on a grand scale at the behest of Henry III in the 13th century, from which time much of the present church dates. The eastern parts, the single main transept and the eastern bays of the nave, were begun in 1245 in Early English style, also used, in conscious imitation, when the master mason Henry Yevele extended westwards in the late 14th century. The choir was located in the nave to leave the crossing free, as at Reims, for use as a coronation theatre. The building retains many original monastic features, including cloisters and outbuildings, but in other ways is untypical of English cathedrals of the time: its great height, its complex flying buttresses, its lack of a crossing-tower, its *chevet*-type east end, the only complete example in England, show a distinct French influence, from a period in which the politics of the two countries were intimately linked.

In the early Middle Ages much of northern Europe's culture had come from Scandinavia, but by the 12th century this had turned round. Constructional knowledge

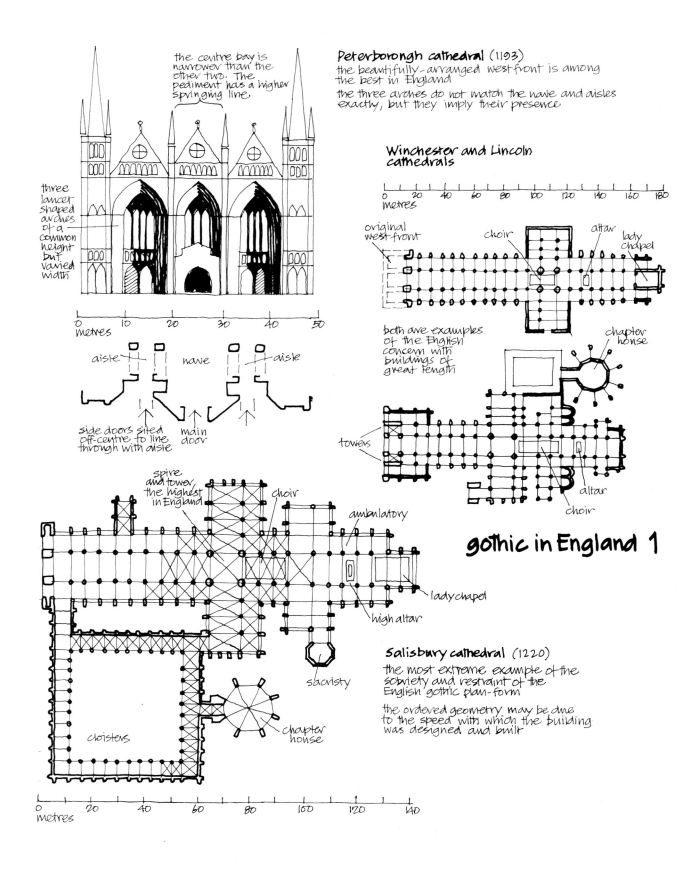

**the centre bay is narrower than the other two. The pediment has a higher springing line.**

## Peterborough cathedral (1193)

the beautifully-arranged west front is among the best in England

the three arches do not match the nave and aisles exactly, but they imply their presence.

**three lancet shaped arches of a common height but varied width**

## Winchester and Lincoln cathedrals

```
0   20   40   60   80   100  120  140  160  180
metres
```

original west front

choir    altar    lady chapel

both are examples of the English concern with buildings of great length

**aisle**    nave    aisle

**side doors sited off-centre to line through with aisle**

**main door**

towers    altar    choir

```
0    10    20    30    40    50
metres
```

spire and tower, the highest in England

choir

ambulatory

lady chapel

high altar

sacristy

chapter house

cloisters

## gothic in England 1

## Salisbury cathedral (1220)

the most extreme example of the sobriety and restraint of the English gothic plan-form

the ordered geometry may be due to the speed with which the building was designed and built

```
0    20    40    60    80    100   120   140
metres
```

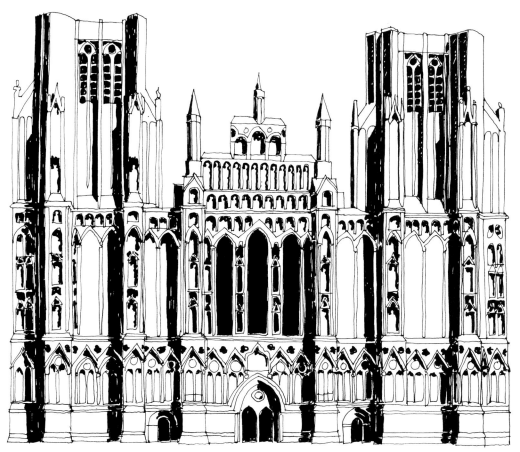

**Wells cathedral** (1180 and later)
The west front, rich with decoration and sculpture,
yet with a strong underlying form, is one of the finest in England

Westminster Abbey with its great internal height, prominent
flying buttresses and chevet-type plan is one of the
most French of English churches

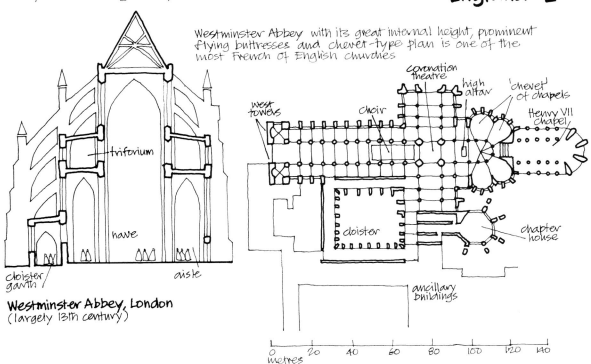

triforium

nave

cloister garth

aisle

**Westminster Abbey, London**
(largely 13th century)

west towers

choir

coronation theatre

high altar

'chevet' of chapels

Henry VII chapel

cloister

chapter house

ancillary buildings

0    20    40    60    80    100    120    140
metres

for the grander building projects of Norway, Denmark and Sweden now came from France and England: the church at Trondheim (1190) was contemporary with, and very similar in design to, Lincoln cathedral; Uppsala cathedral (1273) was begun in an English style and completed in a French one; the nave of Linköping cathedral (1240) was built by a team of English masons.

These importations were superimposed on a long-standing tradition of timber church building. The earliest was at Hemse in Gotland, a simple rectangular building with a pitched roof. The walls were of 'staves', giving a name to the style. These were split logs, plain on the inside and rounded on the outside, butted together side by side and driven into the ground. Sancta Maria Minor, Lund (1020), is the earliest surviving example, and the nave of Greensted church in Essex, almost contemporary, is of similar design. A structural frame with a ground-beam to carry the staves and prevent their rotting had by then been introduced. The buildings were often intricately decorated; the surface carving in the Celtic tradition at Urnes church, Sogne Fiord, Bergen (1125), is a famous example. Urnes also demonstrated a new two-tier structure in which a high, central space, defined by a timber colonnade, was surrounded by a lower aisle. This form culminated at Hoprekstad, at Lorn and above all at Borgund (1150). Here the plan was centralised in the Byzantine tradition. Both the main space and the surrounding aisles were multi-tiered: the drama of the exterior and the spatial richness of the interior were comparable in mood with a gothic cathedral.

Through direct French influence, gothic architecture also developed early in Spain: the cathedral of Ávila, with its *chevet*-type plan was started in 1160. Early Arabic influences persisted, and Spanish Gothic is remarkable for its intricate geometric decoration. A particular feature was a pierced screen of decorative stonework, in the Arabic tradition but adapted to Christian uses. It appears in the cathedral of Burgos (1220 and later) in the form of elaborate internal screen-walls at triforium level and externally on the richly decorative crossing-tower and western towers, the latter crowned with delicate open-work stone spires. The French plan-form is discernible, with its *chevet*-type east end, but other more Spanish features were perhaps demanded by a more elaborate liturgy. The profusion and considerable size of the side chapels is remarkable; so too is the location of the choir which, typically in a Spanish cathedral – as at Reims and Westminster – is located in the eastern part of the nave, leaving the crossing free for rituals and reducing the western nave almost to a narthex.

The cathedrals of Toledo (1227) and Barcelona (1298) are also based on French plans, with Spanish adaptations. Barcelona has a fully-developed *chevet* of nine chapels, with several more outside the main aisles, contained between the great buttresses of the main roof. Toledo's plan strongly resembles Paris or Bourges, with double aisles continuing round the apsidal east end. In contrast to England, cathedrals in both France and Spain were wide in relation to their length; Toledo, over 60 metres wide, takes this feature to its ultimate. It is a grand and monumental building, enlivened by a richly carved interior and fine stained glass.

In the Low Countries and Germany, with their strong Carolingian and romanesque traditions, the gothic style developed, but more slowly. The earliest gothic building in the Netherlands was probably the church of St Gudule, Brussels (1220). Romanesque features are still present in the details, but the plan-form and twin-towered western

# the stave church of Scandinavia

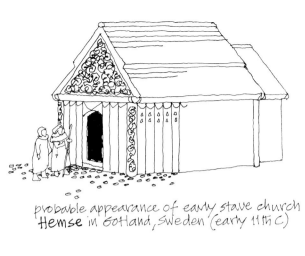

probable appearance of early stave church at **Hemse** in Gotland, Sweden (early 11th C)

the stave church plan in its simplest form at **Urnes** in Norway

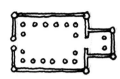

and the more developed form of the second **Urnes** church (1125)

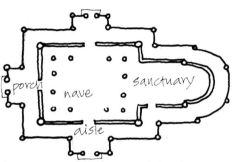

porch    nave    sanctuary

aisle

plan of **Borgund** church in Norway representing the culmination of the style (1150)

the final form of **Urnes** church

carved wood wall panels

tower above nave

aisle

nave

cross section

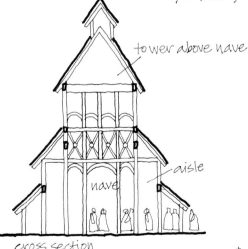

**Borgund** demonstrates the great richness of the style

# Spanish gothic

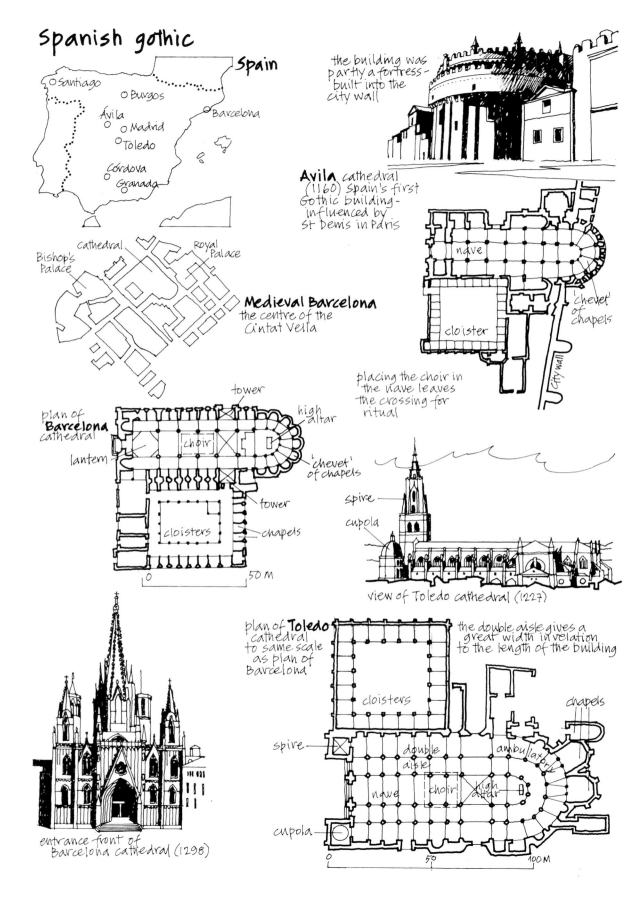

Spain

Santiago
Burgos
Ávila
Madrid
Barcelona
Toledo
Córdova
Granada

the building was partly a fortress - built into the city wall

**Avila** cathedral (1160) Spain's first Gothic building - influenced by St Denis in Paris

nave

cloister

'chevet' of chapels

City wall

Bishop's Palace
Cathedral
Royal Palace

**Medieval Barcelona**
the centre of the Ciutat Vella

placing the choir in the nave leaves the crossing for ritual

plan of **Barcelona** cathedral

tower
choir
high altar
lantern
'chevet' of chapels
tower
cloisters
chapels

0   50 M

spire
cupola

view of Toledo cathedral (1227)

plan of **Toledo** cathedral to same scale as plan of Barcelona

the double aisle gives a great width in relation to the length of the building

cloisters
chapels
spire
double aisle
ambulatory
nave
choir
high altar
cupola

0        50        100 M

entrance front of Barcelona cathedral (1298)

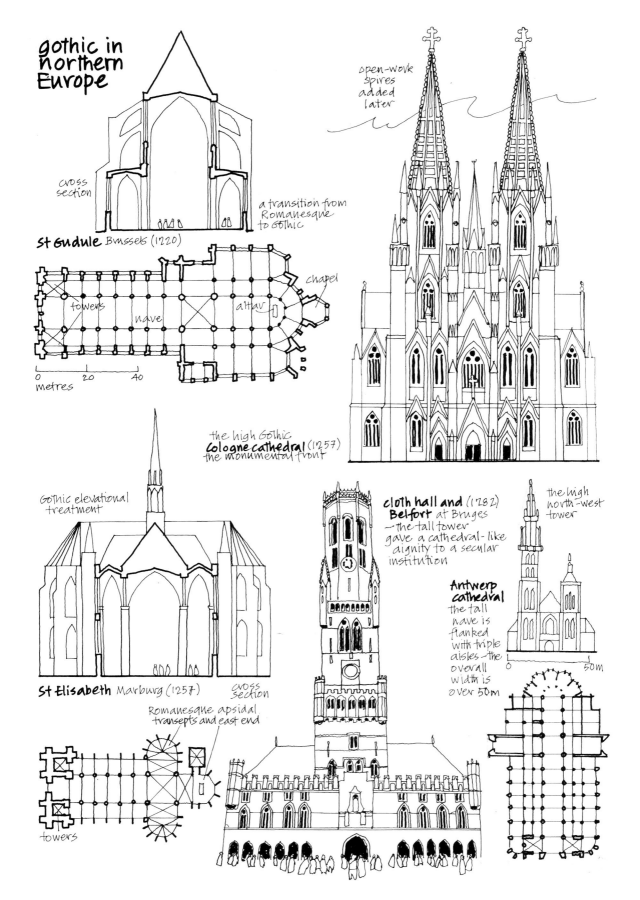

# gothic in northern Europe

cross section

**St Gudule** Brussels (1220)

a transition from Romanesque to Gothic

towers

nave

altar

chapel

0   20   40
metres

open-work spires added later

the high Gothic
**Cologne cathedral** (1257)
the monumental front

Gothic elevational treatment

**St Elisabeth** Marburg (1257)

cross section

Romanesque apsidal transepts and east end

towers

**cloth hall and** (1282)
**Belfort** at Bruges
— the tall tower gave a cathedral-like dignity to a secular institution

the high north-west tower

**Antwerp cathedral**
the tall nave is flanked with triple aisles — the overall width is over 50m

0                50m

façade are in the French gothic style. The cathedral of Utrecht (1254) is a fully-developed French gothic building reminiscent of Amiens. Its single great western tower is an important local feature, prototypical of many in Holland and Belgium. In Germany, the Liebfrauenkirche in Trier (1242), with its round and pointed arches, represents a gradual transition from romanesque to gothic, as does the church of St Elisabeth, Marburg (1257), which, though it has traditional features such as the markedly apsidal transept and east end, is identifiably a gothic building.

Early Gothic in Germany culminated with the cathedral of Cologne (1257) and its derivatives Freiburg (1250) and Regensburg (1275). Cologne, largest of all north European cathedrals, would be remarkable for its size alone: double aisles give it great internal width, its internal height approaches that of Beauvais, and its most striking features are its massive western towers with spires rising some 150 metres above the flat plain of the Rhine, completed centuries later to the original designs. In the Netherlands, the counterpart of Cologne was perhaps the cathedral of Antwerp (1352 and later), a building of no great height but of great width; the basic plan-form is French designed by the master Amel of Boulogne – but characteristic Belgian features, including the monumental north-western tower, are recognisable.

By the 13th century, the Hanse dominated the trade of north Europe. A trade-route was established to Bruges and London in the west and through Danzig and Riga to Novgorod in the east. Cologne, near the geographical centre, profited most, but many other northern towns benefited from the growing trade in wool, metal, timber, furs and manufactured goods of all kinds including cloth. Mercantile buildings were needed. Notable were those of the Netherlands; the great cloth halls at Bruges (1282), with its Belfort, or bell-tower, rivalling that of Antwerp cathedral, and at Ypres (1202), a magnificent building of monumental simplicity, were the finest secular buildings of the 13th century, approaching the size and splendour of the cathedrals and emphasizing that commerce now rivalled religion as a central fact of life.

## PRIMITIVE CAPITALISM

This was also true in Italy which, linked with the east, was able to satisfy European demands for imported goods like silk and spices. Through the Crusaders, the cities of Pisa, Genoa and Venice gained trade concessions in the middle east. Italian *fondachi* or warehouses were established in Syria and Egypt, and middle eastern ones in Venice. In northern Europe, the Church's attacks on money-lending and usury successfully slowed commercial development. But in cosmopolitan Italy, Syrians, Byzantines and Jews, and later western Christians, were free to develop new banking techniques. By the end of the 13th century, Siena, Piacenza, Lucca and Florence had become the banking centres of Europe, introducing non-negotiable bills of exchange, the offering of credit at interest, and a system of double-entry book-keeping.

Two major political events of the 13th century further increased Italian dominance. During the Fourth Crusade of 1204, when the Crusaders were persuaded to turn aside from the Holy Land to sack Constantinople, Venice gained control of the eastern Mediterranean. And the expansion of the Mongol empire, which by the 1240s united most of Asia under one rule, gave Italian merchants easier access to India and China.

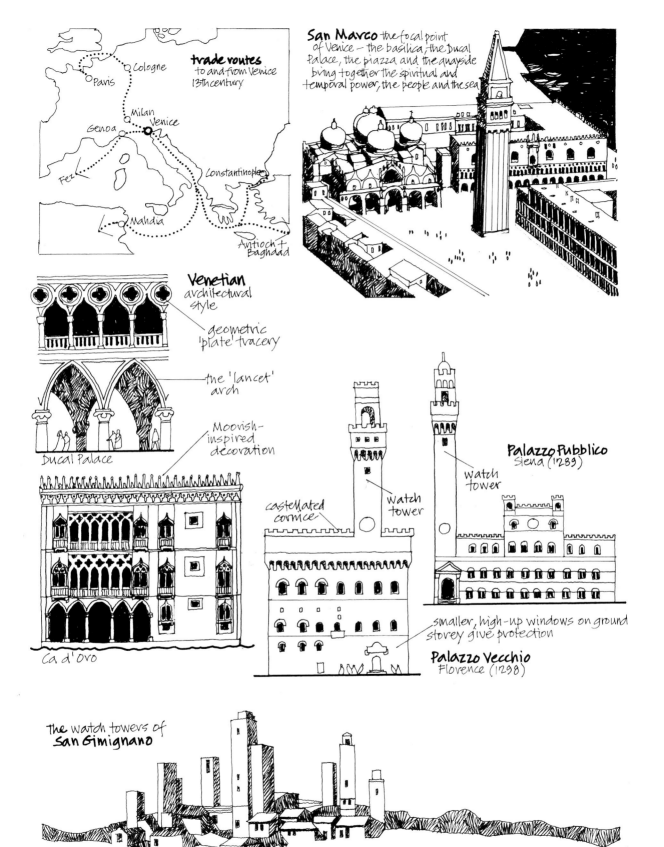

**trade routes** to and from Venice 13th century

Paris
Cologne
Milan
Genoa
Venice
Fez
Constantinople
Mahdia
Antioch + Baghdad

**San Marco** the focal point of Venice – the basilica, the Ducal Palace, the piazza and the quayside bring together the spiritual and temporal power, the people and the sea

**Venetian** architectural style

geometric 'plate' tracery

the 'lancet' arch

Moorish-inspired decoration

Ducal Palace

Ca d'Oro

castellated cornice

watch tower

**Palazzo Pubblico** Siena (1289)

watch tower

smaller, high-up windows on ground storey give protection

**Palazzo Vecchio** Florence (1298)

the watch towers of **San Gimignano**

# the buildings of early capitalism

Inspired by Marco Polo, and his close association with the Great Khan, they made the most of the opportunity.

Primitive capitalism was competitive and brutal, and its architecture had to be both defensive and aggressive. A rich man's house in a congested, high-density Italian town was different from a feudal castle or manor-house, but it shared with them two important tasks: the defence of the owner's property from robbers and rivals, and an aggressive expression of wealth and power. The Torre Asinelli (1109), the Torre Garisenda (1100), both in Bologna, and the 13 towers which still remain of the reputed 72 built in San Gimignano between the 10th and 14th centuries, are good examples. Their grim and featureless elevations were obviously built for defence, but their great height, 70 metres or more in some cases, was not only because of the congested sites or of the need for high look-out positions; it was also a conspicuous demonstration of status.

The urban palazzo of the 12th and 13th centuries was usually a solid block-like building of five or so storeys in heavily rusticated stone. For protection, the barred windows on the lower floors were much smaller than those above, and battlements, machicolations and watch-towers, at least partly functional, made up a characteristic skyline. Some, like the fine Palazzo Vecchio, Florence (1298), were family strongholds. Others, like the Palazzo Pubblico, Siena (1289), were municipal buildings which could serve as places of public refuge in time of trouble.

Of all the medieval *palazzi*, that of the Doge in Venice (1309–1424) is the most splendid. Its position near the cathedral of San Marco, like the palace and abbey at Westminster, publicly brought together secular and spiritual power. The Doge was the chief examining magistrate of the Venetian republic and symbolised the laws on which the city's commerce was based. Unlike the forbidding Palazzo Vecchio, his palace implies public accessibility, with its richness of colour and texture. The lower storeys present a double-storey open colonnade of gothic arches and plate tracery, and the offensive roof-top crenellations of the fortress-house are transmuted into a crest of delicate stone lace-work of Arabic character. The architects, Giovanni and Bartolomeo Buon, also designed the Ca' d'Oro in Venice (1424) which on a smaller scale displays many of the same characteristics, including arcaded ground floor, gothic plate tracery, Arabic skyline and the same lightness of texture and coloration. The style of both buildings is that very specific Venetian version of gothic – owing something to the northern European style of the times, but also drawing on the city's rich Byzantine tradition, its decorative Arabic craftsmanship and, of course, its spectacular wealth.

Venetian influences dominated northern Italy. The pilgrimage church of Sant' Antonio, Padua (1232), though equipped with a *chevet* of chapels in the contemporary French manner, is roofed with seven domes similar in arrangement to San Marco. Some north-European features appeared in Italy during the 12th, 13th and 14th centuries, but there were few wholly gothic buildings. Though the plan-forms of the Venetian churches of Santi Giovanni e Paulo (1260) and Santa Maria Gloriosa (1250) are of a northern, Latin-cross type with transeptal chapels and apsidal east ends, the square vaulting-bays and the use of tie-beams in the nave instead of flying buttresses place the buildings firmly in the Roman tradition.

In the great pilgrimage church of San Francesco, Assisi (1228), pointed rib-vaults and tentative flying buttresses are used, but the building as a whole, part of a vast

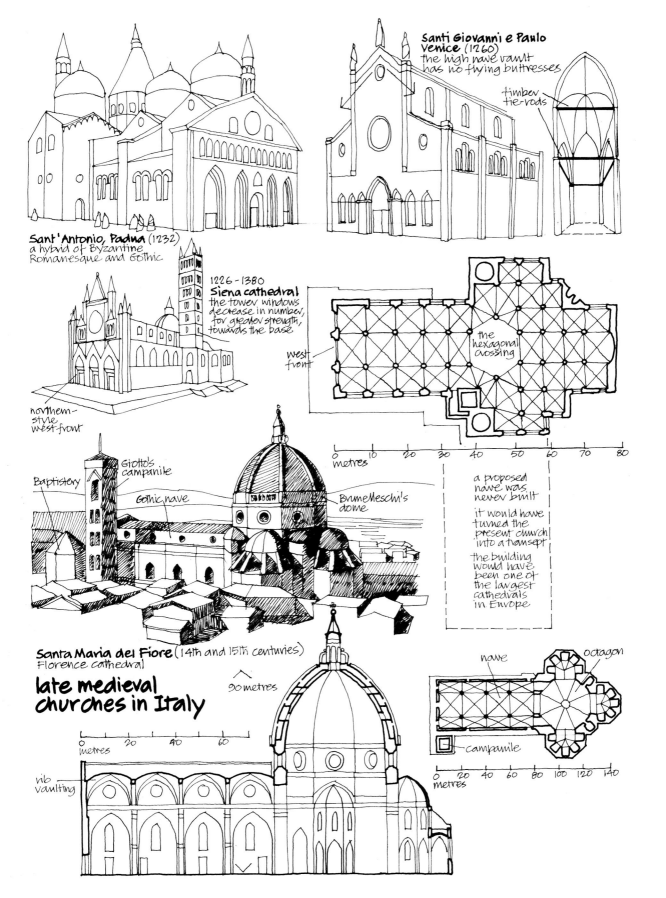

Santi Giovanni e Paulo
Venice (1260)
the high nave vault
has no flying buttresses

timber
tie-rods

Sant'Antonio, Padua (1232)
a hybrid of Byzantine,
Romanesque and Gothic.

1226-1380
Siena cathedral
the tower windows
decrease in number,
for greater strength,
towards the base

west
front

the
hexagonal
crossing

northern-
style
west front

0  10  20  30  40  50  60  70  80
metres

Baptistery

Giotto's
campanile

Gothic nave

Brunelleschi's
dome

a proposed
nave was
never built

it would have
turned the
present church
into a transept

the building
would have
been one of
the largest
cathedrals
in Europe

Santa Maria del Fiore (14th and 15th centuries)
Florence cathedral

late medieval
churches in Italy

90 metres

nave

octagon

campanile

0  20  40  60  80  100  120  140
metres

0  20  40  60
metres

rib
vaulting

monastic complex on a fine hill-top site, has a romanesque simplicity and grandeur. The romanesque tradition persisted in southern Italy, though the proximity to north Africa made Islamic influences strong; the cathedral of Palermo (1170) has a basilican plan with decidedly Moorish elevations. One of the most ambitious projects of the 13th century was the building of Siena cathedral (1226–1380), a grand essay in civic pride. Its ornate west front is north European Gothic but is literally a façade, bearing little relationship to the magnificent and original building behind, a rich composition of semi-circular and pointed vaulting centred on a hexagonal crossing carrying a dome and lantern.

The churches of Venice imply a closer relationship between municipality and church than actually existed: both authorities were suspicious of each other but did what they could to coexist. Florence too, with sound commercial instinct, came to terms with the Papacy by becoming the official collector of papal taxes, to the financial benefit of both parties. A town council could obtain church support by financing religious buildings, and the construction of many magnificent Italian churches from the 12th century onwards owes more to this than to any popular upsurge of religious feeling.

Florence was investing hugely in building, not only in the churches of Santa Maria Novella (1278) and Santa Croce (1294), though these were fine enough, but particularly in the great complex of buildings forming the cathedral of Santa Maria del Fiore. As at Siena, the cathedral was paid for by the city council in an outpouring of civic ambition, and its construction occupied a succession of Florentine designers over a period of 200 years. Under the circumstances, the design is remarkably unified. Arnolfo di Cambio began the construction in 1296. The main focus is the east end, in the form of a Greek cross, centred on a huge octagonal crossing 43 metres wide. Three of the arms, forming sanctuary and transepts, are short apses ringed with chapels, but the western arm is a long rectangular nave of four square vaulted bays lined with aisles. A few gothic elements were used, but the structural system is less adventurous than Chartres or Reims, with none of their dynamic spatial effects internally and no flying buttresses or pinnacles to disturb the tranquil outline, punctuated only by the simple rectangular campanile (1334) designed by the painter Giotto. For years, the city pondered on how to solve the problem of roofing over the unfinished crossing. But for that, the story of western architecture had to move on to another chapter.

# 6 The 14th and 15th centuries

By the start of the 14th century European kings and urban bourgeoisie had formed a *de facto* economic alliance. Together, they were now displacing the Church as the main investor in buildings. One of the most dramatic examples of this was the English king Edward I's castle-building programme – the largest ever undertaken – during his pacification of Wales in the late 13th century. The defeat and death of the Welsh prince Llywelyn the Last in 1282 was Edward's opportunity to create a strong military presence in Wales and, more important, to re-mould its economy. Not only were the great castles built, but many of them were supported by new towns, encouraging the replacement of the Welsh pastoral way of life by an urban one. These Edwardian *bastides* included Conwy, Caernarfon, Beaumaris, Flint, Ludlow and Chepstow, whose regularity of layout resembled that of purpose-built new towns everywhere.

Like the Krak des Chevaliers or the Château Gaillard, Edwardian castles were guarded by rings of concentric walls, but the keep was no longer placed inside. Instead, the outer wall became the strongest line of defence, and the keep, with its living quarters, was replaced by an enormously strong gatehouse, located aggressively at the front. The outer wall was invariably defended by escarpments or ditches and often by a low concentric spur wall intended to keep attackers at a distance from its base. Numerous round towers, to provide flanking fire, punctuated its length and served to divide the upper rampart into sections so that any part which fell to the enemy could be isolated. The north Welsh castles of Conwy and Caernarfon, both begun in 1283, are the largest, strongest and grandest; Caerffili (1267), Harlech (1283) and Beaumaris (1283) the most systematic, ordered and symmetrical.

These castles had only a short life as unassailable defences against medieval hand-weapons. Because of the development of gunpowder – ironically by the kings and bourgeoisie themselves, the only institutions rich and organised enough to manufacture armaments on a large scale – castle walls were no longer safe. And as their owners' wealth increased, they were gradually transformed into grand houses; living apartments were added and windows enlarged, increasing their comfort but reducing their strength. Even during the Wars of the Roses fortified castles and town walls were being overthrown.

By the time of the English Civil War in the mid-17th century, they had become almost obsolete as defences. Rhaglan castle in south Wales, originally a motte and bailey castle of the 12th century, was rebuilt in the 15th and 16th centuries as a luxurious dwelling. After a protracted siege this royalist stronghold fell to the Parliamentary forces in the Civil War. Loches and Chinon, Henry II's two 12th century châteaux in the Loire valley, were remodelled in the 15th century to become two of king Charles VII's favourite houses, but were later abandoned in favour of even more luxurious palaces.

As Church power gradually declined under a succession of weak or corrupt Popes, the ambitions of the nation-states and their kings correspondingly grew. In 1309, Philip IV of France engineered the appointment of a French Pope, setting him up in a palace in Avignon where for seventy years the Papacy underwent a 'Babylonian captivity', subservient to France, worldly, corrupt and powerless. The great papal palace, towering above the city on its cliff-like podium with arched buttresses, looked like a veritable fortress but to its incumbent must also have seemed a prison. In 1378 two rival popes were elected, one in Avignon and the other in Rome, resulting in the 'Great Schism' which brought papal authority to its lowest point and sorely divided the Church. Revolutionaries within the Church, such as John Wycliffe, challenged its right to own secular possessions and condemned many of its dogmas; Johann Huss advocated a return to the Bible as the basis of Christian life; other Christians, following Meister Eckhardt, turned to mysticism to try to purify the faith.

A building which typifies this religious struggle was the cathedral of Albi (1282). Built in the wake of the Albigensian heresy, and the brutal government reprisals in which many local people had lost their lives, it was a building calculated to awe a defeated populace. Built in brick because of a shortage of stone, its narrow-windowed walls rise from a high, solid podium, resembling a castle as much as a cathedral. Its interior, by contrast, is rich with filigree decoration, and its walls and ceiling contain huge late-medieval frescoes, including a terrifyingly salutary 'Last Judgement'.

Paradoxically, amid all this turmoil, the growth of royal or bourgeois patronage meant that the 14th century saw some of the Church's greatest architectural achievements. Fewer new cathedrals were being built, but everywhere, particularly in France and England where the monarchy was making most headway, existing ones were being enhanced and in almost every town and village parish churches were being re-modelled or new ones built.

Philip IV of France (1285–1314) increased taxes, confiscated the property of Jews, befriended the rich bourgeoisie and, in a bitter war, annexed the property of the Knights Templar, who after the fall of the Holy Land had settled in France. One of his main building projects was the enhancement of Reims cathedral, the place of royal coronations. A symbolic sculptured group of the coronation of the Virgin (1290) above the main west door gave implicit assent to the divine right of kings, and the fine west towers (1305) added grandeur to the composition. The rich, decorative style of late French Gothic, of the 14th and 15th centuries, with its curving, flame-like lines, is known as *flamboyant*. It is a style mainly of northern France, where it is seen on the fine south transept front of Beauvais cathedral, on the west front of the abbey church of La Trinité, Vendome, and in Rouen on the church of Saint-Maclou and on the fine 'lantern' crossing-tower of the church of St Ouen.

# the castle in the 13Th and 14Th centuries

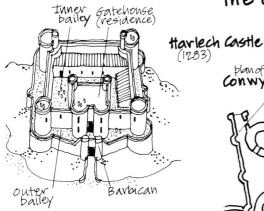

Inner bailey — Gatehouse (residence)

**Harlech Castle** (1283)

Outer bailey — Barbican

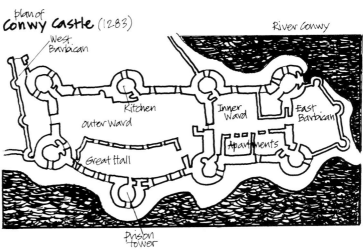

plan of **Conwy Castle** (1283)

River Conwy

West Barbican

Kitchen

Inner Ward

East Barbican

outer Ward

Apartments

Great Hall

Prison tower

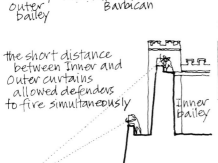

the short distance between Inner and Outer curtains allowed defenders to fire simultaneously

Inner bailey

**Chateau de Pierrefonds** (1390) was heavily reconstructed in the 19th century

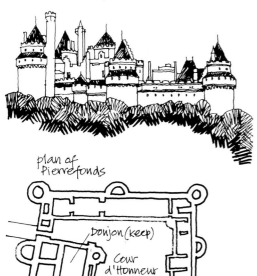

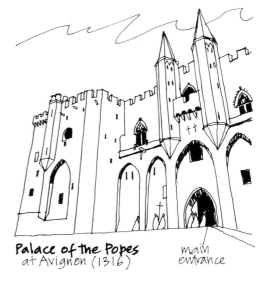

**Palace of the Popes** at Avignon (1316)

main entrance

plan of Pierrefonds

Donjon (keep)

Cour d'Honneur

Chapel

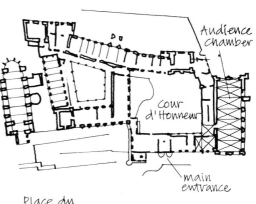

Audience Chamber

Cour d'Honneur

main entrance

Place du Palais

However, the French kings' growing power, calculated to disadvantage the feudal aristocracy, was also beginning to anger the townspeople. When in 1337 Philip VI tried to annexe Aquitaine at the beginning of a protracted struggle for land with the kings of England, he found himself without popular support. This first phase of what became the Hundred Years War brought England victory at Crécy in 1346 and Poitiers in 1356, where the superior tactics and fire-power of a small Anglo-Welsh force defeated a much larger defending army. Many of the French nobility died, and the credibility of the monarchy was ruined. Royal patronage of building works suffered a setback. Whereas the architecture of 12th and early 13th century France had led the world, the late 13th and early 14th centuries were dominated by England.

There came a new and more confident phase of English Gothic. At first geometrically regular, it gradually developed sinuous curves and rich decoration. This 'decorated' style was the local equivalent of the French *flamboyant*. Between 1261 and 1324 the nave and chapter-house and the 'decorated' west front of York Minster were built, and during the 14th century its fine stained glass was installed.

In 1307 the square crossing-tower was added to Lincoln cathedral, at 82 metres the highest in England, and in 1325 its great circular window with flowing 'decorated' tracery. In 1321 a similar central tower was built at Wells. The added stress placed by the tower on the structure below was taken up by four huge 'scissor' arches inserted between the main piers of the crossing; they are unique in medieval architecture and illustrate the ingenuity of their builders in coping with what they assumed – for they had no means of knowing for certain – to be structural necessity.

Indicative of the new splendour of English architecture was Ely cathedral, in particular its Lady Chapel (1321) and the rebuilt nave crossing (1323). The Lady Chapel is about 30 by 14 metres, its rectangular plan the only simple feature. Its walls are formed by arcades of serpentine or 'ogee' arches rising like trees to branch out into a ceiling of decorative rib-vaulting, and the whole is covered in carved foliage of great luxuriance. The central crossing is an undeniably great achievement of 14th-century architecture. Built by the master mason John Attegrene to replace a collapsed tower, it stylishly departs from the simple rectangularity of the rest of the building and forms a high octagonal space. A vast octagonal lantern by the king's carpenter William Hurley, set at an angle to the stone octagon below, further increases the richness of the spatial effect and floods the interior with light.

The finest example of a complete building in 14th-century 'decorated' style is Exeter cathedral. Each of the decorative piers has an engaged pilaster – that is, a vertical column attached to the wall – running vertically up past the triforium to branch into a multiplicity of roof-ribs spreading inwards like palm-fronds to meet the ridge, in a composition of great consistency and imagination. It was a short step from this 'palm' vaulting to the decorative vaulting of Gloucester cathedral, where each group of ribs was designed to the same length, so defining an arc around each support and describing the fan-shape which gives this system its name. Fan-vaulting was not a new structural departure, but mainly a decorative feature; it was adopted by the king's mason Henry Yevele in rebuilding the nave of Canterbury cathedral in 1379, and was to reach a peak in the royal chapels of the 15th and 16th centuries.

Possibly the best example of royal patronage and the finest single creation of any

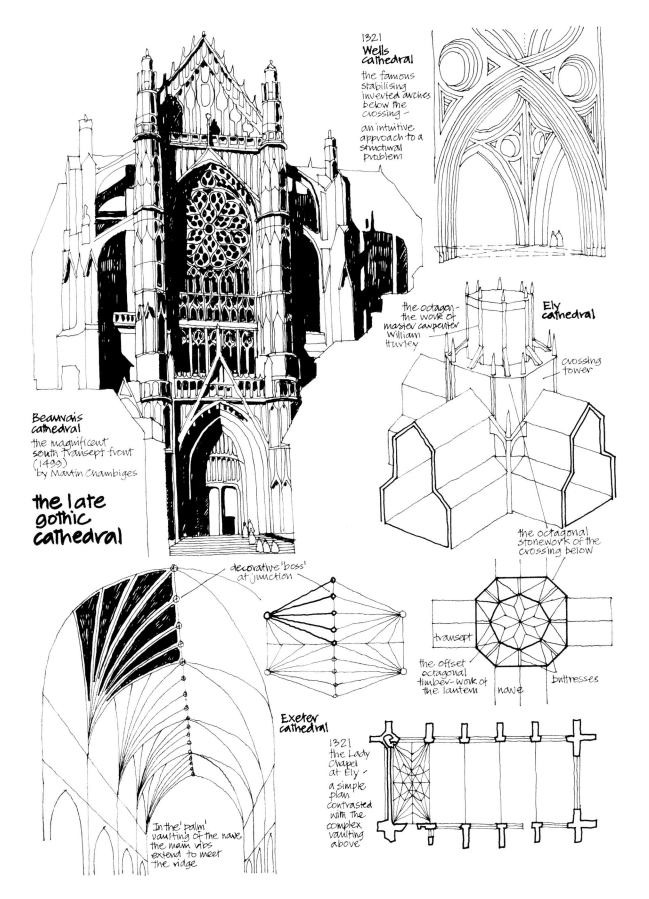

**1321**
**Wells cathedral**
the famous stabilising inverted arches below the crossing —

an intuitive approach to a structural problem

**Beauvais cathedral**
the magnificent south transept front (1499) by Martin Chambiges

# the late gothic cathedral

the octagon — the work of master carpenter William Hurley

**Ely cathedral**

crossing tower

the octagonal stonework of the crossing below

transept

the offset octagonal timber-work of the lantern

nave

buttresses

decorative 'boss' at junction

**Exeter cathedral**

1321 the Lady Chapel at Ely — a simple plan contrasted with the complex vaulting above

In the 'palm' vaulting of the nave the main ribs extend to meet the ridge

medieval craftsman was Westminster Hall, built in 1397 for Richard II (1377-99), an energetic promoter of the arts. For him the Wilton Diptych was painted, and Chaucer is thought to have entertained his court with *The Canterbury Tales*. And for him Hugh Herland the master-carpenter rebuilt the roof of the great hall at the Palace of Westminster. Like the best of gothic building, the oak roof, covering an area of over 70 by 20 metres, is a synthesis of structural and artistic expression, deriving its aesthetic directly from the way in which the mechanical problems were solved. In order to reduce the great span down to a manageable size, horizontal hammer-beams, supported by curved struts from below, were cantilevered from the walls and their ends became the springing points of the arched roof trusses which hang daringly in space. The big curved arches, springing across the central space, are sinewy with carved fluting and the heavy hammer-beams loaded with rich decoration.

In the 200 years since the 12th century, the master-craftsman had become a different man. William of Sens and the unknown master of St Denis, though respected for their ability, had occupied a lowly place in society, but the 14th-century craftsman's increasing influence gave him a higher status. He or his sons might now be educated at a university or marry into the nobility. For a long time the activity of building had been remote, through its technical sophistication, from the everyday life of the common man; now it was becoming socially removed as well.

Late-gothic architecture developed more slowly in Germany, where the 13th-century pattern persisted. The Frauenkirche in Nuremburg (1354), with one large roof covering nave and aisles, was a hall-church in an older tradition, and the cathedral of Ulm (1377) was an intricate building with one high western spire similar to the 13th century cathedral of Freiburg. The cathedral of St Vitus in Prague (1344) was to an imported French design, by the master Mathieu of Arras. It has a *chevet* east end and an array of flying buttresses. Its detail design was taken over in 1353 by Peter Parler, another master with French connections.

The gothic architect's knowledge of structural theory was still very limited, and even achievements like Beauvais or Westminster Hall owed more to experience and intuition than to any precise analysis of the loads and forces involved. Gothic roof-trusses often contained superfluous members of no structural significance. In late-gothic architecture, such elements were used more and more, becoming a kind of mannerism. Buttresses at Prague were decorated with 'blind' window tracery; roof-vaults had free-flying ribs added, through which the true ribs could be seen; pendent vaults were built, hanging like stalactites, with no purpose other than that of surprise and ambiguity.

## FEUDALISM UNDER PRESSURE

In the early 14th century, old and new institutions co-existed in a peculiar kind of transitional society. Italy, often with Church connivance at a process which was actually eroding the old medieval Christian ethic, was pioneering modern commerce, often with aggressive competition between the various cities. Northern Europe was producing manufactured goods, generally in a more pragmatic spirit of co-operation. The trade of raw materials and crafted goods through the Hanse created a lot of wealth. In England,

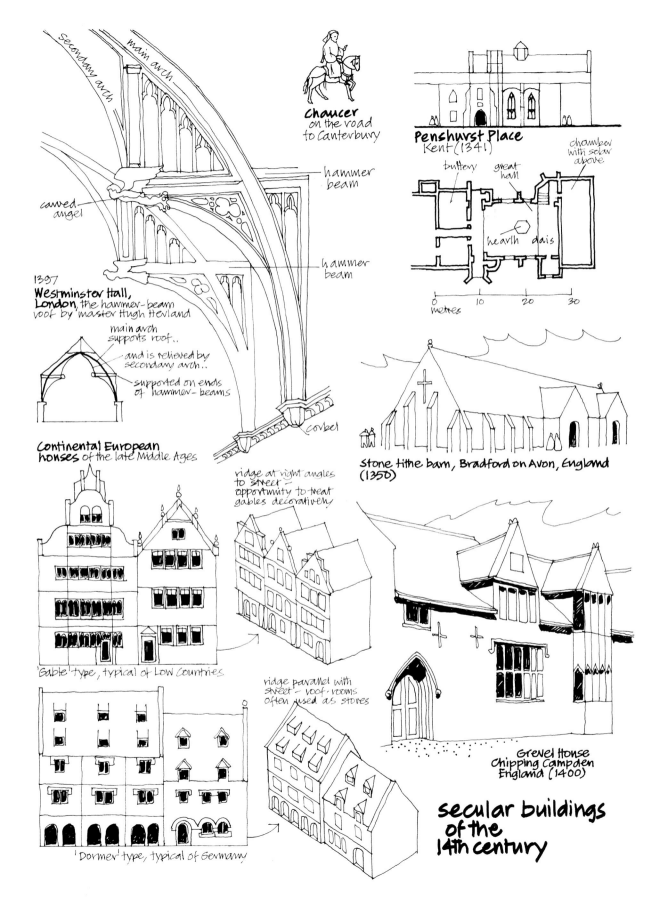

secondary arch

main arch

**chaucer**
on the road
to Canterbury

hammer
beam

carved
angel

hammer
beam

1397
**Westminster Hall,
London,** the hammer-beam
roof by 'master Hugh Herland'

main arch
supports roof..

..and is relieved by
secondary arch..

..supported on ends
of hammer-beams

corbel

**Penshurst Place**
Kent (1341)

buttery

great
hall

chamber
with solar
above

hearth   dais

0        10       20       30
metres

Stone tithe barn, Bradford on Avon, England
(1350)

**Continental European
houses** of the late Middle Ages

ridge at right angles
to street -
opportunity to treat
gables decoratively

'Gable' type, typical of Low Countries

ridge parallel with
street - roof-rooms
often used as stores

'Dormer' type, typical of Germany

**Grevel House
Chipping Campden
England (1400)**

**secular buildings
of the
14th century**

wool production flourished and its success was one of the economic prodigies of the 14th and 15th centuries. As production increased, the advantages of a captive rural labour-force became apparent, and the gradual liberalisation of feudalism was suddenly arrested. Payment for labour ceased, as feudal landlords tried to hold onto their labour-force. As the peasants' condition and status declined, the gap between rich and poor grew wider.

Then in the mid-14th century a cataclysmic event left its mark on almost every aspect of society. An outbreak of bubonic plague, the 'Black Death', spread along the caravan routes from the far east in 1346, through the Crimea into southern Europe in 1348 and to the north in 1350. Between a quarter and a third of the people died in affected areas, with devastating results for Europe: harvests went ungathered and trading all but ceased. But the longer-term effects were catalytic, even positive. An economic recovery took place, and the previous trend towards humanism in the arts, exemplified by the painting of Giotto (1276–1337) and the poetry of Dante (1265–1321), was intensified. In some, a feeling of pessimism and despair produced a pre-occupation with death, reflected in the *memento mori* which appeared repeatedly in the arts, but to others came an attitude of defiance towards accepted religious tenets. Commerce, philosophy, art and architecture were pursued with greater intensity.

The Black Death also intensified the economic contradictions in society since, with the labour-force decimated, land-owners imposed even stricter controls on the survivors. The workers, seeing their labour at a premium, increased their demands for better conditions, and the inherent tensions present in both city and countryside came to the surface. With the Hundred Years' War dragging on, the growing discontent of the ordinary people gave rise to the rebellions of the *Jacqueries* in France in 1358 and the English peasants' revolts of the 1380s. In London, urban workers and peasants, led by Wat Tyler and John Ball and inspired by the idealism of Wycliffe and his 'Lollard' followers, opposed the primitive capitalism of the property-owners with their own primitive communism.

Their efforts, however, were premature; crushed by the forces of the crown the peasants fell back, left behind by the developments of the 14th century. Certainly they had evidence enough that others than they were prospering: Henry Despenser, the avenging bishop of Norwich, for example, to whose fine manor house at South Elmham the first Lollard martyr, William Sawtry, was brought for torture in 1399; or Sir John de Poulteney, the rich London merchant who built Penshurst Place in Kent (1341). By 14th-century standards, Penshurst was a luxurious place to live. Based on the design of the Norman manor house and built in stone, with decorated tracery in the windows, it had a great hall with kitchen and buttery on one side and a withdrawing-chamber on the other, with solar above: a stark contrast with the hovels of the countryside around. Another type of building that presented a perpetual reminder of servility was the tithe-barn. The church's demands for tithes – taxes in the form of goods – was quite marked by the 14th century, and the tithe-barn, often located near the church, was a dominant feature of the landscape.

Cities, too, presented a contrast, between the well-built town-houses of the merchants and the huts and shelters of the poor. Typical of the more substantial English houses was the Grevel House, Chipping Campden (late 14th-century), a translation into stone of forms already familiar in timber, with main ground storey, steeply-pitched roof storey and prominent gabled dormers. Medieval house frontages were generally narrow – between 4.5 and 6 metres – with the ridges of the pitched roofs running at right angles to the streets. The richest merchants could combine two or more plots, forming a wide-fronted property with the ridge parallel to the street.

Large houses of this kind were also built in Germany. Some, in Braunschweig, Nuremburg and elsewhere, were high, with three or more roof storeys, each lit with a line of dormers. Narrow-fronted houses in which the front gable was made a decorative feature were also built in Germany but were more common in Holland and Belgium. Old houses at Ghent, Liège, Middelburg, Utrecht and Malines still survive.

With the growth of capitalism, the Middle Ages in Europe came to an end: the inherent tensions that accompanied the new system – between nation-states and between the classes within them – are features of the modern world. One casualty was the medieval system of scholastic philosophy, that long search begun in Charlemagne's Palace Schools to reconcile reason with religious faith. In its place, many thinkers outside both church and university, and untramelled by their traditions, were developing a new humanistic attitude. In literature, the works of Boccaccio, Petrarch, Froissart, Chaucer, Langland and Villon were dealing with people and their lives rather than with weighty abstractions, and the paintings of Uccello, Fra Angelico, Piero della Francesca, Dürer and van Eyck were moving away from medieval symbolism towards characterisation, to depicting the real world through the use of perspective and, with oil painting, to a new approach to the rendering of light and shade. Inevitably, a comparable attitude developed in architectural design.

In most of Europe it took the form of a late flowering of gothic architecture, craftsmanship and sculpture. A spectacular example is Milan cathedral, begun in 1385 and developed during the 15th century into one of the largest and most decorative cathedrals in the world. Its size and richness reflected the wealth of its sponsor, Visconti, Duke of Milan; its design came from the experience of fifty or more designers from north of the Alps and the result was a combination of Italian, French, and German influences. The nave, with French double aisles, terminates in an apsidal east end, not in the *chevet* form but surrounded instead by a polygonal German aisle. The great height of the main side-aisles effectively reduced the opportunity for a clerestory: the internal effect is dark and solemn like a German hall church, contrasting with the bright, Italian marble exterior, a mass of lacy buttresses, pinnacles and statuary. Finest of all are the three main windows of the apse, with their asymmetrical flowing tracery.

Similar in concept, though very different in execution, is the cathedral of Seville, the largest of all medieval churches. Begun in 1402, it was not completed till 1520. Its great size and unusually rectangular plan came from the re-use of the foundations of a former mosque, parts of which, notably the elegant minaret, were incorporated into the final design. The nave, with double aisles and side chapels of great width, is roofed with massive yet intricate rib-vaulting. The exterior, with triple flying buttresses, is gothic in general character and outline but Islamic in detail.

The 15th-century churches of England were among the finest achievements of late gothic design. Many large projects, some begun centuries earlier, were reaching completion. In the south transept of Gloucester cathedral and in the slightly later choir,

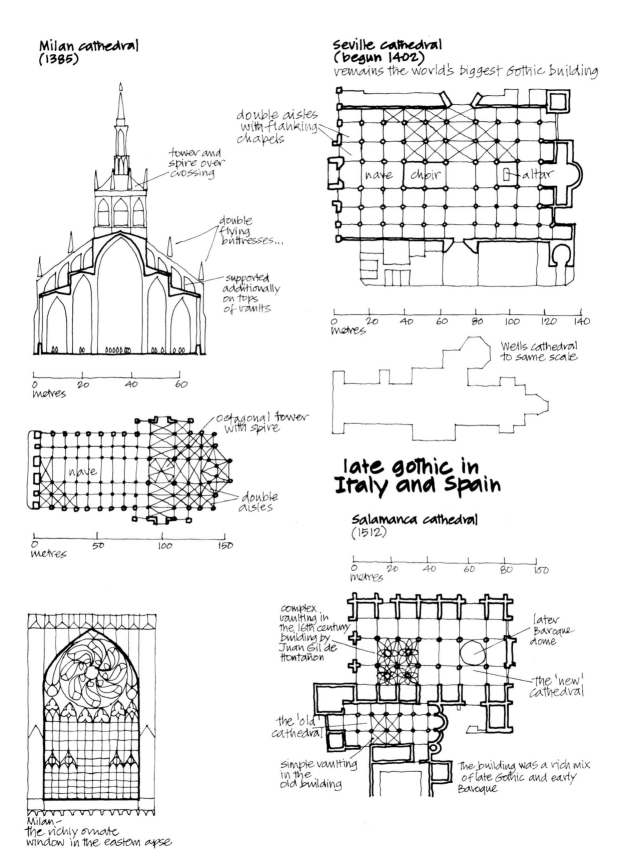

Milan cathedral
(1385)

tower and spire over crossing

double flying buttresses...

supported additionally on tops of vaults

0    20    40    60
metres

octagonal tower with spire

nave

double aisles

0    50    100    150
metres

Milan—
the richly ornate window in the eastern apse.

Seville cathedral
(begun 1402)
remains the world's biggest Gothic building

double aisles with flanking chapels

nave    choir    altar

0    20    40    60    80    100    120    140
metres

Wells cathedral to same scale

# late gothic in Italy and Spain

Salamanca cathedral
(1512)

0    20    40    60    80    100
metres

complex vaulting in the 16th century building by Juan Gil de Hontañon

later Baroque dome

the 'new' Cathedral

the 'old' cathedral

simple vaulting in the old building

the building was a rich mix of late Gothic and early Baroque

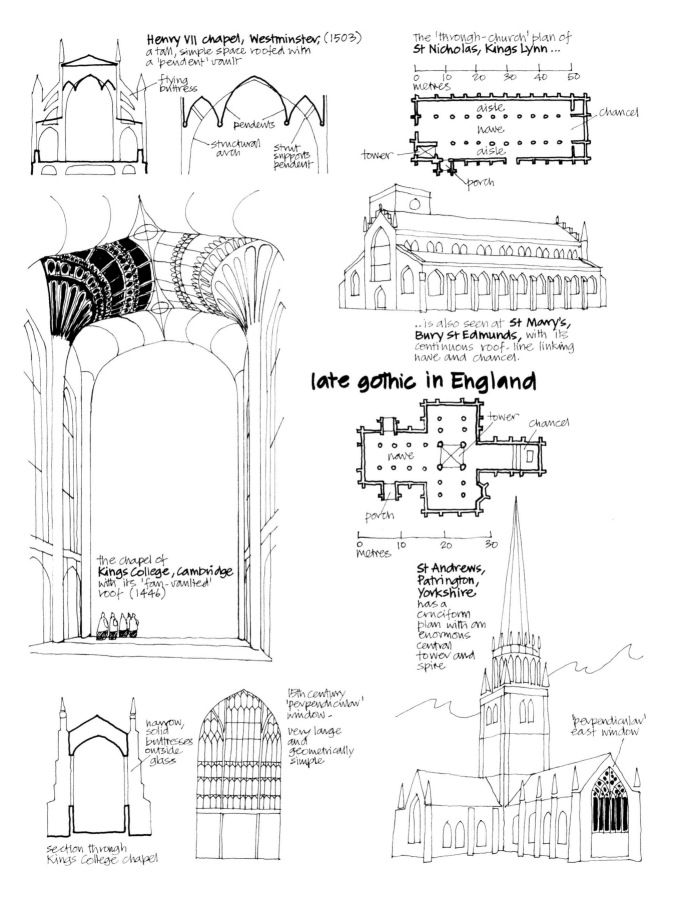

**Henry VII chapel, Westminster, (1503)** a tall, simple space roofed with a 'pendent' vault

flying buttress

pendents

structural arch

strut supports pendent

The 'through-church' plan of **St Nicholas, Kings Lynn**...

0  10  20  30  40  50
metres

aisle
chancel
nave
aisle
tower
porch

..is also seen at **St Mary's, Bury St Edmunds**, with its continuous roof-line linking nave and chancel.

# late gothic in England

tower
chancel
nave
porch

0  10  20  30
metres

the chapel of **Kings College, Cambridge** with its 'fan-vaulted' roof (1446)

**St Andrews, Patrington, Yorkshire** has a cruciform plan with an enormous central tower and spire

'perpendicular' east window

narrow, solid buttresses outside glass

15th century 'perpendicular' window - very large and geometrically simple

section through Kings College chapel

a new, elegant style was seen. This was continued in the magnificent west front of Beverley Minster, finished around 1400, and in a spire added to the tower of Norwich cathedral. In about 1410 a beautiful nave was completed at Canterbury cathedral and fine crossing-towers were built both there (1490) and at Durham (1465). In addition, several important royal chapels were built, among them Henry VI's chapels at Eton College (1440) and at King's College, Cambridge (1446), the chapel of St George at Windsor Castle begun for Henry VII in 1481, and the Henry VII chapel at Westminster Abbey, built in 1503 for his son Henry VIII.

The architectural style of all these amazing buildings, is known as 'perpendicular', and has no parallel outside England. The name derives from the simple regularity of the window-tracery, in contrast to the richness of both English decorated and of French *flamboyant*. This feature has led to theories about a dearth of adequate craftsmen in the years following the Black Death; in fact 15th-century buildings in general, and perpendicular in particular, with its precise, elegant, and amazingly insubstantial stonework, demonstrate medieval craftsmanship at its most technically accomplished.

If King's College chapel lacks anything, it is the ambiguous spatial variety of Early Gothic, which so added to the mystery and excitement, and which has no place in this rational, almost materialistic, building. A simple box, 88 metres long, 12 metres wide and 24 high, its only internal division is a timber choir-screen. The brilliance of the effect comes from the enormous, repetitive windows with their simple tracery, alternating with tall piers whose vertical flutings emphasise their height and continue up to branch into master John Wastell's richest and most intricate fan-vaulting. The vaulting ribs were no longer lines of structural stress, but had become decorative features carved onto the surface of the stone shell built up from a mosaic of panels. This retreat from structural 'expression' culminated in the Vertue brothers' fantastic stone roof of Henry VII's chapel at Westminster, where the real structural arches are almost concealed by an effusion of intricate stone 'pendent' vaults, which hang downwards, seemingly defying gravity.

Royal sponsorship of church building had its parallel in villages and towns throughout Britain, where the local bourgeoisie, many of them enriched by the sudden growth of the wool industry, were following suit. Some churches retained traditional or local forms, but generally the perpendicular style was used, in light, airy churches of great size.

Strong definition between nave and chancel was rejected in favour of 'through churches', with a high, continuous roof linking nave and chancel into one main space, separated only by a decorative pulpitum or rood-screen; St Mary's, Bury St Edmunds, is a good example. Many great churches were newly-built in the perpendicular style; others had new features added, such as the big east window at Patrington, Yorkshire, or the enormous tower, the 'Boston stump', of Boston in Lincolnshire. Finest of all were the timber roofs: the depressed tie-beam type, as at St Cuthbert's, Wells, was used on low-pitched lead roofs, and on steeper pitches a variety of types including the magnificent double hammer-beam, as at March in Cambridgeshire.

The rich and fanciful church designs of England had their counterparts all over Europe, in a last outburst of gothic imagination, from the Church of the Jerónimos at Belém, Portugal (1500), the cathedrals of Salamanca (1512) and Segovia (1522), to the

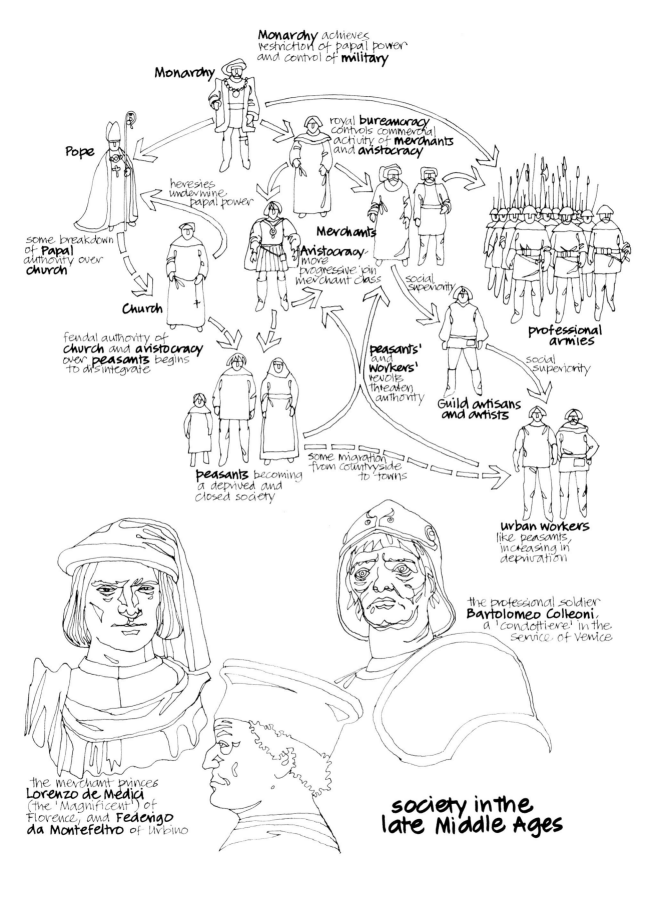

Monarchy achieves restriction of papal power and control of **military**

Monarchy

royal **bureaucracy** controls commercial activity of **merchants** and **aristocracy**

Pope

heresies undermine papal power

some breakdown of **Papal** authority over **church**

Church

Merchants

**Aristocracy** more progressive join merchant class

social superiority

professional armies

feudal authority of **church** and **aristocracy** over **peasants** begins to disintegrate

**peasants'** and **Workers'** revolts threaten authority

Guild artisans and artists

social superiority

**peasants** becoming a deprived and closed society

some migration from countryside to towns

**urban workers** like peasants, increasing in deprivation

the professional soldier **Bartolomeo Colleoni**, a 'condottiere' in the service of Venice

the merchant princes **Lorenzo de Medici** (the 'Magnificent') of Florence, and **Federigo da Montefeltro** of Urbino

# society in the late Middle Ages

west front at Rouen (1509) and the church of St James at Brno (1495). Though clearly gothic in spirit, all these designs were strikingly individual. The growing identity of national culture and the increasing autonomy of the individual designer had taken architecture a long way since the days, three centuries before, when European Gothic had recognisably been that of the Île de France. A common European tradition based on skills and experience handed down through practice rather than theory had yet allowed local styles to emerge and individual talent to flourish.

## THE ARCHITECT'S NEW STATUS

But by the end of the 16th century, though local methods of construction would persist in humble buildings, this tradition was dying out. The lodge system had by now broken down in favour of the guild system. Big buildings were built less by integrated multi-skill teams than by collections of craftsmen of different trades. A designer was often a man of considerable status, now separated by education and class from the craftsmen on the site. His skill might be more intellectual than practical; he became increasingly remote from the building process itself while seeking to control it more and more. The autonomy of the individual craftsman diminished as he was allowed to make fewer and fewer design decisions of his own.

Three developments gave these trends further impetus. The first was the invention by Johann Gutenberg (1400–68) of the moveable-type printing-press, which revolutionised communication and enabled a rapid increase in the transmission of ideas in written form. The medieval tradition of communicating building knowledge by practical example was superseded by the spread of theoretical ideas. The second was the gradual discovery by the Italians of their imperial Roman history. Encouraged by growing secularism, interest in classical pagan authors led to a revived interest in the buildings of ancient Rome. Medieval Italy had remained strangely unaware of its legacy of ancient buildings, except as symbols of a barbaric past and quarries for building materials. The 5th-century baptistery at Florence, remodelled in the 11th century, was vaguely thought to be a Roman building; elsewhere genuine Roman buildings lay half-ruined or, like the Colosseum, provided living-space for squatters. But now, the 15th century saw an unequivocal return to the architectural forms of ancient Rome. Gothic architecture had never taken hold in Italy to the extent that it had in the north, and Italian architects were now ready to return to their own past. Inspiration came not only from the ruins themselves but also from the writings of Vitruvius, a 1st-century Roman architect, whose somewhat suspect and pedantic theories were given the reverence due to a sole authority.

The biggest impetus for the movement usually described as 'the Renaissance' came from the existence in Italy of a unique new class, a merchant aristocracy of unprecedented wealth and power which had drawn into its ranks many of the old feudal nobility and had assumed their education and refinement of life-style. These new 'merchant princes', in the fragmented society of 15th-century Italy, were able to command positions of absolute power, unchallenged by the petits-bourgeois and artisans whose status was gradually degenerating into wage-slavery.

The changes took place more quickly in Italy than anywhere else. Northern merchants were slower to usurp the power of the hereditary aristocracy, and the strength of the northern guilds protected the status of the lower middle classes and artisans, but in Italy the merchant-princes and their families ruled supreme. Despite the Black Death, trade and production were growing and capital formation increased rapidly. No merchant specialised; his activities were spread over banking, money-lending, mining and manufacturing, importing and exporting, building, real-estate and art-dealing. To replace the medieval institutions and now outmoded republicanism of Venice and Genoa came the oligarchic city-states of Milan under the Visconti and the Sforza and Florence under the Medici; through skilful diplomacy and the exercise of great wealth, they each attained the power and influence of much larger states. Painting and sculpture flourished as a result of the patronage offered by these great families to artists like Ghiberti, Donatello, Botticelli and Leonardo, and investment in building dramatically increased.

The medieval architect, invariably a serf, was prized by the ruling classes for his abilities but despised as a manual labourer. Even in 15th-century Florence architecture was still not a profession in its own right. The usual approach to it was through one of the associated crafts: jewellery or silver-smithing, painting or sculpture, masonry or carpentry – all of which still carried the social stigma of manual labour. But with feudalism at an end, status was no longer automatically inherited; it had to be attained. Some artists and architects went to great lengths in fighting for recognition of their special status. Some refrained from manual work; purely intellectual pursuits like philosophy and natural science were socially more acceptable. Others achieved high positions in society through wealth or by marrying into noble families, becoming, in the words of William Morris, 'the great architect, carefully kept for the purpose and guarded from the common troubles of common men'.

High status gave the artist or architect greater freedom to develop his abilities. At the same time, something was lost, for greater independence gradually increased alienation. The static nature of feudal society, for all its limitations on personal development, had at least ensured that a building was the product of a well-defined and close relationship between designer and user. As capitalism developed, society became more fluid and relationships not only more complex and less easily defined but also less close. In 15th-century Florence, however, with capitalism in its infancy, this alienation was not yet far advanced. Moreover, the social milieu within which the architect worked was extremely stimulating: the new bourgeoisie were still an active and revolutionary force with generous and expansive ideas. At this stage, the architect's new-found independence, stimulated by the merchant prince's wealth and dynamism, ensured a great outburst of architectural achievement.

Among the foremost Florentine achievements were those of Filippo Brunelleschi (1377–1446). Starting as a goldsmith and sculptor, he demonstrated his great skill as early as 1401 in a competition entry for the bronze doors of the Baptistery. Gradually he became interested in architecture and by 1410 had already designed a few buildings and visited Rome, where he had measured and drawn the monuments. In 1418 he won a competition for the completion of the cathedral of Santa Maria del Fiore, Florence's most important building. His aim was to construct a dome over the crossing, according to Arnolfo's original intention but without using formwork. To prove his ability to a sceptical Board of Works, he tried out his method on a smaller dome at the church

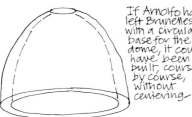

If Arnolfo had left Brunelleschi with a circular base for the dome, it could have been built, course by course, without centering.

each successive stage would have been a structural entity

However, the plan required the building of a dome over an octagonal space

The most obvious answer was a construction of eight ribs with panels spanning between.

The ribs, however, would have required support during construction, until all the panels were in position

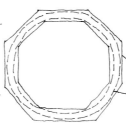

Fortunately, the octagonal base was fairly wide.

Brunelleschi designed an octagonal dome thick enough to contain a circular dome within it and thus to act as a circular dome during construction

# Brunelleschi 1

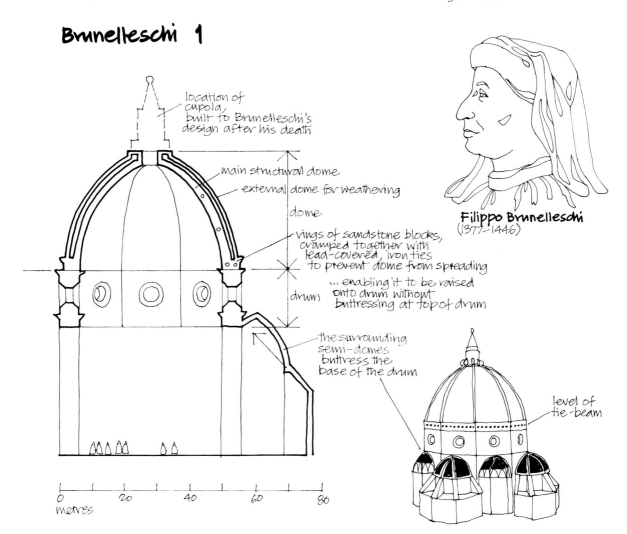

location of cupola, built to Brunelleschi's design after his death

main structural dome

external dome for weathering

dome

rings of sandstone blocks, cramped together with lead-covered, iron ties to prevent dome from spreading

... enabling it to be raised onto drum without buttressing at top of drum

drum

the surrounding semi-domes buttress the base of the drum

Filippo Brunelleschi (1377-1446)

level of tie-beam

0     20     40     60     80
metres

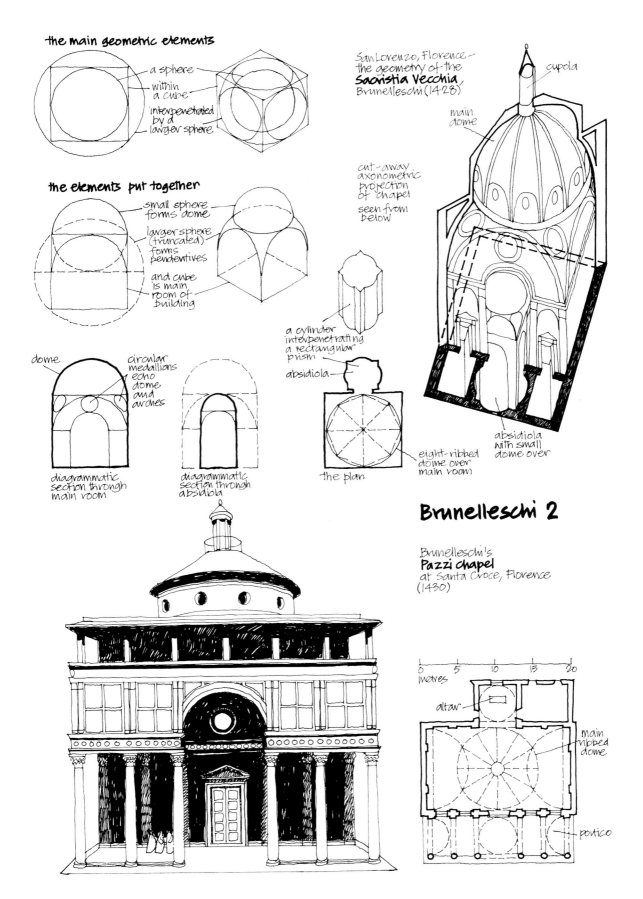

**the main geometric elements**

a sphere within a cube

interpenetrated by a larger sphere

San Lorenzo, Florence — the geometry of the **Sacristia Vecchia**, Brunelleschi (1428)

cupola

main dome

**the elements put together**

small sphere forms dome

larger sphere (truncated) forms pendentives

and cube is main room of building

cut-away axonometric projection of chapel seen from below

a cylinder interpenetrating a rectangular prism

absidiola

dome

circular medallions echo dome and arches

diagrammatic section through main room

diagrammatic section through absidiola

the plan

eight-ribbed dome over main room

absidiola with small dome over

# Brunelleschi 2

Brunelleschi's **Pazzi chapel** at Santa Croce, Florence (1430)

0  5  10  15  20
metres

altar

main ribbed dome

portico

of San Jacopo Oltrarno. The great dome itself was begun in 1420 and substantially complete by 1436. The ingenuity of its box-rib structure, covered with inner and outer skins, together with the incomparable serenity of its outline, won universal admiration. 'Who could be so harsh or envious', asked his fellow-architect Alberti, 'as not to praise our architect Pippo who has built so great a structure high into the sky, so huge as to overshadow all the people of Tuscany?'

## ROME REDISCOVERED

During the building of the Florence dome Brunelleschi was able to devote himself to several other major buildings, an indication in itself of the way the architect's role had changed. In 1421 he was directing the building of a loggia at the Ospedale degl'Innocenti, a simple arcaded cloister carrying an enclosed upper storey and standing on a stepped podium. Much of the detail, including the round columns with their composite capitals and the simple groined vaulting, were Roman in origin, and the elegance of the detail has much in common with the romanesque of San Miniato. However, the whole concept was so clear and unified that it went well beyond its romanesque and even its Roman antecedents.

The intellectual life of Renaissance Italy was the product of the most progressive minds of the day, engaged in a search for an underlying order in a tumultuous world. Just as the painter was beginning to investigate the geometry of perspective and the sculptor was discovering the structure of human anatomy, the architect was becoming interested in the harmony imparted to a building by the choice of mathematically related dimensions. One of the best examples of this is the church of San Lorenzo (1421), a basilican building with a high nave and groin-vaulted aisles, with the sanctuary flanked by two sacristies. The Sacristia Vecchia (1428) on the north side is one of the masterpieces of Italian architecture. Brunelleschi designed this small room as a cube, over which he placed a hemispherical dome. To one side, for the altar, is a small *absidiola*, a double cube with its own small dome. All the wall and ceiling surfaces are white plaster, on which the dark grey of pilasters, arches and applied medallions stand out, emphasising the geometry of the room with great clarity. The effect of liveliness is nevertheless firmly controlled, though in a creative rather than a pedantic way.

The chapel Brunelleschi built in 1430 for Andrea, head of the Pazzi family, at the church of Santa Croce, is a development of his work at San Lorenzo. A small building, with a ribbed dome over a rectangular space, it displays the same interest in the use of simple geometric shapes, again expressed in terms of grey stone ribs against a white background. A particular achievement is the beautifully organised front elevation with its projecting portico, the architrave broken by a semi-circular arch echoing the shape of the dome above.

Brunelleschi is sometimes credited with having been the first to analyse the laws of perspective, which allowed painters accurately to represent-three dimensions on a flat canvas, and architects to investigate spatial effects before they were built. At their best, Brunelleschi's buildings certainly bear this out: his most mature works display a spatial control which could only have come from meticulous pre-planning. In 1436 he designed the church of Santo Spirito, a large latin-cross building which went beyond the simplicity of the basilican San Lorenzo. Tall, arched colonnades separate nave and aisles and are seen against further colonnades formed by the engaged columns which divide the side chapels.

Brunelleschi was an eclectic, deriving his architectural vocabulary from classical, romanesque and even gothic sources with equal readiness. Soon, however, increasing reliance was placed on ancient Rome as the source of architectural inspiration. This was partly due to the influence of Leon Battista Alberti (1404–72), a writer and academic interested in the study of classical literature. His book *De Re Aedificatoria* was published in 1485, the first architectural book to be printed by the Gutenberg method, and the first attempt to lay down a set of theoretical design rules since those of Vitruvius, on which it was largely based. Alberti also designed buildings. In his west façade for Santa Maria Novella in Florence, the decorative flanking 'scrolls' joining nave and aisles, which were to become a feature of church design, made an appearance. And in the Palazzo Rucellai (1451) he brought a modest development of style to the building-form which had begun with the Palazzo Vecchio and been developed and humanised by Brunelleschi in his Palazzo Pitti (1435) and by their contemporary Michelozzo Michelozzi in the Palazzo Riccardi (1444). Alberti adorned his three-storey elevation with three tiers of superimposed orders, a direct reference to the Colosseum of ancient Rome. The Palazzo Strozzi by Majano and Cronaca (1495) is a typical Florentine palace of the time, a solid block-like building with reasonably large and attractive windows on the two upper floors and a massive Roman cornice. Typically, the palazzo was planned around a central *cortile* or courtyard which gave light and ventilation to the interior.

In 1446, a design by Alberti was used for re-modelling the west front of San Francesco in Rimini as a monument to Sigismondo Malatesta, a rich merchant. It was a suitably grandiose design, based partly on the arch of Augustus in Rimini. Alberti was perhaps not typical of the architects of the time, being more academic and theoretical than most, but he did not even stay to see the design executed; instead he sent detail drawings by letter to the resident engineer as work progressed. Alberti's best work was the church of Sant' Andrea in Mantua, begun in 1472, just before his death, and completed 40 years later. A massive, latin-cross type building without aisles and with a crossing-dome on pendentives, it has a grand, Roman character, emphasised by a west front in the form of a triumphal arch.

The three orders appear again in the inner *cortile* of the Palazzo Ducale at Urbino, designed in 1465 by Luciano Laurana for the Montefeltro family. This building is also remarkable for its elegant interior, which includes the famous wall-panel, possibly by Piero della Francesca, showing an imaginary renaissance town drawn in accurate parallel-perspective. Florentine ideas were gradually spreading. The church of the Certosa at Pavia (1453) is essentially a gothic building in character but the west front, designed and sculpted by Giovanni Amadeo, though medieval in spirit, is classical in detail. The Venetian architect Pietro Lombardo introduced the new ideas into Venice, as always, with local variations. His Santa Maria dei Miracoli (1480) was beautifully crafted in marble in the Veneto-Byzantine tradition.

In Rome too the new ideas were pursued with great enthusiasm. Though the Papacy's spiritual influence was low its wealth was growing. In this final century before the

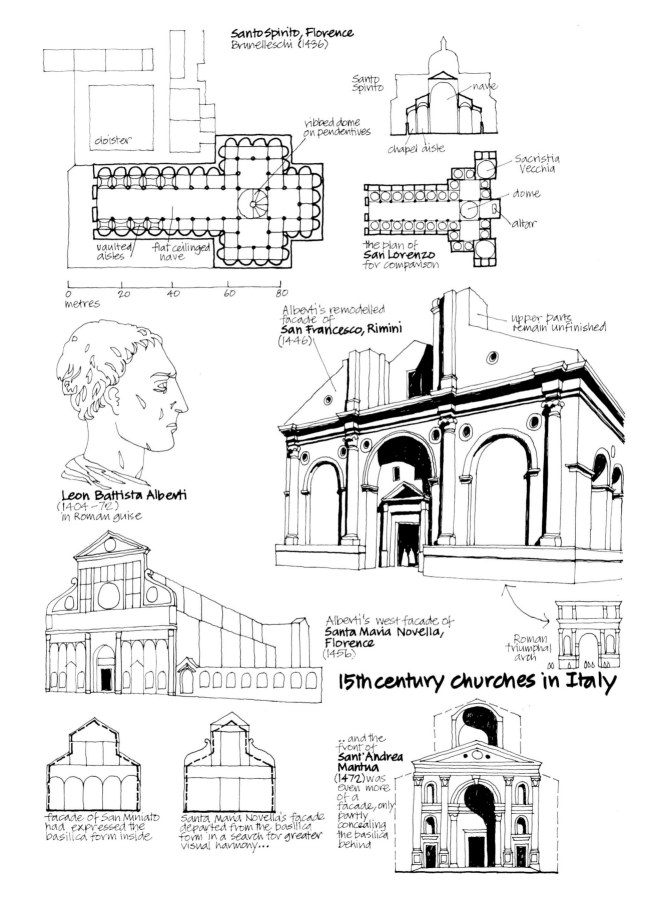

Santo Spirito, Florence
Brunelleschi (1436)

cloister

ribbed dome on pendentives

vaulted aisles

flat ceilinged nave

0   20   40   60   80
metres

Santo Spirito

nave

chapel aisle

Sacristia Vecchia

dome

altar

the plan of San Lorenzo for comparison

Leon Battista Alberti
(1404–72)
in Roman guise

Alberti's remodelled facade of
San Francesco, Rimini
(1446)

upper parts remain unfinished

Alberti's west facade of
Santa Maria Novella, Florence
(1456)

Roman triumphal arch

## 15th century churches in Italy

facade of San Miniato had expressed the basilica form inside

Santa Maria Novella's facade departed from the basilica form in a search for greater visual harmony...

.. and the front of
Sant'Andrea Mantua
(1472) was even more of a facade, only partly concealing the basilica behind

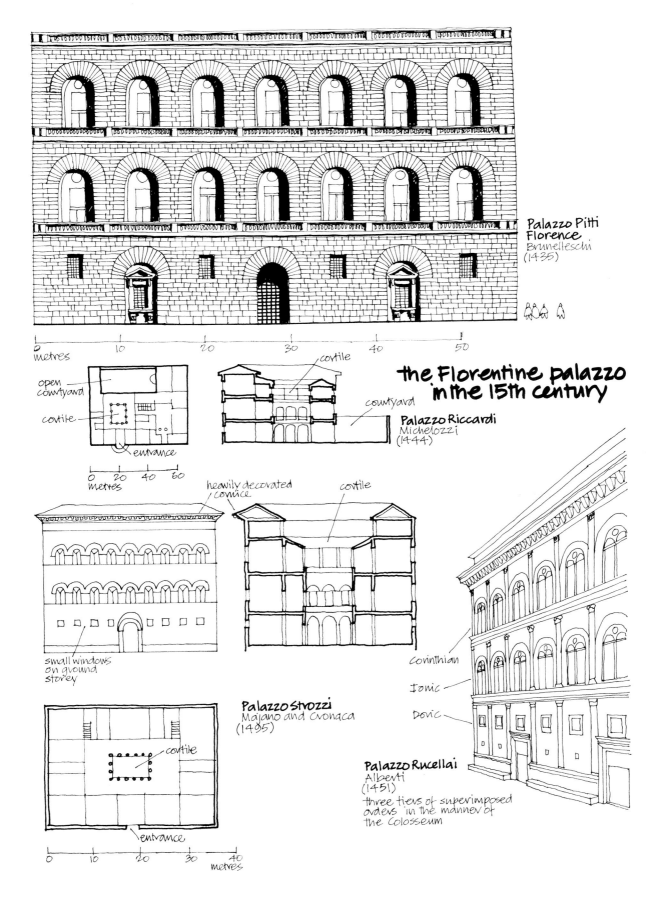

**Palazzo Pitti Florence**
Brunelleschi
(1435)

0 metres 10 20 30 40 50

open courtyard

cortile

entrance

0 20 40 60
metres

cortile

countyard

courtyard

**Palazzo Riccardi**
Michelozzi
(1444)

# the Florentine palazzo in the 15th century

heavily decorated cornice

cortile

small windows on ground storey

**Palazzo Strozzi**
Majano and Cronaca
(1485)

0 10 20 30 40 metres

cortile

entrance

Corinthian

Ionic

Doric

**Palazzo Rucellai**
Alberti
(1451)
three tiers of superimposed orders in the manner of the Colosseum

Reformation, it could at least use this to make an outward demonstration, in building form, of the religious authority it was losing. Its main agent was Donato Bramante (1444–1514). Though from a poor background, Bramante's talents enabled him to train as a painter in Urbino and to develop into an architect occupying in Rome the position that Brunelleschi did in Florence. By the time he had seriously begun work in Rome in 1499, he had already completed several important works in Milan, including in 1492 a magnificent domed east end to the medieval abbey church of Santa Maria delle Grazie. He may have been associated with the building of the Palazzo della Cancelleria in Rome, though it was largely completed by the time he lived there permanently. This fine building, a further development of the Florentine *palazzo* style, was the first big Renaissance building in Rome: built for the wealthy Cardinal Riario, it was a three-storey palace with inner *cortile*, incorporating into one of its wings the whole of the ancient basilican church of San Lorenzo in Damaso.

It was to be expected that in Rome, with its papal ambitions to relive the days of imperial power and with many ancient buildings to serve as models, architecture would develop away from the eclecticism of Brunelleschi towards a historically correct re-creation of the Roman design method. Bramante's work certainly took it in this direction, and led to the so-called 'High Renaissance' period when discovery and experiment were over and architects worked within an accepted framework of conventional knowledge and set formulae. Lesser designers than Bramante made this an excuse for undistinguished buildings, but his Tempietto di San Pietro di Montorio in Rome (1502) is a minor masterpiece. Built to mark the place where St Peter was martyred, it is in the form of a small circular Roman temple, only 4.5 metres across internally, surrounded by a Doric peristyle and surmounted by a drum and dome. Perfect in proportion and form, it was a dignified tribute by the 16th century to its Roman past.

We do not know for certain how medieval churches were used, but it seems likely that the design of the buildings reflected the symbolism of the mass, the Host being prepared in the sanctuary while the people waited in the nave, and the two coming together at the crossing, the symbolic heart of the building. During the 15th and 16th centuries, architects began to look for new meanings. A more grandiose and more abstract conception evolved, of the church building as representative of the cosmos, the most perfect symbol of which was the circle. Alberti in *De Re Aedificatoria* identified nine ideal plan-forms for a church: the circle, and eight polygons deriving from it. For justification he pointed to nature's predilection for spherical forms – the earth and the stars- and for precedent to the Roman Pantheon.

The adoption of this form raised liturgical and architectural problems, hardly significant in such a special building as the Tempietto, but more so in a parish church. The circular plan, reinforced in its effect by a centrally placed dome, implied a central location for the altar and the preparation of the sacramental elements. However ideal in symbolic terms, this was often unsatisfactory in practice – where respectively should the priest and congregation stand? On the other hand, an altar in a niche at the side or end, leaving room for the people under the dome, appeared to banish the most important spiritual element to a subordinate position. Nevertheless, for some time the circular form had considerable currency. Bramante's Tempietto was only one of thirty or more important centrally-planned churches built in Italy during the 15th and 16th centuries.

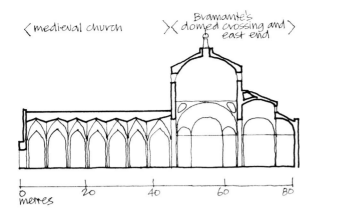

⟨medieval church⟩ ⟨Bramante's domed crossing and east end⟩

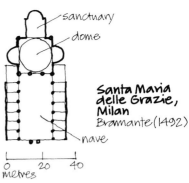

sanctuary

dome

nave

0 20 40
metres

**Santa Maria delle Grazie, Milan**
Bramante (1492)

0 20 40 60 80
metres

entrance to palazzo

entrance to church

# Bramante

**Palazzo della Cancelleria, Rome**
Bramante (1486)

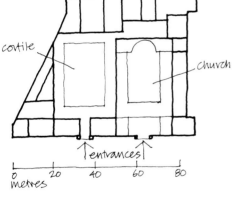

cortile

church

entrances

0 20 40 60 80
metres

**Donato Bramante**
(1444–1514)

Bramante's
**Tempietto di San Pietro in Montorio, Rome**
(1502)

plan

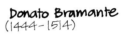

0 5 10
metres

section

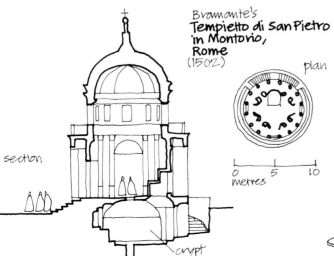

crypt

0 5 10
metres

The architectural ideas of Florence and Rome were slow to spread beyond the Alps. Apart from the powerful dukedom of Burgundy, France was becoming a unified nation, thanks largely to the politics of Louis XI (1461–83), but in the aftermath of the Hundred Years' War social and economic reconstruction was more important than building. England too was becoming unified, but having suffered the Hundred Years' War and the Wars of the Roses, the country had been in no state for economic progress. Richard III was an able administrator but his death in 1485 brought the cunning and ambitious House of Tudor to the throne and Henry VII immediately began to strengthen the monarchy by strict control of the country. The way was open in both France and England for cultural and economic expansion. But richest and most expansive of all the northern countries were the Netherlands. Antwerp, Bruges and Gent had a rich bourgeoisie whose success was based on thriving trade with Italy, Germany, France and England. Van Eyck's famous painting *The Arnolfini Portrait* (1434), besides being significant in the development of Renaissance art, is as good a document as one could wish for of the strong connection between Italy and Flanders.

In Spain and Portugal, in the meantime, events were taking place which would be of great importance to the Europe of the future. The marriage in 1469 between Fernando of Aragon and Isabel of Castile had united their two countries and created modern Spain. Immediately they set about creating a national identity, in a spirit of aggressive expansionism. The aristocracy was firmly controlled, Moslems and Jews were expelled from the country and Torquemada's Inquisition visited on non-believers who remained. The search for new trade, backed by the development of the armed ocean-going ship suitable for both trade and piracy, encouraged a number of epic journeys of exploration. The Portuguese prince Henry the Navigator prompted the exploration of the West African coast, Bernal Diaz reached the Cape of Good Hope, and Vasco da Gama rounded the Cape to India. Cristoforo Colombo, sponsored by Fernando and Isabel, set sail westwards in 1492 in search of another route to India and unexpectedly discovered a new continent. The future development of western culture would no longer be that of Europe alone.

Europe's exploration of the world was stimulated essentially by Italy's competitors, looking for new ways to India and China to break her monopoly of the eastern trade routes. But undreamed-of lands were discovered and their colonisation pushed India and China into the background of men's minds. Conflict arose over possession of the new lands. Suddenly increased sources of silver and gold brought inflation and price increases to Europe as a whole, the merchants prospered, and the poor fell even farther behind, setting the pattern for the economy and class-system of the later industrial age.

Scientific discovery also flourished, though technology did not necessarily benefit. Science had for so long been a branch of philosophy, while technology was the province of the artisan, that the two did not meet immediately. Technical developments continued in the medieval pattern: gradual, pragmatic shifts towards mastery of techniques, still unsupported by general theories. However, man's pursuit of discovery for its own sake was insatiable, and facts were indefatigably catalogued in a way which would allow scientific theories to emerge in the future.

# 7 ENLIGHTENMENT
## The 16th and 17th centuries

'It is a poor disciple', wrote Leonardo da Vinci, 'that does not excel his master'. The new horizons opening up around him had widened man's potential to expand his mind and skills and to use them with greater confidence and freedom. However, by the beginning of the 16th century it was plain that though the medieval system might be collapsing, an oligarchy of a different kind was growing in its place. If some freedoms were gained, others were lost as the 'new princes' of the capitalist world climbed to power and began to dominate politics. Niccolò Machiavelli (1469–1527) recognised this. His treatise *Il Principe*, published in 1513, was written specifically to further his own career at the Medici court, but its realistic analysis of contemporary politics and its practical advice on how to gain and to retain power made it relevant to all such 'new princes'. This *realpolitik* might have been shocking at the time, but it can also be seen as an attempt to bring order to the anarchism of 16th century politics.

Tudor England, whose rulers were as ruthless as any advocated by Machiavelli, had freedom neither of worship nor of speech, nor even, in the case of Thomas More – executed in 1535 for holding unacceptable opinions which yet he had kept to himself – of thought. In 1516 he had written *Utopia*, the story of an imaginary country in which he described in detail, like Plato before him, his view of the ideal human society. More's Utopia was no dream-landscape. His view of society was prescriptive and his ideal state was severe and authoritarian. The Middle Ages had neither admitted nor needed any Utopias. The only ideal society, like that of St Augustine's *City of God*, had been a heavenly one, for which earthly life was no more than a preparation.

As man's reliance on heaven gradually declined, and interest in his own world grew, it became apparent that life on earth, far from being irrelevant, merited serious attention and improvement. Maybe inequality was not pre-ordained but capable of being altered. Maybe the same moral freedom which allowed the rise of unprincipled tyrants would permit those opposed to tyranny to seek a world in which it did not exist. *Il Principe* and *Utopia* are different aspects of the same inquiry, views which continue to recur in European thought: that society can and should be changed for the better, either by working pragmatically within the system, or by presenting an ideal to which all may aspire.

Either way, the improvement of any society is a difficult task so long as it remains dominated by a privileged class. This will be reflected in the architecture of the time. The cathedrals of the Middle Ages, though in many respects the expression of their sponsors' personal ambition, also had the glorification of God as a justification for the enormous wealth expended on them. But post-medieval society needed no such excuses: in the more secular ethos that had developed, great buildings could be undisguised expressions of their owners' wealth and power, and 16th-century palaces attracted the kind of investment and architectural effort which in the 13th century had been given only to God.

Foremost among these were the châteaux of the Loire Valley in France. Like many royal courts of the day, the house of Valois spent much of its time travelling from one place to another, and a chain of great palaces was built to accommodate it. When the food and wine were gone and the cess-pits full, the court would move on, leaving the resident household to clear up afterwards. The great days of the Loire châteaux lasted from the reign of Charles VII in the mid-15th century to that of Henri III, last of the Valois, at the end of the 16th. During this time they developed from medieval châteaux forts, built for protection, into magnificent places of comfort and display. The medieval castle of Blois was extended with a grand courtyard of new buildings centred round the wing of François I (1515), with its spiral processional staircase. At Chenonceaux in 1515 and Azay-le-Rideau in 1518 two ornate chateaux were begun whose picturesque medieval silhouettes were enhanced by their waterside settings. Most magnificent of all, Chambord (1519), though classical in many of its details, was still essentially medieval, its plan-form deriving from that of the concentric castle and its vertically-designed elevations and exuberant roofline from the gothic cathedral.

In 1556, an extension to Chenonceaux was built out on a five-arched bridge over the river Cher, by the master of the king's works, Philibert de l'Orme (1515–70), the first great French architect in the post-medieval sense. An enthusiast for Vitruvius, he had visited Italy in 1533, returning imbued with a spirit of classicism, which he celebrated in his two books *Le Premier Tome de l'Architecture* and *Nouvelles Inventions pour bien Bastir*. But neither his books nor his buildings conveyed a dry academicism, for his was an essentially practical mind with an understanding of building materials. The Château of Anet (1547) used Vitruvian motifs, but re-interpreted them. The chapel, though employing classical detail, was an original composition of bold geometric forms.

The Italians' primary inspiration, the buildings of the Romans, were few and far between in France, and the tradition of gothic craftsmanship too strong to die easily. So throughout the 16th century, French architects gradually assimilated the new influences and evolved both from them and from medieval traditions an indigenous French style, in which de l'Orme's distinctive way of ordering a façade played an important part. His extension at Chenonceaux and his designs for Anet, Fontainebleau, Villers-Cotterets and the Château de Boulogne with their elegant, even severe lower storeys and steeply pitched hipped roofs with decorative dormers, set a pattern for the future which dominated French domestic architecture for about three centuries, equally adaptable to middle-class urban housing, as in the Place des Vosges in Paris by Claude Chastillon (1605), and to the royal palaces of the Tuileries and the Louvre.

The Palais des Tuileries, on the right bank of the Seine in Paris, was named after the tile factories which had once stood on the site. Begun in 1564 by de l'Orme for Catherine de Médicis, in the next century it was added to successively by Jean Bullant, Androuet du Cerceau and Louis Le Vau. The projected plan of three large courtyards was never achieved, but the single group of blocks which was built remained the main residence of French kings and emperors till its destruction in 1871. Linked to the Tuileries and its gardens in one vast formal composition was the Palais du Louvre, begun in the reign of François I on the site of an old medieval château, and gradually built up by a succession of architects into one of the largest palaces in European history.

But the products of royal patronage in France, fine as they were, did not attain the heights of those of papal and bourgeois patronage in Italy, where the 16th century saw much inventive architecture. Among the grandest was the Belvedere courtyard at the Vatican, built in 1503 by Bramante for Pope Julius II and containing a Roman-scale three-storey triumphal feature, a gigantic semi-domed open-air niche, whose only purpose was architectural effect. Of comparable splendour was the Palazzo Farnese (1515), finest of the urban *palazzi* of the time, designed by Antonio da Sangallo, a pupil of Bramante, as a three-storey block in stuccoed masonry enclosing a fine 25-metre square *cortile*. Respect for the legacy of ancient Rome did not prevent the builders from pillaging stones from the Colosseum for the travertine dressings round the windows.

Among the most splendid of Rome's high renaissance buildings was another Palazzo Farnese, built at nearby Caprarola in 1547 by Giacomo da Vignola, a capable architect and a theoretician whose scholarly book *Regola delli Cinque Ordini d'Architettura* was to have great influence in France. The plan of the Palazzo is pentagonal, 46 metres to each face, enclosing a circular *cortile*. The whole composition with its external staircases, ramps and terraces arranged about the hill-top on which the building stands, is powerful and monumental.

## THE MANNERISTS

As time went on, the imagination of designers began to go beyond the Vitruvian rules which inspired Bramante and his circle. A search for variety gave rise to impatience with the rule-book and even with the logic of building construction. Significantly, perhaps, much of the impetus came not from a conventionally-trained architect or craftsman but from a painter and sculptor. The first important manifestation of this 'mannerist' approach was the chapel at San Lorenzo in Florence, designed in 1521 by Michelangelo Buonarotti (1475–1564) to contain the tombs of Giuliano and the younger Lorenzo de Medici. The chapel is the counterpart of Brunelleschi's Sacristia Vecchia but is radically different in mood. Instead of Brunelleschi's lively, essentially architectural logic, Michelangelo's is that of the sculptor. The architecture is intense and distorted, in keeping with the dramatic character of the two sculptures it contains: Michelangelo's own portrait figures of Giuliano and Lorenzo. The interest of the design is centred about four metres up on the two opposing walls, where the seated figures of the two dukes brood over their sarcophagi below. Around these two points, the architectural detail is complex and unconventional. The composition includes pairs of Corinthian pilasters with no entablature whose only function is visually to frame the sculpted figures.

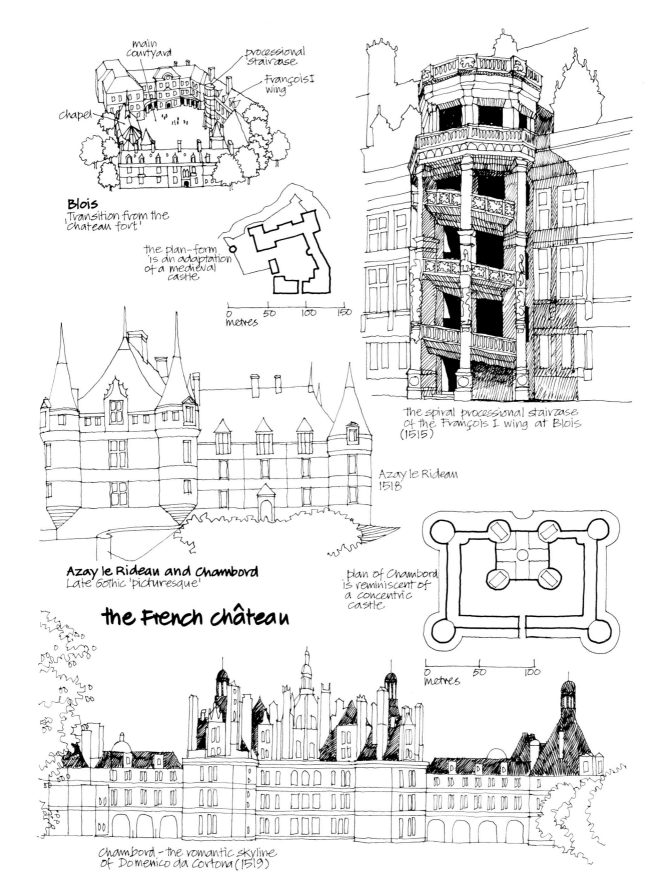

main
courtyard

processional
staircase

François I
wing

chapel

**Blois**
'Transition from the
'château fort'

the plan-form
is an adaptation
of a medieval
castle

0    50    100   150
metres

the spiral processional staircase
of the François I wing at Blois
(1515)

Azay le Rideau
1518

**Azay le Rideau and Chambord**
Late Gothic 'picturesque'

plan of Chambord
is reminiscent of
a concentric
castle.

0        50        100
metres

# the French château

Chambord - the romantic skyline
of Domenico da Cortona (1519)

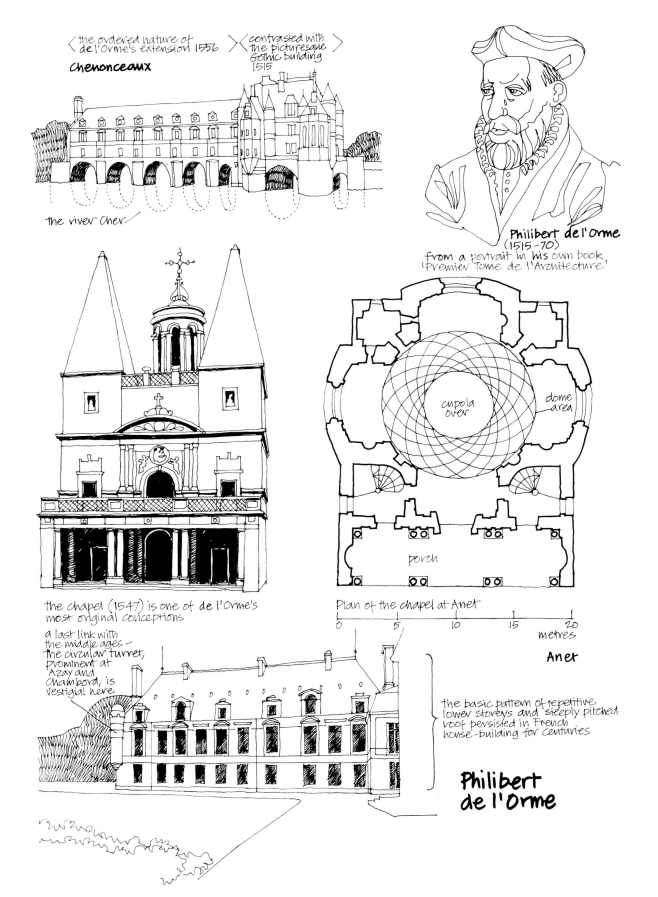

⟨ the ordered nature of de l'Orme's extension 1556 ⟩ ⟨ contrasted with the picturesque Gothic building 1515 ⟩

**Chenonceaux**

the river Cher

Philibert de l'Orme (1515–70)
from a portrait in his own book, 'Premier Tome de l'Architecture'

the chapel (1547) is one of de l'Orme's most original conceptions

cupola over

dome area

porch

Plan of the chapel at Anet

0    5    10    15    20
metres

**Anet**

a last link with the middle ages — the circular turret, prominent at Azay and Chambord, is vestigial here

the basic pattern of repetitive lower storeys and steeply pitched roof persisted in French house-building for centuries

**Philibert de l'Orme**

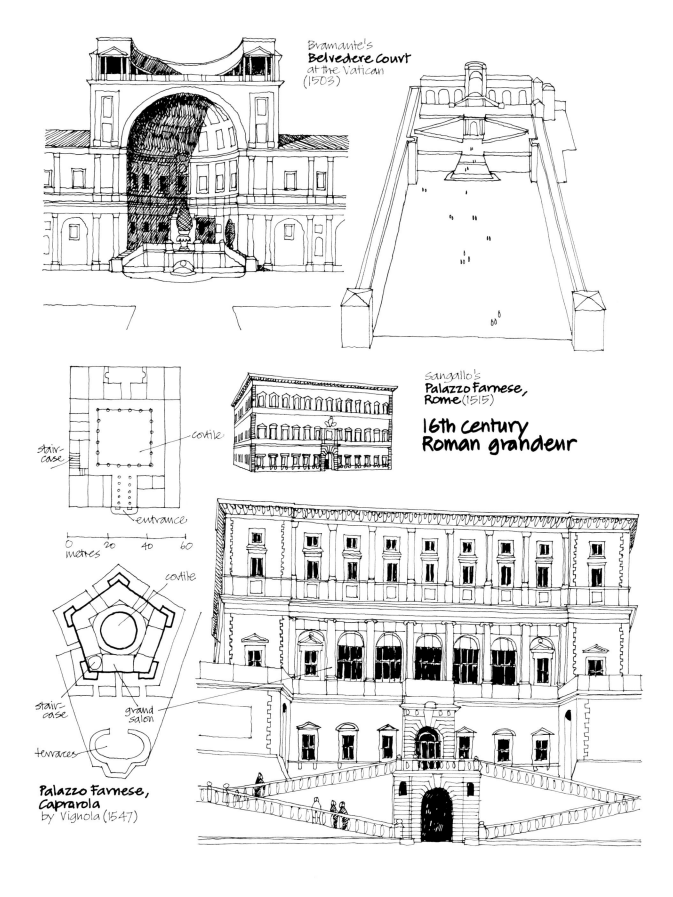

Bramante's
**Belvedere Court**
at the Vatican
(1503)

Sangallo's
**Palazzo Farnese,
Rome** (1515)

# 16th century
# Roman grandeur

staircase

cortile

entrance

0      20     40     60
metres

cortile

staircase

grand
salon

terraces

**Palazzo Farnese,
Caprarola**
by Vignola (1547)

This feature was developed further in the ante-room to the nearby Laurentian Library, designed by Michelangelo in 1524 and built by others in 1559. The curious free form of the triple staircase and the bizarre treatment of the double columns, which instead of standing on a solid base are cantilevered from the walls on consoles, are part of Michelangelo's unconventional treatment. A similar impatience with classical precedent can be seen in the work of Giulio Romano (1492–1546), another who came to architecture from painting. His Palazzo del Te in Mantua, a pleasure resort built for the Gonzaga family in 1525, is a solid, rusticated building with applied Doric pilasters used in a very unacademic manner.

Venice, whose strong Byzantine connections meant that classical architecture arrived relatively late, had not yet rejected it; but her architects were transmuting Roman forms into a highly personal Venetian style, often rich and decorative as at the Library of San Marco by Jacopo Sansovino (1536) or the Palazzo Grimani by Michele Sanmichele (1556). Foremost among the Venetian architects and possibly, for his subsequent influence, one of the most important in Europe, was Andrea Palladio (1508–80). Unlike Michelangelo and Giulio he did not reject classicism, but he did temper it with his own imaginative approach. His adopted home-town of Vicenza is now a monument to his own particular blend of academicism and originality. The Palazzo Chiericati (1550) is a characteristic building, unsensational, harmoniously proportioned, classical in spirit yet sufficiently original in the treatment of its main façade, with its contrast between solid and void, to be highly memorable. Palladio also gave an architectural form to the country houses which rich merchants increasingly preferred to congested urban *palazzi*. Unlike the *palazzo*, the Palladian 'villa' was designed to be seen as part of a landscape and from all sides. Archetypal is the Villa Capra at Vicenza (1552), a square building with a columnar portico on ea.ch face and surmounted by a shallow dome, a revolutionary departure which inspired several imitations.

Palladio's great influence on architectural design lay chiefly with the publication of his famous *I quattro libri dell' Architettura*. It was printed in every European country from 1570 onwards, and did much to publicise classical form and proportion. As he wisely included pictures of his own buildings, it did much to publicise them, too. Palladio's least pretentious buildings are often his most successful. A mason by training, he understood the properties of materials, and though all his buildings display this, it is often the smaller ones that demonstrate with simplicity and directness his mastery of colour and texture and of the use of humble brick and stucco.

He also built the two Venetian churches of San Giorgio Maggiore (1565) and Il Redentore – 'the Redeemer' – (1577). Each is basilican but with a domed crossing which gives a Greek-cross aspect to the east end. The treatment of the western elevation in each case emphasises the basilican form behind, with single-height pilasters on the ends of the side-aisles and giant double height engaged columns on the nave, reflecting the respective heights of the spaces. These 'giant orders' are a distinctive feature of several of Palladio's larger buildings and evoke a feeling of considerable grandeur.

The fine self-confidence of Italian architecture in the 16th century belied the crisis the Papacy was undergoing. The growing reliance of philosophers on reason rather than dogma turned many minds away from traditional forms of faith, and there was almost universal disillusion about the corruption of many of the Church's practices. In

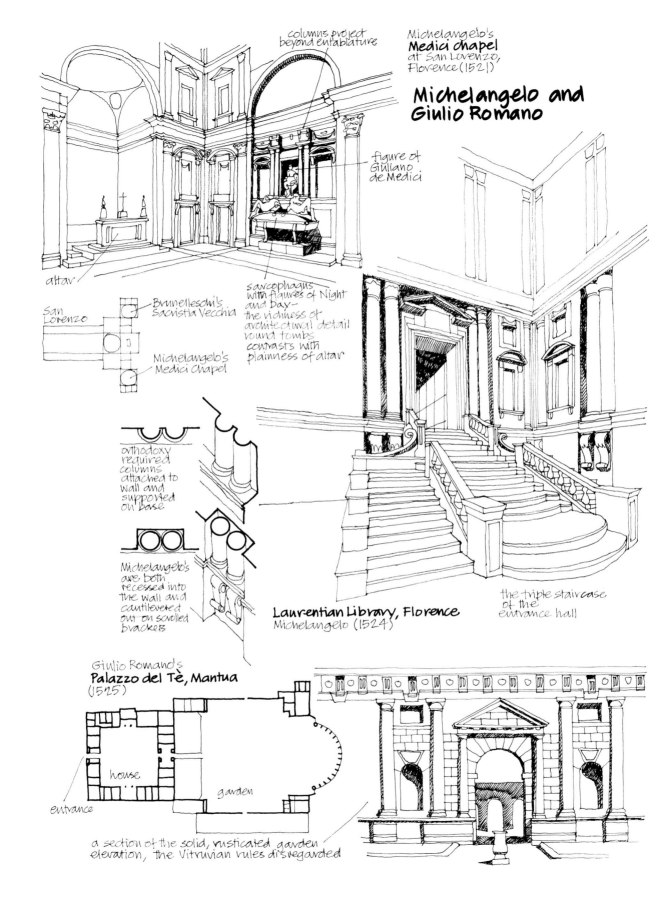

columns project beyond entablature

Michelangelo's **Medici chapel** at San Lorenzo, Florence (1521)

# Michelangelo and Giulio Romano

figure of Giuliano de Medici

altar

San Lorenzo

Brunelleschi's Sacristia Vecchia

Michelangelo's Medici Chapel

sarcophagus with figures of Night and Day — the richness of architectural detail round tombs contrasts with plainness of altar

orthodoxy required columns attached to wall and supported on base

Michelangelo's are both recessed into the wall and cantilevered out on scrolled brackets

**Laurentian Library, Florence** Michelangelo (1524)

the triple staircase of the entrance hall

Giulio Romano's **Palazzo del Tè, Mantua** (1525)

house

garden

entrance

a section of the solid, rusticated garden elevation, the Vitruvian rules disregarded

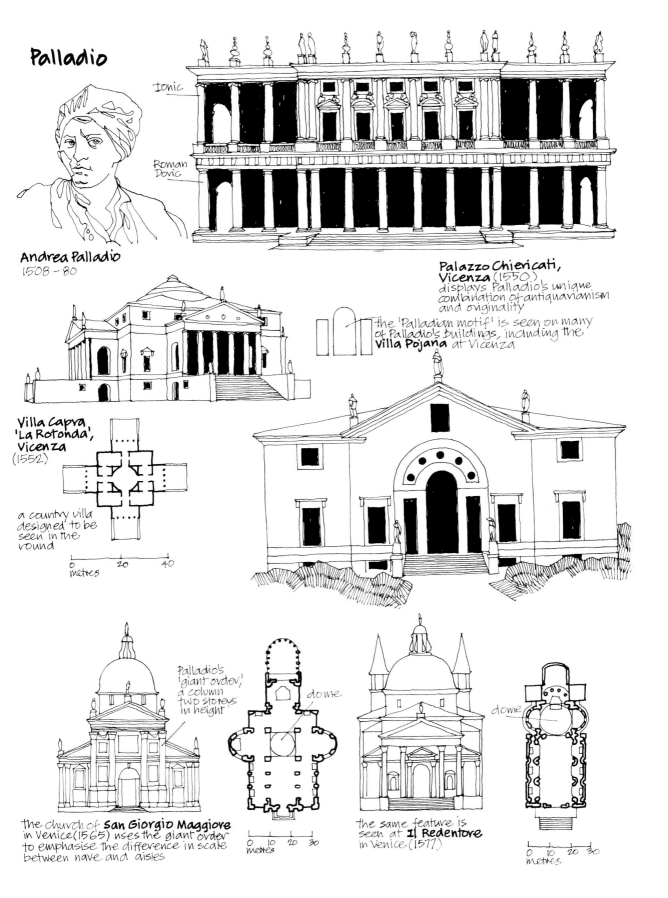

# Palladio

Andrea Palladio
1508 - 80

Ionic

Roman Doric

Palazzo Chiericati,
Vicenza (1550)
displays Palladio's unique
combination of antiquarianism
and originality

the 'Palladian motif' is seen on many
of Palladio's buildings, including the
Villa Pojana at Vicenza

Villa Capra,
'La Rotonda',
Vicenza
(1552)

a country villa
designed to be
seen in the
round

0   20   40
metres

the church of San Giorgio Maggiore
in Venice (1565) uses the giant order
to emphasise the difference in scale
between nave and aisles

Palladio's
'giant order',
a column
two storeys
in height

dome

0  10  20  30
metres

the same feature is
seen at Il Redentore
in Venice (1577)

dome

0  10  20  30
metres

1517, the German priest Martin Luther (1483–1546), who taught that the Bible, not the Church, should be the supreme Christian authority, published his 'Ninety-five Theses' as a head-on challenge to the power of the Pope. Luther was supported by many of Germany's imperial Electors, who sensed that a collapse of papal authority could mean the final removal of obstacles to the free development of capitalism.

Amid much conflict, Luther's Reformation gained ground. Protestantism spread through Germany and, by the efforts of Zwingli and Calvin, to Switzerland, Scotland, England and France. The Catholic church retaliated. A revival of the inquisition in Spain and in Italy began to stamp out open heresy, and this counter-reformation was reinforced by Ignatius of Loyola's new 'Society of Jesus', a fierce monastic order dedicated to intellectual attainment and the conversion of the unbeliever. The Reformation and its consequences left Europe split between a Protestant north and a Roman Catholic south, and brought four destructive wars of religious freedom and political emancipation: within Germany, between Holland and Spain, between Catholics and Huguenots in France and between Spain and England. National unity and self-determination increased, and with them the wealth of the kings and bourgeoisie. Church exemptions from taxes and from civil law were ended, capitalism was boosted as the Church's moral sanctions were removed, and royal treasuries filled with confiscated gold.

But there seems to be no hint in the papal architecture of the mid-16th century of the Church's political problems, except, perhaps by way of reaction, its even greater display of confidence. The Villa Giulia, a country pleasure-resort for Pope Julius III designed by Vignola in 1550, is a model of serenity, with its calm, ordered front façade and a sweeping semi-circular courtyard at the rear which develops into a long succession of terraces, staircases and walled gardens.

Vignola's great church of Il Gesù, designed in 1568 for the Society of Jesus, is another affirmation of confidence. In form it is a more self-assured version of Alberti's Sant' Andrea at Mantua. Its domed, centralised east end was extended into a Latin cross by a lengthened western arm, which foreshadowed a general move in subsequent church planning away from a totally centralised plan. The interior, completed by a succession of later architects, is rich and decorative, while the exterior features a severe west façade which is also a development of Alberti, a basilican elevation complete with the linking scrolls of Santa Maria Novella.

During the whole of the 16th century, while the church was torn apart, the biggest building project of all was proclaiming Christian unity to the world, paid for, ironically, by the sale of indulgences, the practice most criticised by Luther. It began in 1505 with the desire of Julius II to proceed with a long-anticipated demolition of Constantine's ancient basilica of St Peter which was in bad repair. Bramante's scheme for a vast Greek-cross church with a central dome was begun in 1506. In 1513, Raphael revised the design, meaning to change the plan to a Latin cross, but the church's recurrent political crises, a shortage of funds and the changing ideas of successive architects slowed the work drastically. In 1546, amid a period of renewed confidence, it was taken over by the ageing Michelangelo. The construction of his new Greek-cross design proceeded steadily till his death in 1564, when the building was complete as far as the drum of the dome. From models left by him, the dome and cupola were built in 1585, At the turn of the century Carlo Maderna reverted to a latin-cross plan, pulling the nave forward and adding a

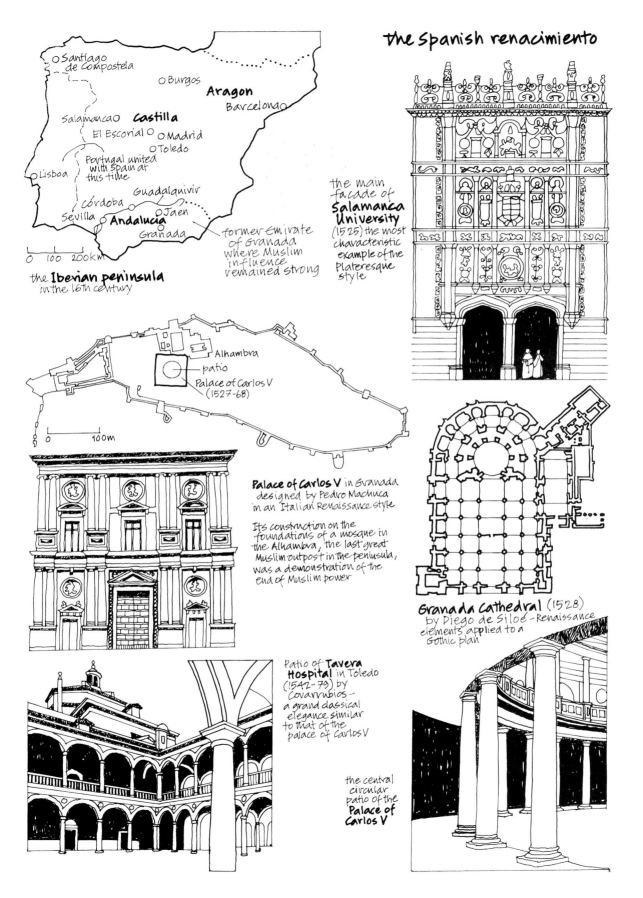

# the Spanish renacimiento

O Santiago de Compostela

O Burgos

**Aragon**

Barcelona O

Salamanca O  **Castilla**

El Escorial O   O Madrid
O Toledo

O Lisboa

Portugal united with Spain at this time

Córdoba

Guadalquivir

Sevilla

**Andalucía**

O Jaen

Granada

former Emirate of Granada where Muslim influence remained strong

the **Iberian peninsula**
in the 16th century

0  100  200km

the main facade of **Salamanca University** (1525) the most characteristic example of the Plateresque style.

Alhambra
patio
Palace of Carlos V (1527-68)

0   100m

**Palace of Carlos V** in Granada designed by Pedro Machuca in an Italian Renaissance style

Its construction on the foundations of a mosque in the Alhambra, the last great Muslim outpost in the peninsula, was a demonstration of the end of Muslim power

**Granada Cathedral** (1528) by Diego de Siloé – Renaissance elements applied to a Gothic plan

Patio of **Tavera Hospital** in Toledo (1542-79) by Covarrubios – a grand classical elegance similar to that of the palace of Carlos V

the central circular patio of the **Palace of Carlos V**

majestic west front. Eventually, in the mid-17th century, Giovanni Bernini's colonnade completed the composition by forming a wide ceremonial piazza at the front; after some 160 years and the efforts of twelve important architects, Julius' memorial was complete.

It is easy to say that St Peter's lacks architectural unity – under the circumstances of its creation, it could hardly be otherwise – and the most criticised feature of this enormous building is the fact that external views of the dome, the centre of the whole design, are obscured by the extreme length and height of the nave. But the building is enormously impressive; not only its size but also its decorative richness give it an appropriate air of solemn grandeur. Bramante's dome would have been low and shallow, like that of his Tempietto, but Michelangelo's is tall and soaring, some 140 metres to the top, supported on four gigantic piers and bound internally by tension chains to prevent collapse. The drum on which it stands, and the cupolas which occupy the corners of the building, all display the projecting, disengaged columns in Michelangelo's most mannerist style. Appropriately, the high altar, with its fine *baldacchino* designed by Bernini, is placed over the supposed tomb of St Peter, and both are located in the exact centre of the dome area, the symbolic focus of the whole composition.

The Pope's main allies in Europe were the catholic kings of Spain, leaders of the 16th century's most powerful empire. Charles V of Spain (1519–56) became Holy Roman Emperor in 1520 and ruled over Sicily, Naples, Sardinia, Austria, Luxembourg and Holland as well as the colonies which his *conquistadores* were assembling in central America. To the New World the Spanish took gunpowder, the horse and the Bible; from it, they brought a seemingly unending supply of gold and silver which enriched the Spanish treasury. The christianisation of Latin America involved the construction of big cathedrals. Those of Lima in Peru and, especially, of Mexico City, the flagship of Spanish colonisation, were huge basilicas, with the great width we associate with Spanish cathedrals, and prominent western towers.

Spain's imported wealth, however, did little to stimulate the economy. Inflation was high, the balance of trade poor. Lavish spending, including on major building projects, threatened to bankrupt the economy. Among the fine buildings of the early 16th century were Granada cathedral, in size and shape comparable with Seville, with a gothic plan given a classical treatment, and Salamanca University, with its splendid gateway. Their ornate detail belongs to a style known as 'plateresque' – *plateria* means silverware – possibly inspired by the intricate metalwork plundered by explorers.

Gradually Italian architectural influences grew stronger. By 1527 Pedro Machuca had begun a great palace for Charles V adjoining the 14th-century Moorish Alhambra in Granada. A two-tier, 60-metre-square block with a circular central courtyard, it assimilated the spirit of Bramante, classical, grand and monumental. The Tavera Hospital in Toledo (1542) by Bartolomé de Bustamente, with its elegant two-tier arched courtyard, was similarly Italianate.

Philip II came to the Spanish throne in 1556 and ruled for the rest of the century. He saw the forcible establishment of Catholicism throughout Europe and the Spanish empire as the best means of achieving a political unity over which he and the Pope would preside. But he was destined to fail. Corruption in his own bureaucracy undermined his strength at home, and his dream of a united Europe was ended by the Dutch protestants' fierce struggle for independence under William the Silent.

The means of achieving dominance collapsed in 1588 when the English, led by Sir Francis Drake, destroyed his entire fleet. The severe, dedicated existence of this troubled king is expressed in the vast Escorial Palace near Madrid, begun in 1599 by Juan Bautista de Toledo and continued by Juan de Herrera. An extensive complex of buildings some 200 metres square on a lonely mountainous site, it had all the necessities for Philip's austerely religious kingship: a central courtyard, dominated by a domed church and flanked by a monastery on one side and a religious college and royal apartments on the other, grand, monastic and austere to the point of grimness.

## TUDOR ENGLAND

Monastic severity was not the style of the Tudor monarchs of England. Henry VII established more than just a new dynasty. Through rigid control of barons and parliament he established a strong rule, stabilising the political life of England and encouraging trade. His son Henry VIII (1509–47) broke from the Pope, created a national church with himself as the head and dissolved the catholic monasteries, seizing their wealth. The firm establishment of the new Anglican church was completed by his daughter Elizabeth I (1558–1603). Her sea-power became pre-eminent in the world, stimulating overseas exploration and colonisation, expanding trade and steadily increasing the country's wealth. Henry and Elizabeth presided over a sequence of cultural achievements including those of Tallis and Byrd, Spenser and Shakespeare.

In contrast to the Escorial, Henry VIII's palace of Nonsuch in Surrey was a pleasure garden, built around two courtyards, on which the collective abilities of craftsmen from Italy, France, Holland and England were lavished. Nonsuch was pulled down in the 17th century, but contemporaries describe it as five storeys high with many towers, pinnacles and statues. The ground storey was stone and the upper ones timber-framed with decorative panelling covered in gilt. There was a three-storey-high banqueting-hall and numerous formal gardens and walks.

However, Henry soon tired of his great palace in favour of an even grander one being erected by his Chancellor, Cardinal Wolsey, at Hampton Court. Built by native-born craftsmen, it depended heavily on the gothic tradition. It is a rambling, informal building, mainly in decorative brickwork, built around four courtyards of different sizes, with many fine features: ornate gatehouses, a chapel, and a Great Hall with a hammer-beam roof by James Nedeham. The work was begun in 1520, and by 1526 Henry's envy was so great that Wolsey had no option but to bestow the palace on his king.

During the 16th century there was a great demand for fine houses by the aristocracy and aspiring merchants of England, and a characteristic style was established. Most house plans were arranged around a great hall, developed from that of the Norman manor but now elaborately panelled in oak, with a decorative wooden roof or elaborate plaster ceiling and a large fireplace and chimney. The hall was the main room of the house and also the main circulation space. A grand staircase at one end gave access to the upper rooms, which included the main withdrawing-room, developed from the Norman 'solar', and that 16th-century innovation, the long gallery. This covered walkway joining all the upper rooms was gradually widened, lengthened and improved as time went on to become an art gallery, a place of recreation and an object of wonder.

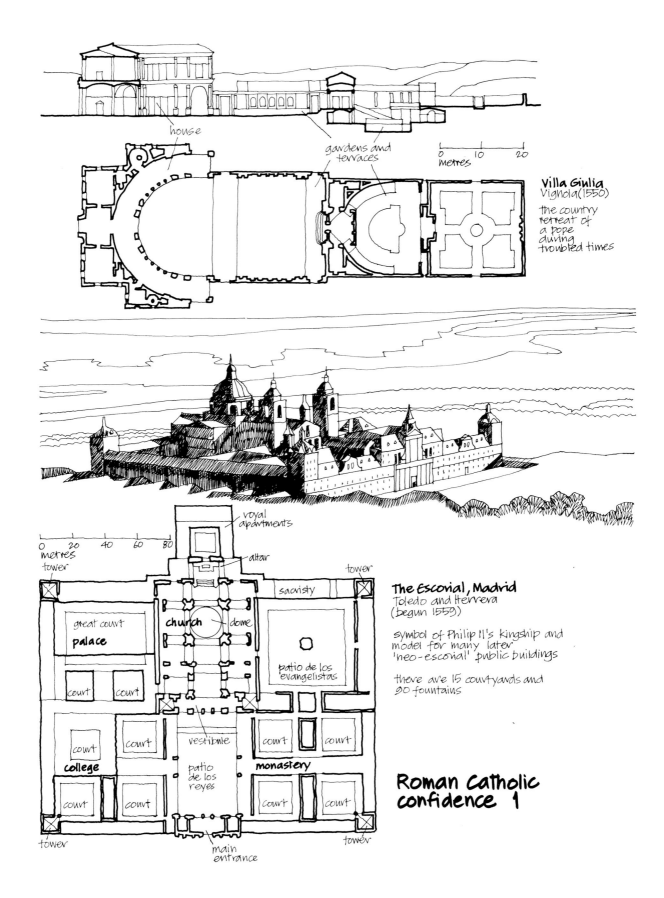

house

gardens and
terraces

0    10    20
metres

**Villa Giulia**
Vignola (1550)

the country
retreat of
a pope
during
troubled times

royal
apartments

altar

0    20    40    60    80
metres
tower

sacristy

tower

great court
**palace**

**church**    **dome**

patio de los
evangelistas

court    court

vestibule    court    court

patio
de los
reyes

court    court

**college**    **monastery**

court    court

tower    main
entrance    tower

**The Escorial, Madrid**
Toledo and Herrera
(begun 1559)

symbol of Philip II's kingship and
model for many later
'neo-escorial' public buildings

there are 15 courtyards and
90 fountains

**Roman Catholic
confidence 1**

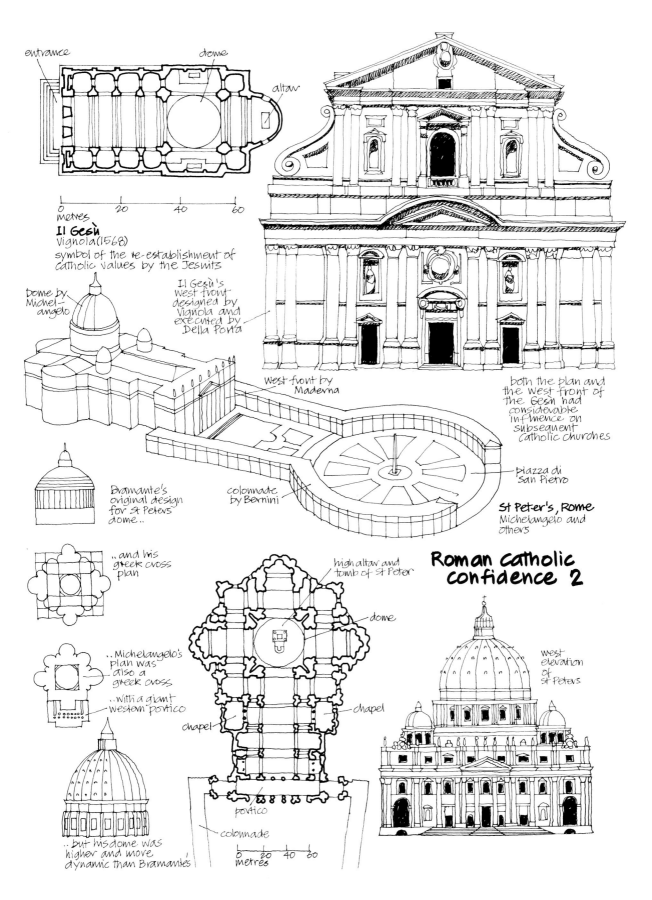

entrance

dome

altar

0    20    40    60
metres

**Il Gesù**
Vignola (1568)
symbol of the re-establishment of
Catholic values by the Jesuits

Il Gesù's
West front
designed by
Vignola and
executed by
Della Porta

Dome by Michel-
angelo

West front by
Maderna

both the plan and
the West front of
the Gesù had
considerable
influence on
subsequent
Catholic churches

Bramante's
original design
for St Peter's
dome..

colonnade
by Bernini

piazza di
San Pietro

St Peter's, Rome
Michelangelo and
others

..and his
greek cross
plan

high altar and
tomb of St Peter

**Roman Catholic
confidence 2**

..Michelangelo's
plan was
also a
greek cross

..with a giant
western portico

dome

chapel

chapel

West
elevation
of
St Peter's

..but his dome was
higher and more
dynamic than Bramante's

portico

colonnade

0    20    40    60
metres

The late-medieval informality of the early 16th century, seen at Compton Wynyates (1525), gave way to a strongly geometric plan, including perhaps a square internal courtyard, and also to a rectilinear external appearance in which large, mullioned windows, often in projecting bays, played an important part. Large houses were usually built in the limestone and sandstone of central and south-west England, and include Longleat (1567), Castle Ashby (1572), Woollaton Hall and Montacute (both 1580). Considerable use was made, in lesser manor-houses, of timber-framed construction and Moreton Old Hall in Cheshire (1559) and Pitchford in Shropshire (1560) are fine examples of Elizabethan black-and-white building.

The richness of these wealthy houses, with their lavish use of timber, contrasts with the cottages and farmhouses of the time. By the late 16th century a drastic shortage of timber in Europe jeopardised economic expansion. Wood had always been used in considerable quantities for building and shipbuilding and the rapid growth of towns and trade were making ever-greater inroads into the forests. In addition, timber had always been used as an energy source. During the 16th century, considerable advances were made in the improvement of water- and wind-mills, but the growing metallurgical industry, in particular, relied on timber for fuel and helped create a crisis which was not fully resolved until alternative energy sources arrived with the industrial revolution of the 18th century. In some parts of Europe, timber prices rose during the 16th century by 1200 per cent. Added impetus was given to the use of brick construction, and timber was used much more sparingly, especially in cheaper buildings. The typical farmhouse or cottage of the time had its framing timbers widely spaced, and more use was made of inferior or mis-shapen wood.

Rural 16th-century England was the scene of a fundamental social change. In a general move towards establishing private property, the old medieval fields were being enclosed – by the landlords – with hedges and ditches, the peasants dispossessed and their hovels pulled down. Added to the thousands of estate workers thrown out of work by the dissolution of the monasteries, the peasants created an enormous unemployment problem, only partly solved by the growth of manufacturing industry. This too was beginning to change rapidly: the wool trade of the 15th century had developed into a thriving cloth industry, requiring factories and a new class of wage-labourers to work them. As the peasants everywhere declined in numbers, society became polarised between the capitalist property-owners and a working class who owned literally nothing but their ability to work – assuming that they could find employment.

'Faith', Luther had said, 'as it makes man a believer, so also it makes his works good.' Now that Protestantism was spreading through Europe, there was less emphasis on monastic contemplativeness than on the development of man's practical talents. Those who embraced the new faith – and many who did not – were happy to use it to justify the pursuit of industry and commerce. The steady economic growth of north European countries during the 17th century, especially Britain and Holland, was due at least in part to their capitalists embracing the 'protestant ethic'. There were more solid reasons too, notably that their wealth was based firmly on manufacturing industry, unlike Italy's which relied on commerce and Spain's which derived mainly from its store of captured gold. So the 17th century saw a rapid build-up of the sea-routes carrying British and Dutch trade to and from their colonies, while Italy and Spain were left in the past.

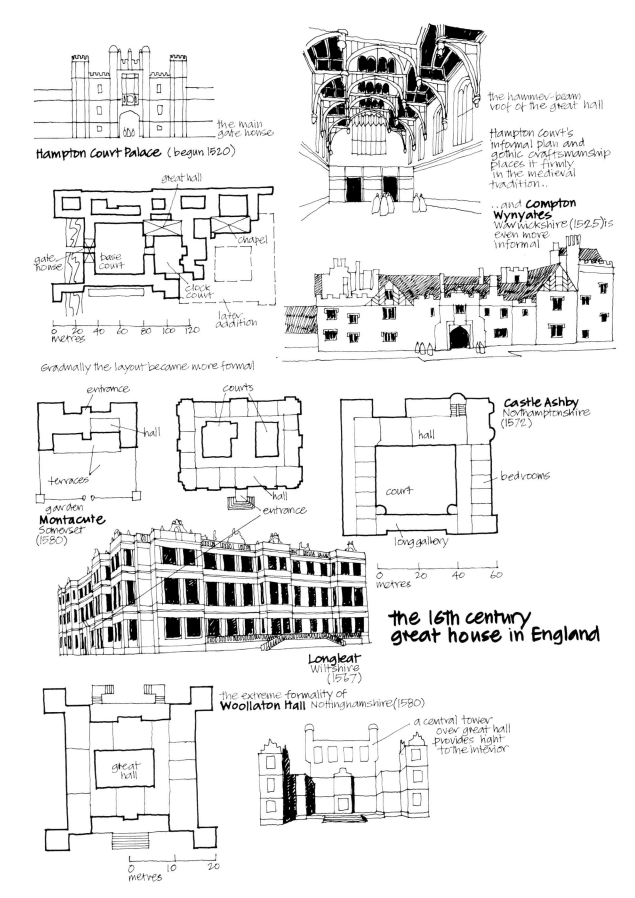

the main gate house

**Hampton Court Palace** ( begun 1520)

the hammer-beam roof of the great hall

Hampton Court's informal plan and gothic craftsmanship places it firmly in the medieval tradition..

..and **Compton Wynyates** Warwickshire (1525) is even more informal

great hall

gate house

base court

clock court

chapel

later addition

0 20 40 60 80 100 120
metres

Gradually the layout became more formal

entrance

hall

terraces

garden

**Montacute** Somerset (1580)

courts

hall

entrance

**Castle Ashby** Northamptonshire (1572)

hall

court

bedrooms

long gallery

0 20 40 60
metres

# the 16th century great house in England

**Longleat** Wiltshire (1567)

the extreme formality of **Woollaton Hall** Nottinghamshire (1580)

a central tower over great hall provides light to the interior

great hall

0 10 20
metres

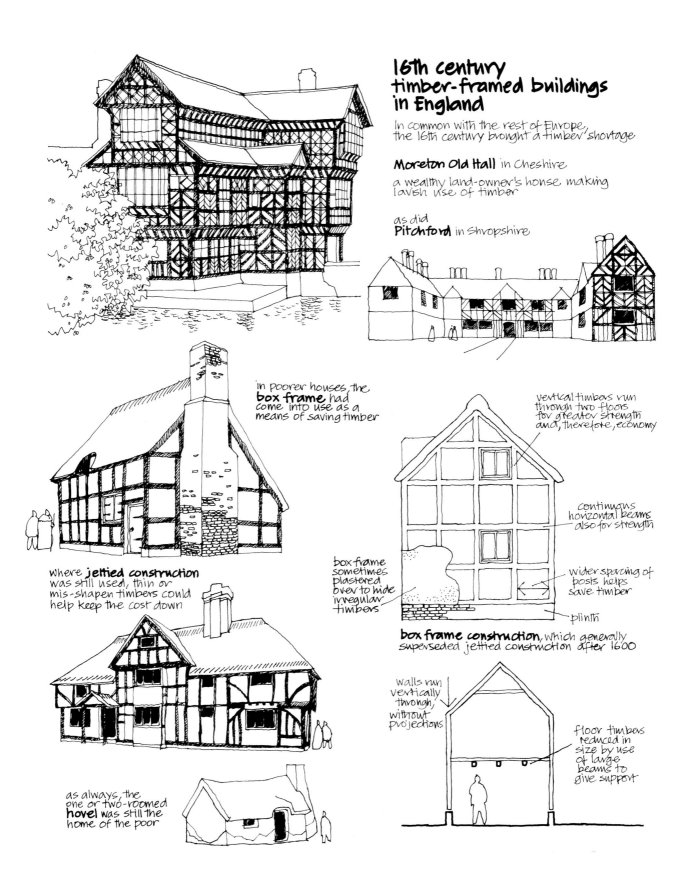

# 16th century timber-framed buildings in England

In common with the rest of Europe, the 16th century brought a timber shortage

**Moreton Old Hall** in Cheshire

a wealthy land-owner's house making lavish use of timber

as did **Pitchford** in Shropshire

in poorer houses, the **box frame** had come into use as a means of saving timber

where **jettied construction** was still used, thin or mis-shapen timbers could help keep the cost down

as always, the one or two-roomed **hovel** was still the home of the poor

vertical timbers run through two floors for greater strength and, therefore, economy

continuous horizontal beams also for strength

box frame sometimes plastered over to hide irregular timbers

wider spacing of posts helps save timber

plinth

**box frame construction**, which generally superseded jettied construction after 1600

walls run vertically through, without projections

floor timbers reduced in size by use of large beams to give support

Great wealth still existed in both countries, however. As a result of the Reformation, the Papacy had suffered a financial setback as its sources of income dried up, but the loyalty of the remaining Catholic countries, and increased taxes, helped to keep the coffers full. Churches and palaces were still built and Italian architecture entered a magnificent autumnal phase. Under the influence of the architects Carlo Maderna (1556-1629), Francesco Borromini (1599–1667) and the great Bernini (1598-1680) a style was developed, rich, bold and powerful, which though still using the Roman vocabulary, broke entirely from the restraints of classicism into an effusion of curving, plastic shapes. The word *barocco* is a jeweller's term to describe a rough pearl or uncut stone, and so the lack of classical refinement in the style of Maderna and his successors has given us 'baroque'. Maderna's nave and west front of St Peter's is a monumental essay in the Corinthian order, with columns almost 30 metres in height. His church of Santa Susanna in Rome (1597) is less grandiose but perhaps more imaginative. Its façade has a rich display of decorative features, groups of orders clustered together, repeated pediments and projecting bays, which build up to emphasise the central entrance.

Bernini, like Michelangelo, was also a sculptor, and had a similar disregard for architectural rules, which he subordinated to sculptural effects. The sweeping curves and false perspective of his colonnade at St Peter's are baroque town design at its finest, as, at the other end of the scale, is his tiny church of Sant' Andrea del Quirinale in Rome (1658). Its central, elliptical dome is the generator for the geomentry of the rest of the building. Its front façade has a projecting semi-circular porch on a stepped podium, together with a curved pair of wing walls which connect the building to the public space in front. The Scala Regia (1663) is Bernini's famous staircase linking the Vatican with the portico of St Peter's. Given a restricted, tapering site he made a virtue out of necessity, and the diminishing perspective and unusual lighting effects of this long indoor space give it great dignity. Bernini's spatial effects were essentially theatrical, designed to draw the viewer into the composition and involve him totally. In the Medici chapel Michelangelo designed the architecture around the sculpture; Bernini, in the Santa Teresa chapel (1646) at Carlo Maderna's church of Santa Maria della Vittoria in Rome, went further. The focal point of the interior, framed like a proscenium by double columns surmounted by a baroque 'broken pediment', is his sculpture of the ecstatic St Teresa and the angel, depicted with stunning realism. The theatrical feeling is enhanced by sculptured angels peering down on the scene from stage 'boxes' above.

Bernini, for all his theatricality, obtained his rich effects by simple means. The architecture of Borromini, his pupil, is by contrast complex and intense. It is typified by the church of San Carlo alle Quattro Fontane in Rome (1638), which though similar in size and shape to Bernini's Sant' Andrea, and roofed with a similar elliptical dome, has a more complex plan-form. Its main façade, following the curves of the interior, is arranged along an undulating plane which gives a dramatic and restless effect.

By the time baroque architecture spread to the rest of Italy, building activity had considerably died down, but there is one major building in Venice by Baldassare Longhena, a contemporary of Bernini, which can stand comparison with those of Rome. This is the church of Santa Maria della Salute (1631), a fantastic, centrally planned building, octagonal on plan, with a high dome mounted on a drum supported by 16 scrolled buttresses. A second, lower dome over the sanctuary, flanked by minaret-like

# Italian baroque 1
## Bernini

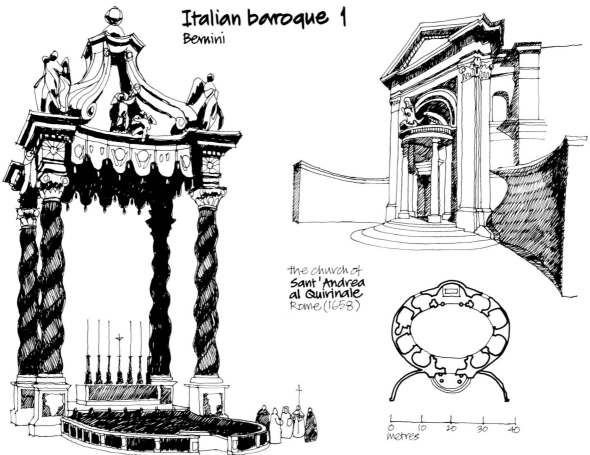

the church of
**Sant'Andrea
al Quirinale**
Rome (1658)

0  10  20  30  40
metres

**the baldacchino**
above the high altar,
St Peter's Rome

the great size helps relate the
human scale to the enormous
space below the dome.

**the Scala Regia** at the Vatican (1663)

perspective diminishes,
steps reduce in size,
and columns get closer

entrance from
St Peters

0  10  20  30  40  50  60
metres

St Teresa and
the angel in the
**Cornaro chapel**
Santa Maria
della Vittoria,
Rome (1646)

the sculptured
group is at the
centre of a
dramatic
composition

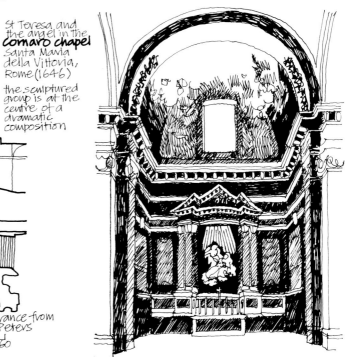

# Italian baroque 2

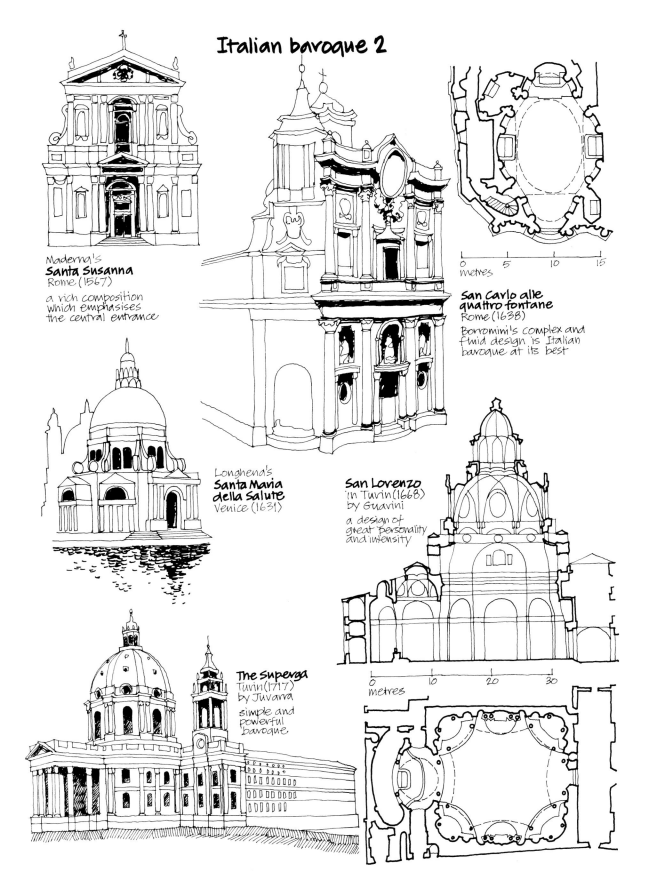

Maderna's
**Santa Susanna**
Rome (1567)

a rich composition
which emphasises
the central entrance

**San Carlo alle
quattro fontane**
Rome (1638)

Borromini's complex and
fluid design is Italian
baroque at its best

0   5   10   15
metres

Longhena's
**Santa Maria
della Salute**
Venice (1631)

**San Lorenzo**
in Turin (1668)
by Guarini

a design of
great personality
and intensity

**The Superga**
Turin (1717)
by Juvarra

simple and
powerful
baroque.

0   10   20   30
metres

towers, gives an almost oriental richness to the skyline. Two other northern architects of great ability, who brought new inspiration to Italian architecture at a time when Rome's was declining, were Guarino Guarini (1624–83) and Filippo Juvarra (1678–1736). Guarini's two great church buildings, San Lorenzo in Turin (1668) and the chapel of the Holy Shroud in Turin cathedral (1667) are very complex spatially, built up out of overlapping ovoid or circular volumes and with domes constructed in complicated intersecting vaulting. Juvarra's work, by contrast, is simple and grand, typified by the Superga in Turin (1717), a church and convent on a hill-top site in which the simple, repetitive convent building and the fine domed church at the front contrast with each other to great effect.

If some southern European towns were entering a period of slow decline, those in the north continued to grow. Ornate town halls in Antwerp (1561) – with its nearby guild houses – Cologne (1569), Ypres (1575) and Gent (1595), picturesque in character and rich in classical detail, indicate expanding wealth. By now, most towns had a lot of factories and workshops, but industry was not yet a mainly urban activity. As long as wind or water power and transport were available, many processes, including the all-important cloth-making, could be carried out in country-cottage workshops where the raw material was easy to obtain. The 17th-century industrialist was often a rural landowner too. The richness of Jacobean country houses demonstrates that though England's income came from trade in the towns, it was also dependent on the productivity of its country estates. Hatfield House in Hertfordshire (1607) by Robert Lyminge for the Earl of Salisbury is among the finest great houses, combining simplicity of conception with richness of detail. The fine craftsmanship of its brick and stone façades, its picturesque skylines and the ordered formality of its layout extending into the landscape around, also have their counterparts at Knole in Kent (1605) and Audley End in Essex (1603).

The early 17th century was a dramatic turning-point for the English kings. The Tudors, though despotic, had preserved a relationship with parliament, but their Stuart successors were more ambitious. The words of James I (1603-25), 'a Deo rex, a rege lex' (the king comes from God, the law from the king), expressed his desire to rule absolutely and were echoed by other monarchs of the time. James's Catholicism in a now-protestant state, his autocracy, his self-indulgence and nepotism were resented, but his successor Charles I (1625–49) went even further. He tried to levy personal taxes on his subjects and when parliament intervened he dissolved it, ruling autocratically, collecting taxes illegally, appointing the catholic William Laud as archbishop and jailing anyone who protested.

## ITALIANATE ENGLAND

The career of the great Inigo Jones (1573-1652) almost exactly spanned the reigns of the first two Stuart kings. Ironically, the architectural expression he gave to this precarious monarchy was one of great serenity. His career began as a stage and costume designer for lavish royal entertainments and he soon progressed to the position of Surveyor of the King's Works, the most important architectural post in the country. He brought to his work a consuming interest in classical architecture and design, which he had studied in Italy at first hand. Classical details had been copiously used in English buildings since

hall

chapel

long gallery over cloister

**Hatfield House**
Robert Lyminge (1607)

**Audley End Essex**
(1603)

# the 17th century in England

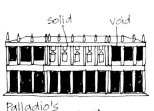

solid     void

Palladio's Palazzo Chiericati

solid   void

**The Queens House** Greenwich Palace
Inigo Jones (1616)

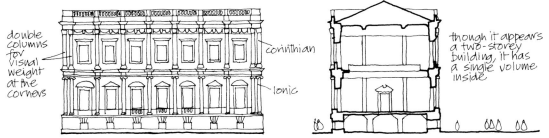

double columns for visual weight at the corners

corinthian

ionic

though it appears a two-storey building, it has a single volume inside

**Banqueting Hall** Whitehall London
Inigo Jones (1619)

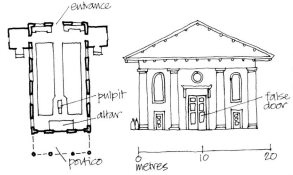

entrance

pulpit

altar

portico

false door

0   metres   10   20

the portico is at the wrong end to present a facade towards Jones' Covent Garden piazza

**St Pauls church**
Covent Garden London
Inigo Jones (1631)

a simple 'barn' in the Tuscan style, the first purpose-made Protestant church in England

**Inigo Jones**
(1573-1652)

Tudor times, but never as part of an integrated philosophy of design. This, however, was what Jones introduced, causing a minor artistic revolution.

For the first time, the English saw what had been seen in France since de l'Orme and in Italy since Brunelleschi: a style of architecture in which every element, and its relationship with every other element, was carefully considered. From the first it was Palladio, with his well-mannered blend of academicism and originality, who appealed most to the English, and Jones's first major English building demonstrated his debt. The elegant Queen's House at Greenwich (1616), built for the wife of James I, is a two-storey stone building with a double-height entrance hall. The lower storey is rusticated and the upper one plain stonework, finished with a cornice and stone balustrade. The south elevation makes more than a passing reference to the Palazzo Chiericati, echoing the proportion and the general mood and simply reversing Palladio's pattern of solid and void.

Jones's other important Italianate building was the Banqueting House at the royal palace of Whitehall in London (1619), the only completed part of an ambitious rebuilding project. The Hall stands on a rusticated stone base and has finely-proportioned two-tier elevations enclosing a single large volume inside. The elevations have superimposed Ionic and Corinthian orders, doubled at the corners for visual strength. The Banqueting Hall was built for the performance of court masques, but in 1649 it became the scene of a grimmer entertainment: Charles I, defeated in the English Civil War by Cromwell's army of parliamentarians, was publicly executed on a scaffold outside. Jones, who never concealed his esteem for his king, was arrested as a collaborator by Cromwell's men and, though later released, survived Charles by only four years.

In central Europe the struggle for religious freedom and political power was as great as in England. The Thirty Years War began in Germany in 1618 with protestant demands for religious toleration. After involving Bohemia, France, Sweden, Denmark and Holland in what had become a struggle for the domination of Europe, it ended in 1648 with the Empire crushed and vast areas of land devastated and depopulated, but having at least ensured German Protestantism. In France, Protestantism was less assured. The new Bourbon monarchy, in the person of Henri IV (1589–1610) aided by his minister Sully, had issued the Edict of Nantes in a spirit of religious toleration which had united the country, increased royal revenues by reducing the extravagant palace-building of the Valois, and improved agriculture and foreign trade. But his successor Louis XIII (1610–43), guided by the formidable Cardinal Richelieu, had a less progressive attitude. He crushed opposition wherever he saw or suspected it, destroying the fortified châteaux of the nobles, subjecting both them and the bourgeoisie to rigorous control, and removing many of the rights of the protestant Huguenots.

The reign of Henri IV had seen many royal public works and works of capitalist enterprise, including the improvement of Paris by civic-design schemes which brought an air of formality and bourgeois affluence to the medieval city. The Place Royale (1605) – now the Place des Vosges – is a square surrounded by the regular façades of *hôtels*, terraced houses built round courtyards with a colonnaded ground storey, two upper storeys and a steeply pitched roof with dormers. The Place Dauphine (1608), on the west end of the Île de la Cité, is triangular, linked at one end to the Pont Neuf, centred on a formal statue of Henri IV.

As Louis and Richelieu gradually engineered a move back to Catholicism and royal absolutism, investment was once again directed towards the building of churches and royal palaces. The Palais du Luxembourg in Paris (1615) was built by Salomon de Brosse for Henri's widow Marie de Médicis. A front *porte-cochère* gives access to a *cour d'honneur* around which the three-storey house is arranged. The treatment is bold and classically simple. Smaller, but more elegant and refined, is the Château de Maisons near Paris (1642), a symmetrical composition with a decorative central pavilion and side wings, designed by François Mansart (1598–1666), the greatest French architect of the period. Though wilful and difficult in his dealings with others, a factor which cost him many aristocratic commissions, he created buildings which are models of restraint and clarity and did much to establish the grave and elegant French classical style of the 17th century. Maisons was designed for a wealthy merchant whose purse and patience were elastic enough to allow the building to be pulled down during construction to enable Mansart to revise the design. The result was his masterpiece and shows his ability to achieve rich effects without recourse to elaborate decoration. The Château de Richelieu (1631) by Jacques Lemercier (1585–1654) was by contrast enormous, though nothing of it now remains; but the equally impressive Vaux-le-Vicomte (1657) by Louis Le Vau (1612–1670) is still intact. It has no *cour d'honneur*; instead, the main rooms, including a big, elliptical salon, look out onto a vast formal garden designed by André Le Nôtre.

The church of the Sorbonne in Paris (1635), designed for Richelieu by Lemercier, is formal and classical, with a simple two-tier elevation and an elegant, high, central dome. Richer in effect is the church of the Val-de-Grace in Paris (1654) by Lemercier in succession to François Mansart. It is similar in outline to the Sorbonne church, but the supporting consoles round the drum of the dome and the scrolls on the entrance façade are part of a more vigorously decorative approach. Most impressive of all is the church of the Hôtel des Invalides (1680) designed by the aristocrat-architect Jules Hardouin-Mansart (1646–1708). It has a Greek-cross plan with a tall, central dome almost 30 metres across, built off a drum with external buttresses in the form of a colonnade of paired orders. To obtain the right appearance externally, Hardouin-Mansart made the external dome considerably higher than the one visible inside. The latter is in effect two domes: a lower one with a central opening through which a decorative upper one is seen.

Richelieu's efforts on behalf of Louis XIII were continued for his successor Louis XIV (1643–1715) by Mazarin and Colbert. They built up the royal treasury through monetary reforms, and during his long reign of 72 years Louis reached a position of unprecedented power. 'L'état, c'est moi', he said, and it was no idle boast. Parliament was not called into session once during his reign, and political life centred entirely on his court. He took charge of the collection and spending of all taxes, making of laws, dispensing of justice and waging of war. The colonies expanded, culture was encouraged, and French manners – as reflected in the plays of Corneille, Molière and Racine, the music of Lully and Rameau, and the painting of Poussin and Claude – were copied by all Europe's high society.

Louis rejected Paris as his capital; instead he built a new one at Versailles, some miles out of the city, housing all the functions of government and his entire court in a single vast building where he could keep his eye on them. The Palace of Versailles is perhaps the most spectacular monument to absolute kingship ever seen in Europe. Built mainly

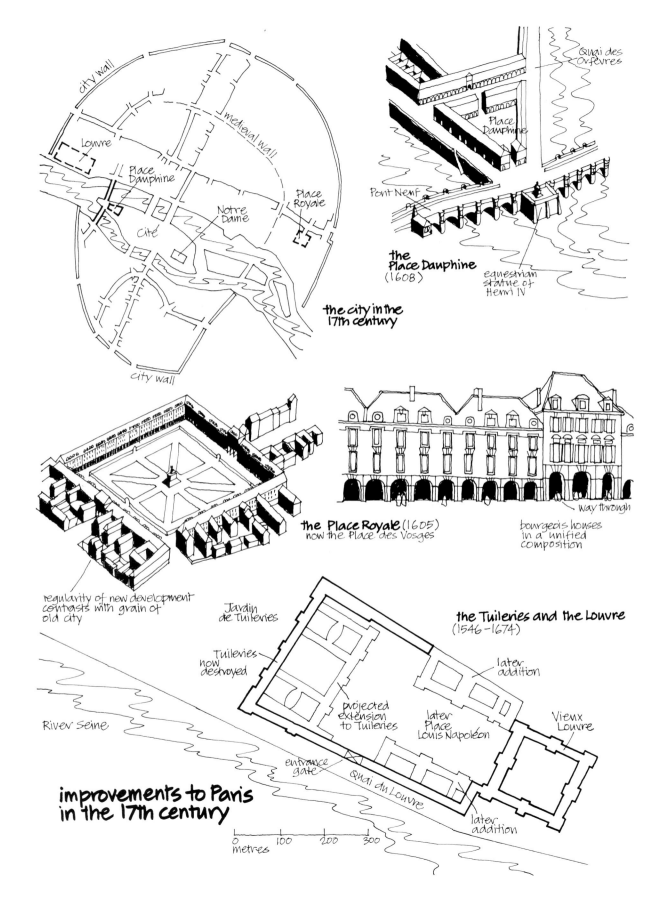

city wall

medieval wall

Louvre

Place
Dauphine

Cité

Notre
Dame

Place
Royale

city wall

the city in the
17th century

Quai des
Orfèvres

Place
Dauphine

Pont Neuf

equestrian
statue of
Henri IV

the
Place Dauphine
(1608)

regularity of new development
contrasts with grain of
old city

the Place Royale (1605)
now the Place des Vosges

Way through

bourgeois houses
in a unified
composition

Jardin
de Tuileries

Tuileries
now
destroyed

projected
extension
to Tuileries

the Tuileries and the Louvre
(1546-1674)

later
addition

later
Place
Louis Napoléon

Vieux
Louvre

River Seine

entrance
gate

Quai du Louvre

later
addition

improvements to Paris
in the 17th century

0    100   200   300
metres

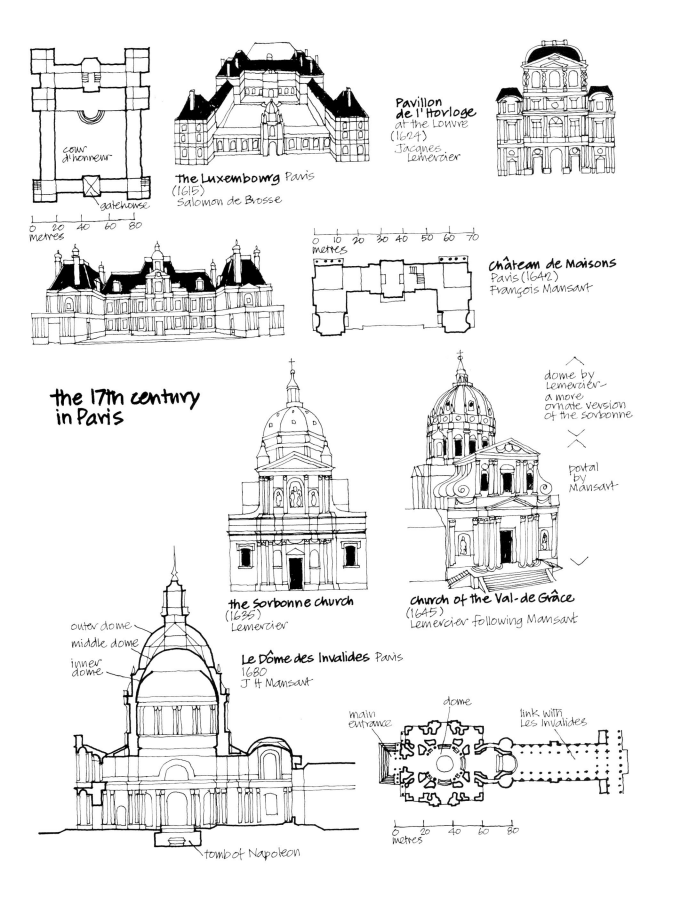

cour d'honneur

gatehouse

0 20 40 60 80
metres

the Luxembourg Paris
(1615)
Salomon de Brosse

Pavillon
de l'Horloge
at the Louvre
(1624)
Jacques
Lemercier

0 10 20 30 40 50 60 70
metres

château de Maisons
Paris (1642)
François Mansart

the 17th century
in Paris

the Sorbonne church
(1635)
Lemercier

church of the Val-de-Grâce
(1645)
Lemercier following Mansart

dome by
Lemercier –
a more
ornate version
of the sorbonne

portal
by
Mansart

outer dome
middle dome
inner
dome

Le Dôme des Invalides Paris
1680
J H Mansart

tomb of Napoleon

main
entrance

dome

link with
Les Invalides

0 20 40 60 80
metres

between 1661 and 1756 by Le Vau and Hardouin-Mansart, it has a front *cour d'honneur* enclosed on three sides by the building. Stretching away on both sides are wings which together add up to a garden façade some 400 metres in length, treated repetitively with an order of giant pilasters on the main storey. The 70-metre-long Galérie des Glaces, designed by Hardouin-Mansart and panelled with mirrors, is the main feature of the luxurious interior, but finest of all are the vast formal gardens of Le Nôtre (1613–1700) which influence the environment for miles around.

The intention was to provide recreation for the palace's hundreds of inhabitants and guests. Close to the building, the woods were cleared to form a wide axial vista in which formal pathways and terraces, decorated with statuary and pools, were set between *parterres*, low ornamental shrub-beds laid out in geometric patterns. At the end a wide canal led apparently endlessly into the distance and on either side formal avenues for riding and driving cut their way into the forests, leading to artificial grottoes and temples, open-air theatres and small lakes, to surprise and delight the jaded aristocratic eye. Radial avenues, like rays emanating from '*le roi soleil*', led out into the surrounding landscape or, from the front of the palace, into the town, symbolically extending the king's domain to the horizon.

The 'grand manner' of Le Nôtre influenced not only garden design but also city planning. From the 17th century onwards, the artistic and philosophical ideas which accompanied the rebuilding of many European city centres, or the founding of new ones in colonies overseas, were to find expression through his architectural vocabulary: the straight avenue forming a vista, the radial or grid layout of routes and the *rond-point* where the routes met.

In 1685, Louis revoked the Edict of Nantes and established Catholicism as the supreme religion. Huguenots left France, many for England, taking with them their skills as craftsmen and entrepreneurs. The economy was further weakened by Louis's extravagances at home and his costly and disastrous military exploits abroad. Taxes were steadily increased. The magnificence of his reign, of which Versailles is the ultimate expression, ironically resulted in France's decline as a world power and in the growing discontent of all classes of society.

## BAROQUE EUROPE

The aftermath of the Thirty Years War brought renewed economic confidence to the Low Countries. Protestantism was firmly established. Holland, having thrown off Spanish domination, was prospering, and Amsterdam and The Hague were overtaking Antwerp as the main outlets for north European trade. The royal household and the merchants were the main patrons and Jacob van Campen their architect. His Mauritshuis in The Hague (1633) for Prince Maurice of Nassau is a rich and well-proportioned adaptation of the Palladian style to Dutch tastes, and his Town Hall in Amsterdam (1648), later the royal palace, is a large stone building, also Palladian in content, with the four main storeys divided into pairs and treated with giant pilasters. A large cupola over the central, pedimented portico is an indigenous feature. His New Church at Haarlem (1645) with its, centralised plan and prominently located pulpit represents a search for a form for protestant worship. Among the finest buildings in 17th-century Belgium

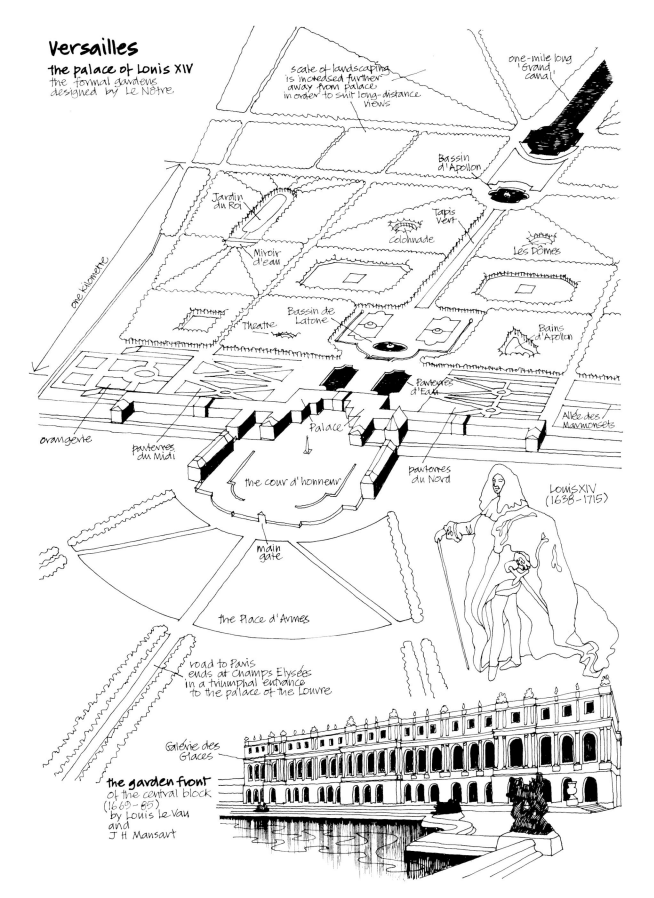

# Versailles
## the palace of Louis XIV
the formal gardens
designed by Le Nôtre

scale of landscaping
is increased further
away from palace
in order to suit long-distance
views

one-mile long
'Grand
canal'

Bassin
d'Apollon

Jardin
du Roi

Tapis
Vert

Colonnade

Les Dômes

Miroir
d'eau

Bassin de
Latone

Bains
d'Apollon

Theatre

one kilometre

Parterres
d'Eau

Allée des
Marmousets

orangerie

parterres
du Midi

Palace

parterres
du Nord

the cour d'honneur

Louis XIV
(1638-1715)

main
gate

the Place d'Armes

road to Paris
ends at Champs Elysées
in a triumphal entrance
to the palace of the Louvre

Galérie des
Glaces

**the garden front**
of the central block
(1669-85)
by Louis Le Vau
and
J H Mansart

were the Guild Houses of the Grand' Place, Brussels (1691), magnificently ornate with classical detail, and with a picturesque skyline reminiscent of earlier ones in Antwerp.

The Thirty Years War left Germany as a confusion of small states, each with cultural and religious autonomy, broadly speaking, a protestant north and a Catholic south. Catholicism remained prominent in Bavaria, Austria and Bohemia, which therefore maintained architectural links with Italy and France. These would reach fruition in the fantastic late-baroque churches of the 18th century, but in the 17th a more sober style prevailed. The Theatine church in Munich (1663), by Agostino Barelli and Enrico Zuccali, is Italian baroque in conception, with two west towers added to a façade not unlike Vignola's Gesú. The Troja Palace in Prague (1679), by the Frenchman Jean-Baptiste Mathey, is Bohemian baroque at its finest, a central block with side wings in a well-ordered design unified by the use of giant pilasters thoughout.

In Russia, the unchallenged power of the monarchy was reaching a peak. The firm foundation given to it by Ivan III and Ivan the Terrible in the 16th century was built on by Peter the Great in the 17th. His policy of opening 'windows to the west' was based on a view of western Europe, especially France, as a model for progress. During his reign (1682–1725) he opened the ice-free ports of the Baltic to western trade, brought the Greek Orthodox church in Russia under Russian control, built schools and hospitals, developed printing and introduced western-style clothing to his medieval Tsardom. He also built a new capital, Petersburg, and employed western architects to design its buildings in a grand, baroque style. The first was Domenico Tressini who was responsible for the Peter-and-Paul fortress and the cathedral, on the fortified island in the Neva where the new city began.

In England, absolute monarchy had died with Charles I. The Civil War had been more than a religious conflict; it was essentially a struggle for power between the puritan bourgeoisie on the one hand and the king and aristocracy on the other. The old feudal powers undoubtedly lost, but as yet the bourgeoisie had not completely triumphed. Oliver Cromwell had dissolved parliament in 1653 and ruled as a religious and military dictator. Bourgeois democracy was thus still denied, though trade, industry and Britain's sea-power were on the ascendant, and building activity continued unabated.

On Cromwell's death, parliament returned and reinstated the catholic Stuart kings. Charles II (1660–85) tried to strip the puritan ministers of their power, but parliament countered by limiting his own, through the Habeas Corpus Act (1679). James II's short reign (1685–8), marked by continuous struggles with parliament, ended prematurely when William and Mary of the protestant House of Orange were invited to the throne in 1688, on parliament's terms: supremacy of parliament over the king and an assured future for Protestantism. A bourgeois 'English Revolution' had taken place, just as a French one would a century later.

One side-effect of Protestantism was its indirect encouragement of scientific research: faith in the written word had greatly encouraged the spread of literacy, and with it the universal spread of ideas, including scientific ones. Science at that time consisted of observing the natural world and recording and classifying it; using the methodology developed by Descartes and Bacon, scientists were now able to construct theories based on observable fact. Galileo, Kepler and above all Newton were able to extend dramatically man's view of himself in relation to his world. In the years to come, science

**the Mauritshuis**
The Hague
(1633)
Jacob van
Campen

a building of
considerable
influence in the
establishment of
the northern
version of the
Italian style

**the New Church**
Haarlem (1645)
by van Campen

a Greek-cross-
in-a-square
plan which set
a trend for
Protestant
churches

intersecting
barrels
forming
central
cross-vault

square
plan

**the New Church** at
The Hague (1649) by
Noorwits and van Bassen

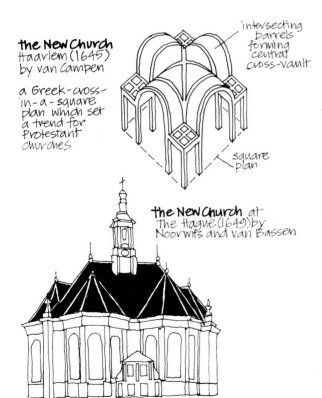

another simple, centralised plan
for Protestant worship

**Guild Houses** at
Grand' Place, Brussels
(1690)

similar in character to
late Gothic examples
like these in Antwerp
(1561)

# the 17th century in
# the Low Countries

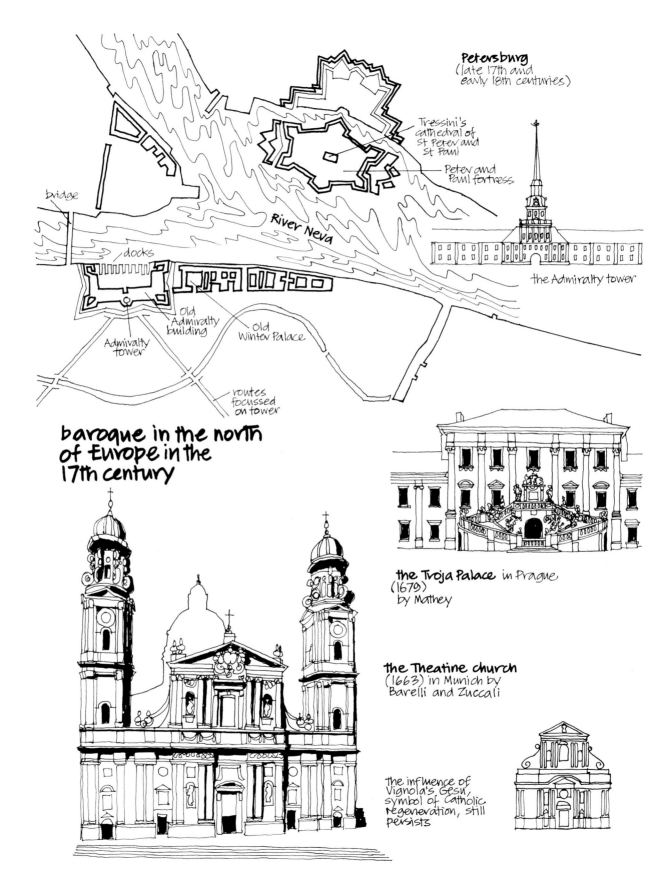

**Petersburg**
(late 17th and
early 18th centuries)

Tressini's
Cathedral of
St Peter and
St Paul

Peter and
Paul fortress

River Neva

the Admiralty tower

bridge

docks

Old
Admiralty
building

Admiralty
tower

Old
Winter Palace

routes
focussed
on tower

# baroque in the north of Europe in the 17th century

the Troja Palace in Prague,
(1679)
by Mathey

the Theatine church
(1663) in Munich by
Barelli and Zuccali

the influence of
Vignola's Gesù,
symbol of Catholic
regeneration, still
persists

would vastly increase man's technological powers, but in the 17th century science and technology were only just beginning to come together. Foremost in the movement was Charles II's Royal Society, founded in 1645 by a group of wealthy dilettanti insatiable for knowledge on every subject from language to astronomy. Bacon, Boyle and Newton were members, and so was Christopher Wren (1632–1723).

By education this greatest of English architects was not an architect at all but a classicist, mathematician and astronomer. Early in his career he wrote that 'mathematical Demonstrations being built upon the impregnable foundations of Geometry and Arithmetick, are the only Truths, that can sink into the mind of man, void of all uncertainty', and he brought this precision to the solving of structural and spatial problems. Coming from a family of royalist sympathisers, he did not progress till after the restoration of Charles II. The brilliance of his mind, his uncommon ability to solve practical problems – such as his ingenious roof for the Sheldonian Theatre in Oxford – and a shared interest in astronomy, soon attracted the attention of the king. In 1666 a disastrous fire swept through the City of London destroying the old gothic cathedral of St Paul, scores of parish churches and hundreds of homes, and Wren was put in charge of the reconstruction.

He had visited France the previous year, where he had met François Mansart and the ageing Bernini – then sixty-seven – who was there on a commission, and seen Maisons, Versailles and the Louvre, and the churches of the Sorbonne and Val-de-Grâce. His education as an architect was founded on this short visit, on the authors he had read – Vitruvius, Alberti, Serlio and Palladio among them – and on such classical buildings as Jones and his pupils had already built in England. His plan for the city, a 'grand manner' exercise of radial routes and *ronds-points*, à la Versailles, would have transformed it, but cost, expediency and indecision prevented it from being carried out. St Paul's and the city churches, however, are among the finest achievements of English architecture.

Fifty city churches were rebuilt between 1670 and the mid-1680s. All were different and all show the ingenuity with which Wren solved the problems of designing for cramped urban sites. He was breaking new ground, for designing a protestant parish church was almost unprecedented: the only existing examples known to Wren were one by Jones in Covent Garden, one in Charenton by de Brosse and possibly Van Campen's New Church. Wren's approach was to design a church as capacious as possible in which everyone could see the pulpit and hear what was said from it. Generally, this suggested a square rather than longitudinal plan and often two tiers of seating. The pulpit was tall and prominent and, as the Word held sway over the Mass, the altar was located out of the way against a side or end wall.

In the densely built-up city, church towers helped to identify the building from a distance. Wren's designs for them were boundless in their imagination and ranged from simple lead-covered cupolas to elaborate stone spires. The steeple of St Mary-le-Bow, almost 70 metres high, is among the finest, as are those of Christchurch, St Michael Paternoster Royal and St James Garlickhythe. The plan-form of St Mary-le-Bow is typical of Wren's ingenuity with on a restricted site, and Christchurch shows the assurance with which he adapted a basilican plan to accommodate a gallery. Interior treatments ranged from the whitewash and panelling of St Benet Paul's Wharf to the rich plasterwork and wood-carving of St Clement Danes. Among the simplest

# Christopher Wren

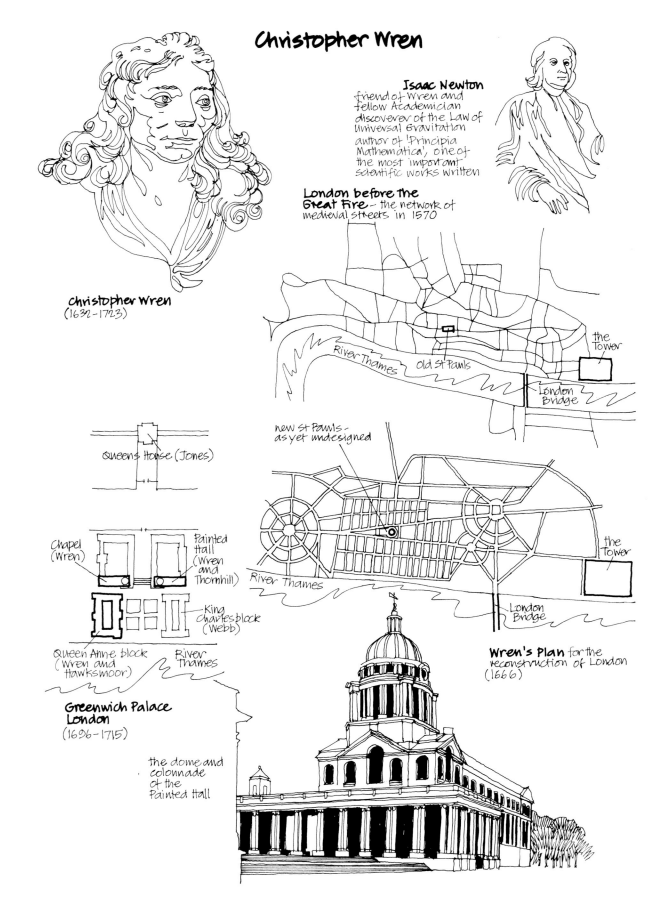

**Isaac Newton**
friend of Wren and
fellow Academician
discoverer of the Law of
Universal Gravitation
author of 'Principia
Mathematica', one of
the most important
scientific works written

**christopher Wren**
(1632-1723)

**London before the
Great Fire** – the network of
medieval streets in 1570

River Thames

Old St Pauls

the
Tower

London
Bridge

Queens House (Jones)

new St Pauls –
as yet undesigned

Chapel
(Wren)

Painted
Hall
(Wren
and
Thornhill)

King
charles block
(Webb)

Queen Anne block
(Wren and
Hawksmoor)

River
Thames

River Thames

the
Tower

London
Bridge

**Wren's Plan** for the
reconstruction of London
(1666)

**Greenwich Palace
London**
(1696-1715)

the dome and
colonnade
of the
Painted Hall

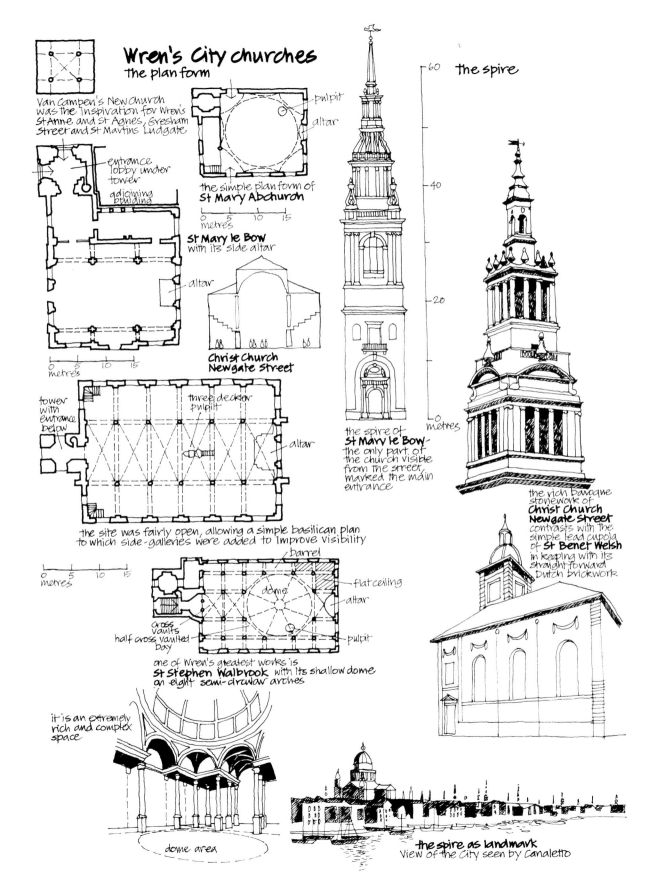

# Wren's City churches
## the plan form

Van Campen's New Church was the inspiration for Wren's St Anne and St Agnes, Gresham Street and St Martins Ludgate.

entrance lobby under tower

adjoining building

**St Mary le Bow**
with its side altar

0  5  10  15
metres

pulpit
altar

the simple plan form of
**St Mary Abchurch**

0  5  10  15
metres

altar

**Christ Church
Newgate Street**

tower with entrance below

three decker pulpit

altar

the site was fairly open, allowing a simple basilican plan to which side-galleries were added to improve visibility

0  5  10  15
metres

barrel
dome
flat ceiling
altar
cross vaults
half cross vaulted bay
pulpit

one of Wren's greatest works is
**St Stephen Walbrook** with its shallow dome an eight semi-circular arches

it is an extremely rich and complex space

dome area

the spire

60

40

20

0
metres

the spire of
**St Mary le Bow** -
the only part of the church visible from the street, marked the main entrance

the rich baroque stonework of
**Christ Church Newgate Street**
contrasts with the simple lead cupola of **St Benet Welsh**
in keeping with its straight-forward Dutch brickwork

the spire as landmark
view of the City seen by Canaletto

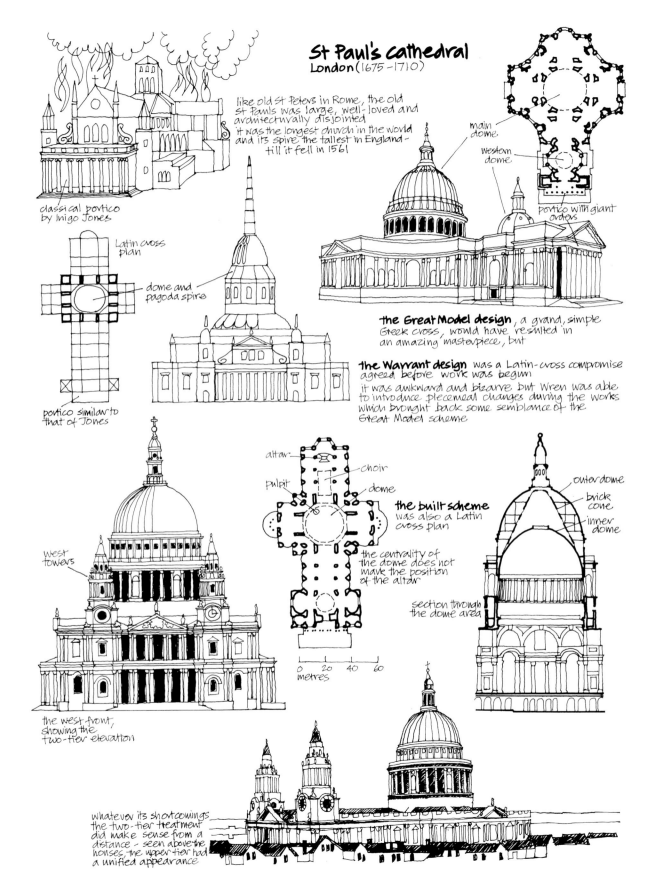

# St Paul's Cathedral
## London (1675–1710)

like old St Peters in Rome, the old
St Pauls was large, well-loved and
architecturally disjointed

it was the longest church in the world
and its spire the tallest in England –
till it fell in 1561

classical portico
by Inigo Jones

main
dome

western
dome

portico with giant
orders

Latin cross
plan

dome and
pagoda spire

portico similar to
that of Jones

**the Great Model design**, a grand, simple
Greek cross, would have resulted in
an amazing masterpiece, but

**the Warrant design** was a Latin-cross compromise
agreed before work was begun

it was awkward and bizarre, but Wren was able
to introduce piecemeal changes during the works
which brought back some semblance of the
Great Model scheme

altar

pulpit

choir

dome

**the built scheme**
was also a Latin
cross plan

the centrality of
the dome does not
mark the position
of the altar

outer dome

brick
cone

inner
dome

section through
the dome area

0    20    40    60
metres

West
towers

the west front,
showing the
two-tier elevation

whatever its shortcomings
the two-tier treatment
did make sense from a
distance – seen above the
houses, the upper tier had
a unified appearance

plan-forms were those of St Mary Abchurch, a dome over a square room, and St Anne and St Agnes Gresham Street, with its simple cross vault supported on four columns. The richest spatially, and one of the great masterpieces of English church architecture of any age, is St Stephen Walbrook, a small building which nonetheless manages to combine rudimentary nave, aisles, transepts and chancel with a central, coffered dome rising off eight semi-circular arches, all into a wonderfully resolved whole.

Stimulated by the domed churches he had seen in France, Wren had long been pre-occupied by the idea of a dome on eight arches for St Paul's. In 1673, after many abortive sketches and models, he produced the design from which the 6-metre-long 'Great Model' was made, a magnificent Greek-cross plan with a lengthened western arm and a central dome only slightly smaller than that of St Peter's. Regrettably, the establishment found it too revolutionary and demanded a latin-cross plan. The result (1675–1710), though still one of England's finest buildings, is a compromise.

The interior is grave and elegant, flooded with clear light through the plain glass windows which Wren preferred. At the centre of gravity is the dome though, unlike St Peter's, the altar is placed farther east, in the chancel. The dome, on its eight huge piers, is as wide as nave and aisles together – a reference perhaps to the octagon at Ely, which Wren knew well. Internally, the dome is a hemisphere and above it is a structural brick cone supporting the cupola. The outer dome, framed in timber and sheathed in lead, is raised high on a colonnaded drum, at the base of which an iron chain prevents spreading.

The external silhouette of the dome is calm, classical and very beautiful, though the lower parts of the façade are more conventional. A two-tier elevation runs all round, the upper tier, with blank windows, acting as a screen wall to conceal the flying buttresses which the gothic plan-form made necessary. Wren abandoned his west portico of giant orders in favour of the weaker-looking design built, but the two west towers are among his finest inspirations, in the rich English baroque which Wren himself invented.

As the king's architect, Wren was called upon to fulfil many large-scale commissions during his long life, and his output was enormous. His last great work (1696–1715) was his improvement of Greenwich Palace, bringing together a number of disparate elements by other architects into a unified, sober and beautifully ordered design. Wren is important not only for his buildings but also for the way in which he looked at architectural problems. The designer of St Paul's had far fewer resources at his disposal than had those who built St Peter's, but his flexible, scientific way of thinking enabled him to find solutions much more quickly. Since Galileo's death in 1642 the science of statics had been developing, and Wren's knowledge, together with his great mathematical ability, probably enabled him to predict with more certainty the stresses in his structures than any architect hitherto. Science and technology were coming together.

# 8 THE DUAL REVOLUTION
## *The 18th century*

'Descartes', the writer Boileau said, 'has cut the throat of poetry', and there is no doubt that during the period in which Cartesian thought dominated Europe, the late 17th and early 18th centuries, an intellectual change was taking place. Politics were now less dominated by religion, public life was becoming less idealistic and more pragmatic, encouraging realism in all things including, to Boileau's evident disgust, artistic expression. Eighteenth-century society was dominated by bureaucrats and professionals, engaged in a singular task. By the mid-17th century exploration had almost ceased and the exploitation of the new colonies, their minerals, crops, animals and people, had begun in earnest. The products of plantations and mines in central America, of herding in America, Australia and South Africa and of trapping in Canada and Asia flowed into northern Europe.

Colonial societies tended to be rigid and authoritarian. Some, like the West Indies, depended on slavery; others, like New England, became harshly egalitarian. Sometimes, as in Spanish America, the culture of the mother country was firmly imposed from above: rigid control by Church and bureaucracy kept the indigenous people in cultural sterility until the end of the 18th century, until the Spanish-American middle class began to challenge the old Spanish aristocracy. In north America there were no cultural achievements to rival those of the educated Spanish-Americans – as late as 1800, Mexico City was still the finest city in the whole of the Americas – but there was an inbuilt strength in the society which came from its diversity: the close-knit puritan groups in the New England states, a European merchant class dominating the eastern seaports, and a freer, frontier society farther west. Political liberty, freedom of thought – including religious belief – and the possibility of moving up the social ladder existed here in a way only dreamed of in Europe.

Mexico City cathedral, completed in the mid-17th century, is a grand building covering some 60 metres by 120 whose great width, west front with twin towers, and central portico, are reminders of Spanish medieval cathedrals, though its detail treatment is classical and restrained. This latter is in contrast to many other Spanish-American churches, in which plateresque decoration found its way home again. Among

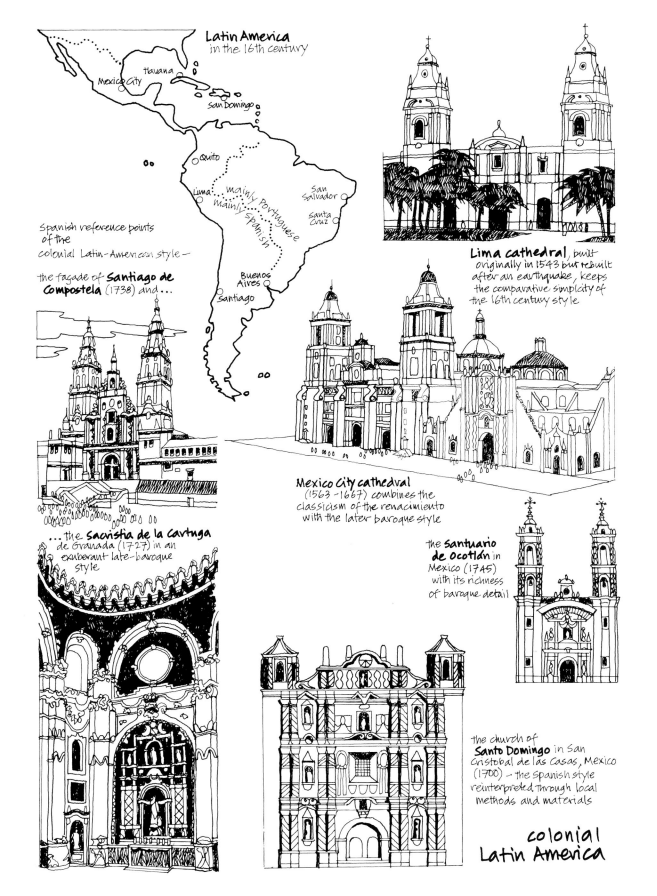

**Latin America**
in the 16th century

Havana
Mexico City
San Domingo
Quito
Lima
San Salvador
Santa Cruz
Mainly Portuguese
Mainly Spanish
Buenos Aires
Santiago

Spanish reference points of the colonial Latin-American style —

the façade of **Santiago de Compostela** (1738) and...

... the **Sacristia de la Cartuja** de Granada (1727) in an exuberant late-baroque style

**Lima cathedral**, built originally in 1543 but rebuilt after an earthquake, keeps the comparative simplicity of the 16th century style

**Mexico City cathedral** (1563 - 1667) combines the classicism of the renacimiento with the later baroque style

the **Santuario de Ocotlán** in Mexico (1745) with its richness of baroque detail

the church of **Santo Domingo** in San Cristóbal de las Casas, Mexico (1700) - the Spanish style reinterpreted through local methods and materials

**colonial Latin America**

colonial
north America
in the
18th century

weather
boarded
sides

central
cluster of
chimneys

shingle roof

jetty belongs
to European
tradition

**Capen House** Topsfield, Mass.
(1683)
a simple, timber-framed house

Doric
portico

brickwork

**Drayton Hall** South Carolina
(1738)
an archetypal plantation house
in Charleston

'**Westover**' Charles City County, Va.
(1730)
brick-built in European style

'**Parlange**' Pointe Coupée, La.
(1750)
in the south the veranda
becomes a major feature

**the Capitol** (State House)
at Williamsburg
(1701)

**plan of
Williamsburg**
Virginia
in the early
18th century

Governor's
Palace

avenue

church

court
house

William
and
Mary
college

powder
magazine

asylum

Capitol
(State
House)

Tazewell
hall

a layout which is classical and
organised - yet unpretentious

0    200    400    600    800
metres

these are the church of Santo Domingo in San Cristobal, Mexico (1700), in which the adopted style of the mother country was translated into local materials, and the pilgrimage shrine at Ocotlán, Mexico (1745), a confection of white stucco and ceramic tiles by the native-born sculptor Francisco Miguel.

North American architecture was more restrained, not only because society was largely puritan but also because the contemporary north-European architecture from which it derived was itself entering a period of rational understatement. In the north-eastern states, the pattern was late 17th-century English or Dutch architecture, though often translated into timber forms. Capen House, Topsfield, Mass. (1683) is representative of many such timber-framed, weather-boarded and shingle-clad small houses. Larger houses might be built in brick and one of the best examples is Westover in Charles City County, Va. (1730), a fine formal building with two storeys and a hipped roof with dormers, equal in both design and craftsmanship to the English houses it resembles. Farther south, the north-European style had to be adapted to the sub-tropical climate. Drayton Hall in South Carolina (1738) is basically English but with the addition of a double-height portico for use as a veranda in hot weather. Farther south still, the veranda became the main feature of the house. In Parlange at Pointe Coupée, La. (1750) a two-storey open gallery runs all round the house giving access and direct ventilation to the rooms.

The design of Protestant churches tended to derive from those of Wren and his successors, but often, like St Michael's Church, Charleston, S.C. (1752), they are re-workings of Wren's vocabulary in terms of timber rather than brick or stone. Williamsburg, Va., a colonial town now preserved largely intact as a living museum, has some fine examples. Here too are William and Mary College (1695) consisting of a central pavilion with two side wings, the Governor's Palace (1706), and the fine Capitol building (1701), H-shaped on plan with a slim central clock-tower. Finest of all, however, was State House, Philadelphia, Pa. (1731), a dignified civic complex in brickwork with stone dressings with a central pavilion surmounted by a magnificent clock tower and open cupola.

With native American resistance to the colonists gradually being overcome, and with the French in Canada defeated in the war of 1756–63, the presence of English troops became a burden, and the taxes paid to London anomalous. Attempts by the ruling Tory party in Westminster to assert English authority met with increasing resentment, and bourgeois activists on both sides of the Atlantic began to plot an end to the old aristocratic regime.

The *ancien régime* seemed nowhere stronger than in France, where Louis XIV's court exercised its apparent domination of Europe. Culturally at least, Europe had not been so unified since the 13th century. Among the ruling classes an understanding had been reached. Determined not to lose power, they had to find a workable formula to retain the status quo. Even the Bourbons, most absolute of monarchs, depended for support on complex political alliances and a rigid bureaucracy, which served to stabilise society and stave off the revolution which England had already undergone.

In art, a kind of unadventurous classicism reflected this era of pragmatism, typified perhaps by the Petit Trianon at Versailles, a small detached house built in the gardens in 1762 by the architect Ange-Jacques Gabriel, for Mme de Pompadour, the mistress of

179

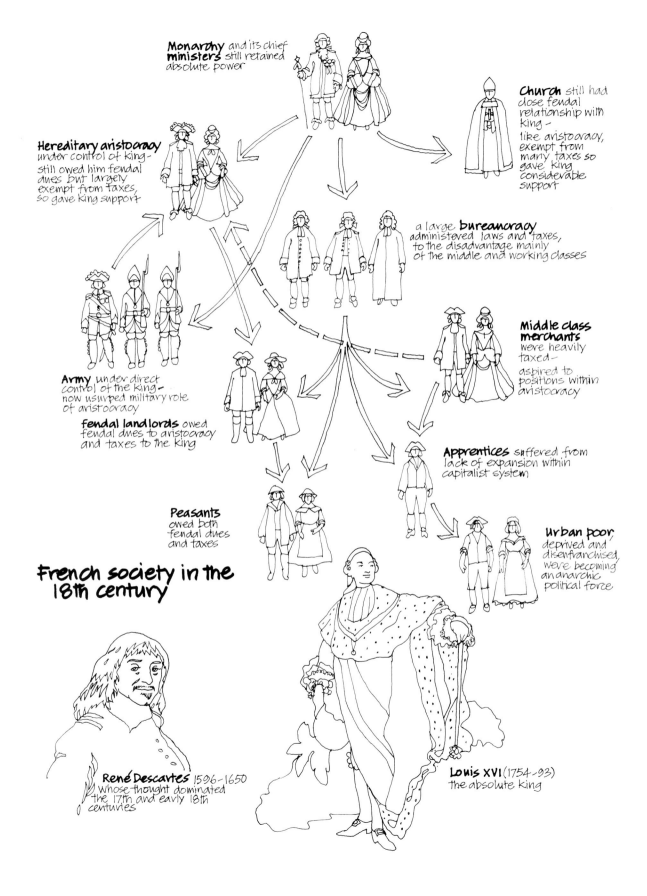

**Monarchy** and its chief **ministers** still retained absolute power

**Church** still had close feudal relationship with king — like aristocracy, exempt from many taxes so gave king considerable support

**Hereditary aristocracy** under control of king — still owed him feudal dues but largely exempt from taxes, so gave king support

a large **bureaucracy** administered laws and taxes, to the disadvantage mainly of the middle and working classes

**Middle class merchants** were heavily taxed — aspired to positions within aristocracy

**Army** under direct control of the king — now usurped military role of aristocracy

**feudal landlords** owed feudal dues to aristocracy and taxes to the king

**Apprentices** suffered from lack of expansion within capitalist system

**Peasants** owed both feudal dues and taxes

**Urban poor,** deprived and disenfranchised, were becoming an anarchic political force

# French society in the 18th century

**René Descartes** 1596–1650 whose thought dominated the 17th and early 18th centuries

**Louis XVI** (1754–93) the absolute king

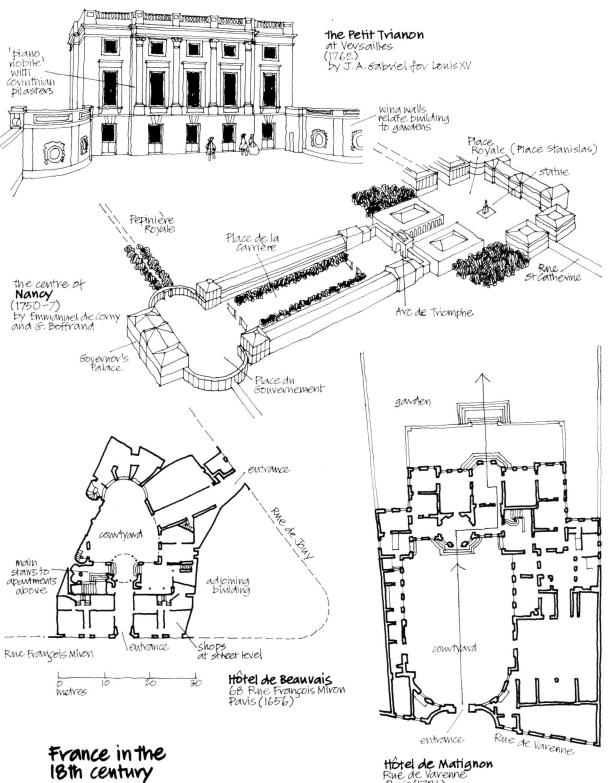

the Petit Trianon
at Versailles
(1762)
by J. A. Gabriel for Louis XV

'piano nobile' with Corinthian pilasters

wing walls relate building to gardens

Place Royale (Place Stanislas)

statue

Pépinière Royale

Place de la Carrière

Rue St Catherine

the centre of
**Nancy**
(1750-7)
by Emmanuel de Corny and G. Boffrand

Arc de Triomphe

Governor's Palace

Place du Gouvernement

entrance

Rue de Jouy

courtyard

main stairs to apartments above

adjoining building

Rue François Miron

entrance

shops at street level

0   10   20   30
metres

**Hôtel de Beauvais**
68 Rue François Miron
Paris (1656)

garden

courtyard

entrance

Rue de Varenne

**Hôtel de Matignon**
Rue de Varenne
Paris (1721)

**France in the 18th century**

Louis XV. It is a three-storey block built in honey-coloured stone, restrained in detail, sedate in mood and beautifully executed. Slightly richer in detail but equally restrained in character is the contemporary civic design scheme for the centre of the town of Nancy, in the Moselle region of north-west France. By the architects Germain Boffrand and Emmanuel de Corny, it was completed in 1757 and consists of three linked squares of different sizes and shapes flanked by public buildings of elegant and restrained classical design.

Typical of the late 17th and early 18th century in France was the rich aristocratic or bourgeois town-house or *hôtel*. Often built on restricted sites in densely built-up areas, they had an ingenuity of planning unnecessary in contemporary English houses. The larger ones might stand behind an entrance courtyard, or *cour d'honneur*, and have a garden behind. The smaller ones might be built on three sides of a smaller entrance court. In the Hotel de Beauvais, Paris (1656), a central entrance flanked by shop units leads to a courtyard, around which the main residence is tightly packed. A later and larger version, the Hotel de Matignon, Paris (1721), has space for a rear garden as well as a front court. The awkwardness of the site places the garden front on a different axis to the front entrance, but the change of direction is managed neatly in the internal planning.

House interiors of the period were often decorated with the spiky ornamentation known as *rocaille*, from which comes the word 'rococo'. Gilded plasterwork in abstract, asymmetrical scrolls and swags, built-in mirrors and delicately-painted walls and ceilings were combined to create an impression of elegance and lightness. Boffrand's interiors for the Hotel de Soubise in Paris (1706) and Jacques Verberckt's intricate carved decorations in Louis XV's apartments at Versailles (1753) were typically rococo, the bold drama and serious purpose of the baroque style having been transmuted into something politer, more elegant and frivolous. The portraits and occasional pieces of artists such as Boucher and Fragonard, in which aristocrats pose in fine costumes, musicians play in woodland glades, and classical figures re-enact scenes from Ovid's *Metamorphoses*, encapsulate the style.

In the electorates and dukedoms of Germany, French manners were followed at court, but other influences were exerted on the architecture. Particularly in the south, where contact with Italy was greater, the 18th century saw an outburst of late-baroque building which had more in common with Guarini than with Gabriel. The hill-top Benedictine monastery of Melk (1702), overlooking the Danube in Austria, is by Jacob Prandtauer. It is a richly-designed domed and twin-towered building of almost Spanish character. Brevnov monastery in Prague (1710) by Christoph Dientzenhofer is a strong, curvilinear building of distinctive baroque character despite its spareness of decoration.

Contemporary churches in Bavaria show less restraint. Still recognisably baroque, with their curvilinear forms and interpenetrating spaces, they are lavishly decorated with rococo ornament and painted designs in an almost overwhelming profusion. St Paulin in Trier (1732) by the Bohemian-born Balthasar Neumann (1687–1753), and St Johann-Nepomuk in Munich (1733) by the brothers Asam, are highly decorative but spatially comparatively simple. However, in the abbey church of Ottobeuren (1748) by the German architect Johann Michael Fischer (1692–1766) and the pilgrimage church of the Vierzehnheiligen (1744) by Neumann, spatial complexity and decorative

# central European baroque

the hilltop monastery of
**Melk** Austria
by Prandtauer
(1702)
'rising from the rock ... like a
vision of heavenly glory'

the monastery of
**Brevnov** Prague
by Dientzenhofer
(1710)
baroque at its most
severe

the altar
of the
fourteen saints

plan at ground level

altar

plan at vault level

the abbey church of
**Ottobeuren** in Bavaria
by J. M. Fischer
(1748)
the decoration acts as
a unifying element

the pilgrimage church of
the fourteen saints
**Vierzehnheiligen**
in Bavaria
by Neumann (1744)

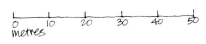

0    10    20    30    40    50
metres

richness are combined. In Vierzehnheiligen, for example, the nave consists of a double interconnecting oval and the sanctuary of a single one; at the side are vestigial circular transepts. The crossing – the focal space in a centralised church – is therefore no more than the joint between four spaces, with the focus of the church, the elaborate altar of the fourteen saints, located in the nave. The interior is alive with rococo decoration – vegetation, fruit, shells, asymmetrical scrolls and swags – which ignores the discipline of the architecture, flowing freely over columns and cornices and linking the building, its statuary and its ceiling paintings into a unified and spectacular whole.

In Russia, the French influence on the Tsar's court and the upper classes extended to its architecture. The summer palace of Petrodvorets, or Peterhof, on the Gulf of Finland (1747) was built for Peter the Great by his French architect Jean-Baptiste Le Blond (1679–1719), the master-planner of Petersburg, and was extended by the Italian Rastrelli. A central three-storey block with a wing on either side emulates Versailles, and its magnificent garden makes spectacular use of fountains and cascades. Francesco Rastrelli (1700–1771) had studied in France and his palace buildings for the empress Elizabeth are strongly reminiscent of Versailles in treatment, with added decorative detail in a Russian style. The summertime Ekaterininsky Palace (1749) at Tsarskoe Seloe or 'Tsar's village', and the Winter Palace on the Neva in Petersburg (1754) are two of his finest buildings. Both use giant orders as the main feature of their long façades – the former is 300 metres long – and both are enlivened with bright colour and decorative detail. Near the Winter Palace is what is perhaps Rastrelli's finest building, the Smolny Convent (1745), with a focal cathedral church surrounded by a courtyard of ancillary buildings. There is no monastic severity here. The buildings, though adopting the basic forms of the Byzantine past, are alive with baroque decoration and bright colour. The centrally-planned cathedral incorporates onion domes, but only as cupolas above larger baroque ones.

## GEORGIAN ENGLAND

During the 18th century, four great powers were beginning to dominate Europe politically. Three of them were authoritarian monarchies: Russia under the Romanovs, pushing her way into Finland, Poland and the Crimea; the Prussian state led by the Hohenzollerns, beginning to dominate Austria and the rest of Germany; Bourbon France, retaining her power in Europe and developing her colonies overseas.

The fourth power was England. The English Revolution had firmly established parliament on the political stage, confirming the rights of bourgeois property-owners to make political decisions. France's bourgeoisie, dominated by the Bourbon court, or those in countries still dominated by the church, looked enviously at their counterparts in Britain. The parliamentary system was much more responsive than the rigid bureaucracy of France. In practice, the needs it responded to were those of the merchants, the planters, the slavers, the farming landlords and the cotton magnates, so in Britain bourgeois power and prestige were correspondingly higher than elsewhere.

In France, entering the aristocracy was the ambition of the successful merchant, but in Britain the reverse was true; the aristocracy, as in Renaissance Italy, were only too glad to enter commerce. In France the spendthrift, idle nobility were dispersing

# imperial Petersburg

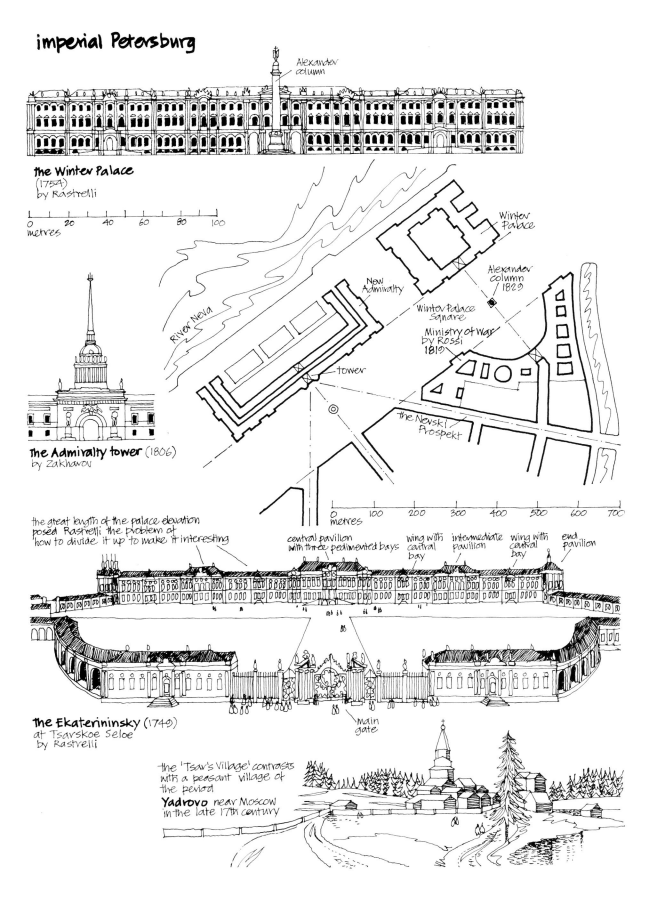

Alexander column

**the Winter Palace**
(1754)
by Rastrelli

0   20   40   60   80   100
metres

River Neva

Winter Palace

New Admiralty

Alexander column 1829

Winter Palace Square

Ministry of War by Rossi 1819

tower

the Nevski Prospekt

**the Admiralty tower** (1806)
by Zakharov

0   100   200   300   400   500   600   700
metres

the great length of the palace elevation posed Rastrelli the problem of how to divide it up to make it interesting

central pavilion with three pedimented bays

wing with central bay

intermediate pavilion

wing with central bay

end pavilion

main gate

**the Ekaterininsky** (1749)
at Tsarskoe Seloe
by Rastrelli

the 'Tsar's Village' contrasts with a peasant village of the period
**Yadrovo** near Moscow in the late 17th century

# Protestant society in the 18th century

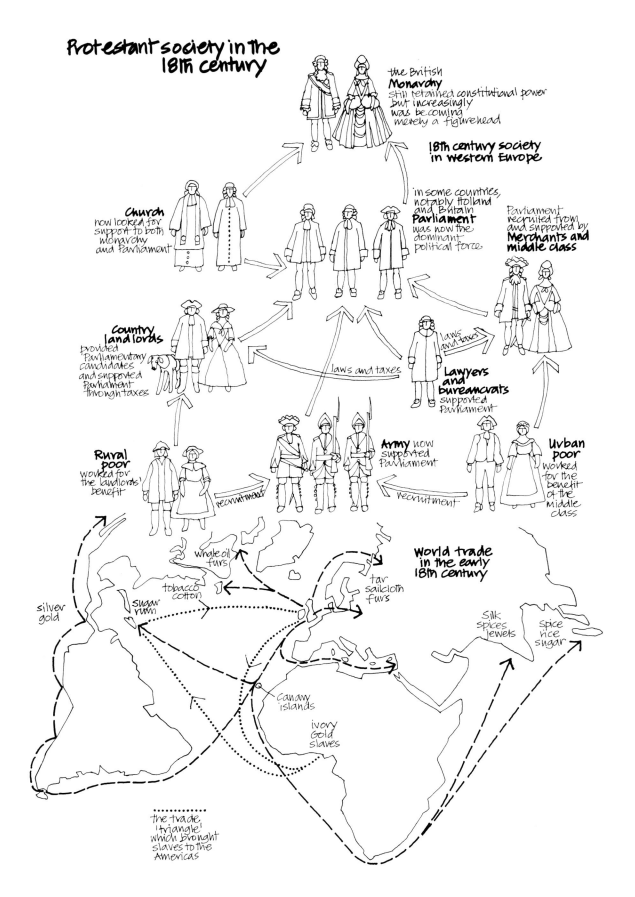

the British **Monarchy** still retained constitutional power but increasingly was becoming merely a figurehead

**18th century society in western Europe**

**Church** now looked for support to both monarchy and Parliament

in some countries, notably Holland and Britain **Parliament** was now the dominant political force

Parliament recruited from and supported by **Merchants and middle class**

**Country landlords** provided Parliamentary candidates and supported Parliament through taxes

laws and taxes

**Lawyers and bureaucrats** supported Parliament

**Rural poor** worked for the landlords' benefit

recruitment

**Army** now supported Parliament

recruitment

**Urban poor** worked for the benefit of the middle class

**World trade in the early 18th century**

whale oil furs

tobacco cotton

tar sailcloth furs

silver gold

sugar rum

Silk spices jewels

spice rice sugar

Canary islands

ivory Gold slaves

the trade 'triangle' which brought slaves to the Americas

capital, but in England it was being conserved and accumulated. In consequence, British economic growth during the 17th and 18th centuries was prodigious and her position as a great power and the strength of her institutions at home were ensured. The major building works of the 17th century – such as Greenwich – had been royal commissions, and the tax that paid for St Paul's cathedral and the city churches had been levied by the king. Now a new group of patrons came to the fore; the palaces of the 18th century were those of new land-owners and successful businessmen.

Blenheim Palace, Oxfordshire (1704), was the gift of a grateful nation to one of its military heroes, the first Duke of Marlborough. The architect, John Vanbrugh (1664–1726), was already engaged on another palace, Castle Howard in Yorkshire (1699), a commission he had obtained through social connections. He had no architectural training – his early success had come from writing plays, like *The Relapse* and *The Provok'd Wife* – but he also had great architectural imagination, which was given direction when he was appointed to assist Wren as royal surveyor. Blenheim, Castle Howard and his later Seaton Delaval in Northumberland (1720) fell into no current architectural pattern. Large, powerful and dramatic, heavy and grossly proportioned, deliberately discordant, they shocked the classical purists of the day. They are in fact among the few achievements of English baroque, highly personal in style and owing little to precedent – except perhaps that their general conformation around a *cour d'honneur* resembles the great French houses of the 17th century.

Vanbrugh stood outside England's prevailing architectural philosophy. The conventional wisdom was in favour of reviving an understated, sedate Palladianism of antiquarian correctness. Mereworth Castle, Kent (1722) is by the Scottish architect Colen Campbell, author of yet another Vitruvian design guide, the *Vitruvius Britannicus*. Mereworth is virtually a reproduction of Palladio's Villa Capra, scholarly, attractive and doubtfully appropriate in the English climate. It has a square plan with a classical portico on each front, and is surmounted by a dome above a central circular hall. Very similar is Chiswick House, London (1725), by the dilettante Lord Burlington and his architect William Kent (1685–1748), the latter a serious student of the work of Jones, and prime mover of the 'Palladian revival' of the 18th century. At Chiswick House, the dome is raised on a drum, through which the hall is lit by clerestories, and the porticos are reduced from four to one. Kent's grandest work, done in conjunction with the local architect Matthew Brettingham, who considered the work to be his, was Holkham Hall in Norfolk (1734), a large, severe, symmetrical composition of a central block surrounded by four similar wings. The plainness of the façades, and the uncompromising regularity, are Palladianism at its most serious and academic.

An integral part of the design of the grand Palladian house was its garden. The characteristic style of the English 18th-century garden was developed first by Kent and continued by his assistant Lancelot 'Capability' Brown (1716–83). It was the exact opposite of the style of Le Nôtre; in place of a strongly-imposed discipline on nature came an artful, informal approach, designed to improve and enhance the natural landscape rather than to re-structure it. Expanses of lawn, dark clumps of deciduous trees, curving routes and natural-looking lakes provided a setting for ornamental bridges, temples and follies. No formal terrace or *parterre* separated the house from its park; instead the informal landscape came up to the very walls. The distinction between the park and the natural landscape beyond was likewise blurred, so that everything the eye could see seemed part of the same composition.

Kent's finest landscape, on which Brown also worked, was at Stowe House, Buckinghamshire, and displays these characteristics perfectly. Brown's own work included the gardens at Croome Court (1751) and Ashburnham (1767). His garden at Vanbrugh's Blenheim (1765), where he swept away much of the original formal landscape, includes a lake which he enlarged to match in scale the bridge which Vanbrugh had built over it.

The Palladian style offered a good workaday solution to the design of many public buildings, and though not all rose above the merely mechanical, there were some notable exceptions. The Senate House in Cambridge (1722) by James Gibbs (1682–1754), a pupil of Wren, is a formal classical block with a central pedimented bay, dignified by the use of giant Corinthian orders. The Horse Guards building in London (1750) by Kent was double sided. From the street frontage in Whitehall, with its *cour d'honneur*, an arch leads through to the more formal side, where a dignified elevation confronts the large parade ground.

Finest of all, perhaps, is Somerset House between the Strand and the river Thames (1776), by William Chambers (1723-96). A large purpose-built government office block, the first such in London, it is built round a fine central courtyard and has a dignified river frontage 200 metres long, broken up into sections, and a central bay surmounted by a small dome. Before the construction of the Thames embankment the building was lapped by the river and had water-gates to allow boats to enter. Similar in character, equally dignified and with a more prominent central dome, is the fine Customs House on the bank of the Liffey in Dublin (1781) by James Gandon (1743–1823), a former pupil of Chambers.

In church building, the influence of Wren persisted well into the 18th century, and the pattern set by him of a short, squarish plan, with galleries and a prominent pulpit, was taken up by Gibbs, designer of St Mary-le-Strand (1714) and St Martin-in-the-Fields (1722), both in London – the former Italianate and rather baroque, the latter more consciously Palladian. More adventurous were the churches of Thomas Archer (1668–1743). St Philip's, Birmingham (1709), has a powerful front tower with concave sides, and St Paul's, Deptford (1712), and St John's, Smith Square (1714), both in London, have centralised plans, the former with a single western spire and a semi-circular portico, the latter with four circular towers flanked with detached columns. In all of them, a richly-moulded baroque and rather un-English style prevails.

The English baroque architect who stands most comparison with Wren and Vanbrugh, however, was Nicholas Hawksmoor (1666–1730). Unlike them, Hawksmoor was trained as an architect, and seldom can there have been such professional dedication. His method was to analyse rigorously every detail in a building and, leaving nothing to chance, to describe it to the builder by copious drawings. He worked with Wren in the royal Office of Works till 1718 when both were dismissed in favour of mediocre but politically acceptable competitors. He shares with Wren much of the credit for Greenwich, and with Vanbrugh worked on Castle Howard and Blenheim. There is much of the baroque spirit of both Wren and Vanbrugh in his work, though his spare, rugged style is undoubtedly his own.

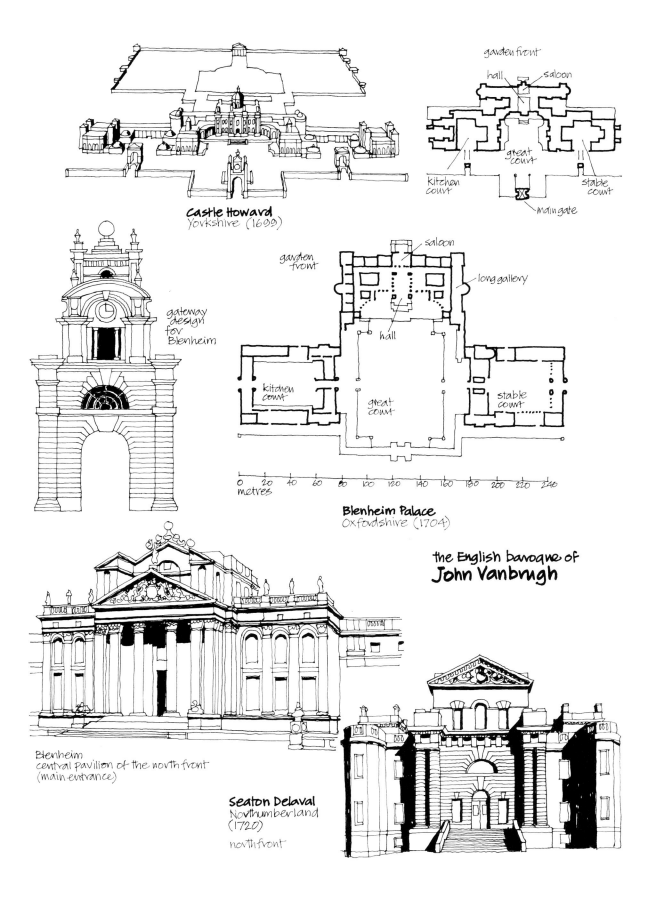

**Castle Howard**
Yorkshire (1699)

garden front
hall
saloon
great court
kitchen court
stable court
main gate

garden front
saloon
long gallery
hall
kitchen court
great court
stable court

0  20  40  60  80  100  120  140  160  180  200  220  240
metres

**Blenheim Palace**
Oxfordshire (1704)

gateway design for Blenheim

the English baroque of
**John Vanbrugh**

Blenheim
central pavilion of the north front
(main entrance)

**Seaton Delaval**
Northumberland
(1720)

north front

Among his masterpieces were six London parish churches built as a result of an Act of Parliament in 1711. The first two, St Alphege, Greenwich and St Anne, Limehouse, were begun in 1712, followed by St George-in-the-East (1715), St Mary Woolnoth (1716), St George, Bloomsbury (1720) and Christchurch, Spitalfields (1723). Each is different in detail though each displays the same interest in strong, unconventional spatial effects internally, and dramatic, powerful statements outside. St Mary Woolnoth has a strange rectangular rusticated tower surmounted by two square turrets, St Anne's tower is strong, geometrical baroque in diminishing tiers, and Christchurch, his masterpiece, has a pointed spire of almost romanesque character above a square tower with two concave sides and a barrel-vaulted portico. The combination of such disparate elements into an 'incorrect' but brilliantly organic whole did not impress his Palladian critics.

The influence of Palladianism was far-reaching, affecting the design of small houses as well as grand ones. We now classify this very English style of architecture, corresponding roughly with the 18th century and the reigns of four kings called George, as 'Georgian'. By the end of the 17th century, a distinctive style had been evolved for the country houses of the well-to-do middle class, partly from the style of Jones, partly from ideas imported from 17th-century Holland, both adapted to English use. The house of Sir Roger Pratt, Coleshill in Berkshire (1662), typifies the style. Now destroyed, it was a compact, two-storey house with a central doorway and vertical sash-windows, Palladian in style, in the manner of Jones's Queen's House. Above the heavy cornice-line, however, instead of Jones's apparent flat roof was a heavy hipped roof, reminiscent of Van Campen's Mauritshuis. This feature, with added dormers and chimneys, became an accepted – and appropriate – method of adapting Palladio's style to the English climate and in the hands of master-builders and local craftsmen it was reproduced up and down the country.

In the towns, the middle classes – merchants, lawyers, agents and clerks – were increasing in number, and the growing need for houses somewhere in standard between a mansion and a worker's hovel was supplied by speculative building. Speculators acquired what land they could, often from the estates of commercially-minded aristocrats, and laid out housing developments. Some – often the landlords themselves acting as developers – realised that an attractive layout including shops and open space would be more commercial, and the Earl of Southampton's development of Bloomsbury in the late 17th century set a pattern, with its related streets, squares and open spaces, for the higher-class estate. Others were interested in obtaining as many houses as possible on their land in closely packed streets.

In both cases, the basic building form was the terraced house, arranged in geometric rows and designed along classical lines. There was usually a basement, an entry floor approached through an ornate street door, a tall upper floor – a 'piano nobile' – with the main rooms, and further upper floors diminishing in height towards the top. Household servants were accommodated in basements or attics. The proportions of doors and windows, their relationship to one another, their diminution towards the top of the building, were set down in pattern books, like those of the carpenter Batty Langley which enjoyed a considerable currency in the early 18th century and which enabled small speculative builders everywhere to put up tolerably stylish buildings. The whole side of a square could be made into more than the sum of its parts if the

# Palladianism in England

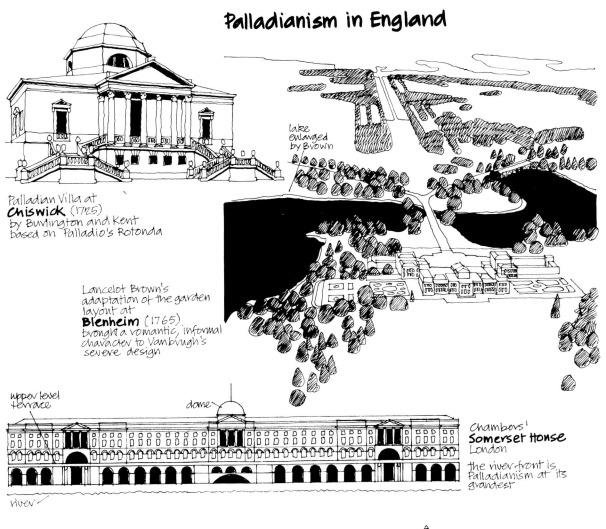

Palladian Villa at
**Chiswick** (1725)
by Burlington and Kent
based on Palladio's Rotonda

lake
enlarged
by Brown

Lancelot Brown's
adaptation of the garden
layout at
**Blenheim** (1765)
brought a romantic, informal
character to Vanbrugh's
severe design

upper level
terrace

dome

Chambers'
**Somerset House**
London

the river-front is
Palladianism at its
grandest

river

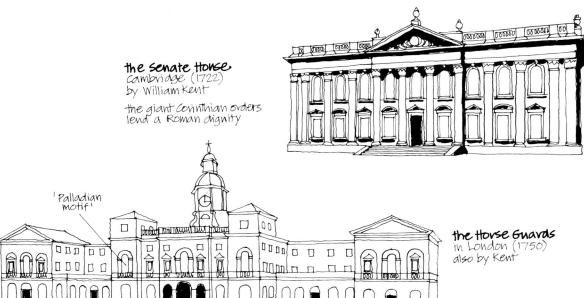

the **Senate House**
Cambridge (1722)
by William Kent

the giant Corinthian orders
lend a Roman dignity

'Palladian
motif'

the **Horse Guards**
in London (1750)
also by Kent

parade
ground

**St Mary-le-Strand**
(1714)
Gibbs' most baroque
design

semi-circular portico

**St Pauls Deptford**
(1712)
an elegant design by Archer
with a Wren-like spire

the portico is a
Palladian motif
transformed by
being projected
into three
dimensions

**St Mary Woolnoth**
(1716)
a four-square
tower over
a square plan

compare
with the
gateway
design
for
Blenheim

entrance

**Christ Church Spitalfields**
(1723)
Hawksmoor's masterpiece

like all Hawksmoor's church plans
**St George's Bloomsbury** is based
on two axes

# English 18th century baroque

centre house were designed as a central feature and the end two as pavilions. That way, the owners had the satisfaction of appearing to live in a palace. Large areas of London, Dublin and Edinburgh were built in this way, but the finest example was the small Somerset town of Bath.

Known to the Romans as *Aquae Sulis* for its medicinal water, Bath was re-discovered around 1720 by fashionable society, and the job of re-planning the town to meet the needs of large numbers of wealthy hypochondriacs fell to the two John Woods, father and son. Using the local sandstone, they built three groups of majestic terrace houses, linked together as part of a sequence of spaces: Queen's Square (1728), The Circus and the Royal Crescent (1754). The buildings in The Circus, three curved blocks forming a circular space, are designed with three main storeys treated, like the Colosseum, with superimposed orders. The Queen's Square houses, like a Florentine *palazzo*, have a rusticated ground storey as a podium, with the two upper floors bound together by giant orders. A central pedimented bay and two end pavilions lend a palatial aspect, and the whole is capped by a heavy pediment which largely conceals the servants' rooms in the roof space.

Though the poor were not deliberately included in the improvements that were taking place, they did benefit in some ways. Improved crops, fewer wars, better transport, gradually-acquired immunity to disease and better medicine were enough to raise their expectation of life, if not their wealth. Most workers still lived in a single-storey dwelling, built in local materials, with a thatched roof. It might have no more than two rooms, one of which contained a brick-built chimney-stack. The water-supply might be far from the house and – though this was almost true of the upper classes as well – sanitation was non-existent. The better cottages, built not by the tenants themselves but by local builders, perhaps for top estate workers, were more varied. Typically two-storeyed, they might be timber-framed and weather-boarded, though as bricks and tiles became more common a greater constructional variety was possible. A steeply-pitched roof might contain the top-floor bedrooms, lit with small dormer windows. Perhaps the most significant feature of the 18th-century cottage was its external regularity. The central, hooded doorway, with glazed sash-windows placed symmetrically on either side, show, if only faintly, the extent of Palladio's influence.

There were other influences on design. A German shoemaker's son called Johann Winckelmann, a poet, classical scholar and Vatican bureaucrat was in Naples in 1748 when engineers working for the King of Naples uncovered the first wall-paintings in the buried town of Pompeii. His published description of the amazing finds as they came to light awoke a wide interest in antiquity. This interest was given a romantic direction by the artist Giovanni Battista Piranesi (1720–78) whose views of Pompeii, Herculaneum and the monuments of Rome, ivy-covered and decaying, and of terrifying, imaginary prison-scenes, the celebrated *Carceri*, were widely published. Starting with Gibbon's *Decline and Fall of the Roman Empire* (1776), there was a renewed interest in the writing of history. The growth of antiquarianism encouraged cultured gentlemen of leisure to study the past for its own sake. This growing passion for the past was not confined to Rome but extended to Etruria, Greece, the far east and to Europe's own medieval heritage. Langley's *Gothic Architecture Improved* (1742), Chambers' *Design of Chinese Buildings* (1757) and Stuart and Revett's *Antiquities of Athens* (1762) were books which had considerable influence.

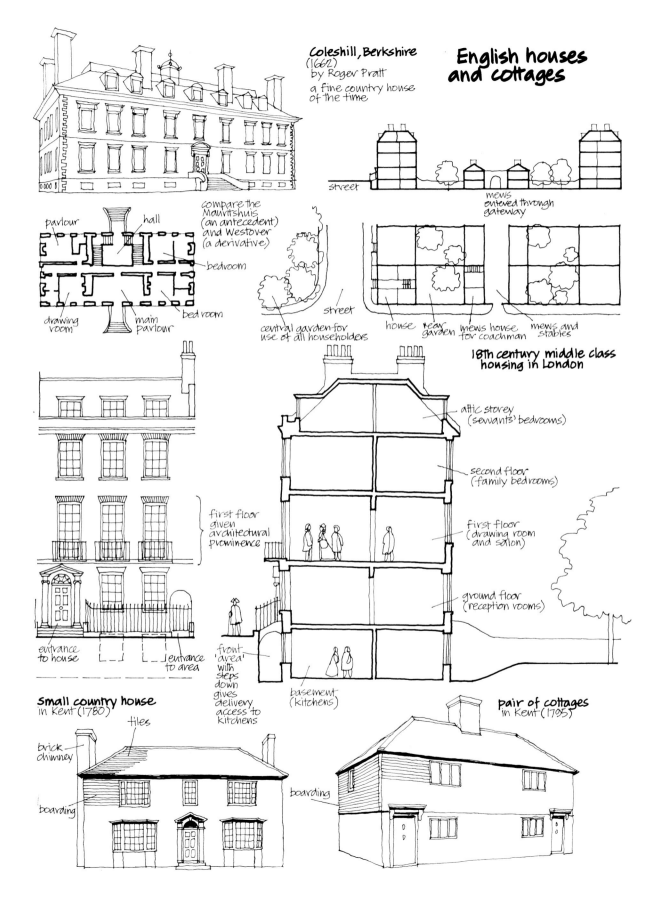

Coleshill, Berkshire (1662) by Roger Pratt
a fine country house of the time

English houses and cottages

parlour    hall

bedroom

drawing room    main parlour    bed room

compare the Mauritshuis (an antecedent) and Westover (a derivative)

street

central garden for use of all householders

street

mews entered through gateway

house    rear garden    mews house for coachman    mews and stables

18th century middle class housing in London

attic storey (servants' bedrooms)

second floor (family bedrooms)

first floor given architectural prominence

first floor (drawing room and salon)

ground floor (reception rooms)

entrance to house    entrance to area

front 'area' with steps down gives delivery access to kitchens

basement (kitchens)

Small country house in Kent (1780)

tiles

brick chimney

boarding

pair of cottages in Kent (1705)

boarding

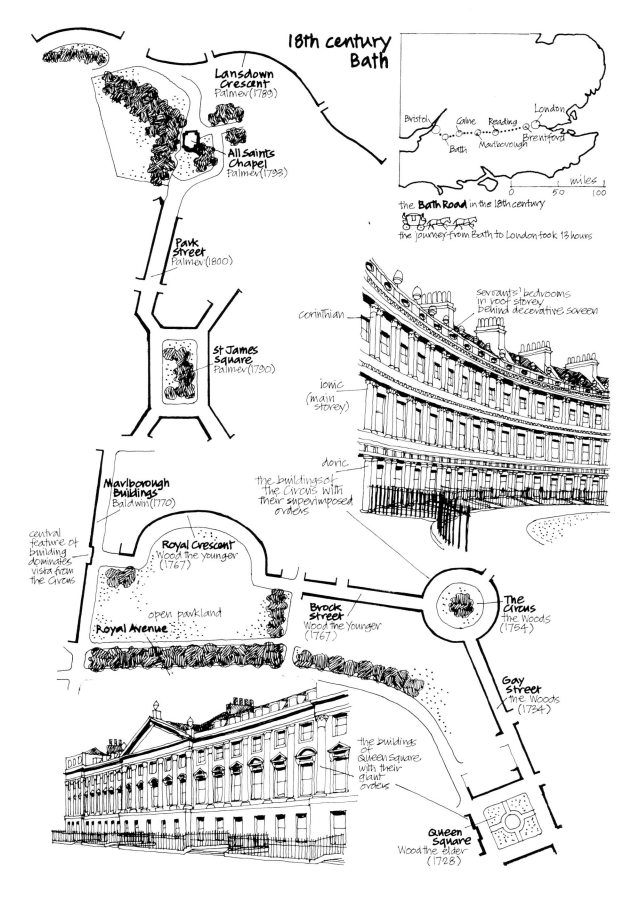

# 18th century Bath

**Lansdown Crescent**
Palmer (1789)

**All Saints Chapel**
Palmer (1793)

**Park Street**
Palmer (1800)

**St James Square**
Palmer (1790)

**Marlborough Buildings**
Baldwin (1770)

central feature of building dominates vista from the Circus

**Royal Crescent**
Wood the younger (1767)

open parkland

**Royal Avenue**

**Brock Street**
Wood the Younger (1767)

Bristol · Calne · Reading · London
Bath · Marlborough · Brentford

miles
0 · 50 · 100

the **Bath Road** in the 18th century

the journey from Bath to London took 13 hours

corinthian

servants' bedrooms in roof storey behind decorative screen

ionic (main storey)

doric

the buildings of the Circus with their superimposed orders

**The Circus**
the Woods (1754)

**Gay Street**
the Woods (1734)

the buildings of Queen Square with their giant orders

**Queen Square**
Wood the Elder (1728)

The Scottish architect Robert Adam (1728–92) studied in Italy and Paris, visited Rome where he measured the monuments and met Piranesi, and returned to England to start a practice with his brothers James and John. Robert's design ability and the business acumen of the other two brought them great success, not only in numerous re-modellings of old houses for wealthy clients, but also in full-blooded ventures into property speculation.

The Adelphi development in London (1768), between the Strand and the river, was the most impressive, a multi-level complex of warehouses, stables, offices and residences which turned a derelict riverside mud-flat into a fashionable area. Robert was by training a Palladian designer but his antiquarian studies had given his work an eclectic aspect. In his travels he had seen Diocletian's Palace at Split, and the riverside frontage of the palatial Adelphi development was a conscious borrowing. A wharf at water level gave access to a vast vaulted basement storage area which formed a podium. A network of narrow streets ran directly from the Strand and gave access to the upper-level terraces. The style of building was elegant and formal, dressed in painted stucco and giant pilasters which were enlivened by Robert's characteristic low-relief decoration. The colours and patterns resemble plaster-work and frescoes Robert would have seen at Pompeii.

They appear again and again in his interior designs for large houses: at Kedleston Hall in Derbyshire (1760), begun by Brettingham as a follow-on from Holkham, and at Osterley (1761), Syon (1762) and Kenwood (1767), all on the fringes of London. In them, rich Roman colour and delicate Hellenistic ornament were used in the most artful way. In his finest works, Robert Adam is also a master of internal spatial effects, both in the way he organises a sequence of spaces of different sizes and shapes, and in the way he divides spaces by free-standing columns and beams, or extends them with alcoves.


## THE NEW PROMETHEANS

Gothic architecture, as we have seen, remained a living tradition at least till the 16th century. After that, it was generally supplanted by baroque and Palladian. Indeed, the very epithet 'gothic', associating the style with the barbarians who overran classical Rome, was first coined as a term of abuse. But to the imaginative mind of the late 18th century, the ivy-covered ruins of medieval buildings, like the abbeys destroyed by Henry VIII, or abandoned French châteaux, summarised all that was romantic and mysterious about the past. Horace Walpole's *The Castle of Otranto* (1764) and William Beckford's *Vathek* (1782) were the first of many 'Gothick' novels – Mary Shelley's *Frankenstein* (1817) ultimately becoming the most influential – in which adventure, mystery and the supernatural were set against the echoing corridors of medieval abbeys and castles.

Architecture followed suit. Walpole had already commissioned the rebuilding of Strawberry Hill (1750), a cottage in Middlesex, in an elegant and delicate medieval style. Beckford went further, commissioning James Wyatt to build a huge house, Fonthill Abbey, in Wiltshire, in 1795. An octagonal tower 85 metres high, a great hall and an elevation some 90 metres in length were features of this extraordinary building. As in most subsequent buildings of this 'gothic revival', its medievalism was superficial

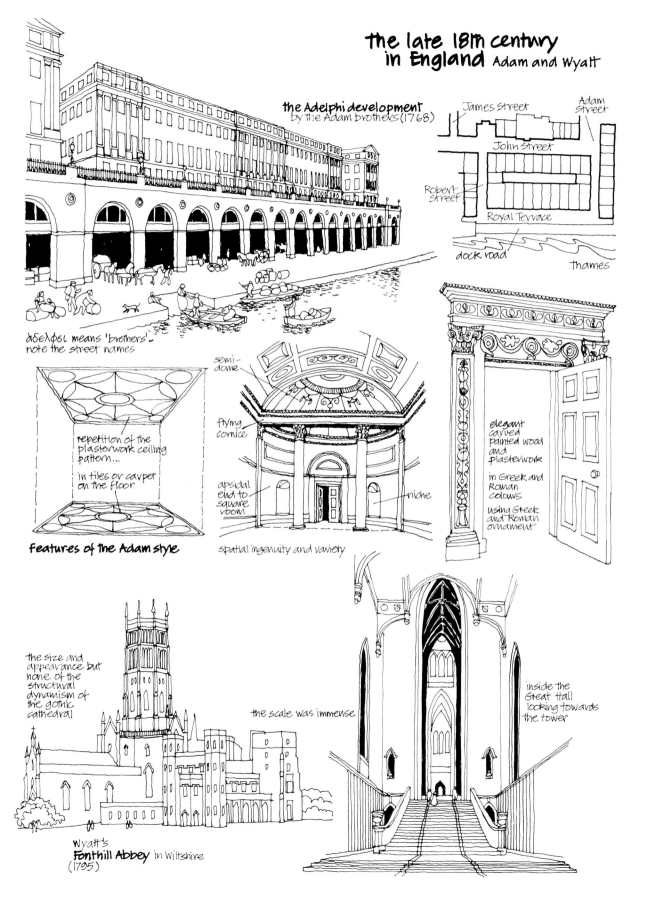

# the late 18th century in England Adam and Wyatt

**the Adelphi development**
by the Adam brothers (1768)

James Street

Adam Street

John Street

Robert Street

Royal Terrace

dock road

Thames

αδελφοι means 'brothers'.
note the street names

**Features of the Adam style**

repetition of the plasterwork ceiling pattern...

in tiles or carpet on the floor

semi-dome

flying cornice

apsidal end to square room

niche

spatial ingenuity and variety

elegant carved painted wood and plasterwork

in Greek and Roman colours

using Greek and Roman ornament

the size and appearance but none of the structural dynamism of the gothic cathedral

the scale was immense

inside the Great Hall looking towards the tower

Wyatt's **Fonthill Abbey** in Wiltshire (1795)

rather than essential – though its tower did emulate several medieval predecessors by collapsing three times, the last in 1825. The house no longer exists.

The more progressive thinkers of the 18th century saw the past as of more than antiquarian interest; rather more fundamentally, it was one of the keys to man's future. The French *philosophes* and their German counterparts differed among themselves over many things; the religious and political attitudes of Rousseau were not those of Voltaire and Diderot, nor Kant's those of Goethe. Among Anglo-Saxon economists and social reformers there were also differences: between Smith and Hume, Gibbon and Bentham, Hobbes and Locke, Jefferson and Franklin. However, they held many basic ideas in common. They were generally hostile to 'revealed' religion, in particular to the church's medieval doctrine of original sin, and looked back with favour on the pre-catholic era of history when men had a greater dignity. They sought for a rational explanation of existence and, believing that human understanding was capable of coming to terms with the problems of the world, looked forward to a better future. Their idea of progress, to be based on values which somehow had been lost, offered society an intellectual challenge.

To some architects, progress meant rejecting the essentially Roman forms associated with the hereditary aristocracy and rediscovering the architecture of an earlier, more essential kind. Ancient Greece or pre-Roman Etruria provided models. James Wyatt, much happier with classical architecture than with Beckford's gothic, based his design for the Radcliffe Observatory, Oxford (1772) on the Tower of the Winds in Athens. The movement of which he was part, whose academic Greek gravitas contrasted strongly with the theatricality of baroque and the frivolity of rococo, became variously known as 'Greek revival' or, more generally, 'Neoclassical'.

Progressive architectural theorists of the late 18th century were caught up by the dynamism of the philosophes. Buildings, it was thought, should express the essential grandeur of man both by their sublimity and by their reference to his dignified past. Sublimity was capable of analysis: buildings should be large, simple, sombre, cavernous and mysterious in a way typified, perhaps, by Piranesi's Carceri. The two greatest exponents of this approach were Étienne-Louis Boullée (1728-99) and Claude-Nicolas Ledoux (1736-1806). Both designed and theorised much more than they built, and the reputation of Boullée at least depends on his drawings, which include designs for an enormous national library, museums, cemeteries and a monument to Isaac Newton, the symbol of the new age, which was to be a vast hollow sphere, 150 metres or more in diameter, representing the universe.

As social awareness increased, new building-types were required; everywhere architects were inventing forms for buildings designed to promote health, welfare and social responsibility: hospitals, prisons, schools, model factories, housing estates, monuments and Temples of the Moral Values. Among Ledoux's finest built works was the model industrial estate built in 1775 for the chemical works of La Saline near Besançon, a complex of factories and laboratories with a nearby residential quarter. The style was robust and consciously primitive, using the Tuscan order and heavily rusticated walls. The same features appeared on the *barrières* or toll-gates of Paris, built in a ring around the inner city in 1785. Only four of the original forty-five now survive, but La Villette with its heavy rotunda and L'Enfer with its strongly rusticated columns represent the geometric qualities of them all.

# The Revolutionaries

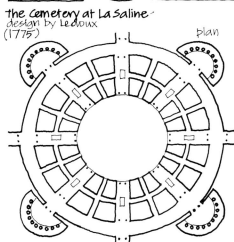

the Cemetery at La Saline
design by Ledoux
(1775)

section

plan

design for a
**Newton Cenotaph**
by Boullée (1784)

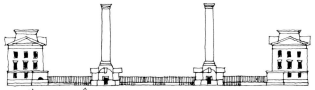

Barrière du Trône

**the Barrières
of Paris**
Ledoux
(1785)

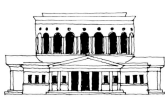

Barrière de
la Villette

Barrière de
l'Enfer

Barrière de
Ménil-Montant

the Rotunda of
**the Bank of England**
by Soane (1788)

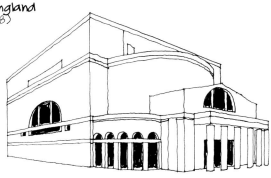

design for the
**Prussian National Theatre**
Berlin
by Gilly (1798)

John Soane (1753–1837) in England and Friedrich Gilly (1772-1800) in Germany were the counterparts of Boullée and Ledoux. Soane's Bank of England (1788), a design which was actually built, was more uncompromising than anything achieved by the others. Stark and austere, it had a magnificent central domed rotunda in which decoration was almost completely eliminated and simplicity of form was everything. Gilly's great work, the Prussian National Theatre designed for Berlin, was never built; but it too shows an uncompromising attitude to geometric purity and surface simplicity. The simple rectangular stage tower set against the hemicyclical auditorium was a concept as suited to the architecture of the 20th century as to that of the 18th.

The group of architects to which Boullée and Ledoux belonged became known as 'the revolutionaries'. On the whole, this described an architectural rather than a social attitude. Ledoux at least was a royalist and an 'architecte du roi', and his designs are oppressive as well as liberating. Nevertheless these *architectes révolutionnaires* were working at a time when the idea of social revolution was part of intellectual life. Jean-Jacques Rousseau, for example, in *Du Contrat Social* (1762) advocated popular sovereignty to attain the supremacy of the 'general will'. In 1775, the theories were put to a practical test as the American colonies, dissatisfied at being taxed without being represented at Westminster, came into open conflict with England. At first, there was no general revolutionary aim – Washington himself was a monarchist and sought only to bring Britain to its senses – but soon the possibility of independence was recognised, stimulated by thinkers like Thomas Paine in his pamphlet *Common Sense* (1776). A revolution took place and independence was gained.

Two years before, Louis XVI had succeeded to the throne of France. In a desperate attempt to unite the three 'Estates', of aristocrats, clergy and people, he recalled the Estates General, an assembly that had not met for two centuries. However, it was too late to resist the demand for popular sovereignty. A newly-formed National Assembly was drawing up a more democratic constitution when on 14 July 1789 a Paris mob stormed the Bastille. This was a 14th century fortress which, like many of its kind, had been converted to a prison. It held some religious and political prisoners and was a hated symbol of the regime. Its rapid fall reminds us how vulnerable a big city was to revolution. Paris, like many others, was essentially medieval, with networks of narrow streets into which revolutionaries could disappear, and with plenty of opportunity for making barricades to frustrate the badly-organised troops. Nor did the comparative remoteness of Versailles give it protection. The mob marched out, over-ran the palace and moved the king and queen back to the city.

The events created a ferment in Europe, with conservatives outraged and fearful, and liberals welcoming the arrival of universal freedom. The European nations banded together against France, to prevent 'liberty, equality and fraternity' arriving in their countries. As it was, of the many guises the revolution went through – Robespierre's Terror, the Directory, Napoleon's rise to power – none was democratic, and popular sovereignty was not achieved. One ruling class, based on inherited wealth, had been removed and was being replaced by another, based on capital accumulation.

# 9 The early 19th century

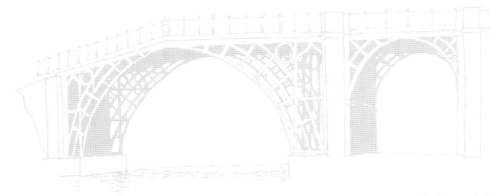

During the 18th century, Britain began developing her role as the 'workshop of the world'. The dominance of the bourgeoisie allowed capital accumulation as never before. Wealth based on land and possessions had been essentially static and unreproducible but capital, by contrast, was fluid and could be re-cycled to create yet more wealth. The real revolution came when capitalism and industrialisation came together. This began with the agricultural reforms of the 18th century, which mechanised farming and appropriated the land for the big landlords, throwing many farm workers out of their homes and jobs. Their move to the towns, looking for work, coincided with another mechanisation, that of the cotton mills. As the labour force and the factory machines came together, productivity suddenly soared, the profits of the new factory owners rapidly rose, and the industrial cities, with Manchester at their centre, grew apace. This was a corollary to the French Revolution: the political freedom promised by the one seemed to be matched by the economic promise of the other.

The intellectual turmoil of this age of revolution is typified by its great artists, who linked the classical world of the 18th century with the modern one of the 19th. After Beethoven's *Eroica* symphony (1804), music could never be the same again. Goethe had a great affinity with the classical world, but *Faust* (1832) introduced concepts – such as the quest for eternal truth, the idea of creative toil and the search for spiritual freedom – which became intellectual hallmarks of modernity.

Architecture had no Goethe or Beethoven. There are several reasons why architects failed at first to make the leap into the 19th century, and why they responded to the new opportunities of the industrial revolution merely by retreating to traditional forms and methods. For one thing, they had worked over the years to achieve status in society. As taste-makers in a world in which taste counted for a great deal, they had created a set of design rules accepted everywhere from Petersburg to Washington. The new techniques threatened their world and understandably they preferred to close their minds to them.

In fact, though the underlying economic structure of society was changing, outwardly the old order appeared to continue: the conservatism of Metternich dominated Italy and the German states, the French revolution had ended in the dictatorship of Napoleon, and the wars against Napoleon allowed George IV of England to bask in the warmth of his people's patriotism.

The liberalism on which industrial capitalism depended, with its ideals of *liberté, égalité, fraternité*, needed to be resisted. There must have been considerable pressure from the old ruling class, and from those of the bourgeoisie who aspired to it, to persist with traditional architectural forms as symbols of continuity in a changing world. They needed a civic architecture to impart grandeur and dignity to their various regimes – from Napoleon's nascent empire to the fast-developing Union of American states. The neoclassical style allowed the politicians of America and France, and elsewhere too, to consider themselves by implication the rightful heirs of democratic Athens or imperial Rome.

The new American capital of Washington was designed by the French architect Pierre Charles l'Enfant (1754–1825) with a grand baroque layout in the style of Versailles, made more magnificent by its riverside location. But the Capitol, the White House and a succession of other government buildings which adorned the site were built as, or remodelled into, severe and elegant Greek-revival monuments. Leading the neoclassical movement in America was Benjamin Latrobe (1764–1820). His early career was associated with President Thomas Jefferson (1734–1826), himself an accomplished architect, whose house Monticello, near Charlottesville, Va. (1770), was an essay in the Palladian style. Together they designed the State Capitol at Richmond, Va. (1789), a fine building in the form of a Greek Ionic temple, which set a pattern for future public buildings. Latrobe's own remodelling of the White House (1807) is a good example, but his best work is perhaps the Roman Catholic cathedral of Baltimore, Md. (1805), with its latin-cross plan and spacious, domed crossing.

In Napoleon's France, civic architecture displayed a similar classical monumentality, for which Roman grandeur rather than Greek democracy was the model. An early forerunner was Jacques-Germain Soufflot's church of Ste Geneviève in Paris (1755), later to become a national shrine known as the Panthéon. Its stark windowless walls, central dome and colonnaded portico recall the mood, if not the detail, of its great Roman predecessor. Pierre-Alexandre Vignon's church of La Madeleine (1806), however, was an almost literal reproduction of a Roman temple. The intended association between Napoleon and the Caesars is clear. The architects Charles Percier and Pierre Fontaine became the Empire's official architects, charged with the task of creating for it a recognisable house style, from wallpaper and ornaments to triumphal arches and palaces. Their work is seen both in Paris and in other big cities of Napoleon's Empire.

Their German counterpart was Karl Friedrich von Schinkel (1781–1841). His two great works in Berlin are the Schauspielhaus (1819) and the Altes Museum (1824). The bold, dramatic massing of these buildings has great integrity and is strongly expressive of the way they are planned, though the elevational detail, relying on the Ionic order, is rather more traditionalist than in the work of Gilly, whose pupil Schinkel was. Schinkel seems to have been influenced by Jean-Nicolas-Louis Durand whose two books, *Nouveau précis des leçons d'Architecture* and *Recueil et parallèle des édifices de tout genre* (1801–2) advocated a formulaic approach, which was adopted in the design of many contemporary public buildings. The Rue de Rivoli in Paris, by Percier and Fontaine, was part of a sweeping improvement scheme for the city initiated by Napoleon in 1811.

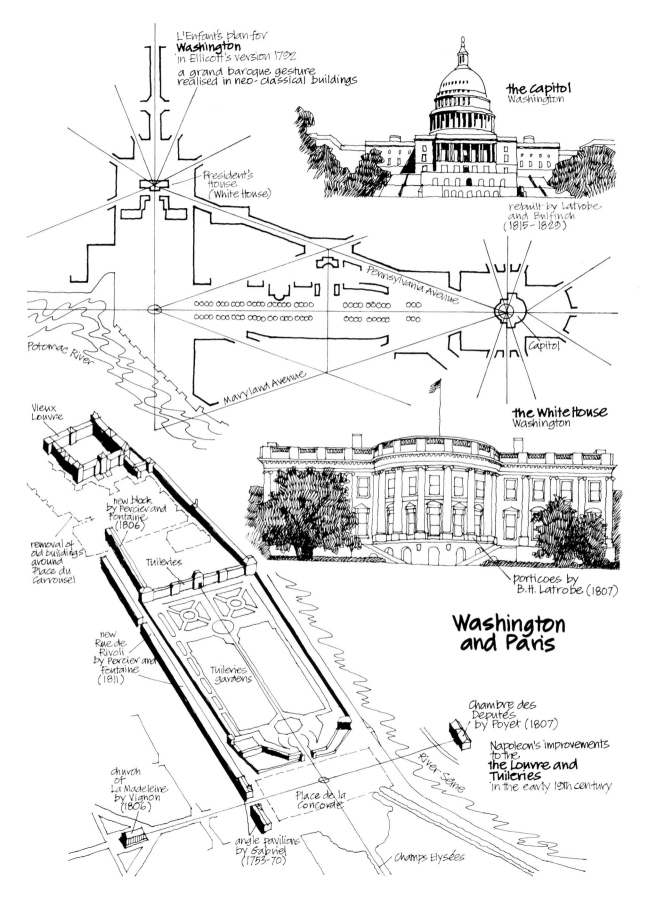

L'Enfant's plan for **Washington** in Ellicott's version 1792
a grand baroque gesture realised in neo-classical buildings

**the Capitol** Washington

rebuilt by Latrobe and Bulfinch (1815-1829)

President's House (White House)

Pennsylvania Avenue

Potomac River

Maryland Avenue

Capitol

**the White House** Washington

porticoes by B.H. Latrobe (1807)

Vieux Louvre

new block by Percier and Fontaine (1806)

removal of old buildings around Place du Carrousel

Tuileries

new Rue de Rivoli by Percier and Fontaine (1811)

Tuileries gardens

church of La Madeleine by Vignon (1806)

angle pavilions by Gabriel (1753-70)

Place de la Concorde

Chambre des Députés by Poyet (1807)

**Washington and Paris**

Napoleon's improvements to the **the Louvre and Tuileries** in the early 19th century

River Seine

Champs Elysées

# Jefferson and Latrobe

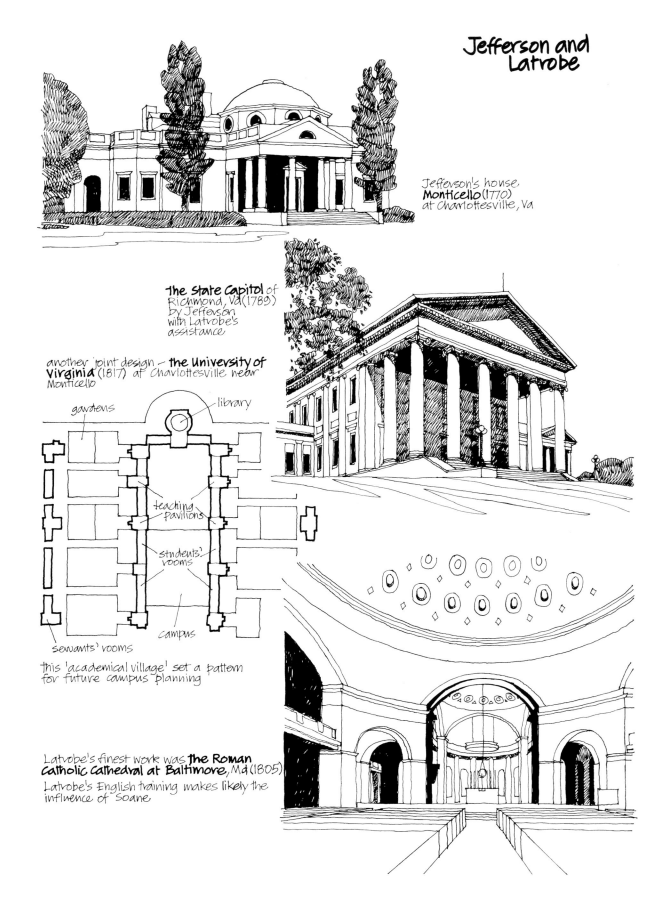

Jefferson's house,
**Monticello** (1770)
at Charlottesville, Va

**the State Capitol** of
Richmond, Va (1789)
by Jefferson
with Latrobe's
assistance

another joint design — **the University of
Virginia** (1817) at Charlottesville near
Monticello

gardens

library

teaching
pavilions

students'
rooms

servants' rooms

campus

this 'academical village' set a pattern
for future campus planning

Latrobe's finest work was **the Roman
Catholic Cathedral at Baltimore**, Md (1805)

Latrobe's English training makes likely the
influence of Soane

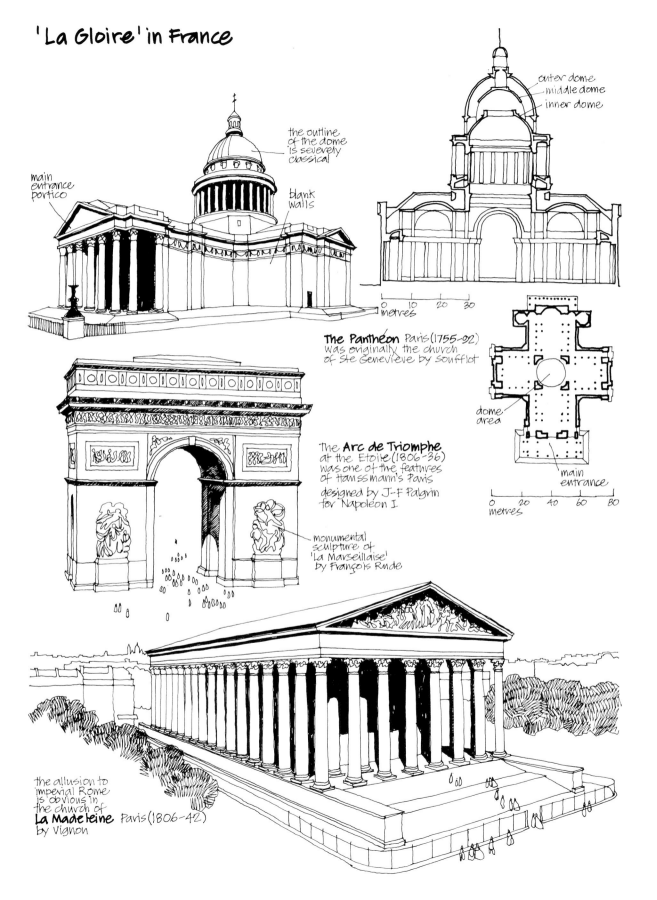

# 'La Gloire' in France

the outline of the dome is severely classical

main entrance portico

blank walls

outer dome
middle dome
inner dome

0  10  20  30
metres

**The Panthéon** Paris (1755-92) was originally the church of Ste Geneviève by Soufflot

dome area

main entrance

The **Arc de Triomphe** at the Étoile (1806-36) was one of the features of Haussmann's Paris designed by J-F Palgrin for Napoléon I

monumental sculpture of 'La Marseillaise' by François Rude

0  20  40  60  80
metres

the allusion to imperial Rome is obvious in the church of **La Madeleine** Paris (1806-42) by Vignon

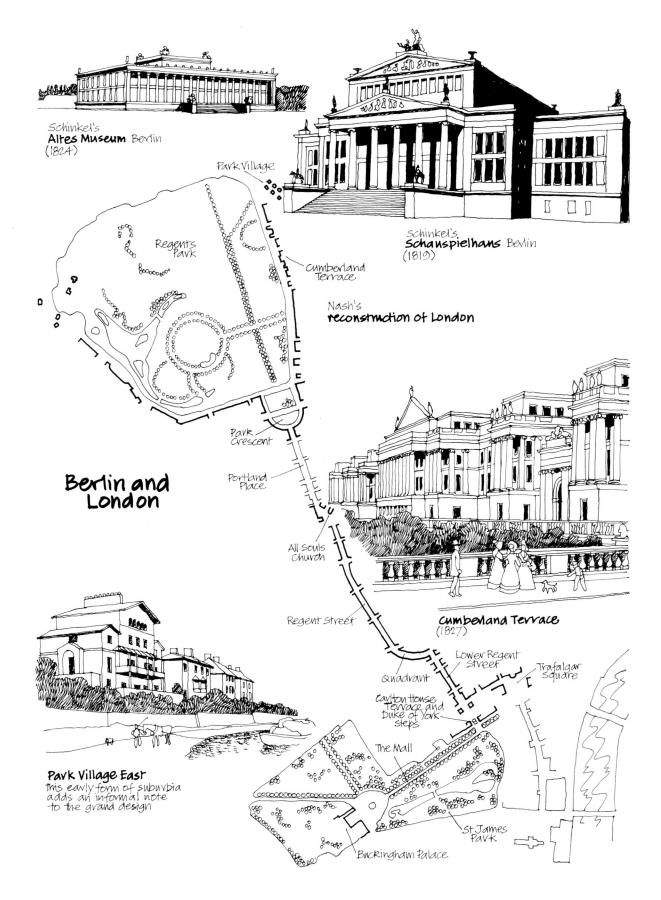

Schinkel's
**Altes Museum** Berlin
(1824)

Schinkel's
**Schauspielhaus** Berlin
(1819)

Park Village

Regents Park

Cumberland Terrace

Nash's
**reconstruction of London**

Park Crescent

Portland Place

**Berlin and London**

All Souls Church

Regent Street

**Cumberland Terrace**
(1827)

Lower Regent Street

Trafalgar Square

Quadrant

Carlton House Terrace and Duke of York steps

The Mall

**Park Village East**
this early form of suburbia
adds an informal note
to the grand design

St James Park

Buckingham Palace

Continuous five-storey residential blocks line the street, with arcaded ground storeys containing shops, in a scheme designed, like Bath, to invest individual bourgeois houses with a collective, palatial dignity.

This approach is seen at its best in the improvements to London of John Nash (1752–1835). A combination of royal patronage, bourgeois support and his own entrepreneurial skill allowed Nash to place his stamp on the West End of London in a way Wren had never been able to do in the City. A sequence of new buildings and public spaces stretching from Buckingham Palace in the south to Regent's Park in the north, demonstrated Nash's mastery over large-scale spatial effects. Unadventurous in style, slipshod in detail and cheap in construction, the elements of Nash's grand design which remain nevertheless impart to London a great theatrical panache. They included The Mall, Carlton House Terrace (1827), Regent Street – later redeveloped – Portland Place, Park Crescent and the terraces of Regent's Park, of which Cumberland Terrace (1827) is probably the best example. The cluster of detached houses and gardens, in various styles, including classical and gothic, which form Park Village (1824) are among the earliest recognisable examples of English suburbia.

## CLASSICAL AND GOTHIC

To the 18th century Palladians, style had been intrinsic, the very essence of architecture. In the 19th century, most architects were still concerned with style and its significance, which prevented them at first from appreciating the structural possibilities of the new industrial materials. Feelings on the subject of style ran high, and Neoclassical and Gothic in particular had firm and even fanatical adherents, ready to do intellectual battle with each other.

The gothic revival, from its tentative beginnings in the 18th century, became firmly established when in 1834 the old medieval palace of Westminster was destroyed by fire. It was decided that the gothic style was most suited to the memory of the old building and would harmonise best with Westminster Abbey and the old Westminster Hall, which still remained. The architect, Charles Barry (1785–1860), was a confirmed classicist and produced a formal, symmetrical plan with an octagonal central hall. The job of converting this into Gothic was entrusted to Augustus Welby Pugin (1812–52), an eccentric and fervent Catholic convert who advocated the gothic style as a matter of religious principle and considered the Italian Renaissance style not only bad architecture but also immoral. Interestingly, his love for Gothic extended to an appreciation of its constructional integrity, and in his book *The True Principles of Pointed or Christian Architecture* (1841) he showed how the decorative aspects of Gothic grew out of its function. His single-minded realisation of the new Palace of Westminster with its romantic silhouette and intricate gothic decoration, coaxed from a specially selected team of Victorian craftsmen, remains one of the finest achievements of English architecture.

Support for the gothic style increased as the influential art critic John Ruskin (1819–1900) weighed in on its side. His book *The Seven Lamps of Architecture* (1849) suggested seven prerequisites for good architecture, among them truth to materials, the beauty of natural forms and the life given to anything which is hand-crafted rather than machine-made. He decided that early Gothic met these requirements, and enlarged on the theme

# the gothic revival

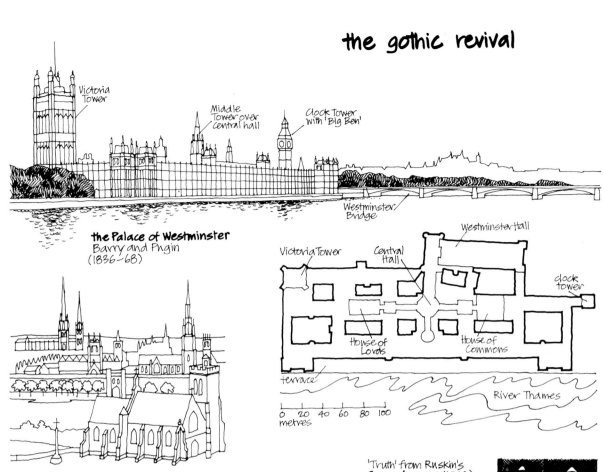

Victoria Tower

Middle Tower over Central hall

Clock Tower with 'Big Ben'

Westminster Bridge

**the Palace of Westminster**
Barry and Pugin
(1836–68)

Westminster Hall

Victoria Tower

Central Hall

clock tower

House of Lords

House of Commons

terrace

River Thames

0  20  40  60  80  100
metres

'Truth' from Ruskin's
**Seven Lamps** (1849)

gothic plate tracery at Beauvais, to Ruskin a perfect balance of design between the shapes of the voids and the simple lines of stone separating them

Pugin's historicism –
'a Catholic town in 1440 and the same town in 1840' from his book
**Contrasts** (1836)

structural ironwork

an illustration from Viollet's **Entretiens** of 1872

'the adoption of architectural forms adapted to our times'

**o'shea**
one of Pugin's craftsmen at work in Oxford

in *The Stones of Venice* (1851) in which he analysed Venetian gothic and attributed its success to the sense of achievement felt by craftsmen in producing it – an important early recognition of the alienating effects of industrial production.

Perhaps the most perceptive theorist of the gothic style was Eugène-Emanuel Viollet-le-Duc (1814-79), the French architect and writer. His interest in gothic was encouraged by enthusiastic friends, including fellow-authors Prosper Mérimée and Victor Hugo. He began as a scholarly restorer of medieval buildings, like the Sainte-Chapelle and Notre Dame, through which he decided that the achievements of the High Middle Ages were the result of laymen breaking free from the bonds imposed by the Church. He was the first to point out, in his *Dictionnaire raisonné de l'architecture française* (1845), that gothic architecture obeyed rational structural laws. Indeed, he went further and drew a parallel between the rib-vaults and buttresses of the Middle Ages and industrial iron constructions of his own day, which architects till then had largely ignored. In his book *Entretiens sur l'architecture* (1858) he tried to awaken architects' interest in the engineering achievements of the 19th century.

Iron construction had been proceeding for some decades, independently of conventional architects. Another class of designers had emerged, ready to fill the role demanded of them by the industrialists. These were the engineers – among them the most agile minds of their generation – who had seized the constructional opportunities offered by the industrial revolution. From ancient times till the 18th century, the technologies of manufacturing, building and travel had developed very little. But the early 19th century was a watershed. From then on, harnessing of energy, scientific application of knowledge and speed of communication allowed industrialism to develop fast.

The industrial revolution took place in England from about 1780 onwards. It reached France, Germany, Belgium and Switzerland in the early 19th century and northern Italy, Catalunya, Sweden, Russia and the USA later in the century. London, its financier, was the first world city to reach a population of one million. In the early 19th century, though ten per cent of Europe's people lived in towns, the figure for England and Scotland was 20 per cent. The basic activity was still agriculture, but now that the enclosures had put an end to the peasant economy, progressive land-owners could experiment with crops, animals and methods. The yields, supplemented by the increasing imports of food from abroad, had become high enough to support a large population. Industry was moving into the towns and, because new large-scale production required a large labour-force, towns were growing up around the industries. Cotton imports grew rapidly, the cloth industry prospered and the cotton-towns grew in size and wealth.

Besides the new technology of the cotton industry, like Thomas Hargreaves' 'spinning Jenny' and Richard Arkwright's 'water-frame', the main technical developments of the age were in the interdependent coal and iron industries. In a small way, coal had been used as a fuel for centuries, but the undreamed-of power it brought to the 19th century came from its use with iron machinery. The early steam-powered machines of Thomas Newcomen and James Watt were developed for mining, to pump out shafts and raise loads. As metallurgy improved, the use of steam-driven machines was rapidly extended to factories, to the fast-growing railways and to the newly developing machine-tool industry.

## THE ENGINEERS

In 1779, the iron-master Abraham Darby III built an arched bridge over the gorge of the River Severn at Coalbrookdale in Shropshire, then an important centre for coal and iron. This elegant structure still remains, a testimony to its maker's understanding of the material, and the first important example in the world of the structural use of cast-iron. During the 18th century, the building of canals and turnpike roads required bridge-building, with the developers all the time pushing their engineers to greater feats of daring. Techniques were still learned by trial and error as well as by analysis. There were often accidents during construction, but the completed projects themselves rarely failed. The engineer Thomas Telford (1757–1834) built several cast-iron bridges. The arched form was found to be the most appropriate to the particular properties of cast-iron, whose high carbon content and granular structure made it strong in compression but weak in tension. When a large-span suspension bridge was needed to carry the Holyhead road over the Menai Strait in Wales (1819), Telford developed chains of wrought-iron, whose directional cellstructure, like the grain in wood, was capable of resisting higher tensile forces.

The coming of the railways began a frenzy of speculative competition, with hastily formed companies placing ever-greater demands on their engineers. The High Level Bridge over the Tyne at Newcastle, designed by Robert Stephenson and begun in 1846, was probably the last great cast-iron bridge, a daring conception in which the bow-and-string principle of the main girders was evolved to lessen the tension in the cast-iron members. Stephenson's other great work was the Britannia railway bridge over the Menai Strait (1850). The total span of almost 300 metres seemed to preclude a suspension bridge like Telford's a mile farther north, despite a rock in mid-stream which would serve for a central pier. Further, an Admiralty requirement for uniform head-room on the underside precluded an arch. The solution was to provide two spans of box-girder construction, massive square tubes of wrought-iron through which the trains ran. This design, based on exhaustive tests and much calculation, was a major step forward in the science of structural mechanics.

Isambard Kingdom Brunel (1806–59) was forced through the competitive nature of the 'railway mania' into rivalry with Stephenson. Like many engineers, he doubted the wisdom of competition. 'The whole world', he wrote, 'is railway mad. I am really sick of hearing proposals made ... The dreadful scramble in which I am obliged to get through my business is by no means a good sample of the way in which work ought to be done.' Projects were pushed ahead too fast, and more construction workers were killed on the railways in England in the first half of the 19th century than in all the battles of the same period – which included the Napoleonic Wars. The engineers themselves saw the professional wisdom of collaboration. Stephenson and Brunel were friends, and exchanged technical knowledge.

Brunel's most famous work is perhaps the elegant wrought-iron suspension bridge over the Avon gorge at Clifton, Bristol, begun in 1829, but his finest is probably the Royal Albert Bridge over the Tamar at Saltash, completed in 1860. Brunel knew Stephenson's Britannia bridge well and the problem he had to solve was similar. The overall span was comparable with Stephenson's, but the central rock did not exist

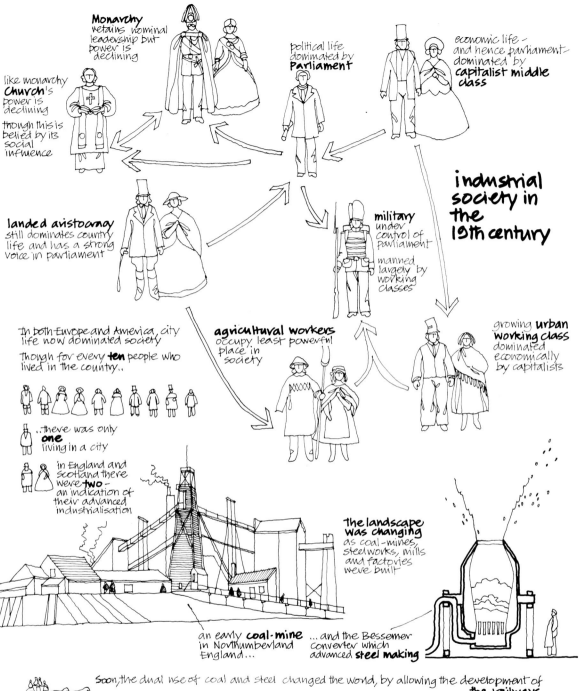

**Monarchy** retains nominal leadership but power is declining

political life dominated by **Parliament**

economic life - and hence parliament- dominated by **capitalist middle class**

like monarchy **Church**'s power is declining

though this is belied by its social influence

**industrial society in the 19th century**

**military** under control of parliament

manned largely by working classes

**landed aristocracy** still dominates country life and has a strong voice in parliament

In both Europe and America, city life now dominated society

Though for every **ten** people who lived in the country..

**agricultural workers** occupy least powerful place in society

growing **urban working class** dominated economically by capitalists

..there was only **one** living in a city

in England and Scotland there were **two** - an indication of their advanced industrialisation

**the landscape was changing** as coal-mines, steelworks, mills and factories were built

an early **coal-mine** in Northumberland England...

...and the Bessemer converter which advanced **steel making**

Soon, the dual use of coal and steel changed the world, by allowing the development of **the railways**

in 1760, five hours in a stage coach could cover **25 miles**

in 1820, five hours' travel on macadamised roads could cover **40 miles**

but in 1860 five hours in a train could cover **170 miles**

Railways created a social revolution, bringing cheap travel even to the poor. More significantly, they allowed the development of trade and capitalism

# early iron engineering 1

Abraham Darby's cast **iron bridge** over the Severn at Coalbrookdale (1779) was the first in the world

Robert Stephenson's masterpiece was the tubular bridge over the Menai straits in Wales, the **Britannia railway bridge** (1850)

31 metres

deck

three arches
post
masonry abutment

masonry pier

central pier on island

wrought iron tube

road

railway

egg-crate construction for stiffness

ribs for stiffness

Stephenson's **High Level bridge** over the Tyne at Newcastle (1846) the last great cast-iron bridge

the tube of the Britannia bridge, through which the railway ran

Brunel's **Royal Albert Bridge** over the Tamar (1860)

wrought iron tubular arch

the concept was similar to the Britannia bridge but the structural method very different

central pier constructed in caisson

**Isambard Brunel** (1806-59)

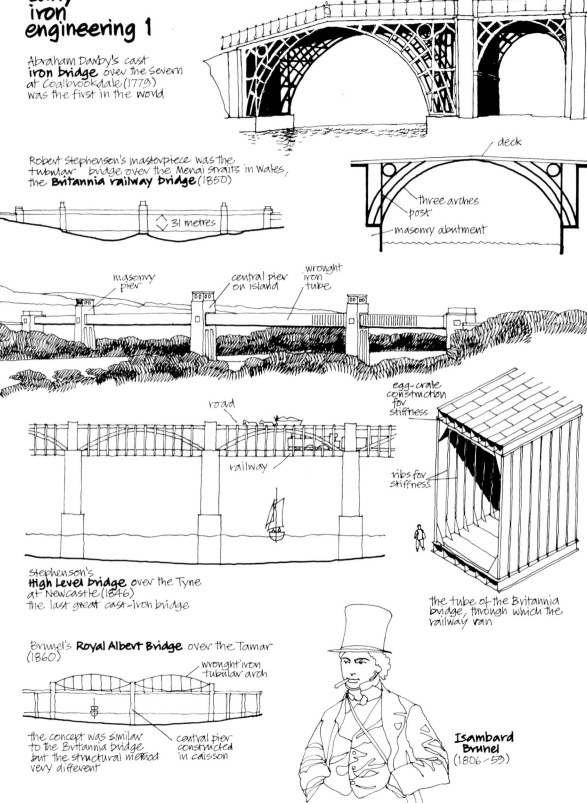

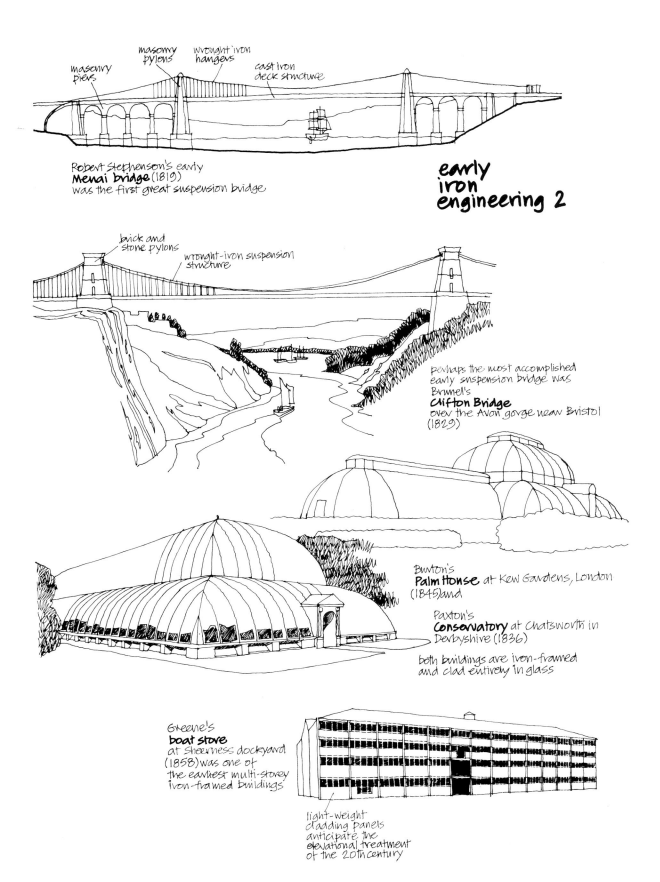

masonry piers

masonry pylons

wrought iron hangers

cast iron deck structure

Robert Stephenson's early
**Menai bridge** (1819)
was the first great suspension bridge

brick and stone pylons

wrought-iron suspension structure

perhaps the most accomplished early suspension bridge was Brunell's
**Clifton Bridge**
over the Avon gorge near Bristol (1829)

Burton's
**Palm House** at Kew Gardens, London (1845) and

Paxton's
**Conservatory** at Chatsworth in Derbyshire (1836)

both buildings are iron-framed and clad entirely in glass

Greene's
**boat store**
at Sheerness dockyard (1858) was one of the earliest multi-storey iron-framed buildings

light-weight cladding panels anticipate the elevational treatment of the 20th century

and Brunel was obliged to build a central pier in mid-stream, inside a pressurised iron caisson which was an engineering feat in itself. As before, a flat underside was required: Brunel's solution was two spans of arched wrought-iron tubes carrying the bridge deck slung below.

Iron was coming into use for buildings as well as bridges, though seldom for conventional building-types and never, as yet, by conventional architects. The beautiful conservatory at Chatsworth, Derbyshire (1836), was designed by Joseph Paxton, a garden superintendent. Some 90 metres long, framed in curving bars of cast-iron and wood and clad entirely in glass, this building had numerous progeny including the equally elegant Palm House at Kew Gardens, designed by Decimus Burton – one-time assistant to Paxton – and Richard Turner in 1845. The boat-store at the naval dockyard, Sheerness, on the Isle of Sheppey, by Col. Godfrey Greene (1858), was a large, simple four-storey building on a rectangular grid of cast-iron columns with wrought-iron beams, and Oriel Chambers in Liverpool (1864) by Peter Ellis was a fine five-storey office building, completely framed in cast-iron, which used this new material in a rich and ornate way.

The railway stations of the period express perfectly the division which still existed between conventional architecture and the adventure of iron engineering. London's King's Cross (1850), one of the earliest of the great termini, was designed by an engineer, Lewis Cubitt. Apart from a small Italianate clock-tower stuck on for architectural effect, its plain brick entrance façade is unpretentious, and in keeping with the double-span arched train-shed behind. But at Paddington (1852) the front of Brunel's amazing train-shed, with its three wrought-iron framed spans intersected by cross-vaults, was disguised with a pretentious hotel building designed by the architect Philip Charles Hardwick. At St Pancras Station (1865) the juxtaposition of engineering and architecture resulted in one of the century's most bizarre masterpieces. At the rear was the spectacular train shed by the railway engineer William Henry Barlow, a single curving span of 75 metres, 30 metres in height. At the front were the neo-gothic turrets and pinnacles of George Gilbert Scott's Midland Hotel. The whole ensemble, with its logical handling of movement and its great symbolism – such as the open end of the great train shed leading passengers on their way – was a monument to the adventure of train travel – until its 'refurbishment' in the 21st century contorted its circulation patterns and cluttered its powerful architectural forms.

The pompous façades of the stations were designed with an ulterior purpose: the Inigo Jones style of Bath Queen Square, the Tudor of Bristol Temple Meads, and the baroque of Newmarket Station were to make the railways respectable to a suspicious public. Approaching Euston through Philip Hardwick Senior's fine Doric *propylaeum* (1840) redolent with feelings of history and culture, the traveller might feel himself bound on some epic pilgrimage.

This unashamed use of architectural style for the associations it evoked became more explicit during the 19th century. Successful businessmen with a sense of tradition could imagine themselves successors to the Medici when they entered Charles Barry's Traveller's Club (1829) or Reform Club (1837), both designed like Florentine *palazzi* – with the central *cortile* translated into a roofed-in saloon to suit the London climate.

The last great manifestation of neoclassical in England was St George's Hall in Liverpool (1840–54) by Harvey Lonsdale Elmes. A massive and monumental building

the Italianate tower is the only architectural frivolity in a serious, engineer's design

Cubitt's
**Kings Cross station**
(1850)

the two arches on the front elevation reflect the double train-shed behind

# London's railway stations

Brunel's
**Paddington station**
(1852)

the cross-vault intersecting the main span marks the position of the station-master's office

train shed

hotel

at **St Pancras station** (1865)
Barlow's train shed is concealed by Scott's Midland Hotel

E U S T O N

Hardwick's entrance to
**Euston station** (1840)
was the grandest of all

on an island site, combining the unlikely functions of concert hall and assize courts, with its clear articulation of the separate elements within the overall mass, it is firmly in the tradition of Gilly. Neoclassical had overtones of Athenian democracy, and was an accepted style for law-courts. It appears again in the gigantic Palais de Justice, Brussels (1866), with its high central tower. By the Belgian architect Joseph Poelaert, the design here is more eclectic, heavier and more overbearingly powerful than in Elmes's more restrained classical design. Equally powerful and monumental is the United States Capitol in Washington, where the central feature, with its high rotunda and dome, were added in 1851. The architect of this prestigious remodelling of the original Palladian building was Thomas Ustick Walter, whose previous work included a scholarly Corinthian-style design for Girard College in Philadelphia (1833).

In America, neoclassical gained greater acceptance than in England. Its use for country mansions, particularly in the south, was a natural progression from Palladianism, and the typical plantation house, with hexastyle Doric portico, dates from this period. So does a development in timber-framing which was to be a major American contribution to building techniques for smaller houses – the perfection of the 'balloon-frame' system – used for timber buildings in Europe since the 16th century but now improved to an extent which allowed it to remain in common use until the present day. Instead of the independent structural frame of earlier centuries, the frame was made an integral part of each wall, floor or roof element, turned into a diaphragm by timber sheathing. Greater economy of timber brought cheap, decently-built houses to all levels of the social scale.

In fact, 19th-century society, despite growing prosperity and despite revolution, was still very unequal. The black slaves in America, European peasants and industrial workers everywhere formed a submerged majority whose rights were ignored. Industrial capitalism expanded, supported by the theories of liberal economists such as Adam Smith, whose *Wealth of Nations* (1776) promoted the free market, and David Ricardo, author of *Principles of Political Economy* (1817), who advocated free trade. Meanwhile, the conditions of the poor worsened. The essays of Revd Thomas Malthus rejected progressive ideas about social reform, arguing that a balanced society would be achieved naturally, through population growth and the resulting mass starvation.

With industrial capitalism, the old personal relationship between employer and employee had broken down. The rewards due to a worker now depended not on ability but on the uncertainty of an anonymous market. Entrepreneurs grew rich at the expense of the workers, for whom long hours, poor conditions and low pay had become endemic. Their old craft skills, from which they might have derived satisfaction, were required less and less, and their families suffered from the social uprooting which industrialisation had brought.

## UTOPIAN IDEALS

Progressive thinkers began to be more critical. John Stuart Mill recognised the value of individual liberty, the need for greater democracy and for social reform. The French philosopher Saint-Simon, a Christian and socialist, believed in the abolition of private property, while his compatriots Fourier and Proudhon, in the tradition of the *philosophes*, believed that the ideal future lay in the development of man's reason,

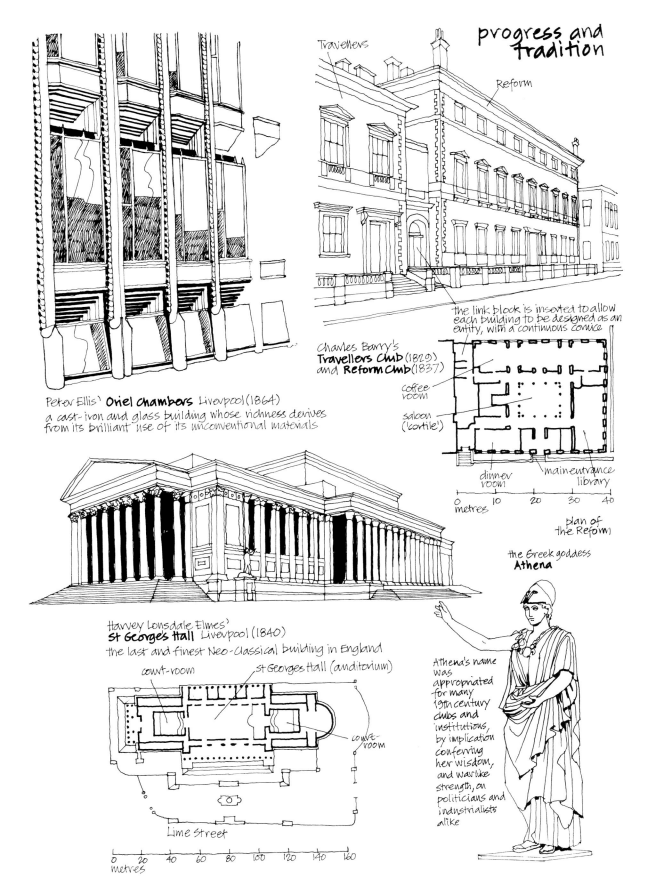

Travellers

Reform

the link block is inserted to allow each building to be designed as an entity, with a continuous cornice

Peter Ellis' **Oriel Chambers** Liverpool (1864)
a cast-iron and glass building whose richness derives from its brilliant use of its unconventional materials

Charles Barry's
**Travellers Club** (1829)
and **Reform Club** (1837)

coffee room

saloon ('cortile')

dinner room

main-entrance library

0    10    20    30    40
metres

plan of
the Reform

the Greek goddess
**Athena**

Harvey Lonsdale Elmes'
**St George's Hall** Liverpool (1840)
the last and finest Neo-classical building in England

court-room

St George's Hall (auditorium)

court-room

Lime Street

0    20    40    60    80    100    120    140    160
metres

Athena's name was appropriated for many 19th century clubs and institutions, by implication conferring her wisdom, and warlike strength, on politicians and industrialists alike

# north American timber construction

the dignity of the timber Doric portico at the **Orton Plantation House** Wilmington N.C. (1734 and later)...

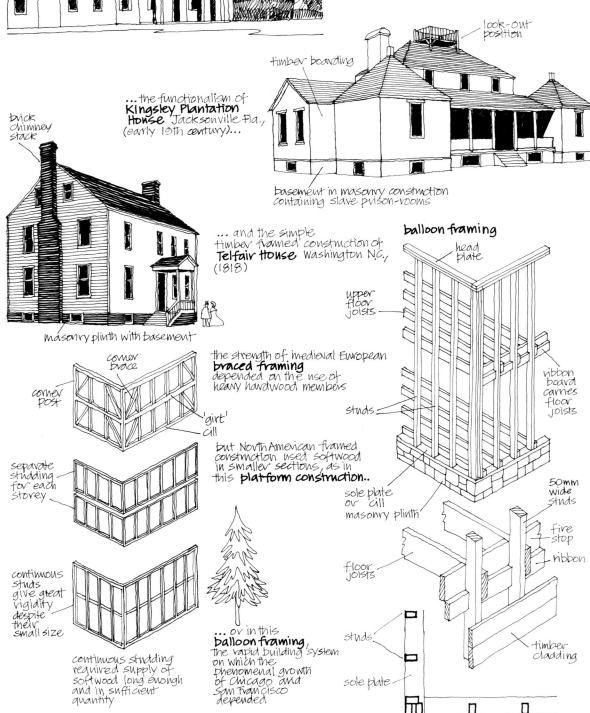

look-out position

timber boarding

...the functionalism of **Kingsley Plantation House** Jacksonville Fla., (early 19th century)...

basement in masonry construction containing slave prison-rooms

brick chimney stack

masonry plinth with basement

...and the simple timber framed construction of **Telfair House** Washington N.C., (1818)

corner brace

corner post

'girt'

cill

the strength of medieval European **braced framing** depended on the use of heavy hardwood members

separate studding for each storey

but North American framed construction used softwood in smaller sections, as in this **platform construction**..

continuous studs give great rigidity despite their small size

... or in this **balloon framing**, the rapid building system on which the phenomenal growth of Chicago and San Francisco depended

continuous studding required supply of softwood long enough and in sufficient quantity

## balloon framing

head plate

upper floor joists

studs

ribbon board carries floor joists

sole plate or cill

masonry plinth

50mm wide studs

fire stop

ribbon

floor joists

studs

sole plate

timber cladding

from which would come a moral, healthy and truly anarchical society. Thinkers like Condorcet, Godwin and Mary Wollstonecraft believed that society could be bettered, and social critics began to address the problem of poverty and its appalling effects on human life. In England, where industrialisation was most developed and its effects most acute, various Acts of Parliament in the early 19th century eliminated some of the exploitation of women and children. And the Welsh industrialist Robert Owen (1771–1858) devised practical schemes to avoid it.

Owen, with one fortune made in the textile industry and another through marrying a millionaire's daughter, took over a factory for 2000 people in 1799 at New Lanark near Glasgow, which he developed into a world-famous model community. In a scheme which today may appear paternalistic, even autocratic, but which then was a big advance on the brutalities of the market system, he built blocks of flats, a school, a shop selling goods to his workers at advantageous prices and community buildings which included an Institution for the Formation of Character. He later sank his entire fortune into a 20,000-acre farming community in Indiana, USA.

Owen's method was essentially to work within the system to alleviate the worst of its effects. He looked hopefully to a millennium in which Unity and Justice would prevail. There were others, however, who saw that the situation was too urgent to wait for gradual improvement. Thousands of workers and their families in the fast growing industrial cities still lived in the most terrible conditions.

> Here one is in an almost undisguised working-men's quarter, for even the shops and beerhouses hardly take the trouble to exhibit a trifling degree of cleanliness. But all this is nothing in comparison with the courts and lanes which lie behind, to which access can be gained only through covered passages in which no two human beings can pass at the same time. Of the irregular cramming together of dwellings in ways which defy all rational plan ... it is impossible to convey an idea ... He who turns in thither gets into a filth and disgusting grime, the equal of which is not to be found. The only entrance to most of the houses is by means of narrow dirty stairs and over heaps of refuse and filth.

This description by Friedrich Engels (1820–95), writing in 1844 of *The Condition of the Working Class in England*, is of the Old Town in Manchester, the pre-industrial centre of the city hurriedly adapted with makeshift hovels and shacks to house the sudden influx of population. The nearby New Town, built by local builders to exploit the demand for living space, was scarcely better. Engels found a greater regularity of layout, but the houses were no more spacious, usually built back to back, lit and ventilated only from internal light-wells and with walls only half-a-brick – that is $4\frac{1}{2}$ inches – in thickness. Homes, tanneries and gas-works were crowded together on the banks of stagnant canals which received factory waste and untreated sewage. Drainage and clean water supplies were non-existent, and disease was endemic.

Engels concluded that the desperate class-struggle which he saw around him was the result of the economic structure of the modern world. In 1844 he established a life-long friendship with Karl Marx (1818–83) who, with Engels' close collaboration, became the first and greatest thinker to describe the multiple causes and effects of industrial society by means of a coherent methodology – which included an analysis of its past and a vision of the future.

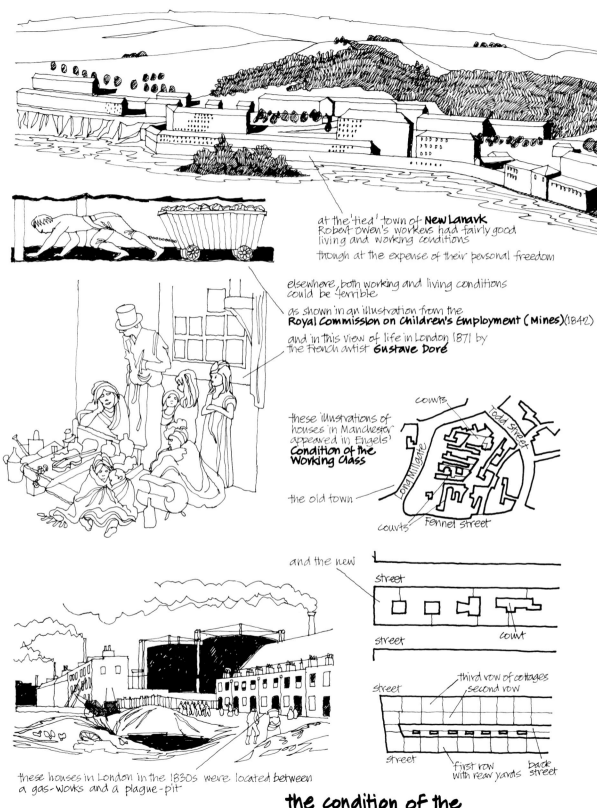

at the 'tied' town of **New Lanark**
Robert Owen's workers had fairly good
living and working conditions

though at the expense of their personal freedom

elsewhere, both working and living conditions
could be terrible

as shown in an illustration from the
**Royal Commission on Children's Employment (Mines)** (1842)

and in this view of life in London 1871 by
the French artist **Gustave Doré**

these illustrations of
houses in Manchester
appeared in Engels'
**Condition of the
Working Class**

courts

Todd Street

Long Millgate

the old town

courts    Fennel street

and the new

street

street

court

street    third row of cottages
second row

street

first row    back
with rear yards    street

these houses in London in the 1830s were located between
a gas-works and a plague-pit

# the condition of the
# working class

Through his writings, such as *Capital* (1867), Marx formulated an approach to the problems of the industrial age. Beginning with a dream of what *could* be – of all men working in a creative collaboration with the world around – he showed how far the capitalist system fell short of this. Full of inherent tensions, capitalism would eventually be destroyed by worsening crises of its own making, but positive steps could be taken towards replacing it with a classless society by taking power from the bourgeoisie, through a workers' revolution.

During the early 19th century, in fact, the working-class movement was gathering strength. In 1848, Europe was once more in a state of revolution – the first in which the workers as a class played a significant part. It began in France where it challenged not only the king but also bourgeois liberalism, then spread to Italy, where it was bound up with the struggle for independence from Austria, and to Germany, Switzerland, Holland, Belgium and Scandinavia. The struggle was short and violent and ended almost everywhere with the re-establishment of the old order.

But Europe changed as a result. The ruling classes in general were less assured, more prepared to adapt and concede. The bourgeoisie, though now stronger economically than ever before, were less confident in the liberal idea of unlimited progress for its own sake. Henceforward the development of capitalism was more pragmatic and realistic. And the workers, though defeated, had at least entered the political arena and gained greatly in strength and confidence.

At the time of the French Revolution in 1789, artists had supported the cause of freedom and liberty, the ideology of the liberal bourgeoisie. Now it was apparent what revolution had really achieved: not freedom for humanity as a whole but the fragmentation of society and the alienation of the individual. When Napoleon declared himself Emperor, Beethoven famously ripped up the title-page of the *Eroica*, with its dedication to his former hero. Critics of society began to sympathise openly with progressive aims: Byron with the Greeks under the Ottoman Turks, Stendhal with the Italians under French occupation, and Pushkin with the dissident Decembrists in Russia. The poetry of Baudelaire was a protest against bourgeois *mores* and Courbet's painting showed his strong sympathy for the common people.

Architects and engineers had no such freedom of expression. The nature of their profession and the way it had developed placed them firmly with the ruling classes, whose main means of communication they now were. The great architectural and engineering works which were to follow 1848 – uniquely impressive, popularly appealing – could be used to give a false air of unity to a divided society.

# 10 VICTORIAN VALUES
*1850–1914*

After the 1848 revolution Napoleon Bonaparte's nephew became president of France. Within four years he had engineered a coup d'etat and proclaimed himself Napoleon III. France had entered its Second Empire. The emperor was shrewd and cynical, whose methods in some ways anticipated the dictators of the 20th century. He was careful to appease both the influential industrialists and the troublesome workers, by handing out attractive concessions. At the same time he was stern and repressive with minorities, the schools and universities, and the press. Under him, France entered its real industrial revolution. Banks were founded, factories and railways built and major public works begun. An ornate neo-renaissance addition to the Louvre by Louis Visconti and Hector Lefuel (1852) established a new *Deuxième Empire* style.

One of the greatest works of the Second Empire was the reconstruction by Baron Haussmann of the centre of Paris, which turned the old medieval city into a grand baroque gesture. New landmarks, like the Bois de Boulogne, the Place de l'Étoile and the Opéra were linked by a network of grand boulevards, beneath which ran new water mains and sewers. The new streets were uniformly wide and lined with blocks of bourgeois apartments, similar in conception to those of the Place Royale and Rue de Rivoli, but of standard height and formulaic elevational treatment which made them rather less elegant, if more economical. Typically they had four or five storeys of flats above a ground floor of shops and were two rooms deep, the outer and grander ones facing the street and the inner ones a narrow light-well disdainfully known as a *cour anglaise*.

Architectural effect was not Haussmann's only consideration. After the revolutionary street-fighting of 1848, security was also an aim. Between 1853 and 1869 small buildings around the palaces and barracks which might offer cover to attackers were swept away. The opportunity was taken to destroy other areas of potential opposition. The Boulevard St Michel cut a swathe through the university quarter, then and since a source of radical discontent. The radiating street-pattern, inspired by Versailles, was given a new meaning. Along the boulevards, troops could be deployed in all directions, and from a single *rond-point* at the centre, a small detachment of artillery could control an entire district.

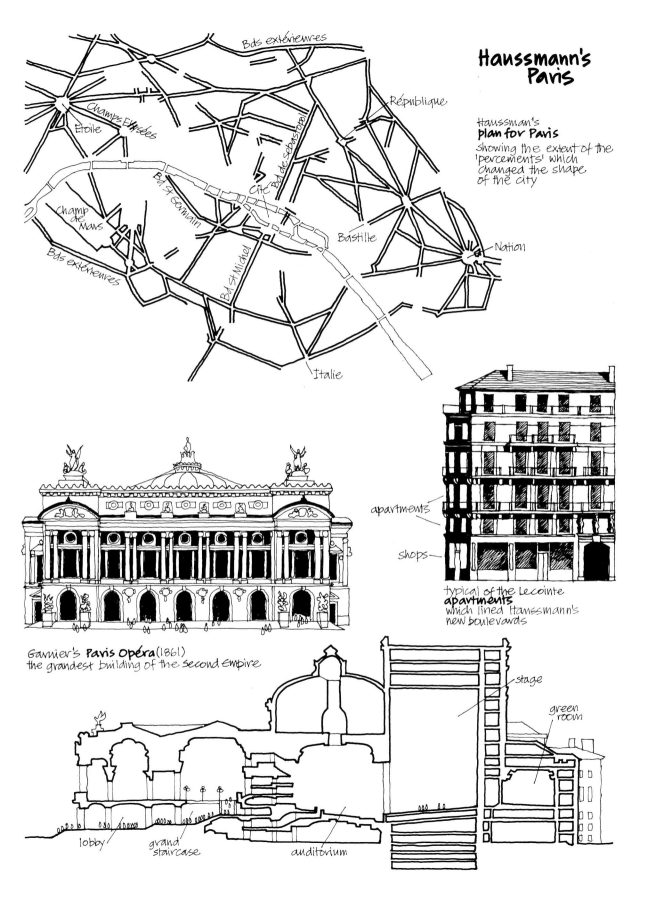

# Haussmann's Paris

Bds extérieures

République

Champs Elysées

Etoile

Bd de sébastopol

Cité

Bd St Germain

Champ de Mars

Bd St Michel

Bastille

Nation

Bds extérieures

Italie

Haussman's **plan for Paris** showing the extent of the 'percements' which changed the shape of the city

apartments

shops

typical of the Lecointe **apartments** which lined Haussmann's new boulevards

Garnier's **Paris Opéra** (1861) the grandest building of the second Empire

stage

green room

lobby

grand staircase

auditorium

Paris was not the only city fearful of an enemy within. In 1858, the walls of Vienna were demolished at the command of the emperor Franz Josef and replaced with the *Ringstrasse*, a broad avenue designed by Ludwig Forster, to form a defensive belt round the old city centre. It separated the Hofburg Palace, in the centre, from working class districts further out. Like the Paris boulevards, it allowed the quick distribution of troops and provided useful lines of fire.

The Ringstrasse was lined with grand public buildings, such as the Vienna State Opera, begun in 1861 by the architects August Sicard von Sicardsburg and Eduard van der Nüll, in a florid renaissance style. Even grander was the Paris Opéra by Charles Garnier, also 1861, which epitomises the bourgeois opulence of the Second Empire. Here the rich neo-renaissance style of the New Louvre was used to invest the fashionable activity of theatre-going with a ceremonial grandeur. The stage area is enormous, with a high tower suitable for flying the numerous scene changes required by *Les Huguenots* or *Guillaume Tell*. The auditorium is large and decorative, but comparable in size and even richer is the entrance hall, with painted ceilings, gilded statuary, ornate chandeliers and grand *escalier d'honneur*, a place for the fashionable opera-goer to see and be seen in a performance to rival that on the stage.

The Opéra was a key building in the development of the Second Empire style. This was codified by the École des Beaux Arts in Paris, brought under state control in 1864 by Napoleon III, which began to propagate a dry, academic approach to design. Certain selected styles of the past – imperial Roman, Renaissance, Baroque and French late Gothic and early Renaissance – provided a set vocabulary for successful architects to use. Through its students, Beaux Arts influences spread over the world. Canada with its French traditions, and the USA with its much-travelled students, were particularly receptive. The French Gothic of the Ottawa Parliament buildings (1861) by Thomas Fuller, and the Italian renaissance-style Vanderbilt Mansion in New York (1879) and the French renaissance-style Biltmore House at Ashville, N.C. (1890), both by Richard Morris Hunt, are good examples.

In Britain the dominant style of the second half of the 19th century was still neo-Gothic. Under the influence of the powerful 'Oxford Movement' of conservative and traditionalist theologians, advocates of the gothic style had become more confident. The church of All Saints, Margaret Street, London (1849), was built by William Butterfield as a major centre of High Anglicanism. Its polychromatic brick and faience work was a re-creation of the richness of the medieval style in modern terms, and the ingenuity of its planning, on a congested urban site, is worthy of Wren. In the same tradition were the simple yet richly textured churches of George Edmund Street, notably those of St James the Less, Westminster (1858) and of St Philip and St James, Oxford (1860). The Victorian gothic high noon continued with the spectacular Albert Memorial in London (1863) by George Gilbert Scott, and the fine Manchester Town Hall (1868) by Alfred Waterhouse. It perhaps culminated in 1871 with Street's complex and romantic design for the Law Courts in the Strand, London, though as a style it continued well beyond the end of the century. Waterhouse's gothic Prudential Assurance building in London was not finished till 1906, at which time Giles Gilbert Scott's gothic Liverpool Cathedral was scarcely begun.

Gothic had also become an appropriate style for the country-houses of the wealthy, especially those of a romantic or eccentric disposition. Scott's Waverley novels, the first

# neo-gothic

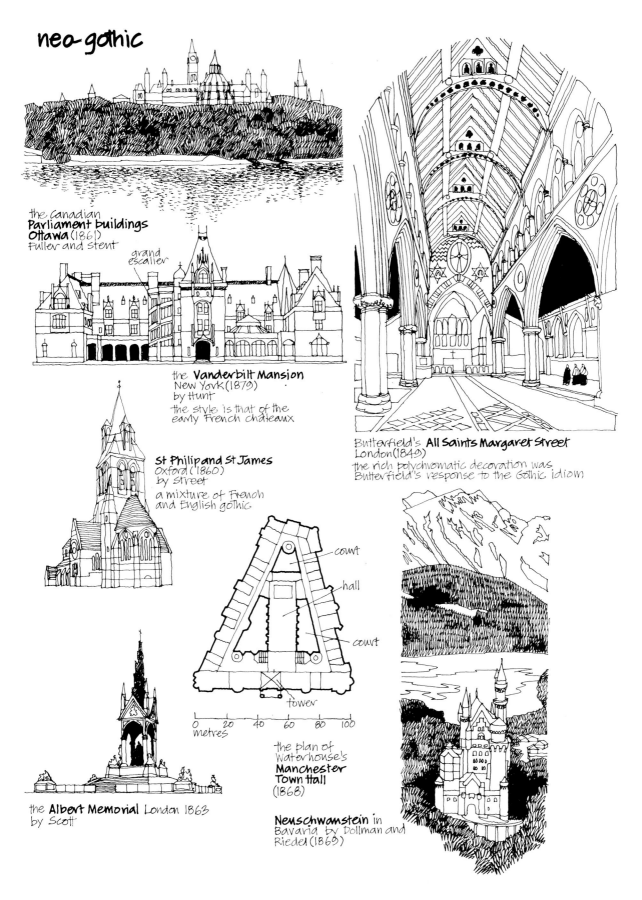

the Canadian
**Parliament buildings
Ottawa** (1861)
*Fuller and Stent*

grand
escalier

the **Vanderbilt Mansion**
New York (1879)
by Hunt
the style is that of the
early French châteaux

**St Philip and St James**
Oxford ('1860)
by street

a mixture of French
and English gothic

Butterfield's **All Saints Margaret Street**
London (1849)
the rich polychromatic decoration was
Butterfield's response to the Gothic idiom

court

hall

court

tower

0   20   40   60   80   100
metres

the plan of
Waterhouse's
**Manchester
Town Hall**
(1868)

the **Albert Memorial** London 1863
by Scott

**Neuschwanstein** in
Bavaria by Dollman and
Riedel (1869)

one published in 1816, and Tennyson's *Idylls of the King* (1856), continued to arouse the interest of poets, painters and composers in the Middle Ages. Simultaneously, Wagner was celebrating medievalism through *Tristan und Isolde* and *Die Meistersinger*. Architects responded, and produced many neo-gothic sham castles. In 1857 Napoleon III commissioned Viollet-le-Duc to restore the Château de Pierrefonds, which was in ruins. Though both scholarly and spectacular, the result was more of an imaginative rebuild than a restoration. Cardiff Castle in south Wales, and the nearby Castell Coch, had also been real enough, but after their reconstruction (1868 and 1875) by William Burges for the Marquess of Bute they became fine examples of medieval scholarship combined with happy decorative invention. Romantic castles began to appear on the hillsides and forests of southern Germany and Austria. Most romantic of all was the mountaintop *Schloss* of Neuschwanstein (1869) built by Georg von Dollman and Eduard Riedel for Wagner's friend and patron Ludwig II of Bavaria. The whole ensemble, site and building, projects an image of Ludwig as a fairy-tale hero.

Romantic images were not confined to rich, eccentric princes. As city centres grew more foul, the middle classes, assisted by the expansion of suburban railways, moved out of town to newly-built, speculative suburbs. In England, for example, the aim was to escape the filth and noise of the city by re-creating some half-remembered image of the country mansion – or at least the country cottage. So, in emulation of Nash's Park Village, each house was if possible built 'detached', standing within its own plot, even when the plot was so narrow that the houses almost touched. Closer to the centre, the houses built for petty bourgeois shopkeepers and clerks might for economy be in continuous terraces, but even here the rural image was maintained by the provision of vestigial front gardens. The architectural style was often a debased and highly eclectic Gothic, with high-pitched roofs, frequent dormers and gables, stone or polychrome brick walls with stuccoed or artificial stone window and door surrounds, adorned with factory-produced, neo-Ruskinian foliage. Fine examples of the type include the detached houses of north Oxford, along the Banbury and Woodstock Roads.

But if most architects and builders were still concerned with creating an image of the past, there were now a few others, gradually increasing in number, with a more progressive attitude. The 'railway mania' of the earlier part of the century had left a legacy of structural knowledge which, under the influence of Viollet-le-Duc and others, architects began to use. The pioneer was Henri Labrouste, who built the Bibiliothèque Ste Geneviève in Paris, as early as 1832. Here a plain, rectangular renaissance-style façade contained an elegant two storey library space, framed with slender cast-iron columns, carrying plaster ceilings reinforced with metal mesh. The Parisian churches of Ste Clotilde (1846) by the German architect Franz Christian Gau, and St Eugène (1854) by Louis-Auguste Boileau, made considerable use of ironwork, the former in the roof, the latter as a complete structural frame. The Halles Centrales in Paris (1853) by Victor Baltard, the city's main wholesale market till their demolition in 1971, were a vast complex of iron-framed pavilions separated by circulation routes and roofed almost completely in glass. Of the major Paris railway stations with iron roofs the Gare de l'Est (1847) by François Duquesney and the Gare du Nord (1862) by Jacques Ignace Hittorf, another German-born architect, are the earliest and finest.

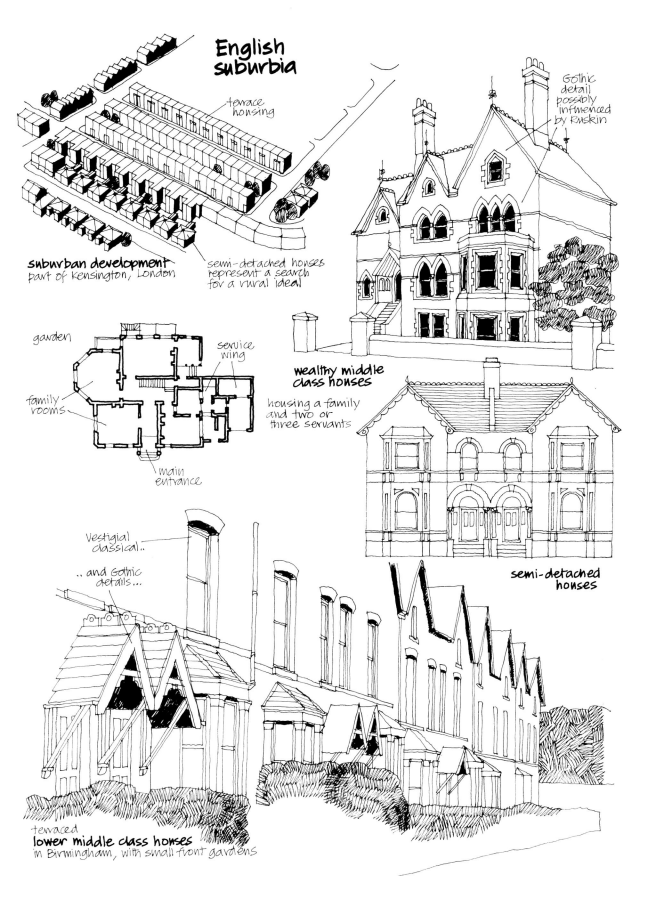

# English suburbia

terrace housing

**suburban development**
part of Kensington, London

semi-detached houses represent a search for a rural ideal

Gothic detail possibly influenced by Ruskin

garden

service wing

family rooms

main entrance

**wealthy middle class houses**

housing a family and two or three servants

**semi-detached houses**

Vestigial classical..

.. and Gothic details...

terraced
**lower middle class houses**
in Birmingham, with small front gardens

**iron and glass**

**Les Halles Centrales**
Paris (1853)
by Victor Baltard

a completely iron-and-glass
structure, part of Haussmann's
reconstruction of the city

the main portico
of the
**Gare du Nord**
Paris (1862)
by J. I. Hitorff
Ionic decoration
on an iron structure

**Galleria Vittorio Emanuele II**
Milan (1829)
by G. Mengoni

a religious form in a
new, secular context

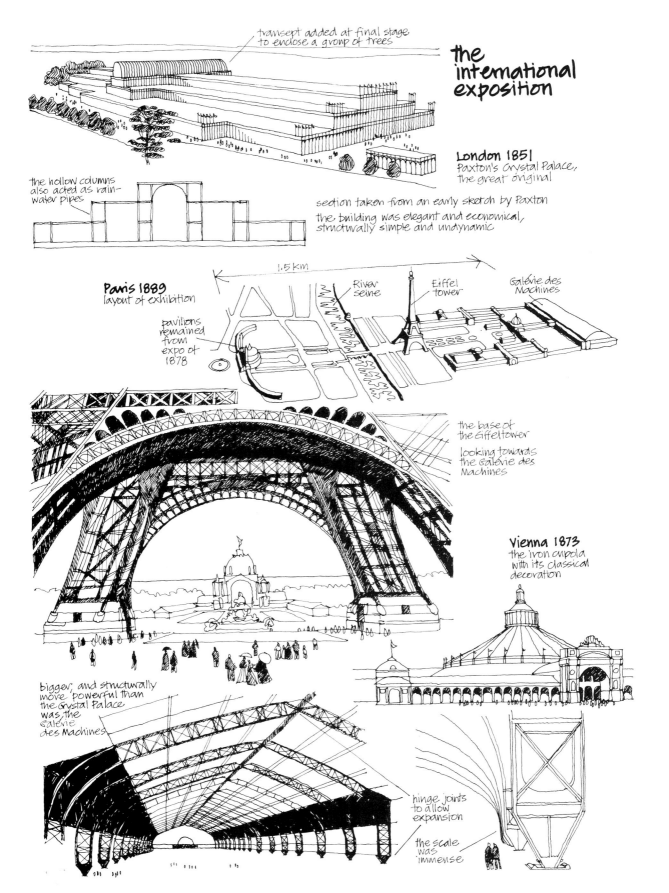

transept added at final stage to enclose a group of trees

# the international exposition

**London 1851**
Paxton's Crystal Palace, the great original

the hollow columns also acted as rain-water pipes

section taken from an early sketch by Paxton

the building was elegant and economical, structurally simple and undynamic

**Paris 1889**
layout of exhibition

1.5 km

River Seine

Eiffel tower

Galérie des Machines

pavilions remained from expo of 1878

the base of the Eiffel tower

looking towards the Galérie des Machines

**Vienna 1873**
the iron cupola with its classical decoration

bigger, and structurally more powerful than the Crystal Palace, was the Galérie des Machines

hinge joints to allow expansion

the scale was immense

As industry expanded, it needed more and more outlets for its manufactured goods. During the 19th century, Europe's exports increased rapidly; England's, worth £100 million in 1854, had increased to £250 million by 1872. Domestic sales too, were strenuously promoted. Cities changed from being periodic outlets for market produce to permanent shopping centres selling manufactured goods. Regent Street and the Rue de Rivoli were elegantly colonnaded to protect their fashionable clients from the weather, and pedestrian shopping streets, completely roofed over with iron-and-glass-vaulted arcades, became quite common in the larger cities. The earliest major example was the Galerie d'Orléans, Paris (1829), by Pierre Fontaine. The finest remaining ones are the Galleria Umberto I in Naples (1887) designed by Emanuele Rocco in emulation of the splendid Galleria Vittorio Emanuele II in Milan (1829) by Giuseppe Mengoni. Both take the form of a pair of paved pedestrian streets, intersecting at right angles, lined with dignified shopping façades and continuously roofed with iron-and-glass barrel-vaulting. The cruciform plans and the domed crossings make them superficially like cathedrals, but the mood is very different: humane, matter-of-fact and unmysterious in a way appropriate to a secular rather than religious meeting-place.

## WORKSHOP OF THE WORLD

Capitalism needed to expand continuously to allow increased consumption to stimulate production. Through international expositions, nations could display their art and technology to the world. The first was the Great Exhibition in London in 1851. Many cities followed suit: Paris in 1855 and 1867, Vienna in 1873, and Paris again in 1878, 1889 and 1900. Because a confident display might invoke the confidence of the customer, expenditure was lavish, and the architects and engineers responded with a vigour and assurance which resulted in some of the finest buildings of the century.

Joseph Paxton's Crystal Palace, built in Hyde Park, London, in 1851, was the culmination of cast-iron building technology. Designed in haste and erected in the remarkably short time of nine months, it showed a mastery of the iron techniques which Paxton had tried out at Chatsworth. It was famous not only for its elegance but also for its great size, 125 by 560 metres on plan and 22 metres high, tall enough to enclose an existing group of mature elm trees. Perhaps more significantly, it was pre-fabricated in sections off the site, a factor which contributed to it short construction time, but which demanded scrupulous pre-planning, remarkable for the period.

With the common use of wrought-iron, and then steel, exhibition structures became even more ambitious. Vienna 1873 saw the building of a gigantic iron cupola, over 100 metres in diameter, and Paris 1889 gave the world two engineering masterpieces. One was the Galerie des Machines, by Victor Contamin, a vast hall 430 by 120 metres on plan and 45 metres high at the apex, clad entirely in glass. Its innovative structure was based on the 'portal frame', that is, on columns and beams joined rigidly together. This caused the transfer of stresses from beam to column, and permitted wider spans for a beam of given depth. The structure was a succession of paired L-shaped frames placed together to form arches and braced laterally by steel framing, in what was then the widest span ever built. The same exhibition also presented the world's highest structure, Gustave Eiffel's famous tower, an elegant lattice of steelwork curving parabolically

# national grandeur and civic pride

**the Reichstag building**
Berlin (1884)
by P. Wallot

**the Victor Emmanuel monument**
Rome (1885)
by G. Sacconi

**the Palais de Justice**
Brussels (1866)
by J. Poelaert

**copenhagen city Hall**
(1893)
by M. Nyrop

**the Rijksmuseum** Amsterdam
(1877) by P. Cuijpers

Edvard Erichsen's statue of Hans Andersen's
**Little Mermaid** is also a symbol of
Copenhagen

from a wide, four-footed base to a height of some 300 metres. Both were conceived in terms of steel, higher in tensile strength than either cast- or wrought-iron. Considering that steel-making was relatively new, it says much for both Contamin and Eiffel that they mastered the material in such a confident way, in the face of criticism from rival engineers who predicted that their buildings would not stay up.

The architectural form of a great medieval church came only partly from the need to enclose a large space. It also expressed society's social and religious aspirations. Its relevance to the actual needs of society was probably less than is commonly supposed, but it had much value as a visual and social focus to the town, and also as a symbol, invoking concepts about God, the Church and the world. In a great building like Durham or Vézelay, function and symbolism were combined in a perfect unity of form and content. But the structural masterpieces of the industrial age, though dazzling in terms of form alone, had no such content. They performed no central social function – the Eiffel Tower had no real function at all – and were not symbols of any central philosophy of their time, except in evoking generalised feelings of pride in the achievements of the age. Their underlying purpose, like most major projects under capitalism, was the stimulation of capitalism itself and the promotion of economic growth. This is an architectural paradox of the modern world, that is, the greatest resources and the highest technology being used on buildings of least social value.

Perhaps the greatest and most prophetic critic of the effect of capitalism on architecture was the English poet, designer and revolutionary, William Morris (1834–96). Even in an age of giants, Morris stands out for the variety of his talents and the vigour of his approach to life. He learned architecture with Street, he painted with the Pre-Raphaelites, wrote novels and poetry, and founded a design firm for the production of textiles, wallpapers, stained glass and illuminated books. All this he did within the context of a political philosophy which, by the 1870s, had reached a similar standpoint to that of Marx, and which made him more and more active in the socialist movement. For Morris, art and politics could not be separated. 'I do not want art for a few', he said in a famous passage from one of his many lectures, 'any more than education for a few, or freedom for a few.' He hated capitalism not only because it brought wage-slavery and alienation, but also because it created ugliness. The future, he was sure, would depend on the workers gaining freedom to expand their minds and skills and beginning once again to create the kind of beauty that the medieval cathedrals showed them capable of.

The nearest he got to demonstrating this was in the design of the Red House, built for him and his new wife Jane, in 1858 at Bexleyheath in Kent. The architect was his colleague Philip Webb (1831–1915), though the project was actually a collaboration between him, Morris and several of their artist friends, who provided internal decorations and purpose-made furniture. In a simple brick and timber construction, with tiled roof and wooden windows, it was designed artfully, to reflect the older traditions of craftsmanship which Morris wanted fervently to reinstate.

Morris's sympathy with the Middle Ages is often criticised as an unreal nostalgia, and his preference for crafted goods over machine-made ones is interpreted as a dogmatic hatred of the machine which denies his own aim of 'art for the people' – the implication being that art can only be brought to the people by machine production. However, these views of Morris fail to incorporate his role as a socialist. Far from being a historicist – as Pugin and Ruskin both were – Morris had a positive, and frequently expressed, view of the future which was decidedly not a re-creation of medieval England. In it, machinery had an important part to play as a background force to relieve man from toil and to free him to develop his talents. His art would not be just one more machine-made commodity imposed on him from outside, but something to which he himself would give expression. Clearly capitalism, with its invention of imaginary needs, its waste, pollution and inequality was not able to create this kind of society.

In the meantime capitalism was still expanding. Under Bismarck and Moltke, Prussia's military successes against Austria in 1866 and France in 1870 were the prelude to a spectacular economic expansion. Italy, created by Garibaldi and Mazzini out of a number of separate states in 1860, and now united under Victor Emmanuel II, also emerged as an industrial power. The United States was now colonising the west, building railways, expanding its industry, commerce and agriculture. The Civil War of 1861–65 had established the ascendancy of the industrial north-east over the agrarian south, and allowed industrial capitalism to expand. Immigrants came from Europe, escaping political repression and poverty, who became a ready-made work-force for the industries of the eastern cities: New York, Boston, Chicago, Philadelphia and Pittsburgh expanded rapidly as industrial and commercial centres. Even Russia, though excluded from western Europe since the Crimean War (1853–6), was making attempts to become capitalist. Alexander II was a reactionary autocrat, but he still saw the expediency of liberal reforms, such as emancipating the serfs, setting up the *zemstva*, or local government bodies, and allowing the formation of limited companies.

Capitalism had more apologists than critics; to many it seemed to represent all that was best in civilisation. To historians like Theodor Mommsen there were similarities between 19th-century Germany and ancient Rome; to Jacob Burckhardt the industrial age fulfilled the promise of the Italian Renaissance. There were architectural apologists too, of course, who executed official commissions by drawing parallels between the present and its glorious heritage. The Reichstag in Berlin (1884) by Paul Wallot was appropriately pompous and baroque, while the monument near the Capitol in Rome (1885) designed by Giuseppe Sacconi to commemorate Victor Emmanuel, the first king of a united Italy, was an extraordinarily grandiose invocation of the imperial past.

In northern Europe there were fewer pretensions to imperial destiny, and public buildings were designed within a more democratic domestic tradition. The Rijksmuseum in Amsterdam (1877) by Pierre Cuypers and the City Hall in Copenhagen (1893) by Martin Nyrop are both unpretentious buildings of gothic or early renaissance character. Their picturesque outline, their use of local brick and their small-scale elevations make them more humane than the pomposities of contemporary Berlin and Rome. The Stock Exchange (1898) and the Diamond Workers' Union (1899) in Amsterdam, both by Hendrikus Berlage, represent a move beyond traditionalism. The simple design of their brick exteriors and the straightforward structural expression of their interiors point the way to the functionalism of the 20th century.

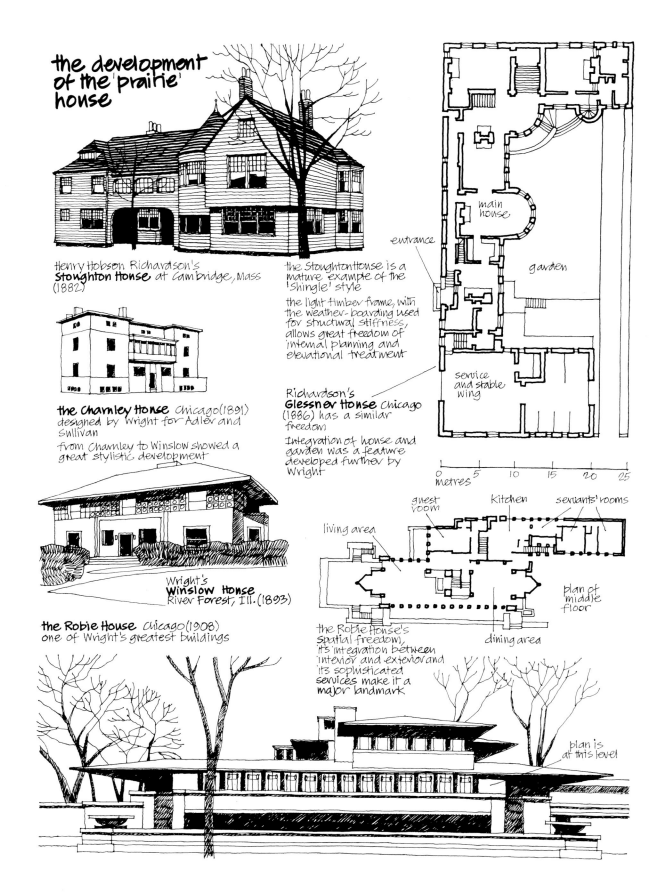

# the development of the 'prairie' house

Henry Hobson Richardson's **Stoughton House** at Cambridge, Mass (1882)

the Stoughton House is a mature example of the 'shingle' style

the light timber frame, with the weather-boarding used for structural stiffness, allows great freedom of internal planning and elevational treatment

entrance

main house

garden

service and stable wing

**the Charnley House** Chicago (1891) designed by Wright for Adler and Sullivan

from Charnley to Winslow showed a great stylistic development

Richardson's **Glessner House** Chicago (1886) has a similar freedom

Integration of house and garden was a feature developed further by Wright

0  5  10  15  20  25
metres

Wright's **Winslow House** River Forest, Ill. (1893)

guest room

Kitchen

servants' rooms

living area

plan of middle floor

dining area

**the Robie House** Chicago (1908) one of Wright's greatest buildings

the Robie House's spatial freedom, its integration between interior and exterior and its sophisticated services make it a major landmark

plan is at this level

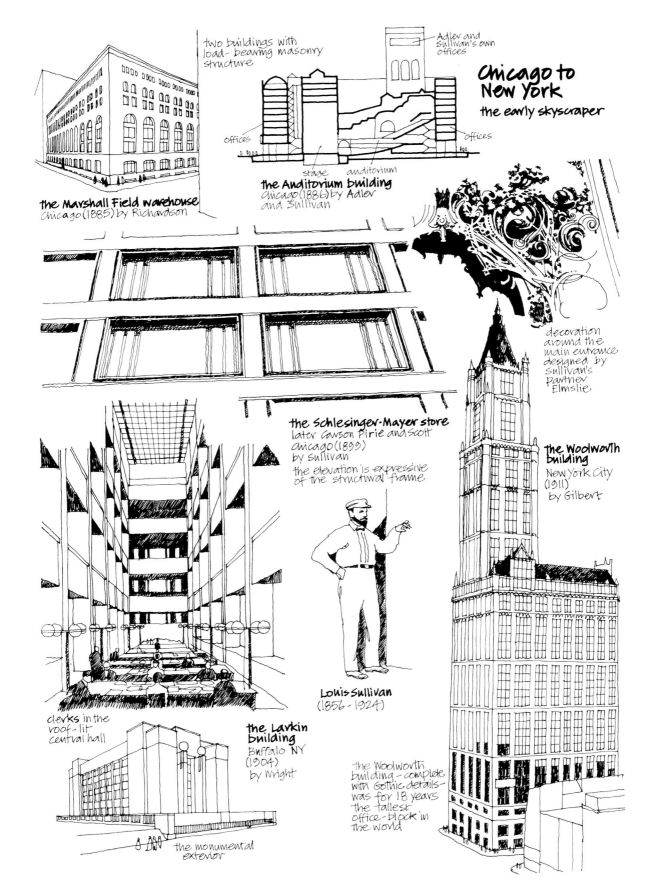

two buildings with load-bearing masonry structure

Adler and Sullivan's own offices

# Chicago to New York
## the early skyscraper

the Marshall Field warehouse
Chicago (1885) by Richardson

Offices

Offices

stage    auditorium

the Auditorium building
Chicago (1886) by Adler and Sullivan

decoration around the main entrance designed by Sullivan's partner Elmslie.

the Schlesinger-Mayer store
later Carson Pirie and Scott
Chicago (1899)
by Sullivan

the elevation is expressive of the structural frame

the Woolworth building
New York City (1911)
by Gilbert

Louis Sullivan
(1856 - 1924)

clerks in the roof-lit central hall

the Larkin building
Buffalo NY
(1904)
by Wright

the monumental exterior

the Woolworth building - complete with Gothic details - was for 18 years the tallest office-block in the world

## THE INDUSTRIAL CITY

In the United States, too, traditional European forms were discarded as architects evolved an indigenous approach to design. The architecture of McKim, Mead and White still showed Beaux Arts influences, with formal plans and strictly controlled elevations. Beginning with the Villard Houses in New York in 1884, they began to specialise the architecture of the wealthy bourgeoisie: grand houses, churches, university buildings and clubs. Henry Hobson Richardson, on the other hand, was more experimental. His style was more romantic, drawing freely on influences as disparate as Romanesque and Arts and Crafts, and is seen clearly in his Trinity Church, Boston, (1872). In his Stoughton House in Cambridge, Mass. (1882), he explored a loose and informal plan arrangement, and lightweight wall claddings, exploiting the greater freedom offered by a structural frame. Frank Lloyd Wright (1869–1959) in his early houses, whether of load-bearing or framed construction, also demonstrates an interest in free-flowing, interpenetrating spaces.

Wright, born in Wisconsin of Baptist parents, was something of a pioneer, who grew up with a love of the countryside and a distaste for city life. He learned his craft with the big-city architects Dankmar Adler (1844–1900) and Louis Sullivan (1856–1924) for whom he worked in Chicago till 1893. Sullivan, whom he revered, was the only architect Wright would accept as having influenced him, though the influence came more from Sullivan's attitude than from his style, that is, the concept of architectural honesty, embodied in Sullivan's famous dictum, 'form follows function'. This misunderstood phrase did not mean that beauty of form arose *inevitably* out of the expression of function, but that honesty of expression was an essential aspect of a beautiful building. In fact, Wright had little sympathy for the office-buildings which were Adler and Sullivan's stock-in-trade, and began to concentrate on the firm's private houses. The Charnley House (1891) was largely Wright's work, a simple geometric brick block of three storeys, with external elevations of unadorned brick and stone, and a dramatic full-height, roof-lit hall inside.

Wright set up on his own, developing a personal style which began to express what he felt about the relationship between man and nature. His early houses in the Oak Park and Riverside suburbs of Chicago, now known as the Prairie houses, were clearly conceived with a more elemental landscape in mind. The Winslow House at River Forest, Ill. (1893) and the famous Robie House in Chicago (1908) were his first mature works. The latter in particular demonstrates an interest in interlocking spaces, a blurring of the distinction between interior and exterior, terraces that link the house to the landscape around, and flat or low-pitched roofs that over-sail the walls and integrate the whole composition. Conceived as a true expressions of its simple materials, generally brick and timber, and with integral rather than applied decoration, it represents Wright's search for a rugged American architecture owing nothing to the European past. With it, American architecture came of age.

There were two other major works of these early years: the Unity Temple in Oak Park (1906) and the seven-storey Larkin Company administration building at Buffalo, NY (1904). The former was not a dramatic statement but two simple rooms linked together by an entrance lobby. Heavy, simple concrete walls and a flat roof were part of a straightforward conception. The latter, till its destruction in 1950, remained unique among office buildings. It was built in brick, heavily modelled into plain, vertical slabs, like the pylons of an Egyptian or Mayan temple. Inside, a central five-storey-high hall was surrounded by tiers of galleries containing office space, and the whole was lit from a vast central rooflight. The Larkin building, simple, vertical and dramatic, and the Robie House, subtle, complex, calm and horizontal, soon became Wright's two most admired buildings and had a strong influence on the ideas of the European avant-garde.

Rising land values in the fast-growing city centres were encouraging developers to build ever higher. This was given an impetus from the 1860s onwards by the use of Elisha Otis's new electric elevator. The ten-storey Home Assurance building in Chicago (1884) was the first steel-framed office block. Designed by the engineer-architect William le Baron Jenney, it is now recognised as the world's first 'skyscraper'. The form began to appear in many US cities, but mainly in Chicago, where the stimulus of rebuilding after the great fire of 1871 was leading to an economic recovery. At first, the buildings had load-bearing external walls as well as steel framing, which required large foundations to carry the enormous loads. Examples of this included Richardson's seven-storey Marshall Field warehouse (1885) and the ten-storey Auditorium building (1886) by Adler and Sullivan.

Adler and Sullivan became experts in the field of skyscraper design. In their Wainwright building in St Louis, Mo. (1890), their Guaranty building in Buffalo, NY (1896), their Gage building in Chicago (1898) and their Schlesinger-Mayer store (1899), also in Chicago, they developed the characteristic repetitive elevational treatment which we now associate with office towers. Heavy external walls were dispensed with. The structural supports, that is the columns and the floorslabs, perhaps faced with some simple material like tiling, became the main features of the elevations. Decoration was used sparingly, though Sullivan was given occasionally to outpourings of rich, decorative detail, much of it designed by his assistant George Grant Elmslie. Skyscraper construction moved dramatically to New York City with the Woolworth building (1911) designed by Cass Gilbert, a protegé of McKim, Mead and White. An enthusiast for Beaux Arts design, he designed a building which looks more historicist and less uncompromising than Sullivan's, but its height of 240 metres – 50 storeys – still makes it a remarkable technical feat.

Steel was not ideal for structural frames. Though quick to erect, it was not fireproof, and de-formed drastically under intense heat. It was also expensive, and by the 1880s a cheaper alternative was developed. The long French tradition of civil engineering, fostered throughout the 19th century by the École Centrale des Travaux Publiques, resulted in the development by Joseph Monier during the 1880s of reinforced concrete. This is a composite material, in which concrete, with its high compressive strength and high resistance to fire, is given tensile strength by the steel reinforcing rods embedded within it. An added advantage is its plasticity, its ability to assume the shape of the moulds in which it is cast. The engineers François Coignet and François Hennebique, in their pioneering work in the eighties and nineties, used this plasticity to advantage, finding it particularly appropriate for arched bridge construction.

The engineer-architect Auguste Perret (1874–1954) was among the first to exploit the new material in buildings. His early block of nine-storey apartments at 25bis Rue

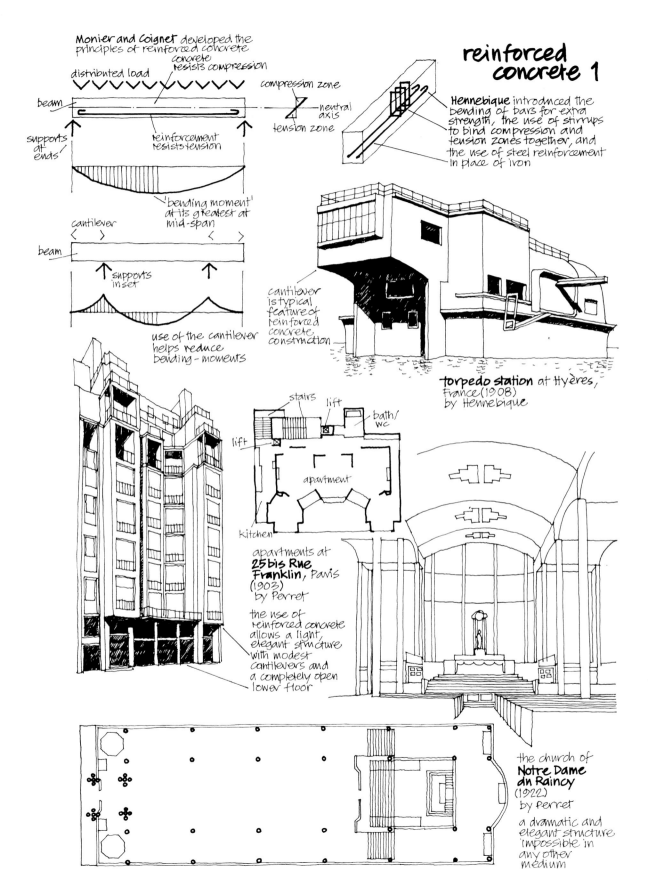

Monier and Coignet developed the principles of reinforced concrete concrete resists compression

distributed load

beam

compression zone

neutral axis

tension zone

supports at ends

reinforcement resists tension

'bending moment' at its greatest at mid-span

Hennebique introduced the bending of bars for extra strength, the use of stirrups to bind compression and tension zones together, and the use of steel reinforcement in place of iron

cantilever

beam

supports inset

use of the cantilever helps reduce bending-moments

cantilever is typical feature of reinforced concrete construction

torpedo station at Hyères, France (1908) by Hennebique

stairs

lift

lift

bath/wc

apartment

kitchen

apartments at 25 bis Rue Franklin, Paris (1903) by Perret

the use of reinforced concrete allows a light, elegant structure with modest cantilevers and a completely open lower floor

the church of Notre Dame du Raincy (1922) by Perret

a dramatic and elegant structure 'impossible' in any other medium

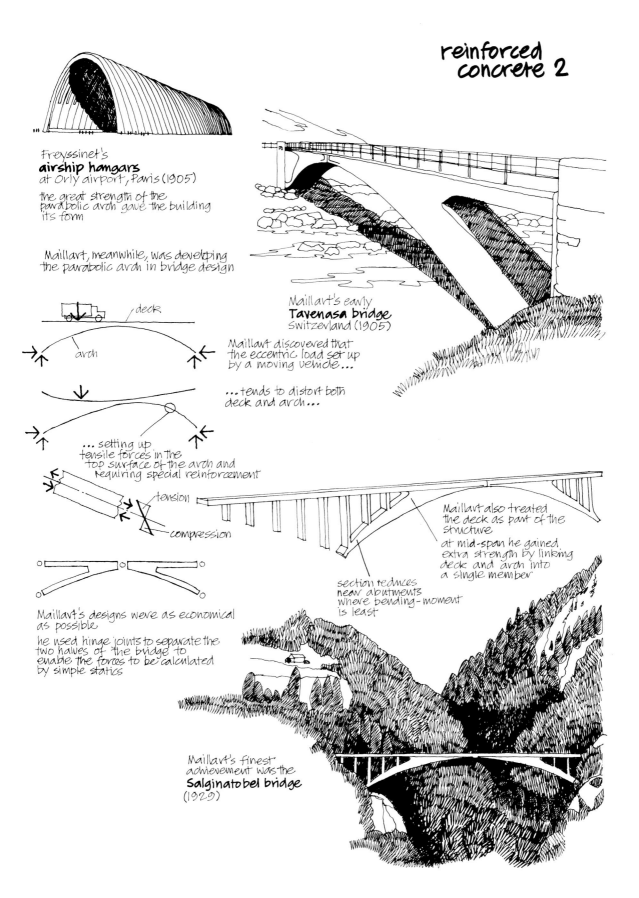

Freyssinet's
**airship hangars**
at Orly airport, Paris (1905)

the great strength of the
parabolic arch gave the building
its form

Maillart, meanwhile, was developing
the parabolic arch in bridge design

deck

arch

Maillart discovered that
the eccentric load set up
by a moving vehicle...

...tends to distort both
deck and arch...

... setting up
tensile forces in the
top surface of the arch and
requiring special reinforcement

tension

compression

Maillart's designs were as economical
as possible

he used hinge joints to separate the
two halves of the bridge to
enable the forces to be calculated
by simple statics

Maillart's early
**Tavenasa bridge**
Switzerland (1905)

Maillart also treated
the deck as part of the
structure

at mid-span he gained
extra strength by linking
deck and arch into
a single member

section reduces
near abutments
where bending-moment
is least

Maillart's finest
achievement was the
**Salginatobel bridge**
(1929)

Franklin near the Trocadéro in Paris (1903) has an exposed concrete frame inset with decorative panels. Though it is predominantly rectilinear, there are bold recessions and projections on the front elevation, a freedom which comes from its frame construction. In his church of Notre Dame du Raincy, Seine-et-Oise (1922), the spatial openness of late gothic is translated into modern materials. The thin-shell concrete vaulting supported on slim pillars, and the perforated concrete screens which serve as windows, give an air of lightness even greater than that of the Sainte Chapelle.

The influence of the École Centrale spread into Switzerland and Germany, resulting in the foundation of the Polytechnic at Zurich in 1854 and numerous *Technische Hochschulen* during the seventies and eighties. In 1895, the École itself became the École Polytechnique, an institution which has continued to influence French public life beyond merely training engineers. One of its pupils, the engineer Eugene Freyssinet, brought an analytical approach to design. His two airship hangars at Orly near Paris (1905) were simple, economical and conceived very much in terms of reinforced concrete: vast, folded slabs curved into the form of parabolic arches some 60 metres to the apex. Further advances were made by the Swiss engineer Robert Maillart (1872–1940), a student of Zurich Polytechnic, who is known particularly for using, from 1908 onwards, 'mushroom' construction in heavily loaded buildings – that is, the formation of wide heads to concrete columns to help spread the loads – and for his curved-slab bridge designs, first used at Tavenasa in 1905. They reached their greatest elegance at Salginatobel in 1929, in which a deeply-arched slab spans the gorge, supporting at its mid-point the flat slab of the roadway.

Through the industrial revolution, architecture had assumed many different forms, and the turn of the century presented a vivid contrast between extremes: on the one hand, Sullivan, Perret and the engineer-architects developing a 'functional' aesthetic which derived from the structural method; on the other, a persistent attitude that, irrespective of structure, architecture was mainly a matter of 'style'. To the traditionalist, 'style' meant reproducing the styles of the past, but in the 1890s a feeling was growing among the more progressive stylists that the modern age should have its own style. The client group was the bourgeoisie of a new group of countries entering, and profiting from, the industrial revolution – now not only Britain, France and Germany, but also Belgium, Bohemia, Russia, Catalunya. For a brief decade, a design movement came and went, taking its name from a shop selling modern goods, opened in Paris in 1895: *l'Art Nouveau*. Designers, artists and architects everywhere seemed concerned with the same new aesthetic, based on limp, flowing curves like the tendrils of growing plants and twisting wind-blown forms like flames, which contrasted strongly with the ordered geometry of Classicism and the stiffness of neo-gothic, to say nothing of Sullivan's new functionalism.

Art Nouveau emerged with the interior designs of the Belgian architects Victor Horta (1861–1947) and Henri van de Velde (1863–1957). In Horta's masterpiece, the Hotel Tassel at 6 Rue Paul-Émile Janson, Brussels (1892), the decorative iron main staircase is a forest of flowing curves. The curving iron façade of the Maison du Peuple (1896) and the department store *l'Innovation* (1901), were further essays in the style. Van de Velde designed the interior of *l'Art Nouveau* itself and went on to design buildings and interiors in Germany enhancing his reputation in Europe, especially in furniture design. In France Hector Guimard (1867–1943) designed the Castel Béranger in the Rue Fontaine at Passy (1894) with its sinuous wrought-iron entrance gate, and worked for the Paris Métro. The entrance to the Bastille station (1900) is a vegetable growth of ironwork and glass, an architectural statement which belongs very much to its time, owing little in its lines and form to any period of the past.

In one major respect Art Nouveau was traditional: it was essentially decorative, even two-dimensional, and did not radically appraise the spatial possibilities of the new materials. Among architects, the two main exceptions to this rule stood somewhat on the edge of the movement. The first was the Catalan architect, Antoni Gaudí (1852–1926), an enigmatic, ascetic figure whose buildings are among the most personal ever constructed. His style, while recognisably Art Nouveau, grew out of his own national culture. His early Casa Vicens in Barcelona (1878) and his two blocks of apartments, the Casa Batlló (1905) and the Casa Milá (1905) show a mastery of form and space, rare in Art Nouveau and eccentric in the extreme. Much depends on his use of concrete to achieve flowing shapes, imbedded with shards of pottery and glass and clusters of decorative metalwork.

His masterpiece, begun in 1883 and still unfinished now, was his extension to the neo-gothic church of La Sagrada Familia in Barcelona, a commission of great importance to the forces of right-wing Catholicism to which he responded with architectural fervour. Gradually the existing neo-gothic design was transformed, first into Gaudi's own version of gothic; then, with the addition of the four clustered transept spires and the strange, angular shapes of the internal arcades, the composition became a huge abstract sculpture, incomplete and hardly usable as a building but dramatically powerful as an image.

Gaudi's patron was Eusebi Güell, the aristocratic industrialist, and benefactor of his home city of Barcelona. For him, Gaudi built the early Palau Güell (1885), the charming public resort of the Parc Güell (1900), and at his patron's Owenite factory and model village of Santa Coloma de Cervelló, what is perhaps his most original building, the crypt of the unfinished Güell Chapel. Its complex, organic pillars and vaults were designed by practical experiment: by hanging up a network of loaded chains and allowing their weight to discover natural angles of repose.

The other exception to the art nouveau norm was the Scot, Charles Rennie Mackintosh (1868–1928), who was studying at the Glasgow School of Art when Art Nouveau caught the attention of young designers. He quickly came to public attention by winning a competition in 1896 for the design of a new School of Art. The building is as personal as those of Gaudí, but very different: disciplined and tensely organised, severe yet with touches of frivolity, designed to the last detail. Both inside and out, an art nouveau delicacy of detail contrasts with the tough, plain character of traditional Scottish stone. On the front elevation, large airy studio windows adorned with elegant wrought-iron brackets alternate with massive stone piers, and on the later west elevation the three tall oriel windows which light the library, framed up in light bronze-work, form a rich and dramatic contrast to the mass of stonework which surrounds them.

The rest of Mackintosh's work shows the same startling contrasts – from the rich, elegant interiors for Miss Cranston's chain of Glasgow tea-rooms, of which *The Willow* in Sauchiehall Street (1904) was the finest, to the simple yet original country houses

a wallpaper design by
**William Morris**
with the flowing lines
and two-dimensional
character later to be
associated with Art Nouveau

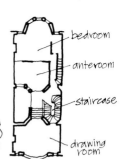

bedroom
anteroom
staircase
drawing room

**6 Rue Paul-
Emile Janson**
Brussels (1892)
by Victor Horta

Horta's plan is
fairly conventional
but the decoration
is highly original

this is the
staircase

**rocking chair**
of 1903
designed by
Henri Van de Velde

Guimard's iron
gateway to the
**Castel Beranger**
in Paris (1894)

the iron and glass
facade of the
**Maison du Peuple**
Horta's building for
the Parti Ouvrier
Belge in Brussels
(1897)

SORTIE  ENTRÉE

one of Guimard's
three standard designs
for Métro entrances
at the **Bastille** Paris
(1900)

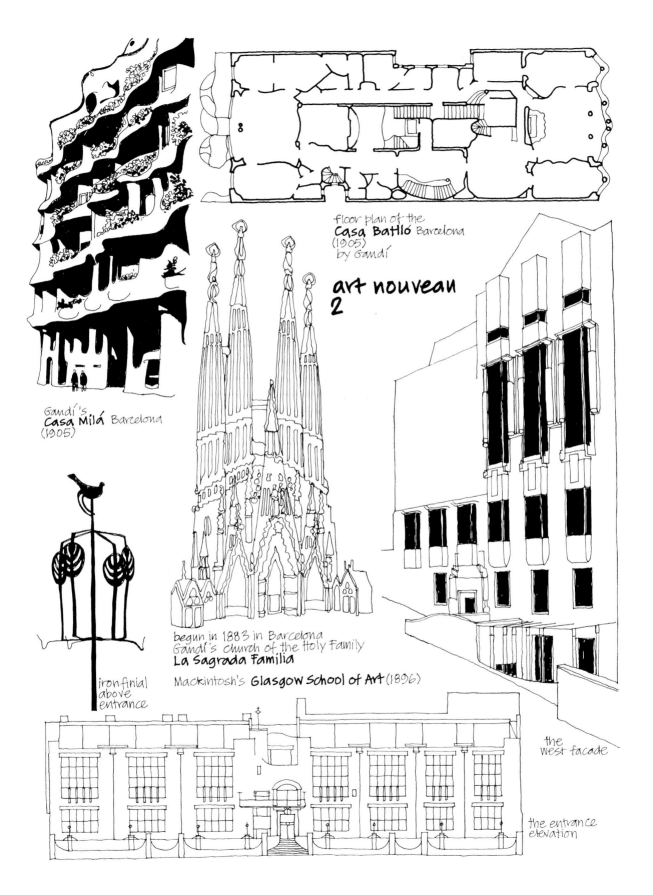

floor plan of the
**Casa Batlló** Barcelona
(1905)
by Gaudí

**art nouveau
2**

Gaudí's
**Casa Milá** Barcelona
(1905)

begun in 1883 in Barcelona
Gaudí's church of the Holy Family
**La Sagrada Familia**

Mackintosh's **Glasgow School of Art** (1896)

iron finial
above
entrance

the
west facade

the entrance
elevation

Windyhill (1900) and Hill House (1902). Mackintosh's spare, cool interiors, often plain and white, did much to form a transition between the excesses of Art Nouveau and the more restrained approach shortly to emerge. His major contribution to architecture was his ability to manipulate space: his interiors, enclosed here by solid walls, there by light screens, now low and constricted, now tall and free, anticipate the exciting spatial adventures of the 20th century.

## ESCAPING THE 19TH CENTURY

Mackintosh's interest in simple, vernacular architecture as a reaction against the 19th century was part of a growing movement. It had its origins in Webb's Red House but from about the 1880s onwards was promoted by figures like Arthur Mackmurdo and Charles Ashbee by the formation of societies, guilds and schools – the most significant being London's Central School of Arts and Crafts, founded by William Lethaby, who became its principal in 1902. 'Arts and Crafts' principles were seen in the houses of Richard Norman Shaw (1831–1912), of Edwin Lutyens (1869-1944) and of Charles Annesley Voysey (1857–1941), all of whom were influenced by the ideas of Morris and Webb.

From neo-gothic, Shaw moved to a mature, restrained and elegant brick style, seen best in his own house in Hampstead (1875), his Swan House in Chelsea (1876) and his suburban housing estate Bedford Park to the west of London (1880). Lutyens, rich and successful, was given the task of expressing the imperial grandeur of his time, in great country houses, churches and official buildings, which culminated in his grandiose designs for the government buildings in New Delhi (1913). But he was also a sensitive designer of smaller-scale houses, often enriched by the gardens of Gertrude Jekyll, like The Orchards, Godalming (1899), and Folly Farm, Sulhampstead (1905). Voysey too was a master at integrating an unpretentious house with its surrounding garden and landscape. Of the three, his architecture is the least formal, the least derivative, most consciously belonging to some long-standing tradition of local building. Annesley Lodge in Hampstead (1895), Broadleys and Moor Crag at Lake Windermere (1898) and The Orchard, Chorley Wood (1899) demonstrate his eloquent and original style.

In the early 19th century, artists had often been ready to celebrate the promise of the industrial age. By the end of the century, the contradictions of late capitalism, with the gap between rich and poor as wide as ever, and the old regimes hanging tenaciously onto power, brought disillusionment. Many painters, for example, rejected bourgeois society and its artistic forms, turning, like the French Impressionists, to greater abstraction, or finding inspiration, like the Russian Narodists, in peasant art. Society in return scorned, misunderstood or merely ignored them. Even some architects, who by definition need a client to bring their work into being, developed a separatist attitude. Various exhibitions, held around the turn of the century by artists, architects and their supporters, had a spirit of defiance. The Impressionists mounted their *Salon des Refusés*, and a group of Bavarian and Austrian designers set up the 'Secession', whose name expressed their intransigent, break-away attitude. Their exhibitions included work by Mackintosh and his Scottish contemporaries, by Otto Wagner (1841–1918), J. M. Olbrich (1876–1908), Josef Hoffman (1870-1956), Adolf Loos (1870–1933) and Peter Behrens (1868–1940).

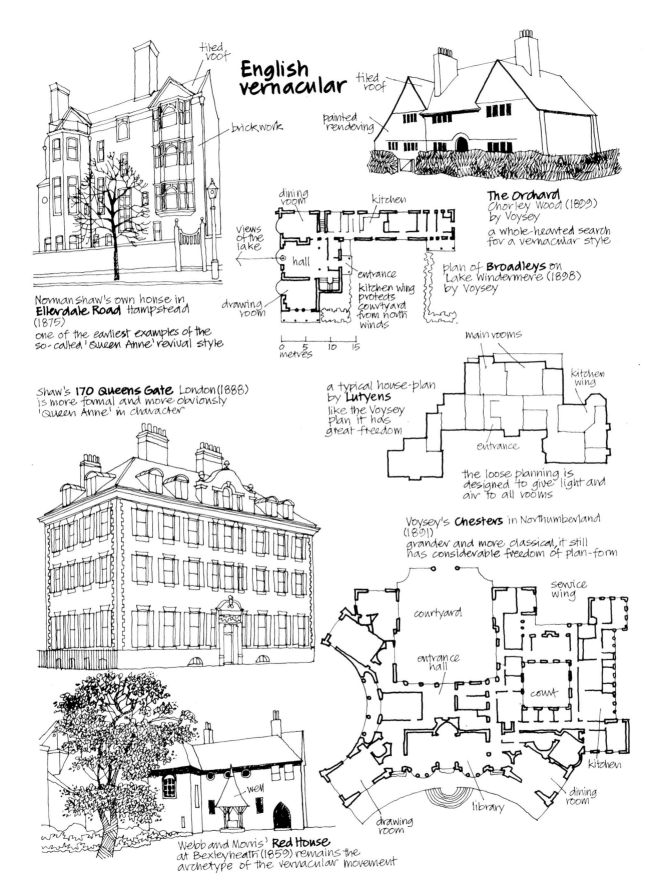

# English vernacular

tiled roof

brickwork

tiled roof

painted rendering

**The Orchard**
Chorley Wood (1899)
by Voysey
a whole-hearted search
for a vernacular style

dining room

kitchen

views of the lake

hall

entrance

drawing room

kitchen wing
protects courtyard
from north winds

0   5   10   15
metres

plan of **Broadleys** on
Lake Windermere (1898)
by Voysey

Norman Shaw's own house in
**Ellerdale Road** Hampstead
(1875)
one of the earliest examples of the
so-called 'Queen Anne' revival style

Shaw's **170 Queens Gate** London (1888)
is more formal and more obviously
'Queen Anne' in character

main rooms

kitchen wing

a typical house-plan
by **Lutyens**
like the Voysey
plan it has
great freedom

entrance

the loose planning is
designed to give light and
air to all rooms

Voysey's **Chesters** in Northumberland
(1891)
grander and more classical, it still
has considerable freedom of plan-form

courtyard

service wing

entrance hall

court

kitchen

well

drawing room

library

dining room

Webb and Morris' **Red House**
at Bexleyheath (1859) remains the
archetype of the vernacular movement

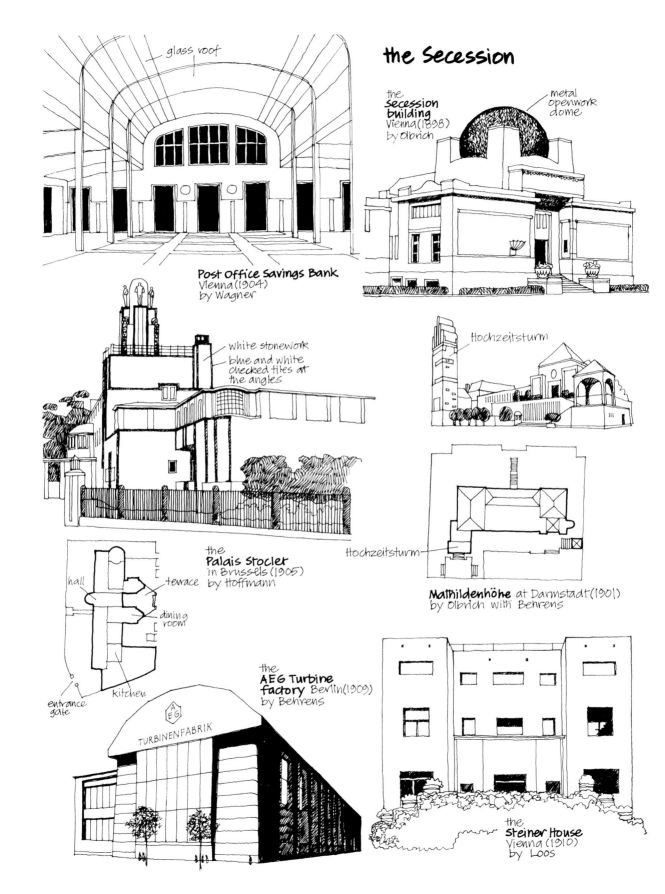

glass roof

# the Secession

the **Secession building** Vienna (1898) by Olbrich

metal openwork dome

**Post Office Savings Bank** Vienna (1904) by Wagner

white stonework

blue and white checked tiles at the angles

Hochzeitsturm

Hochzeitsturm

**Mathildenhöhe** at Darmstadt (1901) by Olbrich with Behrens

hall

terrace

dining room

kitchen

entrance gate

the **Palais Stoclet** in Brussels (1905) by Hoffmann

the **AEG Turbine factory** Berlin (1909) by Behrens

A E G

TURBINENFABRIK

the **Steiner House** Vienna (1910) by Loos

glass panels

**the Werkbund exhibition**
at Cologne (1914)

Taut's Glass pavilion

brick piers

steel and glass panels

**the Faguswerk factory**
workshop block
at Alfeld (1911)
by Gropius and Meyer

Gropius and Meyer's administrative pavilion

glazed staircases

some of the details resemble the houses of Wright

# the Deutscher Werkbund

bent wood and metal **reclining chair**
by Hoffmann (1905)

Berg's 'Jahrhunderthalle'
at Breslau
(1913)

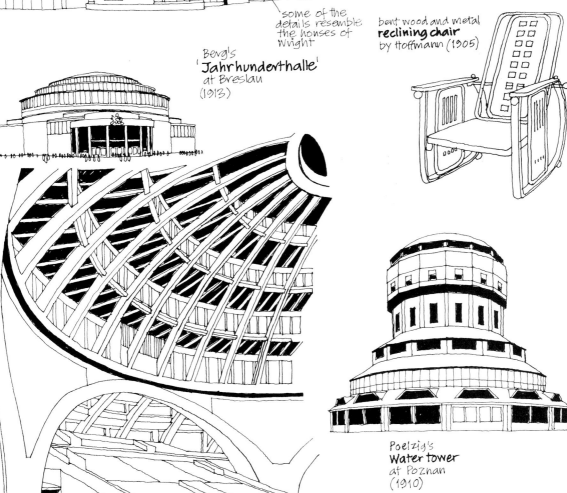

Poelzig's
**Water tower**
at Poznan
(1910)

Wagner, a professor at the Vienna academy, had an influence on numerous gifted students, including Olbrich, Hoffman and Loos. His best-known work is the Post Office Savings Bank building in Vienna (1904) with its barrel-vaulted glass interior, uncompromisingly modern in design even today. Olbrich was the designer of the light-hearted little Secession building in Vienna (1898) the headquarters of the movement – a small rectangular block covered with a metalwork dome – and of the houses of the Mathildenhöhe at Darmstadt (1901), part of an artists' colony founded by the Grand Duke of Hesse and planned by Olbrich, with Behrens, as a group of cool, low buildings whose simple design moved away from the vegetable forms of Art Nouveau. The centrepiece of the composition was the 45-metre 'Wedding Tower' or *Hochzeitsturm*, an original design incorporating a crest of five rounded fin-like pinnacles.

Even more simple and direct are the works of Loos and Behrens. The former's early buildings, such as his houses near Lake Geneva (1904) and the Steiner House in Vienna (1910), are plain and rectilinear, in keeping with his uncompromising, even doctrinaire, design philosophy. 'Ornament', he famously said, 'is a crime'. Behrens, influenced by the total design approach of Morris, brought to his appointment as chief architect to AEG, the Berlin electricity company, a comprehensive design attitude which tackled everything from buildings to stationery. His AEG Turbine Factory (1909) has a strongly classical feeling which makes it unusually dignified for an industrial building, but it is a classicism of mood rather than of detail. It is a symmetrical, hall-like building, steel-framed with a barrel roof, great expanses of glazing set between the steel columns, and rusticated concrete piers on the end walls as bold as the work of Giulio Romano.

In 1907, the Deutscher Werkbund was formed in Germany, an association of architects, designers and artists wanting to apply higher design standards to industrial products, and industrial techniques to building design. Winning over the industrialist demanded a more cautious architectural approach, and the first Werkbund exhibition in 1914 displayed a kind of stripped-down classicism. The only significant exceptions were Bruno Taut's crystalline little Glass Industries pavilion, conceived in terms of its unconventional materials, and parts of the administrative building which, though it had a rigidly classical plan and symmetrical elevations, was relieved by the exciting circular staircases at the corners. The designer of the latter was Walter Gropius (1883–1969), an assistant in Behrens' office who, with Adolf Meyer, had already designed a factory building at Alfeld for the Fagus company, makers of shoe-lasts and other metal goods. The Fagus workshop block (1911) is one of the great works of modern architecture, a long, rectangular three-storey building with its clearly-seen framework of piers alternating with light infill panels of glass and steel. Even though the conception was still classical, the designers emphasised that this was no traditional structure by keeping the corners free of piers, which they set back some 3 metres, cantilevering the floor-slabs out in a way only possible in steel or reinforced concrete. The fully-glazed corners, appearing here for the first time, became a hallmark of 20th-century design.

The main body of Werkbund architects, Behrens and Gropius included, kept within the principles of classical composition. Others, however, were interested in devising new forms and concepts, among them the Werkbund 'expressionists' Max Berg (1870–1947) and Hans Poelzig (1869–1936). Berg designed what was possibly the most original building of the time, the Centennial Hall – the *Jahrhunderthalle* – in Breslau (1913).

design for an
**electricity
station** ('1913)..

...and design for an **airship hangar**
(1913)
both by Sant'Elia

Constantin
Brancusi's
sculpture
**bird in
space** (1919)

sculpture
**unique forms
of continuity in
space** (1913)
by Umberto
Boccioni

Sant'Elia's
design for
**La Città
Nuova**
(1914)

high-rise buildings, bridges, elevators,
subways and access decks combined in
a powerful and persistent image of
the future

# futurism
in Italy

design for an
**apartment block**
by Mario Chiattone
an associate of
Sant'Elia (1914)

**Marinetti** -
chief theorist
of Futurism

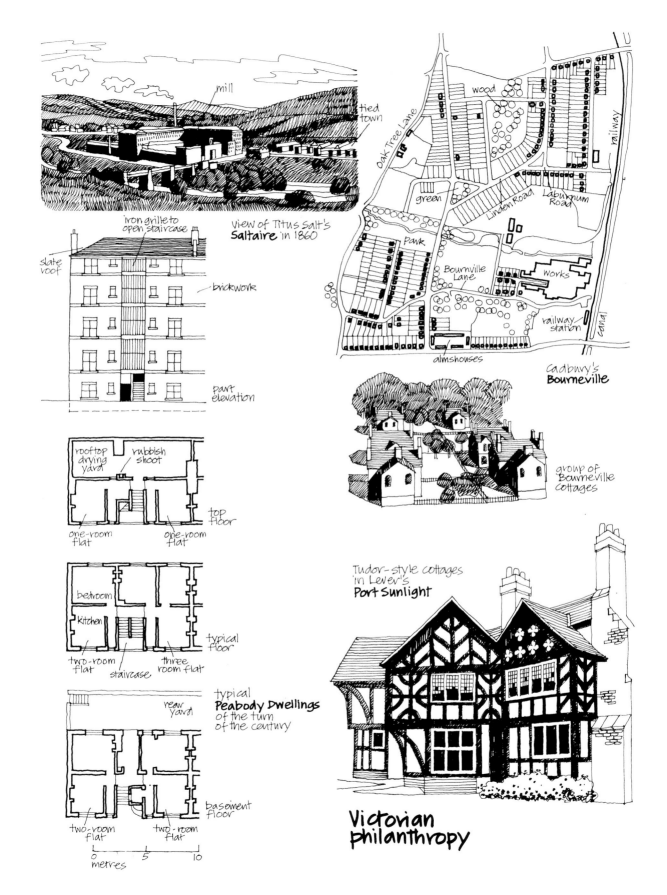

mill

tied town

view of Titus Salt's **Saltaire** in 1860

iron grille to open staircase

slate roof

brickwork

part elevation

Oak Tree Lane

wood

railway

green

Linden Road

Laburnum Road

Park

Bournville Lane

Works

railway station

canal

almshouses

Cadbury's **Bourneville**

rooftop drying yard

rubbish shoot

top floor

one-room flat

one-room flat

group of Bourneville Cottages

bedroom

kitchen

typical floor

two-room flat

staircase

three-room flat

Tudor-style cottages in Lever's **Port Sunlight**

typical **Peabody Dwellings** of the turn of the century

rear yard

basement floor

two-room flat

two-room flat

0      5      10
metres

# Victorian philanthropy

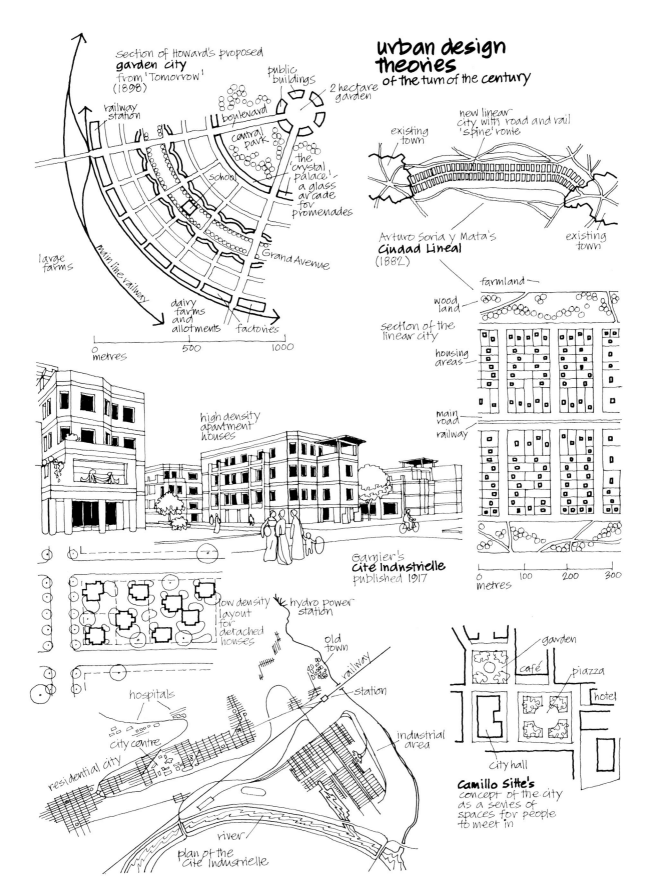

# urban design theories
## of the turn of the century

section of Howard's proposed **garden city** from 'Tomorrow' (1898)

railway station

public buildings

2 hectare garden

boulevard

central park

the 'crystal palace' - a glass arcade for promenades

school

Grand Avenue

large farms

main line railway

dairy farms and allotments

factories

0   metres   500   1000

existing town

new linear city with road and rail 'spine' route

existing town

Arturo Soria y Mata's **Ciudad Lineal** (1882)

farmland

wood land

section of the linear city

housing areas

main road

railway

0   metres   100   200   300

high density apartment houses

Garnier's **Cité Industrielle** published 1917

low density layout for detached houses

hydro power station

old town

railway

station

industrial area

hospitals

city centre

residential city

river

plan of the Cité Industrielle

garden

café

piazza

hotel

city hall

**Camillo Sitte's** concept of the city as a series of spaces for people to meet in

Externally this circular, domed building with its projecting portico is reminiscent of some enlarged Pantheon; but internally its vast circular space, 65 metres across and spanned by a huge ribbed, reinforced concrete dome, is a 20th-century conception going beyond Behrens. Poelzig's vast steel-and-brick circular water-tower at Poznan (1910) and his chemical factory at Luban (1911), an agglomeration of tall brick-built blocks whose semi-circular windows express the character of the material used, were also a reaction against academic Classicism.

Most vociferous of all in the fight against Classicism was the short-lived Futurist movement, founded by a group of Italian painters and the writer Marinetti in 1909. Proclaiming their cause in successive Manifestos, they set out to express the dynamism of the new machine age. For them, 'a roaring motor-car which runs like a machine-gun is more beautiful than the Winged Victory of Samothrace'. Though it had a nationalistic agenda, Futurism was also partly revolutionary in intent – at one stage during its decade of existence it was looking to 'an end to the architecture of big business' – and so it was perhaps not surprising that it failed to find commercial sponsors. The designs of its visionary architect, Antonio Sant' Elia (1888-1916), were never built, though his brilliant pre-visions of the modern world, of glass towers and multi-level transport interchanges, were fulfilled by proxy, through his continuing influence on 20th-century architects.

William Morris had seen the end of capitalism as a pre-condition to creating a better society. For some Secession architects however, and even more the Werkbund and its followers, an accommodation with capitalism was the best way forward. This reflects the debate that split the political Left in the late 19th century, between the respective advocates of revolution and of gradualist reform.

The growth of trade unions in the 19th century put the workers in a stronger position. Strikes against bad pay and conditions brought gradual improvements to factories and housing standards. 19th-century philanthropists, inspired like Owen both by Christian charity and commercial expediency, also helped make life better. Saltaire, near Bradford, a town built for his workers by the industrialist Titus Salt in 1853, has much in common with New Lanark. The rural site on the river Aire was provided with 800 houses, a church and four chapels, public baths and wash-houses, hospital and school, all in a Venetian gothic style. The vast mill building was at one side, a constant reminder of the town's *raison d'etre*. Port Sunlight in Cheshire (1888), a tied town built by W. H. Lever the soap magnate, and Bournville near Birmingham (1895) by George Cadbury the chocolate and cocoa manufacturer, continued the tradition. The neatly packed terraces of Saltaire were rejected in favour of garden-city planning, with a large number of detached cottages with their own gardens. Street names such as Laburnum, Sycamore and Acacia reinforced the rural image.

For the workers who remained in the cities, numerous charitable trusts like Peabody (1862) and Guinness (1889) began to provide improved housing. Estates were built, with tenement blocks in parallel rows far enough apart to allow sunlight and air to penetrate the windows. Typically five or six storeys with common staircases leading to self-contained flats, the estates were high-density, utilitarian and authoritarian, but in privacy and comfort they were infinitely better than the old back-to-backs. Then in 1897 the new London County Council began the world's first local-authority flats on a riverside site at Millbank. For the first time public money was being used to house the poor. The style chosen by the LCC's designers was that of Norman Shaw. What was good enough for the middle classes was good for the workers too.

However much cities might be improved, it was evident that they had inherent disadvantages, among them the congestion, inefficiency and high costs which came from unplanned growth. A new type of planned city combining the liveliness and opportunity of the old city, the spaciousness of the countryside and the efficiency of a logical layout, was suggested in 1898 by Ebenezer Howard, a City of London clerk, in his book *Tomorrow*. Important features of Howard's city were its small size – 32,000 people was the optimum – and the sense of identity which came from its being self-contained rather than just another suburb of a metropolis. In this it differed from the rival theory of the Spanish transport engineer Arturo Soria y Mata who in 1882 had proposed his *Ciudad Lineal*, a continuous pattern of urban growth stretching through the countryside on either side of a rapid-transit 'spine' route, incorporating both old and new urban centres.

In England, the mildly reformist utilitarian ideas of Howard proved appealing, and in 1905 the first of his 'garden cities' was begun, as a private venture, at Letchworth in Hertfordshire, followed by another at Welwyn. Individual houses with gardens, in the tradition of Nash, of Bournville and of English suburbia in general, were interspersed liberally with open spaces and parks, which resulted in low densities and a big land-take, with plenty of light and air but little of the dynamism of the big traditional city.

On the continent, low-density suburban living was less of a tradition, and most theories of town-planning were still based on the formal baroque approach of Haussmann and the Beaux Arts school. In 1889 the book *Der Städtebau* by the Austrian architect Camillo Sitte (1843-1903) proposed to adapt Beaux Arts planning by creating irregularities in a town design to obtain attractive, informal effects. It was, however, the French architect Tony Garnier (1869-1948) who overthrew the Beaux Arts approach with a complete scenario that still plays a major part in architectural thinking. Garnier built little, but his reputation is assured by his design for an imaginary *Cité Industrielle* prepared before 1904 and published in 1917. Like Howard's, it was for a city of about 30,000 people, but Garnier planned his city in linear form, like that of Soria y Mata, to allow for expansion. For the exercise, he chose a real site near his home town of Lyon.

As in Howard, the industrial area was to be set apart to minimise pollution, and the focus of the town was a centre containing civic buildings, hospitals, libraries and entertainment. Garnier designed the buildings in some detail, including the hydro-electric station, the municipal abattoir, factories and housing. The houses would be varied in size and type to suit not incomes but different families' needs. They would include both detached houses and groups of four-storey apartment blocks giving higher densities towards the city centre. The main structural material was to be reinforced concrete, and the plain, simple style of the buildings is reminiscent partly of the French engineers and partly of the stripped classicism of the Werkbund. But perhaps the most significant aspect of the *Cité Industrielle* was its socialism – in the tradition of Proudhon and Fourier – which distinguished it from the modified *laissez-faire* proposals of Howard. Garnier presents us with an alternative prototype for the modern city – purpose-designed and publicly owned. The intellectual foundations had been laid for the development of modern architecture.

# 11 THE HEROIC AGE OF MODERNISM

*1914 to 1945*

*The Interpretation of Dreams* by Freud and T. S. Eliot's *Prufrock*, Schoenberg's *Verklärte Nacht* and *The Firebird* by Stravinsky, *Les Grandes Baigneuses* by Cézanne and Picasso's *Les Demoiselles d'Avignon* – we may remember with surprise that all these archetypal works, which still define Modernism, are over a century old, belonging to the first decade of the 20th century. Architecture, with Voysey's 'The Orchard', Perret's flats in the Rue Franklin and Wagner's Savings Bank, was also becoming recognisably modern. Yet this was still a Europe dominated by kings, Kaiser and Emperor, their ministers and chancellors, and the stifling cultural apparatus which supported them. Artists and designers struggled to break free.

In the last years of the 19th century, capitalism had undergone a long, deep recession. Early entrants to the industrial revolution, particularly Britain – earliest of all – were worst hit. The newly industrialising countries, like Germany and the USA, were not held back, as Britain was, by the primitive technology of coal and iron. They entered their own industrial revolution on a second phase of technology – of steel, electricity, petrochemicals, the automobile, telecommunications. These were potentially liberating, open to all kinds of social possibilities, but in practice the industrial machine served the ruling class.

This was most apparent in Germany where the rigidity of the class system, the prevailing philosophy of state power, and the Prussian army brought capitalism under government control. Coal and iron production, scientific research, and its practical applications in the electrical, chemical and petroleum industries were put at the disposal of the state. In contrast to the rugged individualism of early British capitalists, Germany promoted monopoly capital. AEG, and those other great combines employing the Werkbund architects and their circle, became part of a system of 'cartels', in which supplies and prices were controlled by agreement between competing companies, to the mutual benefit of them all. Railways were built with military strategy in mind. Compulsory military training helped support the whole structure. By 1917 most institutions were in effect controlled by High Command.

Germany was not the only nation to rely on an arms economy. Capitalism depended on overseas markets, to supply industry with raw materials and labour and as outlets for manufactured goods. The end of the 19th century saw many of the old and new industrial powers competing, militarily if necessary, to annex colonies and open up new markets. The sought-after 'balance of power' in Europe became progressively more difficult to maintain. Arms races inevitably lead to conflict, and thus Europe entered the cataclysmic First World War (1914-18). The enormous loss of life destroyed an entire generation of young men. It also brought down many of the old regimes, ended the balance of power and bankrupted the treasuries. Europe was open to influences from elsewhere.

One such was the USA, which had recovered more quickly from the recession. It had huge resources of land, minerals and forests. It had an expanding workforce, stimulated by the skills of refugees from European repression. Its capitalists were more able to adapt. The teeming cities and the great skyscrapers were the most visible signs of their energy. Here, the developers were the emerging private corporations, whose broad financial base was intended to give protection from fluctuations in the market. Resisting state controls, they relied instead on controlling and expanding their markets through monopoly, or advertising, or both. The whole world became a legitimate sphere of influence, including Europe, which had already relied on the USA's military help in the War. The American model of capitalism was one that would dominate the 20th century.

## THE RUSSIAN EXPERIMENT

There was an alternative model, that of Russia, which between 1905 and 1922 underwent a great political turmoil and emerged transformed. The Tsar was opposed both by the bourgeoisie, who had missed out on their own liberal revolution, and by the urban workers, who suffered appalling conditions. In October 1917 the latter, under the leadership of Lenin (1870–1924) accomplished the world's first workers' revolution. The tasks ahead were formidable: to spread the revolution itself to all of the Empire, withdraw from the First World War, combat the White counter-revolution, repel invasions from several capitalist countries, and deal with problems of poverty and famine. Amid all this, a new kind of society was waiting to be created. Russia was attempting to go from the past into the future, without being impeded by the capitalist present. The first years saw a great intellectual ferment, as the new 'soviets', or workers councils, struggled with these ideas.

From the start it was understood that artists and designers could help create the new society. This was promoted by Lenin's cultural commissar Anatoly Lunacharsky, a returned exile with strong cultural connections with the avant-garde in the west. So from 1917 to the late 1920s Russian artistic ideas were among the foremost in the world. Tsarist Russia had arrested its progressive thinkers, and many intellectuals were resigned to leading aimless lives in café society. Now groups of artists and architects suddenly found both freedom of expression and a task to carry out. Abstract art, typified by the 'supreme' restraint of Kasimir Malevich's *Black Square on a white Ground*, could be put at the service of the revolution.

From this period came the early films of Sergei Eisenstein, including *Strike* (1924) and *Potemkin* (1925), the revolutionary poetry of Vladimir Mayakovsky, and the early symphonies and operas of Dmitri Shostakovitch. Art and architecture were examined for their social relevance and were taken into the streets in the form of festivals and concerts, symbolic constructions, murals, posters and slogans. The most famous example was Vladimir Tatlin's design (1919) for a great spiral tower to celebrate the Communist Third International. Intended to exceed Eiffel's in height, it was conceived, as Brecht might have said of it, 'with a splendour that only a beggar could imagine' There was famine, there was no steel to build it with, but it was made in a small-scale wooden mock-up, to be dragged through the streets on demonstrations, remaining a potent image of the new world promised by the revolution.

Partly through Malevich and notably through his pupil, the architect-artist Eleazar (El) Lissitzky (1890–1941), a relationship was established between architecture and abstract painting, initiating a search for an architecture of comparable simplicity and purity. Lissitzky's best known work is the abstract revolutionary poster of the Civil War period, *Beat the Whites with the Red Wedge*. In a series of art-works he called PROUNS, partly two- and partly three-dimensional, he bridged the gaps between painting, sculpture and architectural design.

The state was tolerant of artistic variety: traditionalists, formalists and progressives were given full rein, and many design organisations were formed. They included ASNOVA, a 'Rationalist' movement led by Nicolai Ladovsky (1881-1941) whose followers, despite its name, valued intuition and perception. Another was OSA, formed by the 'Constructivists' and led by the brilliant Vesnin brothers, Victor, Leonid and Alexander, who had a rational, productivist approach. For them, 'things created by modern artists must be pure constructions, devoid of the ballast of representation'. In 1920, at Lenin's request, ASNOVA founded the Higher State Technical and Artistic Studios, known for short as VKhUTEMAS. The school had over 2000 students and brought together Rationalists and Constructivists – both Ladovsky and the Vesnins taught there – into an influential powerhouse of new thinking. It also brought together art and architecture, the former represented by Aleksandr Rodchenko, who was head of the basic course, by Liubov Popova, Aleksandra Ekster, and both Malevich and Tatlin.

Soviet architecture developed rapidly under the influence of VKhUTEMAS. A new society needed not only new buildings but also new kinds of building, many of them unprecedented. They included working men's clubs, like the Zuyev, by Ilya Golossov (1926) and the Rusakov, by Konstantin Melnikov (1927). The revolution depended on communication, in which two new journals played a key part. The Vesnins produced a scheme for the Leningrad *Pravda* building in 1924 and Grigory Barkhin one for Moscow *Izvestiya* in 1927. All these building displayed similar characteristics. They were rectilinear, with concrete and steel framing and often large areas of glass, elegantly balancing, like abstract paintings, the patterns of solid and void.

The most influential building of all, which had a huge influence on 20th century architecture, was the NARKOMFIN apartment block, designed by Moisei Ginzburg (1928). Built for Moscow government workers, it was a demonstration of the semi-communal living which the new utopian society would bring. The private spaces were the bedrooms. Other activities, from eating, and doing the laundry, to caring for the children, were accommodated in communal spaces. The form of the glass and concrete building perfectly reflected this. The long, elegant bedroom block

poster for S. M. Eisenstein's film **Potemkin** 1925 which recalled the revolution of 1905

one of El Lissitzky's 'Prouns' 1919 which he looked upon as a transition between painting and building-design

this one is called **Bridge I**

# soviet constructivism

'To whom + for what purpose + what = how'
El Lissitzky 1931

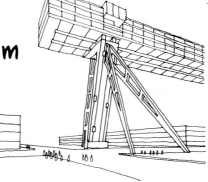

a **Wolkenbügel** designed by El Lissitzky and Mart Stam 1924, an office building on legs, high above the main roads of Moscow

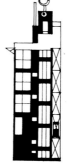

the Vesnin brothers' design for the **Pravda** building Moscow 1924

the Tatlin **tower** designed to celebrate the third International 1919 as a gigantic communications centre with radio, film studios and meeting rooms

the radio masts were a major part of Soviet architectural thought

an important way of educating people in remote rural areas

River Volga

— farmland

— parkland

— housing

— green belt and highway

— industry

— railway

the Vesnins' design for a **Palace of the People** 1922

diagram of Miliutin's linear plan for **Magnitogorsk** 1929

was deliberately repetitive, as if to reflect that in this society, for the first time ever, everyone was equal. The communal accommodation was attached, in spaces designed around their function.

The need to increase factory production and to improve living conditions stimulated the planning of many new towns. Vladimir Semenov, in his proposals for the expansion of Moscow, Stalingrad and Astrakhan adopted Garnier's principles of zoning, to separate the housing areas from the noise and pollution of industry. He also perceived the town as a constantly changing phenomenon, which needed space to expand into. This idea was developed by Nicolai Milyutin (1889–1942), who made proposals for the expansion of Magnitogorsk, Stalingrad and Gorki. He advocated a form developed from Soria y Mata's linear town. The zones were narrow, parallel strips of land running through the countryside, incorporating the old town centres where they occurred: a railway zone, a factory, workshop and technical college zone, a green belt with a main highway, a residential zone, a park and sports area, and a wide belt of farmland. Travel along the routes was rapid and efficient, and travel across them was made easy by the short distances involved. Like Ginzburg, Milyutin anticipated a new social system, including the communal ownership of possessions, equality of the sexes, and communal child care.

During his last years, Lenin thought increasingly about the implementation of Marx's main objective: how to achieve democracy and allow all citizens to participate creatively in their own future. But by 1926 power had been assumed by Stalin (1879–1953) who began to restructure the economy, by collectivising agriculture, putting forward Five-Year Plans for industry and bringing Russia's institutions under strict state control. To reduce opposition he purged the country of intellectualism, stamping out progressive ideas, controlling freedom of expression and assassinating or deporting those who resisted. Under the control of cultural commissars, art and architecture relapsed into representationalism, pseudo-naiveté or banal neo-classicism. Many artists moved to the west.

Western Europe, like early revolutionary Russia, was in intellectual ferment. The break-up of the old empires after the War – Austrian, German, Turkish and Russian – left a number of developing new states and a republican spirit in the air. Mass education was becoming universal, the spirit of experiment and inquiry spread widely and artistic life flourished.

Not so the economies. The post-War reparation payments imposed on Germany forced her to drive her industry strongly towards exporting, creating high employment and also high inflation. The victors, on the other hand, experienced lower inflation but ever higher unemployment, and were burdened with the debt of war-loans from America. The promise to the soldiers had been 'homes fit for heroes', but they came back shattered by the traumas of history's most devastating war to countries whose economic problems were too great to allow the eradication of their squalid slum-housing.

European Marxists looked to Russia as an example. In 1919 there had been abortive revolutions in western Europe too, but by the late 1920s there seemed little hope of engineering a similar social revolution in the west. Besides which, to those who recognised the oppression, Stalinist Russia was less and less useful as a model. Nevertheless, there was a growing confidence among progressive architects that better living conditions for all were almost within reach. The answer, it was thought, lay not so much in any structural change to society as in the proper harnessing of technology: new materials and techniques would bring new architectural forms to cities, ending overcrowding and squalor.

At the head of this movement was the Bauhaus, the industrial-design school founded at Weimar in 1919 by Walter Gropius. Following the Werkbund, Gropius placed his hopes on a closer relationship between 'the best artists and craftsmen on the one hand and trade and industry on the other'. However suspect the idea might be of forming close links with German industry in order to achieve progressive social aims, the Bauhaus was innovatory at least in its teaching methods. The student began in an atmosphere of monastic dedication. He or she then underwent a rigorous three-year course which began by clearing the mind of pre-conceptions, and continued by teaching a craft in the workshop. Only then did he or she proceed to the study of industrial design.

At first, the design style of the Bauhaus was essentially romantic and expressionist, in keeping with the philosophy of the mystical Johannes Itten, head of the *Vorkurs*, the basic course with which the students started. But in 1922 two events occurred which changed this. The first was a meeting in Düsseldorf which brought together progressive designers from both Russia and the west, and ended in the formation of a 'Constructivist International'. The second was an exhibition of Soviet design arranged by Lunacharsky in Berlin. The effect was to persuade Gropius to change direction, and to adopt Constructivism as the Bauhaus style. Itten went, to be replaced by the Hungarian Constructivist László Moholy-Nagy.

## ARCHITECTURE AND THE BAUHAUS

The most tangible result of this change was the Bauhaus building itself, designed by Gropius when the school moved to Dessau in 1925. It consists of three blocks, in an informal yet organised group. At the centre of gravity are the entrance and the all-important workshop block, which link eastwards by means of an assembly hall to a small tower of studio-flats for the students and northwards via a bridge over the access road to the classroom block. The fully-glazed workshops contrast with the more solid walls of the classrooms and the residential tower.

Gropius meant the building to be a manifesto, a demonstration of a rational design approach. So great was its influence, however, that it created an instant 'Bauhaus style', rather to the displeasure of Gropius, who rejected the very idea of style and demanded the working out of solutions from first principles. It is difficult, now that the formal vocabulary of this great building has passed into our architectural language and is used every day in the unthinking concoction of undistinguished buildings, to appreciate its originality. For just as gothic began at St Denis, so was the Bauhaus the first major building in which all the features of 20th-century architecture were brought together as a unified and convincing whole. It has an order which derives not from the imposition of any neo-classical rules of symmetry or proportion but from the logic of its structure, and a richness of effect which comes not from applied decoration but from its design detail. And its subtlety of form and spatial variety do not come from pre-conceived design formulae but are essentially the result of an ordered solution to the planning of the building.

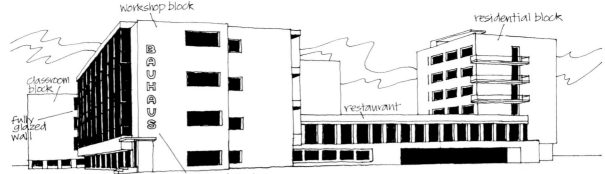

Workshop block

BAUHAUS

classroom block

fully glazed wall

Bauhaus lettering by Herbert Bayer

restaurant

residential block

Walter Gropius
**the Bauhaus building**
at Dessau 1925

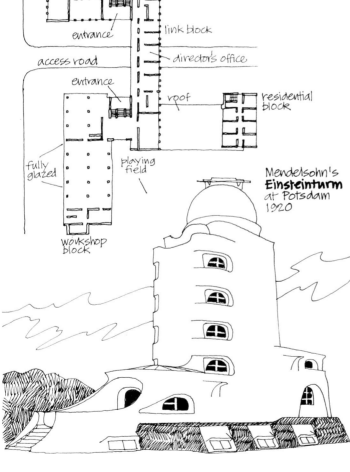

classroom block

entrance

access road

entrance

fully glazed

playing field

workshop block

link block

director's office

roof

residential block

# rationalism and expressionism
## the Schocken store Stuttgart 1926 by Mendelsohn

Mendelsohn's
**Einsteinturm**
at Potsdam
1920

Mendelsohn
design for a car-factory
1914

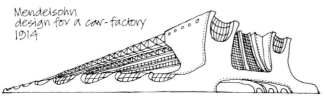

S

# rationalism in the Netherlands

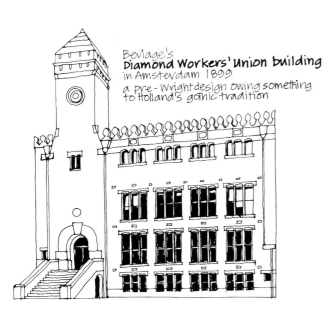

Berlage's
**Diamond Workers' Union building**
in Amsterdam 1899
a pre-Wright design owing something
to Holland's gothic tradition

Logotype for **De Stijl** by van
Doesburg and Huszar 1917

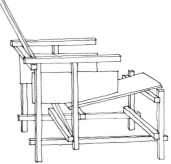

Rietveld's
**Red Blue
Chair**
1917

**Villa** at Huis ter Heide
by Rob van t'Hoff 1916
has definite links with
the work of Wright

Rietveld's
**Schroeder
House** at Utrecht
1924

design for
**seaside houses** 1917
by Oud

**Town Hall** and **Vondelschool**
at Hilversum by Dudok
1929 and 1926

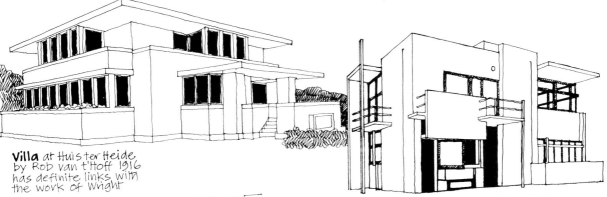

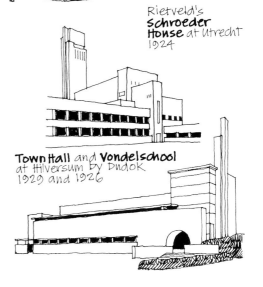

**van Nelle factory** in Rotterdam by
Brinkman, Van der Vlugt and Stam
1928

At first, the Bauhaus courses placed little emphasis on architecture. In 1927 Gropius remedied this by appointing the Swiss architect Hannes Meyer to the staff. On Gropius's resignation the following year to devote more time to his own work, Meyer took over the school. To him, building was first and foremost a social activity, and he found the aesthetic preoccupations of the Bauhaus artists lacking in social purpose. His revision of the curriculum included not only the extension of the scientific and investigative side of the course, but also an increased emphasis on the architect's social responsibilities. Meyer's Marxist views, and his encouragement to the students to participate in political activity, brought a reaction from the conservative Dessau authorities. In 1930 he was asked to resign. Looking back on his two years as director, he was able to claim, 'I taught the students to relate building to the community; I weaned them from the formalistic, intuitive approach and taught them to undertake basic research; I showed them how to put the needs of the people first.'

Meyer's socialism and his materialist design methods were not common among architects of his generation. Politically, the prevailing attitude was a kind of liberal humanism. In design, the methodology was intuitive rather than scientific, even in the Bauhaus, with its claims of rationality, and certainly so in the case of architects like Erich Mendelsohn (1887–1953), an expressionist designer with more in common with the Werkbund architects than with the rationalist Meyer. Mendelsohn's Einstein Tower at Potsdam (1920) was an individualistic vision of the new age, a curious, solid, seven-storey laboratory surmounted by a domed observatory. A composition of sweeping, streamlined curves, it might be said to demonstrate the plasticity of reinforced concrete. The fact that it was built in plastered-over brickwork did not negate the conception: the intention was to symbolise modernity rather than to use its technology. Mendelsohn also designed a store in Stuttgart for the Schocken company (1926) in which his predilection for bold curves was disciplined by a formal structural system; the result was one of the finest of early modern buildings, intellectual in approach and dynamic in effect.

The expressionist approach of earlier years was being superseded by what later became known as the 'international style'. The architectural features of the Bauhaus building became almost universal among the progressive architects: asymmetry, rectangularity of form, and the lightness which derived from the fact that frame construction had emancipated the external wall from its old load-bearing function. Colours were often restrained with walls painted white or pastel colours to emphasise a departure from the heaviness and gloom of neo-classicism. Much use was made of steel and reinforced concrete, which enabled unusual effects of lightness, space and precision – although where traditional materials could obtain a mechanistic effect they might be used without compunction, the look of modernity being more important than the actuality.

Many architects were approaching modernism in the company of painters and sculptors, which sharpened their sense of form and space if not their scientific methodology. Notable among them were the Dutch architects known, from the title of the magazine they began in 1918, as *De Stijl* – simply, 'the style'. Their aim, couched in the resounding terms of the art manifestos of the time, was to reject the old which was 'based on the individual' and discover a harmony, through purity of form and colour, which was by contrast 'universal'. Their art and architecture, at its most pure, was purged of all forms except the most severely rectangular and of all colour except black, white and the three primary colours.

Their chief theorist was Theo van Doesburg, also a lecturer at the Bauhaus, and their style is typified by that of the artist Piet Mondriaan (1872–1944) who carried cubism to a logical conclusion with his own pure, rectilinear painting.

De Stijl architecture began with Hendrikus Berlage, Rob van t'Hoff, Jan Wils and Jacobus Oud, whose early work dated from an exhibition in Holland in 1910 of the work of Wright, and showed distinct echoes of the Larkin Building and the Robie House. But the seminal works of the movement were two by the architect Gerrit Rietveld (1888–1965). The first was the 'Red-Blue' chair of 1917, in which the elements of a chair were reduced to their bare essentials: a flat sheet of plywood for the seat and another for the back, both supported on a frame of overlapping painted wooden bars. Van Doesburg saw in it the 'silent eloquence of a machine'. The second was the Schroeder House (1924), a small two-storey building in a suburb of Utrecht. Its exterior was treated like the projection of a Mondriaan painting into three dimensions, a complex of flat planes – walls, floor-slabs, roofs, canopies, balconies – all overlapping, projecting and intersecting with each other to form an exciting architectural expression of *De Stijl's* stated desire 'for number and measure, for cleanliness and order'.

In 1922, Oud left *De Stijl* to pursue a more rational, less purely sculptural approach, and his blocks of workers' flats at Hoek van Holland (1924) are his attempt to apply the ideas of *De Stijl* to a realistic social aim. William Marinus Dudok was another rationalist, whose rectilinear style owes something to *De Stijl* but is calmer and less sculptural in effect and shows a stronger appreciation of the properties of materials, in particular of brickwork. His Vondelschool in Hilversum (1926) and the influential Hilversum Town Hall (1929) are among his best works – brick buildings in which horizontal masses are carefully balanced against verticals. Among the finest of Holland's rationalist buildings is the factory in Rotterdam (1928) designed for the Van Nelle tobacco company by Brinkman, van der Vlugt and the Bauhaus-trained designer Mart Stam. Like the Bauhaus workshop building, the main eight-storey block has a concrete frame – in this case with mushroom-headed columns – and is clad with a curtain-wall of glass.

## THE NEW SPIRIT

In 1923, a book called *Vers une Architecture* was published in Paris. It was a fighting manifesto advocating the adoption of a new attitude to architecture, and the implication of the title was that no current architecture really deserved the name.

> A great epoch has begun. There exists a new spirit. There exists a mass of work conceived in the new spirit; it is to be met with particularly in industrial production. Architecture is stifled by custom. The 'styles' are a lie.

The writer was a thirty-six-year-old Swiss, Charles-Édouard Jeanneret (1887–1965), who was to become the greatest and most influential architect of the 20th century. In his youth, he had been indifferent to architecture, but a succession of experiences acted as a catalyst to change his life: a tour of Europe in 1907, ending in Paris, where he discovered Notre Dame, the Eiffel Tower and above all, Auguste Perret, for whom he worked for a time; a visit to Greece in 1911, where the Acropolis was a revelation; and a permanent return to Paris in 1917, where he met the post-cubist painter Amédée

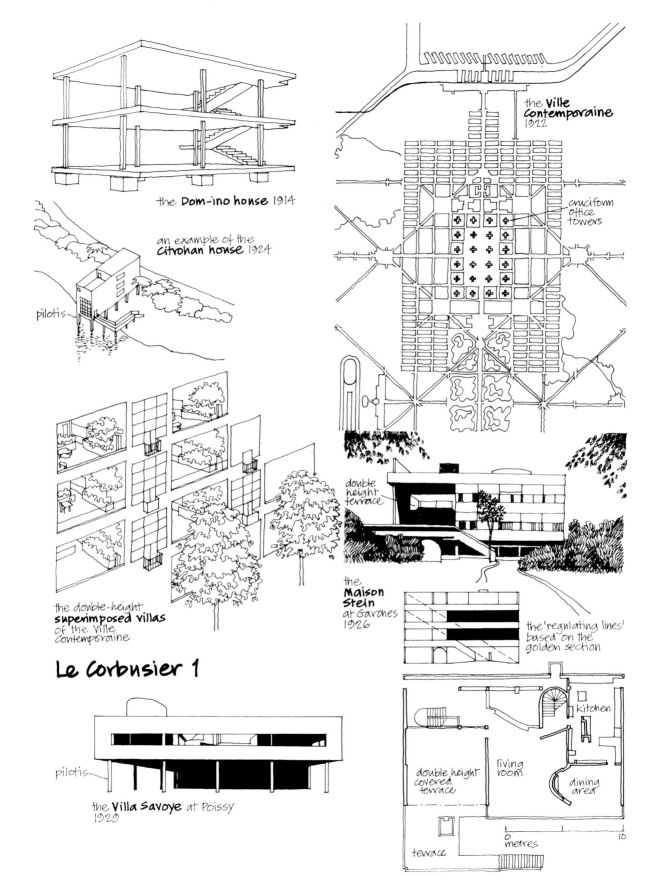

the **Dom-ino house** 1914

an example of the
**Citrohan house** 1924

pilotis

the **Ville
Contemporaine**
1922

cruciform
office
towers

the double-height
**superimposed villas**
of the Ville
Contemporaine

double
height
terrace

the
**Maison
Stein**
at Garches
1926

the 'regulating lines'
based on the
golden section

# Le Corbusier 1

pilotis

the **Villa Savoye** at Poissy
1929

kitchen

double height
covered
terrace

living
room

dining
area

terrace

0                    10
metres

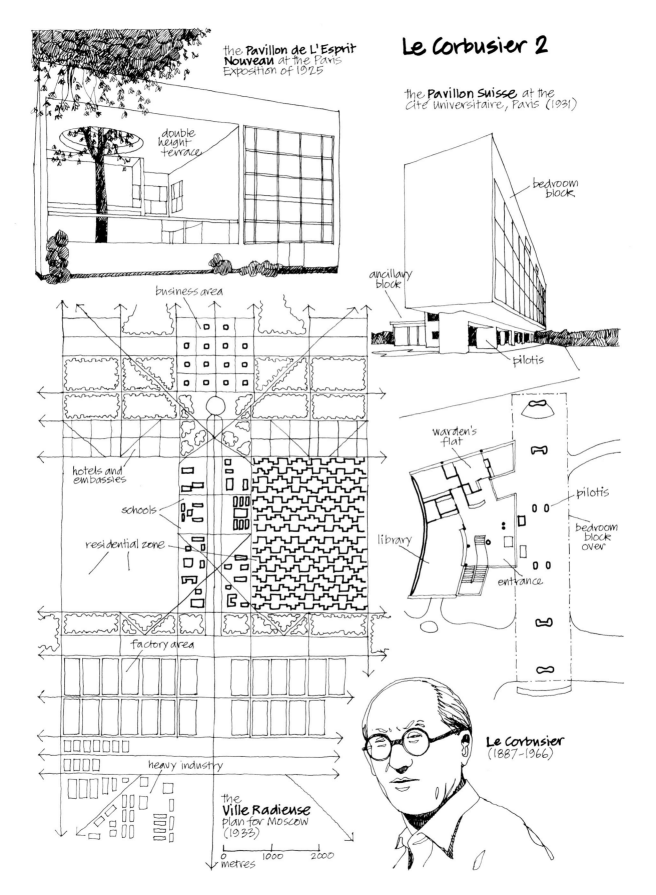

the **Pavillon de L'Esprit Nouveau** at the Paris Exposition of 1925

double height terrace

# Le Corbusier 2

the **Pavillon Suisse** at the Cité Universitaire, Paris (1931)

bedroom block

ancillary block

pilotis

business area

hotels and embassies

schools

residential zone

factory area

heavy industry

warden's flat

library

entrance

pilotis

bedroom block over

the **Ville Radieuse** plan for Moscow (1933)

0   1000   2000
metres

**Le Corbusier** (1887-1966)

Ozenfant with whom in 1920 he founded a paper called *L'Esprit Nouveau*. This he used as a vehicle for his now rapidly forming ideas about painting, architecture and town design. He had become a new man, and it is significant that at this point he left his old identity behind, and became Le Corbusier.

Like Stravinsky or Picasso he was always pursuing new ideas, and the richness of his thought kept him permanently ahead of critics and imitators. However, several continuous threads ran through his work, traceable to his formative years. The simple bold forms of his early cubist paintings, enhanced by carefully placed colour, translated well into his architecture. His early contact with Perret gave him an interest in modern materials – steel, glass, reinforced concrete – and in their structural and spatial possibilities. With Ozenfant he shared a passionate belief in the new machine age and the achievements of its structural engineers, naval architects and car designers. Greece gave him an interest in harmonious proportion, and Italy encouraged the liberal humanistic philosophy which gave him a utopian vision of the future.

One of his greatest talents – shared with Garnier, whose work he knew well – was the ability to see urban problems at every scale, to see the design of a living unit within its larger context, and conversely to design cities in the knowledge of how they were intended to work at the small scale. The design of small houses and of master plans for whole regions were part of the same problem. As early as 1914 he designed a prototype 'Dom-ino House', a framework of six columns, two floor-slabs and a roof, which offered flexibility in the location of internal partitions and external walls. In 1922 he published the first of his major contributions to town-planning theory, *Une Ville Contemporaine de 3,000,000 d'Habitants* in which the ideas of Garnier became a dramatic vision of the future. Le Corbusier's own innovations were significant. He understood the concept of density and how it builds up in intensity towards a city centre – resulting in his case in 60-storey office towers – and an appreciation of the implications of high-speed road and rail movement, which here for the first time became an integral part of town design.

The residential areas of his *Ville Contemporaine* contained many of the ideas which he later published as the 'Citrohan House' (1924): housing-units with spacious, double-height living-rooms corresponding to two ordinary storeys; houses and flats with integral roof-gardens or balconies to provide private outdoor space; buildings raised off the ground on *pilotis* to allow the landscape to flow uninterrupted underneath. In 1925, the Citrohan House was given concrete form, and became the *Pavillon de L'Esprit Nouveau* at the Paris *Exposition des Arts Décoratifs*. The rational 'new spirit' of Le Corbusier's innovative design, and the constructivist panache of Melnikov's Soviet pavilion, contrasted strongly with the other exhibits, most of them in the jazzy 'Art Deco' style to which the exposition gave its name. The international jury offered Le Corbusier first prize, but this was blocked by the French jury-member amid an atmosphere of shrill criticism by the French architectural establishment.

Then came two early masterpieces, the elegant Maison Stein at Garches (1926) and the beautiful Villa Savoye at Poissy (1928). The former is a simple three-storey block, based on Esprit Nouveau principles, with an integral roof-terrace and an inset, double-height garden area, the whole bound together by a system of harmonious proportions founded on the golden section. The latter summarised all his ideas to date, and marked the beginning of his architectural maturity. A two-storey house, it consists of a main upper storey designed as a simple, rectangular white box, with a single line of horizontal windows. This is raised on twelve concrete *pilotis* which form a loggia around the deeply recessed entrance floor, and give the impression of a building which floats above the landscape. From the main level, an internal ramp leads to the roof, which contains a penthouse and terrace. Wright's earthy Robie House seems to grow organically out of the ground. The floating Villa Savoye is an expression of pure, Voltairean rationalism, precise, geometric and man-made, deliberately detached from nature.

In 1926 the international style came to England when Behrens built a two-storey house, 'New Ways', for Wenman Basset-Lowke, a Northampton industrialist, previously a patron of Mackintosh. Houses for the businessman Francis Crittall by the English architect Thomas Tait at Silver End in Essex (1928) and another by the New Zealander Amyas Connell, 'High and Over' at Amersham, Buckinghamshire, (1929), gradually established a kind of Bauhaus-inspired cubism, which was to grow freer and more expressive during the 1930s when the ideas of Le Corbusier became better known.

Le Corbusier's most influential early building was perhaps the Pavillon Suisse, a hostel for Swiss university students at the Cité Universitaire in Paris. Built in 1931, it formed a prototype for many later buildings where the basic design problem was that of assembling a number of repetitive units together with a complex of ancillary accommodation. Le Corbusier's solution, in the manner of the NARKOMFIN apartments, was to house the identical units, the students' bedrooms, in an elegant, regular slab-block which emphasised their repetitive nature. The communal accommodation – offices and common rooms was in a single-storey rear block, as free in shape as the bedroom block was regular. Further emphasis was given to the distinction by lifting the slab-block off the ground on *pilotis*, the only link being a staircase tower.

During the late twenties and early thirties, the liveliness of architectural and artistic ideas, and the freneticism of the jazz and cinema age, contrasted with the grimness of the gradually deepening depression. Inflation and unemployment grew, the former at its worst in Weimar Germany and the latter in France and Britain, and everywhere there was less capital available for building. In 1929 the Wall Street crash seemed to threaten the very continuance of capitalism. Russia, on the other hand, under Stalin's direction, was entering its first Five Year Plan (1929–33). To observers in the west, her relative economic stability seemed admirable. But at that time the implications were little known: collectivisation also meant the liquidation of the Kulaks as a class, the opening of the Gulags, and drastic limits on personal freedom.

Le Corbusier was interested in Russia and in 1928 had prepared a design for the Centrosoyus in Moscow. As a result he had been denounced in the west as a communist, although he probably saw Russia as no more than a vehicle for his architectural ideas. In 1933 he prepared a plan for Moscow which took his theories one step further: this was the famous *Ville Radieuse*, or Radiant City, in which, possibly under the influence of Milyutin's linear city plan of 1929, the concept of planning for expansion entered his thinking.

The economists of the west did not understand or accept Marx's analysis of the crisis of capitalism – that periodically there would be a crisis of over-production, goods would remain unsold, and cut-backs and layoffs would follow, further reducing society's spending power and creating a spiral of decline. Nevertheless, it was still clear that if the capitalist system was to survive, some change was necessary. An emergency world conference on economic planning was held in 1933 but came to no conclusions. The United States was reluctant to share Europe's problems and in Europe itself each nation seemed prepared to go it alone. One economist who did understand the problem of crisis was John Maynard Keynes (1883–1946). *His General Theory of Employment, Interest and Money* (1936) offered a solution. An enlarged public sector, based on taxation, would keep up the demand for the products of industry and so avert the crisis. State intervention in the market found few supporters and Keynes was largely ignored at the time – though his ideas were to become highly influential in later years.

## ARCHITECTURE AND FASCISM

The rise to power of Benito Mussolini (1883-1945) was in general tolerated by the Italians, who were ready to accept his brutalisation of political life for the sake of his welcome plans for increased employment, grand public works and national glory. Concessions given to the church won papal support, and from about 1922 onwards Italy appeared once again to have a purpose which awoke echoes of imperial Rome. The building of factories, power-stations, railways, airports and roads stimulated the economy, and at once presented architects with a dilemma – to reject the vicious regime or to accept it in order to obtain commissions. An uneasy, ambivalent attitude prevailed, with many architects, including some of genius like Giuseppe Terragni (1904–42), mentally glossing over Fascism in order to put their architectural ideas into effect. Terragni, like Sant'Elia, was born in Como and was conscious of an architectural debt to his great predecessor. His works, mostly in Como, included a monument to Sant'Elia and the dead of the Great War – a structure distinctly Sant'Elian in style – the Casa Giuliana and the Novocomum, both of them blocks of flats in a rich modern style, and a little infants' school known as the Asilo Sant'Elia. His best-known work is the Casa del Fascio in Como (1932), now the Casa del Popolo, a plain, rectangular, beautifully-proportioned four-storey block of offices around a central courtyard.

In the mid-1920s Adolf Hitler (1889–1945) began his rise to power in Germany. By 1932, his National Socialists were the biggest political party. The Weimar government's attempts to crush Hitler failed and he was eventually asked to form a government himself. A series of dramatic social reforms restored national pride and evoked memories of Prussian greatness: a public works programme, a national labour service, government support for the armaments industry, for manufacturers and farmers, and the introduction of conscription. Germany's rapid economic expansion blinded most eyes to the Nazis' repressive treatment of dissenters, communists, Romanies, Christians and Jews. As in Italy, factories, power-stations, railways, airports and the system of *autobahnen* became the symbols of national regeneration.

Even more symbolic were the stadia. Through international athletics and party rallies Hitler hoped to demonstrate Aryan supremacy to the world, and here the symbolism went beyond Prussia for inspiration, to ancient Greece and Rome. Hitler's own interest in architecture led him to befriend and give office in 1933 to a young German architect, Albert Speer (1905–81), who was to create for the Reich 'buildings ... such as have not

# architecture of fascism

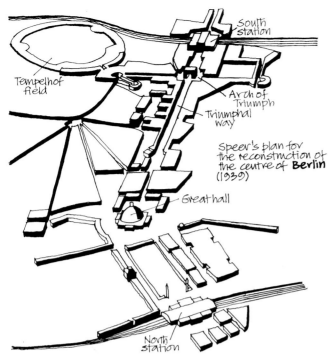

Tempelhof field

South station

Arch of Triumph

Triumphal way

Speer's plan for the reconstruction of the centre of **Berlin** (1939)

Great hall

North station

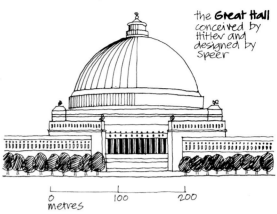

the **Great Hall** conceived by Hitler and designed by Speer

0 metres    100    200

In Nazi **Germany** ponderous neo-classicism became the official style

In **Italy** the Fascists at first welcomed Terragni's progressive approach

But increasing Nazi influence on Mussolini brought Piacentini's traditional style into official favour

Marcello Piacentini's **Via Roma** in Turin (1938) was typical of his neo-classical style

Ginseppe Terragni's **Novocomum flats** (1927) and **Casa del Fascio** (1932) both in Como

been created for four thousand years'. A stadium was built in Berlin to house the 1936 Olympics, but a massive reconstruction planned for the centre of the city – to include a great domed hall, a processional way flanked by new public buildings, a triumphal arch and a new railway terminus – was overtaken by the Second World War. Speer's early training was within the Werkbund-Bauhaus orbit but his association with the Nazis put an end to any aspirations he might have had for modernism: a style was required which evoked the past, and a weighty neo-classicism was thought appropriate. Speer's most impressive architectural accomplishment however was probably his stage-management of the 1934 Nuremburg Rally, for which most of Goering's stock of searchlights was brought to the Zeppelin Field. The effect was beyond Speer's expectations:

> The hundred and thirty sharply defined beams, placed around the field at intervals of forty feet, were visible to a height of twenty to twenty-five thousand feet .... The feeling was of a vast room, with the beams serving as mighty pillars of infinitely high outer walls. Now and then a cloud moved through this wreath of lights, bringing an element of surrealistic surprise to the mirage ...

Henderson, the British Ambassador wrote that 'the effect, which was both solemn and beautiful, was like being in a cathedral of ice.' But theatricality and grandeur disguised a vicious regime. The repression of minority groups only hinted as yet at the horrors to come, but already an exodus of dissident intellectuals, liberals, communists and Jews was under way. The treatment by the Nazis of the Bauhaus was typical.

When the Dessau authorities forced Meyer's resignation in 1930, his place as director was taken by Ludwig Mies van der Rohe (1886–1969). Mies had long been connected with the Werkbund-Bauhaus tradition, having worked for Behrens between 1908 and 1911, and had made a brief excursion into expressionism with his richly-designed and exciting 'project for a glass skyscraper' in 1919. With the establishment of the rational Bauhaus style in the 1920s, however, Mies found his true metier, and his architecture gradually became more spare, calm and elegant. Housing projects in Berlin and Stuttgart established his name. These included a housing development at the Weissenhof Exhibition in Stuttgart in 1927, where he gathered together the work of sixteen progressive architects, including Behrens, Gropius, Poelzig, Taut, Stam, Oud and Le Corbusier. The centrepiece was an elegant four-storey black of flats by Mies himself.

His move towards studied understatement reached a peak with his design for the German pavilion at the Barcelona exhibition of 1929. Designed almost as a house – indeed the same principles were used at the Tugendhat House at Brno, Czechoslovakia, the following year the pavilion was the epitome of Mies's careful yet confident attitude to design. The richest of materials were used – onyx, marble, tinted glass, chromed steel – and the most restrained of concepts: a small, asymmetrical, single-storey flat-roofed building, integrated spatially with a courtyard containing a pool. Divided by the simplest and most carefully-placed partition walls, the whole building was a sequence of elegant and varied spaces, given added lustre by the materials used. The pavilion contained no exhibits: the exhibit was the building itself.

The Barcelona Pavilion was catalytic. Modernism flourished under the Spanish Republican government during the 1930s. The Catalan architect Josep Lluís Sert (1902–83) founded GATEPAC, the Grupo de Artistas y Técnicos Españoles, devoted to the

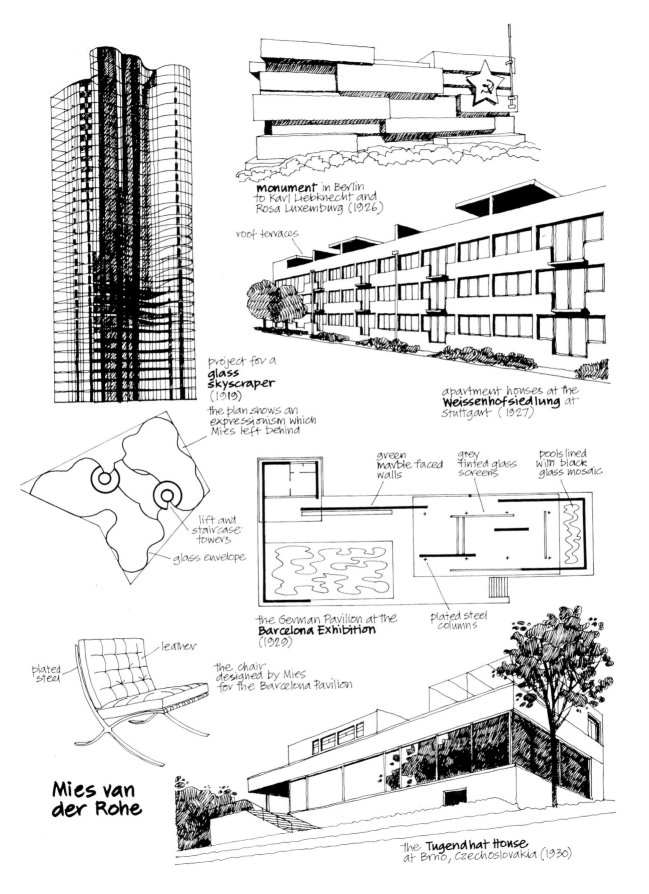

**monument** in Berlin to Karl Liebknecht and Rosa Luxemburg (1926)

roof terraces

project for a
**glass skyscraper**
(1919)

the plan shows an expressionism which Mies left behind

lift and staircase towers

glass envelope

apartment houses at the **Weissenhofsiedlung** at Stuttgart (1927)

green marble faced walls

grey tinted glass screens

pools lined with black glass mosaic

the German Pavilion at the **Barcelona Exhibition** (1929)

plated steel columns

leather

plated steel

the chair designed by Mies for the Barcelona Pavilion

## Mies van der Rohe

the **Tugendhat House** at Brno, Czechoslovakia (1930)

development of modern design. But building of any kind was soon threatened by the Spanish Civil War (1936–9). During the worst years Sert managed to design a number of fine buildings, including the Central Dispensary in Barcelona (1935) and the Spanish Pavilion at the Paris world fair of 1937. The latter is most famous for Picasso's painting *Guernica*. The Basque town had just been bombed by the Nationalists, with Nazi help, as Franco's forces pushed their way into Spain.

When Mies took over the Bauhaus, he and Gropius tried to eradicate its Marxist past, apparently believing that architecture was apolitical and that, if this were made clear for all to see, it would be possible to co-exist with Fascism. The Nazis disagreed. By 1932 the Dessau district was governed by them and they forced the Bauhaus to move to Berlin. In 1933 Hitler himself came to power, and the school was once more under scrutiny. Hitler's architectural taste, and that of his cultural advisors, tended towards traditionalism and kitsch. To them, the Weissenhof was innately alien, a veritable 'Arab village'.

There was worse. Seven years earlier, Mies had designed a monument in Berlin to the communist martyrs Rosa Luxemburg and Karl Liebknecht. The fact that he had fulfilled the commission for architectural and humanitarian rather than political reasons was lost on the suspicious Nazi cultural advisors. To them, the Bauhaus was Bolshevist and un-German, and it was forced to close. For four years Mies continued working in Germany, but at the invitation of the American architect Philip Johnson, he left in 1937 for the United States, where his appointment as head of Chicago's Armour Institute – later the Illinois Institute of Technology (IIT) – began a new chapter in his own life and in that of American architecture.

During the thirties and forties, American and British cultural life was considerably enriched by intellectuals leaving Europe. Some of the architects settled in England, and others paused there briefly before crossing the Atlantic, leaving behind a handful of new buildings and a deep impression on the minds of their more progressive British colleagues. Gropius collaborated with Maxwell Fry on the design of a house in Chelsea (1936) and another at Sevenoaks in Kent (1937). Fry's 'Sun House' in Hampstead (1936) was fully worthy of his eminent partner. Together they built the Impington Village College in Cambridgeshire (1936). Marcel Breuer collaborated with Frederick Yorke, on houses at Bristol (1936), at Eton (1938) and on a long, low, elegant brick-built house, raised on *pilotis*, at Angmering in Sussex (1937). The Russian Serge Chermayeff built a house at Rugby (1934) and one at Halland, Sussex (1939), and with the great Mendelsohn designed a house in Chelsea (1936) and the fine De La Warr Pavilion at the Sussex seaside resort of Bexhill (1935). The firm 'Tecton', set up by Bertold Lubetkin, another Russian émigré, built several houses, two enclosures at London Zoo, the Highpoint flats at Highgate (1936–8) and the Finsbury Health Centre, London (1938–9). To some British conservatives, modern architecture was as alien as it was to Hitler. The De La Warr Pavilion was criticised not only because of its modernist design, but because Mendelsohn was a foreigner and a Jew – though his supporters argued that it was all right really, because Chermayeff his partner was a member of the RIBA. And when Lubetkin came to design the second phase of the otherwise purist Highpoint Flats, he mollified his critics by introducing Greek caryatids as supports for the entrance canopy.

the discovery in 1923 of Tutankhamun's tomb
created a vogue for Egyptian design as in
this **table clock** by Meyrowitz

design on **elevator doors**
in Wall Street office block
of the early 1930s

the Art Deco style became popular
after the Paris Exposition of 1925
where it was featured in all the
pavilions except Le Corbusier's
Purist 'Pavillon de L'Esprit Nouveau'

it was used in hotels, cinemas
and commercial buildings to
express an opulent kind of
modernism..

..as in these gilt metal gates
in the ballroom of **Claridge's**,
London (1929)...

.. or the metalwork pinnacle
of the **Chrysler building**
New York by William van Alen
(1929)

white-painted
render

steel
windows with
horizontal
glazing bars

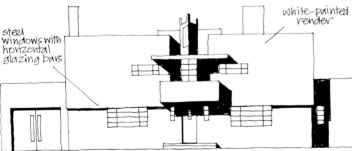

modernistic styling was applied to small, speculative
houses as in this example of the early 1920s
in England

tiles

brickwork

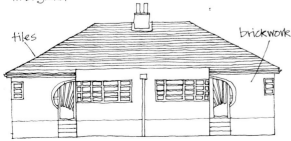

even the most traditionally designed
speculative houses incorporated fashionable
details, like the 'sun-burst' doors on these
1930s 'semi-detached English bungalows'

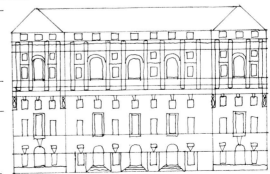

where designers clung to classical styles, the
result was often inappropriate to the
increased height of the buildings. This London
office building is composed of two designs.

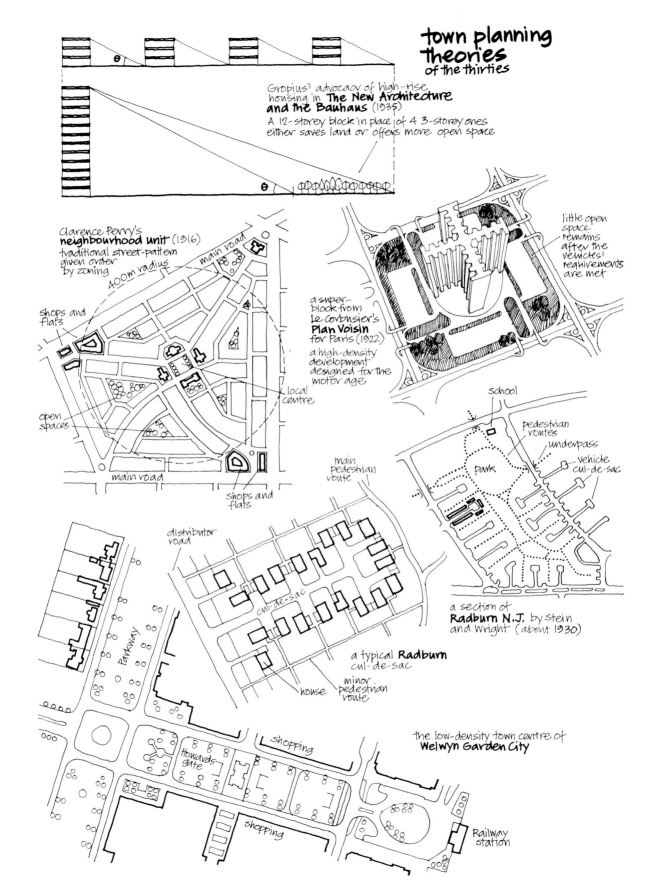

# town planning theories
of the thirties

Gropius' advocacy of high-rise housing in **The New Architecture and the Bauhaus** (1935)

A 12-storey block in place of 4 3-storey ones either saves land or offers more open space

Clarence Perry's **neighbourhood unit** (1916) traditional street-pattern given order by zoning

400m radius

main road

shops and flats

open spaces

local centre

main road

shops and flats

a super-block from Le Corbusier's **Plan Voisin** for Paris (1922)

a high-density development designed for the motor age.

little open space remains after the vehicles' requirements are met

school

pedestrian routes

underpass

vehicle cul-de-sac

Park

a section of **Radburn N.J.** by Stein and Wright (about 1930)

main pedestrian route

distributor road

cul-de-sac

a typical **Radburn** cul-de-sac

house

minor pedestrian route

Parkway

the low-density town centre of **Welwyn Garden City**

Howards gate

shopping

shopping

Railway station

Like Hitler, Franco associated Modernism with Bolshevism. When he came to power in Spain in 1939, he instituted a formal, classical approach to design. Barcelona not only had a modernist culture, it had also been the last Republican stronghold to fall, so was punished accordingly. The repression of Catalan culture lasted throughout Franco's long dictatorship, and many progressive designers emigrated. Sert left for New York in 1939, where he worked in urban design. By 1937, both Gropius and Breuer had moved to Harvard, where they went into partnership and continued teaching, and in the early 1940s Mendelsohn and Chermayeff also moved to America.

In Britain, they left behind a small group of architects and planners whose confidence that a utopian future could be achieved through modern architecture was expressed by the increasing spatial and structural accomplishment of their buildings: the *Daily Express* offices in Fleet Street (1933) by Ellis and Clarke; the Peter Jones Store in Sloane Square, London (1935) by Crabtree, Slater and Moberly; and a number of fine houses by Amyas Connell, Basil Ward and Colin Lucas, which explored many of the design ideas currently interesting Le Corbusier. Using concrete to achieve the rigidity of structure necessary for exciting spatial effects, they built a succession of houses at Ruislip (1935), Redhill and Henfield (1936), Wentworth and Moor Park (1937), culminating in the splendid 66 Frognal, Hampstead (1938).

These pioneer developments were still taking place against a background of public indifference or hostility. A gulf lay between this small group of architects, sure that they had the answer to society's problems, and a public which insisted on going elsewhere for its buildings. The most acceptable style for public buildings was heavy and neoclassical – even though modern structural methods were now common. The result was often a steel-framed, multi-storey building whose baroque stonework was not only out of character but also out of scale with the increased height that the steel frame made possible. In cinema and hotel design, modernism was more permissible, though it seldom took the form of anything more than fashionable applied decoration: the jagged forms of 'jazz modern' or the streamlined shapes of Art Deco.

Cities were still growing at the rate of the industrial revolution, placing enormous demands on space as industry and housing, encouraged by the development of suburban railways and arterial roads, pushed their way out into the countryside. In the city centres, densities were drastically increased as land scarcity put building sites at a premium and the cheaper land at the outer edges of the city was used with prodigality.

## THE DEPRESSION YEARS

Britain's building industry survived reasonably well during the twenties and thirties, and the expansion of the suburbs continued, unaffected by the slump. Nineteenth-century suburbs had represented the desire of the middle classes to escape the city, but now suburbs were being built for lower-middle class and working-class occupation too. The working-class suburb of Becontree in Essex, built between 1921 and 1934 by the LCC for a population of 90,000, was the largest single housing estate in the world. At the other end of the scale, unplanned and piecemeal development was taking place, as individual householders looked for plots on which to put their ideal houses.

Stylistically, the suburban house was often an unhappy mixture of mis-applied historical details derived from such varied sources as the houses of Voysey and those of Tudor England. There were many compensations however: two-storeyed, with front and rear gardens and space for a car, they were a great improvement on those left behind in the crowded city-centre. As a base for family life, they represented the aspirations of a large part of the population. But there were also disadvantages. At this time the local authorities' planning powers were weak: most of the existing controls were in the form of public health bye-laws, the creation of which had been an urgent task in the 19th century. Drainage, lighting, ventilation and space around buildings were thus controlled and ensured certain minimum standards for the house itself. But there was little machinery for making basic decisions about land-use. Estates were built without sufficient open space, because no-one was responsible for providing it; the provision of shops was haphazard; journeys to school might be long and difficult; estates as large as small towns had no focus for their social life.

There was often no architectural focus either: these houses, offering desirable features individually, were monotonous and stereotyped when repeated in their thousands. It was this feature above all which aroused the scorn of progressive architects and set them searching for other ways of designing mass housing to give it more architectural coherence.

One approach was represented by the ideas of Le Corbusier and Gropius; the former in *Vers Une Architecture* and the latter in his book *The New Architecture and the Bauhaus* (1935) were already beginning to show how houses could be piled on top of each other to form regular high-rise blocks and how the space saved could provide landscape for the benefit of all. What was lost, of course, was the autonomy of the individual plot, and the close relationship of the dwelling to the ground. Le Corbusier, with his experience of the long-standing French tradition of flat-dwelling in both cities and suburbs, was prepared to accept this. Less understandably, many of his English colleagues were, too. The desirability of replacing suburbia by high-rise buildings set in park-land became the conventional wisdom for architects, many of whom made their living designing detached houses for wealthy clients.

Another approach was represented by Howard's ordered, balanced garden-city idea which, perhaps because of its nearer approximation to the suburban ideal, continued to have some influence. The approach remained undeveloped in practice, however. Letchworth and Welwyn were very slow to grow – at the end of the 1930s their combined population was less than 40,000 – and the only other major example was Dame Henrietta Barnett's Hampstead Garden Suburb, begun in 1907. On the other hand, many theoretical ideas were being put forward in the United States, where a growing tradition of suburban living made the garden-city idea attractive.

In 1916, the American planner Clarence Perry coined the phrase 'neighbourhood unit'. This idea added a new dimension to garden-city theory by suggesting that each family needed to identify with its local area. This could be done, he suggested, by giving each neighbourhood distinct boundaries and certain specific facilities to act as social foci. Each area would contain about 5000 people – enough to support an elementary school – and would be about a kilometre across, so that the maximum walking-distance to the school and community facilities at the centre would be no more than 400 or 500 metres.

The high car-ownership in America meant that its planners had to consider how to integrate traffic movement into the design of housing. In the late 1920s a four-square-kilometre new town was begun at Radburn, NJ, by the City Housing Corporation. The intention was to build the first American garden city, housing 25,000 people in a number of neighbourhoods based on the Perry principle. The designers, Clarence Stein and Henry Wright, were able to try out their own ideas too, the most important being to separate pedestrian and vehicle movement. Each residential super-block, surrounded by distributor roads, had a central greenway, a pedestrian area onto which all the houses faced. Each greenway was linked to the next by an underpass below the surrounding roads and so it was possible to walk through the town without even seeing a motor vehicle. Radburn was never completed, but the idea, with its emphasis on amenity and safety, remained a major feature of housing philosophy.

In the city centres, particularly those of New York, Chicago and Philadelphia, rising land values pushed office buildings higher and higher. The archetypal New York skyscraper appeared during the 1920s. Wall Street became a forest of tall buildings and even higher ones began to appear in the mid-town area. The City Zoning Ordinance required set-backs on successive floors as the buildings increased in height, which produced the characteristic tapering profile of the New York Life building by Cass Gilbert, of the Chrysler building by William van Allen, and of William Lamb's Empire State building, all designed in a characteristic 'Art Deco' style. At a height of 370 metres, the Empire State was for some time the tallest building in the world. Slightly more modernistic in character was Raymond Hood's Rockefeller Centre, a complex of buildings and spaces dominated by the RCA building, and incorporating an outdoor ice-rink and the Radio City Music Hall.

These spectacular buildings contrasted poignantly with urban unemployment and poverty during the Depression. And in the prairies the 'dustbowl' disaster was leading to a desperate search for work, sending thousands of 'Okies' overland to California. Work was scarce here too, and the gap between rich and poor just as wide. The archetypal Californian luxury house, in Art Deco or Spanish style, ingeniously planned, on a steep hillside site, belongs to this period. These early years of the European presence in the United States also resulted in some fine modern buildings, representing a first real contact with the international style. In 1926, the architect Rudolf Schindler built a house at Newport Beach, Calif, and the following year, Richard Neutra built the Health House near Los Angeles. Both architects were Austrian émigrés with early connections to Wagner and Loos, and the client for both houses was Philip Lovell, an American doctor. The prominent concrete balconies of both houses, the wide windows letting in the sun, and sliding back to let in the breezes, epitomised Lovell's firm views about the relationship between good architecture and good health.

Meanwhile, at IIT, Mies began to re-plan the campus, designing the new buildings as simple, elegant glass boxes, and bringing an unequivocal statement of the machine aesthetic to his adopted country. By now, Gropius too had moved to the USA. In 1938 he built himself a house in Lincoln, Mass., in which he reinterpreted traditional New England timber construction in an innovative way. Even Wright, most American of architects, came as near during the 1930s as he ever did to the international style. His house Falling Water for Edgar Kaufman, at Bear Run, Pa. (1936), was built above a

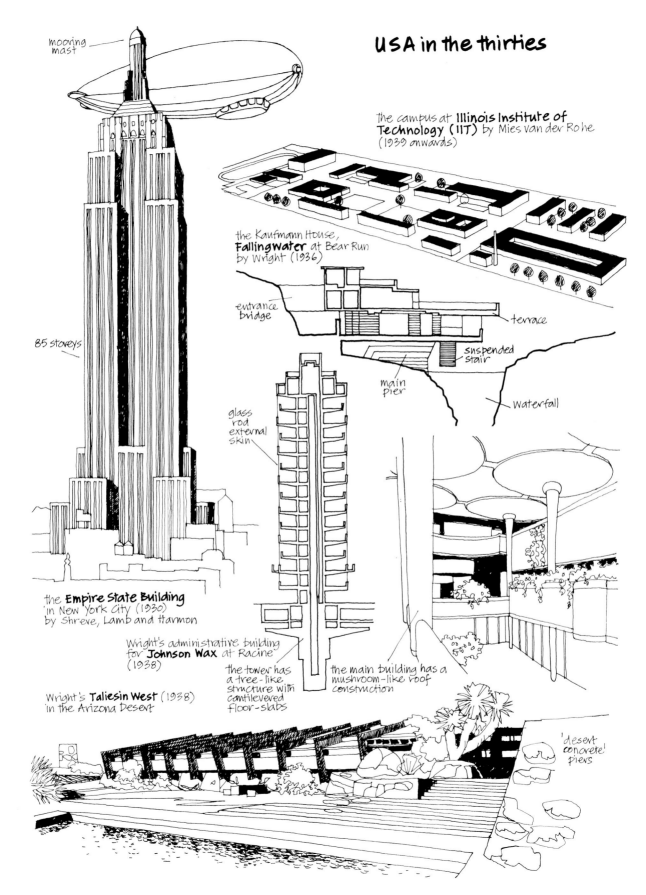

# USA in the thirties

mooring mast

85 storeys

**the Empire State Building**
in New York City (1930)
by Shreve, Lamb and Harmon

the campus at **Illinois Institute of Technology (IIT)** by Mies van der Rohe (1939 onwards)

the Kaufmann House,
**Fallingwater** at Bear Run
by Wright (1936)

entrance bridge

terrace

suspended stair

main pier

Waterfall

glass rod external skin

Wright's administrative building
for **Johnson Wax** at Racine
(1938)

the tower has
a tree-like
structure with
cantilevered
floor-slabs

the main building has a
mushroom-like roof
construction

Wright's **Taliesin West** (1938)
in the Arizona Desert

'desert concrete' piers

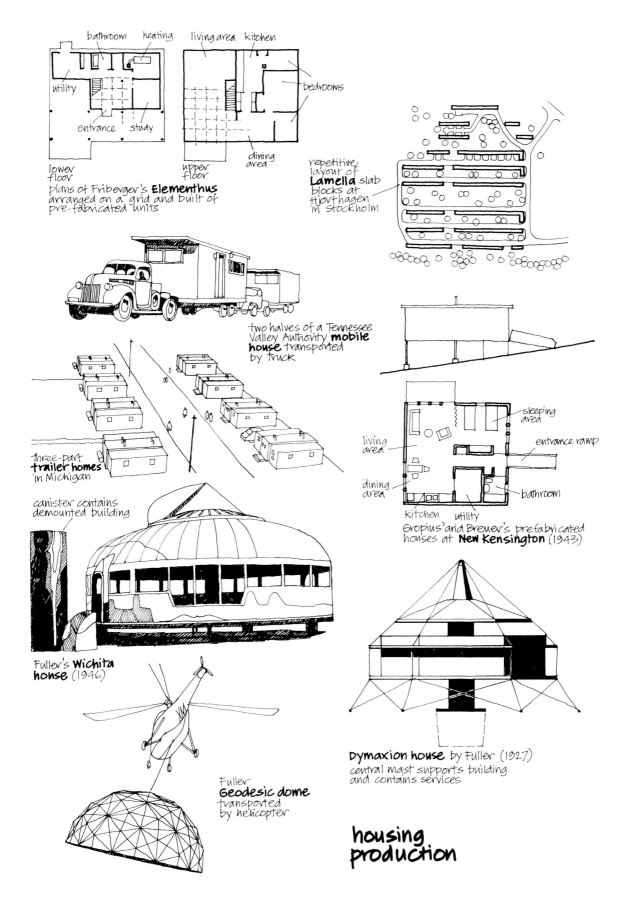

bathroom   heating   living area   kitchen

utility

bedrooms

entrance   study

dining area

lower floor

upper floor

plans of Friberger's **Elementhus** arranged on a grid and built of pre-fabricated units

repetitive layout of **Lamella** slab blocks at Hjorthagen in Stockholm

two halves of a Tennessee Valley Authority **mobile house** transported by truck

three-part **trailer homes** in Michigan

sleeping area

entrance ramp

living area

dining area

bathroom

kitchen   utility

Gropius' and Breuer's prefabricated houses at **New Kensington** (1943)

canister contains demounted building

Fuller's **Wichita house** (1946)

Fuller **Geodesic dome** transported by helicopter

**Dymaxion house** by Fuller (1927)
central mast supports building and contains services

housing production

waterfall, and was as romantic a conception as any of his prairie houses. At the same time, its prominent, white reinforced-concrete cantilevers gave it an air of undecorated simplicity, rare in Wright's work. A similar simplicity characterised his administration building for the Johnson Wax company at Racine in Wisconsin (1938). There was no decoration, and its brick and glass were used-in a strong, original and honest manner. The great richness of the building came mostly from its spatial ingenuity combined with structural discipline, with giant, mushroom-headed columns as a major feature.

The same year, by contrast, Wright produced the most organic and most American of all his buildings. Taliesin West was built in 1938 as a studio-house where he and his students could develop their architectural ideas in monastic seclusion. The building is a romantic response to a spectacular desert site near Phoenix in Arizona which for Wright was the epitome of the frontier. A long, low, tent-like structure, with a roof of canvas and cedar-wood supported on massive piers of 'desert concrete' – boulders held together with cement – it has ancient Mayan, and even Biblical, overtones.

In 1938 Taliesin could hardly have seemed more remote from the political situation in Europe. The growing tensions between the three rival political systems – Stalin's state-capitalism, the Fascism of Italy and Germany, and the struggling capitalism of the other countries – was given a new urgency by German rearmament. The First World War had had both political causes and political effects – the collapse of the old European regimes – but did nothing to resolve the contradictions of a crisis-ridden economic system. The Second World War – though Hitler's politics were undoubtedly its catalyst – was essentially the result of that unresolved economic crisis.

# 12 WELFARE CAPITALISM
## *1945–1973*

The Second World War was hugely destructive. The victims of the Great War had mainly been combatants, but now, entire civilian populations were decimated or displaced. Cities all over the world, from Hiroshima, to Berlin, to Rotterdam to Coventry, had been destroyed. At first, the world economy was slow to recover. The ravaged infrastructure and the social and economic disruption created a painful age of austerity.

However, two factors came together to aid recovery. The first was the technological advance which, paradoxically, the War had created. Nuclear fission, rocketry and aerospace, communications technology, the science of lightweight and synthetic materials, the widespread use of factory production and of prefabrication, not to mention the state controls of industry which had made the various war efforts so effective, all combined to create a technological base on which to build. The second was a general determination that physical reconstruction should be accompanied by social and economic reform, to banish for ever the inequalities and the stagnation of the inter-War period.

Both socially and architecturally, Sweden provided a model for western Europe. Having remained neutral, she had escaped physical destruction and was making steady social progress. A humane, social-democratic government had been in office since the early 1930s, and had established a high standard of living, publicly-provided social services, free education and good industrial relations.

The Weissenhof exhibition in Stuttgart in 1927 inspired a similar one in Stockholm in 1930. The co-ordinator, and designer of several of the buildings, was the architect Sven Markelius. The mixed layout of public buildings, houses, flats and urban landscape, more organised and more varied than the Weissenhof, created an exciting yet realistic image of the city of the future. The Swedish political system encouraged new ideas in housing. Among these was the 'lamella' house. Here, lightweight timber floors, made up of members which spread the stresses in all directions, allowed large spans, and resulted in wide-fronted, shallow houses, giving daylight to all rooms, in contrast to the narrow-fronted introspective houses of Swedish tradition. Lamella houses, in regular, continuous rows, were to make a considerable, if utilitarian, impact on many European townscapes. A typical application was the Hjorthagen area of Stockholm, with workers' houses designed by Hakon Ahlberg. Then, in 1937, the architect Eric Friberger evolved his *elementhus*, or 'element' house which, as its name suggests, consisted of prefabricated units. It was flexible enough to be used for a variety of family sizes, and could even be extended or reduced as the family size changed.

Tower blocks of flats provided higher densities than the lamella terrace, and began appearing in Sweden even before the Second World War. The country's social-democratic ethos favoured communal, rather than private outdoor spaces. Sun-balconies might be provided in blocks of flats, but at ground level the land was usually communal, with public landscaped areas stretching right up to the walls of the houses. The provision of common spaces was a feature of Swedish planning, and was typified by the building of 'collective' houses for families whose parents were at work, with communal restaurants, kitchens, laundries and day-nurseries, the first of which was designed by Markelius for Stockholm in 1935.

Post-War recovery in the capitalist west depended on international co-operation. The economist J. M. Keynes was instrumental in setting up the World Bank and the International Monetary Fund. Many governments adopted the principles laid down in his *General Theory*, and created strong public sectors, based on general taxation. Famously, Keynes had suggested that it made economic sense for the authorities to pay men to dig a hole in the morning and fill it in again in the afternoon. The money they earned would be ploughed back into the economy and stimulate demand. But how much better if their labour were used to create products of social value.

In Britain the 1942 Beveridge Report had suggested how such a programme of social benefits might be achieved. The Labour government of 1945 brought Keynesian economics and social reform together in what the planner Colin Buchanan later called a 'burst of noble legislation'. Education, health and social security systems were set up and many of the country's major functions, like agriculture, the docks, the coal-mines and the railways, were nationalised. Public sector employment increased from about 9% before the War, to 25% after it.

Improving the physical environment was integral to this programme. The County of London Plan (1943) by J. H. Forshaw and Patrick Abercrombie proposed the replanning of the London region, the rebuilding of devastated areas and the setting-up of a ring of new towns on the other side of an encircling 'green belt' which limited the spread of the city. Decentralisation, it was felt, would not only relieve urban congestion, but would also make populations less vulnerable to attack from the air. To provide the machinery for this, the New Towns Act (1946) and the Town and Country Planning Act (1947) gave Britain the most powerful and advanced land-use planning laws in the world. Public benefit was the main aim. The legislation even included provision for claiming back for the public the equivalent of the increased land value that resulted from a planning permission.

In the forties, the British system was still only a system, and not much had been achieved on the ground. But an important example of what could be done was provided by the United States. President Roosevelt's New Deal (1933–41), a response to the Depression, had introduced the country to the concept of state control of the economy and the carrying-out of major public works. In 1933 the Tennessee Valley Authority

(TVA) was set up to direct federal funds to an area of great social and economic need. Then, under acute wartime conditions, with production strained and one-third of the population still badly housed, state control was extended to the housing industry. A crash programme was set up to design and build factory-produced homes both temporary and permanent, both communal and self-contained. The TVA itself pioneered low-cost prefabricated housing delivered in sections to the site on flat-bed trucks. Gropius and Breuer collaborated in the design of prefabricated housing at the aluminium company town of New Kensington in Pennsylvania.

The lessons learned from wartime factory production seemed appropriate for meeting the challenge of post-war rebuilding. Not only had management become more efficient but new techniques had been evolved, often with the extra stimulus of material shortage. Among the more interesting were those of Richard Buckminster Fuller (1895–1983) the designer and inventor. As early as 1927 he had designed and built his prototype 'Dymaxion' house, consisting of two hexagonal metal decks suspended from a central mast which contained the services. The intention was to apply the efficiency and precision of car-building techniques to house construction. The Wichita House (1946) was a prototype metal house produced on the assembly line of an aircraft company, to be packed in a crate and sent anywhere it was needed.

Fuller's most successful work however, was in the science of 'geodesics'. This technique involved the building-up of curved forms – in Fuller's case, domes – by linking together a number of pre-fabricated elements, regular in form, triangular or hexagonal. The connectors were aligned along 'great circles', lines representing the shortest possible distance across the curved surface, and resulted in strong yet extremely light structures: a geodesic dome might easily weigh $\frac{1}{20}$th of an equivalent span in more conventional construction. It was often an advantage, particularly for the military, which helped Fuller develop his ideas, that his buildings were light enough to be picked up bodily and moved elsewhere. Many thousands of Fuller domes were manufactured in aluminium, plywood, plastic, corrugated steel, prestressed concrete or kraft paper and were used for houses, factories, warehouses and exhibition buildings, both temporary and permanent. Fuller later progressed into the realm of 'tensegrity' structures, in which a distinction is made between members in compression and members in tension, allowing each to be more efficiently and economically designed. The furniture designer and film-maker Charles Eames (1907–78) shared Fuller's interest in technology and his own house in Santa Monica, Calif. (1949), built from standard manufactured parts, did much to demonstrate the simple elegance that such an understated approach could obtain.

## MEDIUM AND MESSAGE

The architectural language of the twenties and thirties was now well known. Air travel, newscasting and publishing – including architectural magazines like *Domus*, *Casabella*, *Architectural Forum* and *Architectural Design* – made its scope truly international. Culturally, as the theorist Marshall McLuhan noted, we now lived in a 'global village'. As the world economy recovered, spectacular new buildings became the *lingua franca* of designers everywhere. An office tower for the Brazilian Ministry of Education in Rio de Janeiro (1943) demonstrated this commonality. Designed by the Brazilian architects Oscar Niemeyer and Lucio Costa, with Le Corbusier as consultant, it was a synthesis of cultures.

In London, an international exhibition, the Festival of Britain, was held in 1951, exactly 100 years after Prince Albert's Great Exhibition. It was intended to celebrate post-War recovery and, despite all the austerity, architects and designers did their best to create the cheerful image of an innovative, optimistic future. The only permanent building on the site was the Royal Festival Hall, designed by a team of London County Council architects led by Robert Matthew. It was perhaps Britain's last great building of the international style, with all the formal purity and spatial richness of the great buildings of the thirties – though now sadly diminished by an ill-conceived 'refurbishment'.

The Italian engineer Pier Luigi Nervi (1891–1979) built two fine exhibition halls at Turin (1948–50) whose elegant reinforced-concrete roofs combined structural efficiency with a romantic delicacy of expression. In Rome, a design team led by Eugenio Montuori built Termini railway station (1951), whose clarity of planning and dramatic curving concrete roof influenced much subsequent station design.

Mies van der Rohe's two tower-blocks of luxury flats at 860 Lake Shore Drive, Chicago (1951) and his Farnsworth House at Plano, Ill. (1950) were a move towards ever greater subtlety and refinement. This was a kind of almost negative architecture, containing pure, simple spaces which the inhabitants could use how they wished. Eero Saarinen's (1910–61) General Motors Technical Centre at Warren, Michigan (1951) consisted of luxurious, Miesian buildings in a large, open landscape, planned at the scale of the motor-car in a demonstration of conspicuous consumption.

But just as international Modernism was establishing itself, some of its former champions were moving on. Le Corbusier, for example, began a search for a less refined, more assertive personal style. His amazing pilgrimage chapel of Notre Dame du Haut at Ronchamp in France (1950) was an intriguing combination of functionalism and pure sculpture. Its puzzled critics saw its bizarre, hybrid structure as a betrayal of the principles of modern architecture, perhaps without appreciating the rigorous functionalism of the building's planning, nor the fact that Le Corbusier was also a post-Cubist painter and sculptor of some distinction.

Another personal style was that of the Finnish architect Alvar Aalto (1898–1976). Before the War he had been a practitioner of a fairly straightforward international style of design, demonstrated by the Viipuri library (1927), a factory with workers' housing at Sumila (1936) and his best-known early work, a large tuberculosis clinic at Paimio (1929), built in reinforced concrete. Partly because of their cost, modern materials like steel and concrete were alien to Finnish building experience, and Aalto became increasingly interested in the building techniques of local tradition, and the restrained architectural character which resulted – small-scale, low, modest buildings built in load-bearing masonry or, especially, timber.

His experiments in the 1930s in the design of bent-wood furniture ran parallel with the growth of the Finnish plywood and laminated timber business, which remains today one of the country's principal manufacturing industries. He was thus able to combine a feeling for Finnish tradition with a perception of the most up-to-date techniques it

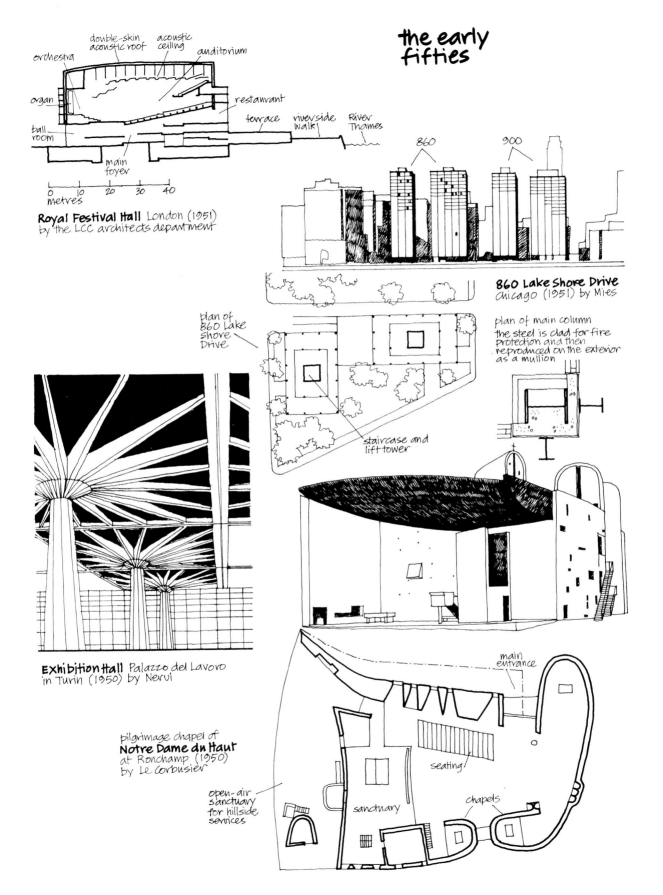

orchestra

double-skin
acoustic roof

acoustic
ceiling

auditorium

organ

restaurant

ball
room

terrace

riverside
walk

River
Thames

main
foyer

0   10   20   30   40
metres

**Royal Festival Hall** London (1951)
by the LCC architects department

860

900

**860 Lake Shore Drive**
Chicago (1951) by Mies

plan of
860 Lake
shore
Drive

plan of main column
the steel is clad for fire
protection and then
reproduced on the exterior
as a mullion

staircase and
lift tower

**Exhibition Hall** Palazzo del Lavoro
in Turin (1950) by Nervi

main
entrance

seating

pilgrimage chapel of
**Notre Dame du Haut**
at Ronchamp (1950)
by Le Corbusier

chapels

open-air
sanctuary
for hillside
services

sanctuary

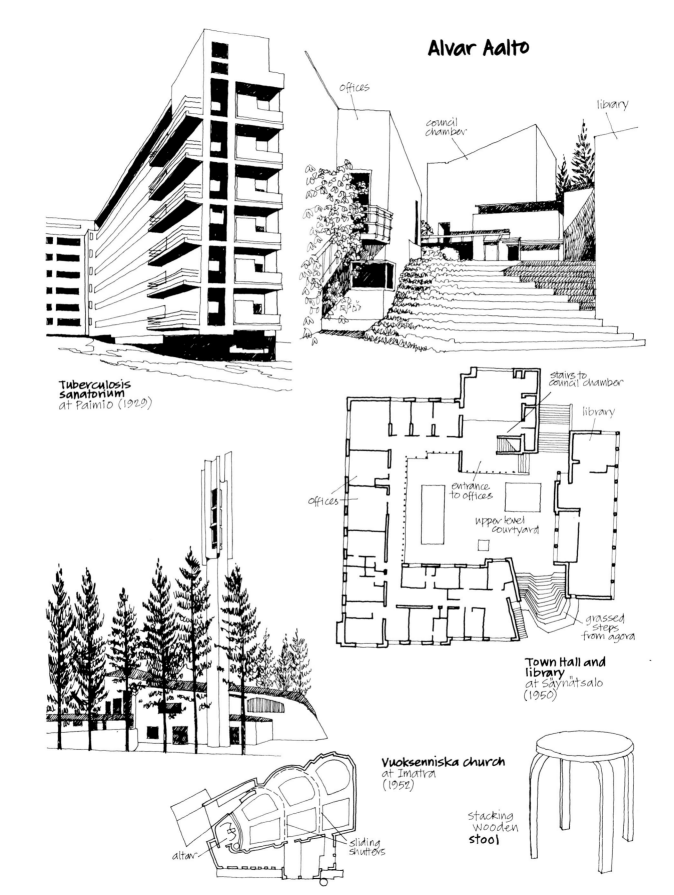

# Alvar Aalto

**Tuberculosis sanatorium** at Paimio (1929)

offices

council chamber

library

stairs to council chamber

library

offices

entrance to offices

upper level courtyard

grassed steps from agora

**Town Hall and library** at Säynätsalo (1950)

**Vuoksenniska church** at Imatra (1952)

altar

sliding shutters

Stacking wooden **stool**

had to offer, and to synthesise the two into the most personal, most self-contained, least fashionable style of any of the great modern architects. His buildings have the spatial richness of Wright's, but without Wright's clutter of decoration; they have a Miesian precision without verging on oversimplification; and they have much of Le Corbusier's grandeur without his occasional grandiosity.

Aalto's post-war reputation rests mainly on two buildings. The first was his beautiful village hall for the tiny island of Säynatsälo. This was perhaps a more important commission than its small size and humble location would suggest: Finland's highly decentralised economy placed great importance on local life. The design of a village hall inevitably says much about the relationship between people and authority. Säynatsälo was a new town for 3000 people, for which Aalto prepared the plan. At its centre was a loosely-planned 'market' area, a main meeting-place recalling the agora of ancient times. At one side were placed the village hall and library, regularly planned around a small courtyard, linked to the market-place by a set of steps. The characterful brickwork and pitched timber roofs of these small buildings give an air of informality and approachability absent from the design of most other civic buildings in Europe or America, either before or since.

His second great building was the Vuoksenniska church at Imatra (1952), contemporary with Ronchamp and an interesting contrast. Both buildings are highly sculptural and spatially and structurally free. But where Ronchamp is a bold composition of parabolic curves, Imatra is complex and intense. Ronchamp stands as a monument on an open hill-side, but Imatra lies low among pine-trees, with only its tall elegant tower to mark it from a distance. It consists of three interlinked compartments, separated or opened up at will by sliding screens, with a huddle of ancillary rooms round the edge. Three copper-clad hump-back roofs cover the three compartments, canted at one side to provide large areas of high-level glazing above the surrounding walls. The idea is simple, but the shapes themselves, and the detailing, are asymmetrical and complex.

Ronchamp was not Le Corbusier's only work of the period. In 1946 he began construction of a building in the suburbs of Marseille which became perhaps the single most influential architectural work of the Post-War years. This was the *Unité d'Habitation de grandeur conforme*, completed in 1952, a massive housing project to rehouse the shipyard workers from the Vieux-Port quarter of the city destroyed in the War. Le Corbusier saw it as an opportunity to put into practice the theoretical ideas of his Ville Contemporaine and Ville Radieuse, and the Unité was only the first of a number of blocks intended to restructure the whole social life of Marseille.

The scale of the building was immense. An entire suburb of 1600 people was to be housed in a single rectangular block, 140 metres long and 24 deep, 20 storeys and more in height, containing not only living space but also shops and sports and play areas. The block was aligned north-south, with aspects to both east and west, allowing all the units – mostly duplexes, ingeniously interlocking around a central access corridor – to receive both morning and evening sun. *Soleil, espace, verdure*, was Le Corbusier's approach. The 'espace' came partly from the double-height living-rooms, on the Citrohan principle, opening onto private open-air balconies, while the 'verdure' was the Provençal landscape, visible not only around the building but also below it, between its giant ground-floor *pilotis*.

Le Corbusier's early interest in prefabrication was apparent in the construction. The main frame was an 'in situ' – that is, 'poured-in-place' – skeleton of reinforced-concrete columns and beams, within which the wall and floor panels of the flats were located, isolated from the main structure, for sound insulation, by pads of lead. Much of the repetitive cladding, including the sun-screens or *brises-soleil*, was precast and lifted into position. The dimensional control implicit in the use of precast elements was given extra point by the use of the 'Modulor', a system of harmonious proportion recently devised by Le Corbusier, based on the principles of the Golden Section.

At the time, one of the more startling things about the building was its surface texture. The idea of concrete as a smooth, precise material – which had informed much of the architecture of the 1920s, including Le Corbusier's own – was here set aside in recognition of its being a plastic material, dependent for its shape on the shutter-boards within which it is cast. It appeared in the Unité, heavily-textured, marked with the knots and grain of the formwork, totally in keeping with the elephantine scale of the building itself.

Le Corbusier followed the Unité with a pair of small houses for private clients, the Jaoul family, in the Parisian suburb of Neuilly (1954). Here the same roughness of detail is apparent – rustic brick walls and heavy concrete floorslabs, with low, barrel-vaulted roofs. The reversion from the machine aesthetic of the Villa Savoye to this earthiness could hardly have been more dramatic. The same aesthetic continued into his two final *chefs d'oeuvre*, the Parliamentary buildings at Chandigarh, new capital of the Punjab (1950–65), and the monastery of La Tourette (1960) near Lyon. The main feature of Chandigarh was the Capitol, a group of four buildings – Palace, Secretariat, Assembly and Supreme Court – enormous in scale but all but dwarfed by a vast, open landscape shaped by Le Corbusier's cosmic geometry. The combination of spatial complexity and textural roughness – intellectual yet technically primitive – seems highly appropriate to the function and the location. And the use of stark, exposed concrete could hardly be more appropriate than among the severe, disciplined Cistercians of La Tourette, in a simple, block-like building whose cunning roof-shapes made the plain interiors glow with light.

Le Corbusier's concrete work helped give birth to a new international style, and his term for it – *béton brut* – gave rise to the name 'brutalism'. Stirling and Gowan's low-rise Langham housing development at Ham Common, London (1958), had the roughness of the Maisons Jaoul. Churchill College, Cambridge (1960), by Sheppard, Robson and Partners, though made of exposed brick and concrete, was rather neater and politer a building. The use of this tough and rugged style for institutional buildings was perhaps understandable but sometimes lacking in sympathy. Aldo van Eyck's orphanage at Amsterdam (1958) and Vittoriano Viganò's Instituto Marchiondi (1959), an institute in Milan for deprived boys, perhaps provide unnecessarily harsh environments.

In the United States, brutalism was softened with touches of luxury, as in the elegantly-ribbed exposed concrete of Paul Rudolph's Art and Architecture building at Yale (1959). Japanese architects were particularly receptive to it. Here the strong forms of *béton brut* were used in a way which resembled the over-lapping baulks of timber in traditional Japanese construction. Among the best examples were two early works by Kenzo Tange, his building for the Yamanshi Broadcasting company at Koufu

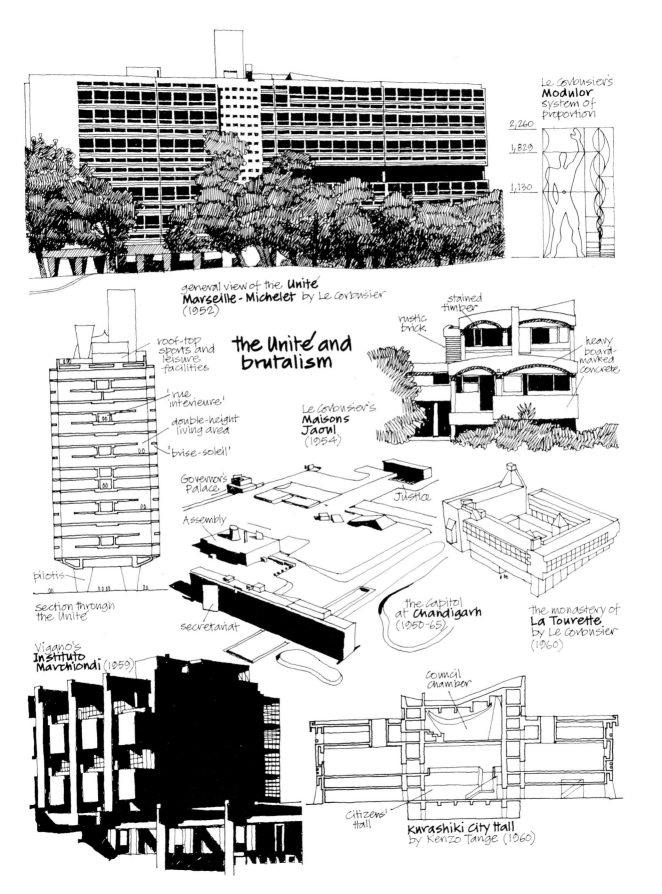

Le Corbusier's
**Modulor**
system of
proportion

2,260

1,829

1,130

general view of the **Unité
Marseille - Michelet** by Le Corbusier
(1952)

roof-top
sports and
leisure
facilities

**the Unité and
brutalism**

stained
timber

rustic
brick

heavy
board-
marked
concrete

'rue
intérieure'

double-height
living area

'brise-soleil'

Le Corbusier's
**Maisons
Jaoul**
(1954)

Governor's
Palace

Justice

Assembly

pilotis

section through
the Unité

secretariat

the Capitol
at **Chandigarh**
(1950-65)

the monastery of
**La Tourette**
by Le Corbusier
(1960)

Vigano's
**Instituto
Marchiondi** (1959)

Council
chamber

Citizens'
Hall

**Kurashiki City Hall**
by Kenzo Tange (1960)

(1967) and his magnificent City Hall at Kurashiki (1960). But perhaps the most fitting application of the properties of *béton brut* was in the small evangelical Church of the Atonement built by Helmut Striffler in 1965 on the site of the Dachau concentration camp in Bavaria, a partly underground building approached by a broad set of steps and contained, with appropriate symbolism, inside a strong, jagged, ribbed-concrete retaining-wall. Its uncompromising modernity was in direct contrast to the classicism and kitsch favoured by the Nazis.

## HIGH-RISE LIVING

Of all Le Corbusier's late buildings, the Unité had the widest influence. Among other things, it encouraged everywhere the building of high-rise flats for family living, a piece of conventional wisdom which was to persist for longer than it deserved. It should be said that the original concept of the Ville Radieuse, with its emphasis on spacious landscape, on community facilities within the block and on upper-level gardens for every flat, would have done much to counter the sense of isolation and the lack of outdoor space which have been major criticisms of high-rise living. The Unité itself fell somewhat short of the theory – certainly the small balconies were little substitute for high-level gardens – but the numerous subsequent imitations and mis-applications of Le Corbusier's ideas fell shorter still.

One of the better follow-ups was the Alton housing estate designed by the LCC architects, led by Robert Matthew, for the London suburb of Roehampton (1952–9). In this, the Ville Radieuse was translated from Provence to a romantic landscape of English parkland. It consisted of five slab-blocks of duplex flats, a number of tower-blocks, and lower terraces of flats and houses, all set in a luxurious landscape of lawns and trees. The tall blocks were neater and politer versions of the Unité. One of the biggest differences was the absence of Le Corbusier's communal spaces. The Unité contained shops, cafés, a bar, a health clinic, crèche, nursery, club and play areas. Though such facilities were provided at Roehampton, they were nearby, rather than in the blocks themselves.

The idea of community was uppermost in the minds of Lewis Womersley, the Sheffield city architect, and of Jack Lynn and the design team of the Park Hill flats (1961). This massive slum-clearance project, stretched out across a rocky hill-side in the city centre, consisted of a number of slab-blocks linked at various levels by continuous 'access-decks', from which opened the doors of every flat. The decks, over three metres wide, were the backbone of the scheme. Used both by people and by lightweight delivery trucks, they were intended to work like traditional streets – not only as a means of getting about, but also as places for people to meet and for children to play in. The concept was similar – though more thoroughgoing in its application – to the internal access corridor of the Unité.

The reason for simulating a traditional street, rather than actually building one, was a question of density. It was thought important to conserve as much land as possible, so Park Hill was in effect three streets of houses piled on top of one another. There was no other way of achieving the high densities required, for the scheme had to contain 500 people per hectare of land. Neither the Unité nor the Alton estate was built at a very high density; the main reason for tall buildings had been the retention of as much as possible of the living landscape below. But inevitably, few sites were in areas of landscape. Inevitably too, higher densities meant less open space, fewer places for children to play and an increase in the psychological pressures that occur when privacy is at a premium. Denys Lasdun's 16-storey 'cluster-block' of flats at Bethnal Green, London (1956), made the best use of a restricted site by providing outdoor spaces at the upper levels for sitting out and talking to neighbours. But other schemes were being built whose design and density were placing considerable strains on their inhabitants, producing isolation and loneliness where there should have been a sense of community, and exposure and insecurity where there should have been privacy.

It must always be recognised that the new blocks of flats provided much lighter, warmer and healthier accommodation than the old slums the tenants were moving out of. Yet in urban areas all over the world high blocks of flats continued to pose social problems. The alienation of high-rise living was shared by tenants in the towers of the peripheral Glasgow estate of Red Road and in the 26-storey blocks of Co-Op City in New York. The malaise of the high-density *banlieues* in Paris had its counterpart in the *superbloques* of Caracas. The petty crime and vandalism on the Southwark estates in south London were also seen at the vast Pruitt-Igoe redevelopment in St Louis, Mo.

On the green-field sites of the new towns, there was the opportunity for a different approach. Here, low-rise housing provided a better home environment for a family, and the acres of green space made for healthier and cleaner surroundings. The early 1950s saw the development of new communities outside many major cities in Europe and America. In Scandinavia, they were mostly treated as satellites to their parent cities: Årsla, Vällingby, Farsta and Täby to Stockholm, Bellahøj to Copenhagen and Tapiola to Helsinki. Small in size, with their own community centres but depending largely for shopping and employment on the city, they were like well-planned suburbs. At their best, they were idyllic, as at Tapiola with its wide variety of buildings set in a spectacular landscape of forests and lakes.

In Britain, by the late 1960s, almost a million people had been housed in twenty-one new towns, eight of them – such as Harlow, Stevenage and Basildon – near London. Larger in size and farther from the centre than their Swedish counterparts, they were as self-contained as possible. They were divided, according to the theories of Perry, into neighbourhoods of 5000 to 10,000 people, each area being planned to exclude through-traffic, often on the Radburn principle. However, the spacious, spread-out housing made for long travelling distances. Though some towns, such as Runcorn near Liverpool, provided efficient bus-services or, like Glasgow's new town of Cumbernauld, were designed compactly enough to encourage walking, in general it was necessary to rely on the motor-car. New towns demanded a certain affluence.

British and Swedish new towns were publicly financed. The relative lack of public enterprise in north America encouraged the private development of new towns. The best-known are perhaps Kitimat, BC, in Canada, built by the aluminium company Alcan, and Reston, Va., near Washington DC, financed by a variety of private interests. The latter, a series of neighbourhood 'villages' set in a landscape of boating lakes, golf-courses and riding-schools, was an unashamed demonstration of middle-class luxury. This feature was shared, to a lesser extent, by many modern new towns, their expansive, successful economies attracting the fairly young, resourceful and economically active.

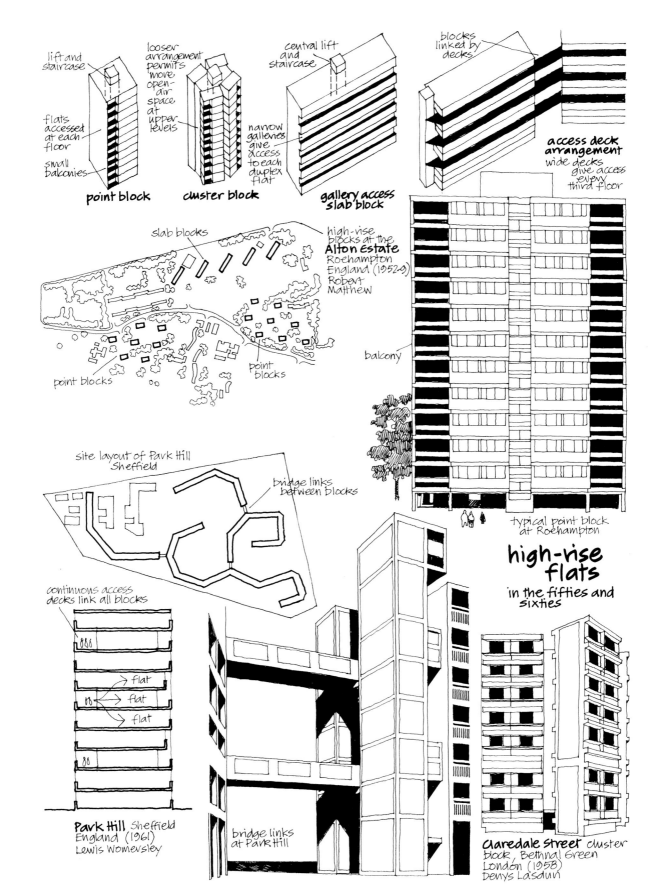

**point block**

lift and staircase

flats accessed at each floor

small balconies

**cluster block**

looser arrangement permits more open-air space at upper levels

**gallery access slab block**

central lift and staircase

narrow galleries give access to each duplex flat

**access deck arrangement**
wide decks give access every third floor

blocks linked by decks

slab blocks

high-rise blocks at the **Alton Estate** Roehampton England (1952-9) Robert Matthew

point blocks

point blocks

balcony

typical point block at Roehampton

# high-rise flats
in the fifties and sixties

site layout of Park Hill Sheffield

bridge links between blocks

continuous access decks link all blocks

flat
flat
flat

**Park Hill** Sheffield England (1961) Lewis Womersley

bridge links at Park Hill

**Claredale Street** cluster block, Bethnal Green London (1958) Denys Lasdun

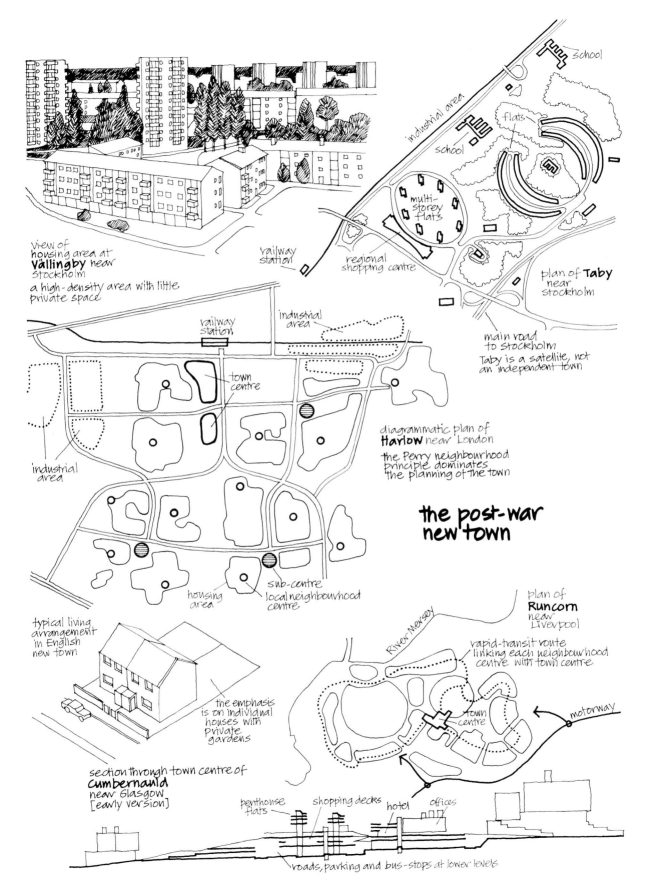

view of
housing area at
**Vällingby** near
Stockholm

a high-density area with little
private space

railway
station

school

industrial area

school

flats

multi-
storey
flats

regional
shopping centre

plan of **Taby**
near
Stockholm

main road
to Stockholm

Taby is a satellite, not
an independent town

railway
station

industrial
area

town
centre

diagrammatic plan of
**Harlow** near London

the Perry neighbourhood
principle dominates
the planning of the town

the post-war
new town

industrial
area

housing
area

sub-centre
local neighbourhood
centre

typical living
arrangement
in English
new town

the emphasis
is on individual
houses with
private gardens

plan of
**Runcorn**
near
Liverpool

River Mersey

rapid-transit route
linking each neighbourhood
centre with town centre

town
centre

motorway

section through town centre of
**Cumbernauld**
near Glasgow
[early version]

penthouse
flats

shopping decks

hotel

offices

roads, parking and bus-stops at lower levels

New towns, with their emphasis on self-contained living, on car-borne mobility, on the shopping centre as the focus of communal life and on the lavish provision of recreation, tended to emphasise the material welfare of this highly active group to the relative exclusion of others.

New-town house design tended to be unadventurous. It was important in attracting people from the cities to provide the same kind of safe, marketable product that they would have looked for in suburbia. It was instead the captive population remaining in the cities, often the poor, the very young and the elderly, who provided the opportunity for architectural experiment. After the war, many European cities began to place considerable emphasis on solving their housing problems through 'industrialised building'. Complete buildings, manufactured in sections in the factory, could be assembled on site by a small, efficient work-force. In Russia, Denmark and Sweden, the long winters made it sensible to transfer as much working-time as possible from the building site to the factory. For economic and practical reasons, the most favoured systems were those using heavyweight pre-cast concrete units in the form of wall and floor panels, bolted together at the junctions. France, with its tradition of reinforced-concrete engineering, was soon among the foremost in the field. The 'Camus' and 'Coignet' systems became widely known.

Economies of scale encouraged the use of repetitive, identical wall units. Furthermore, as each wall panel was load-bearing, it had to be placed vertically above the one below, often resulting in flat elevations of considerable banality. But the advantages of system-building lay in its precision. Steel shuttering could be used to obtain a precise concrete finish, electrical conduit could be installed in the walls before erection, and complete *hjertet* or 'heart' units – fully fitted bathrooms and kitchens – could be delivered to the site and merely lowered into place.

Industrialised building was never as economical as more conventional types of construction, and had to be heavily subsidised. It was popular with politicians, however, who through its conspicuous architectural forms and its quick construction times could be seen to be making an attack on the housing 'problem'. The most spectacular example of heavyweight industrialised building in Britain was the Aylesbury Estate, built during the late 1960s in Southwark, London. This displayed the advantages and disadvantages of the approach, both the precision of its individual components and, with over 2000 dwellings, the dullness of endless repetition. The blocks were planned along continuous temporary 'crane-ways', making the layout rectangular and the blocks themselves economically, but depressingly, long.

In 1968, a heavyweight panel system-built tower block, Ronan Point in the Canning Town estate in east London, partly collapsed, like a pack of cards, as the result of a gas explosion which might have caused much less damage in a traditionally-built building. The stringent safety measures which immediately came in added further costs to a form of development which many people already had misgivings about, and heavyweight panel building suffered a setback.

But there must be fewer doubts about the more successful lightweight systems devised for school-building in England during the post-war years of material shortage. Using a specially devised system of standard components, the Hertfordshire Council, under their County architect C.H. Aslin, were able to build 100 schools during the nine

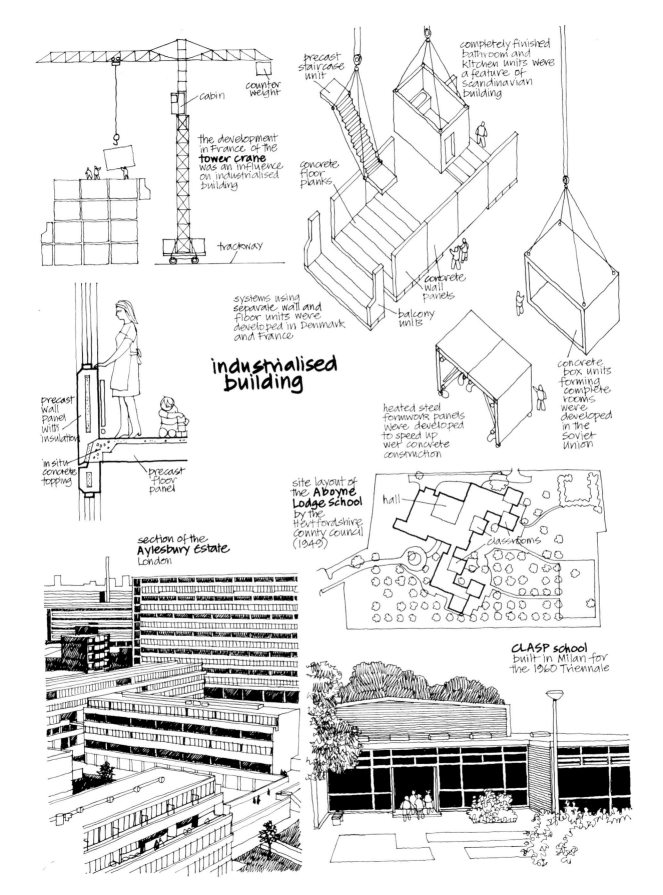

cabin

counter weight

the development in France of the **tower crane** was an influence on industrialised building

trackway

precast staircase unit

completely finished bathroom and kitchen units were a feature of scandinavian building

concrete floor planks

concrete wall panels

balcony units

systems using separate wall and floor units were developed in Denmark and France

heated steel formwork panels were developed to speed up wet concrete construction

concrete box units forming complete rooms were developed in the Soviet Union

# industrialised building

precast wall panel with insulation

in situ concrete topping

precast floor panel

site layout of the **Aboyne Lodge School** by the Hertfordshire County Council (1949)

hall

classrooms

section of the **Aylesbury Estate** London

**CLASP school** built in Milan for the 1960 Triennale

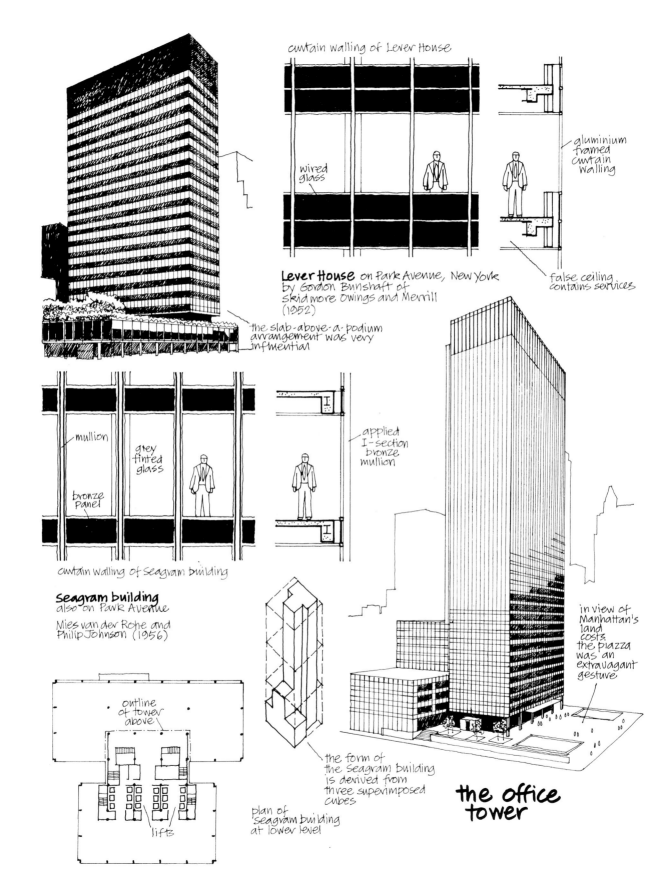

curtain walling of Lever House

wired glass

aluminium framed curtain walling

**Lever House** on Park Avenue, New York by Gordon Bunshaft of Skidmore Owings and Merrill (1952)

the slab-above-a-podium arrangement was very influential

false ceiling contains services

mullion

grey tinted glass

bronze panel

applied I-section bronze mullion

curtain walling of Seagram building

**Seagram building** also on Park Avenue

Mies van der Rohe and Philip Johnson (1956)

outline of tower above

lifts

plan of Seagram building at lower level

the form of the Seagram building is derived from three superimposed cubes

in view of Manhattan's land costs, the piazza was an extravagant gesture

**the office tower**

years following 1946. In 1955, the CLASP system – Consortium of Local Authorities Special Programme – was begun by the Nottinghamshire Council under the County architect Donald Gibson. CLASP was a lightweight steel frame, suitable for one- and two-storey buildings, as flexible in its uses and as elegant in its application as the heavy concrete systems were inflexible and ponderous. CLASP had a wide variety of components for different situations, including spring-loaded joints to cope with subsidence from underlying coal mines, and a great variety of external appearance was possible. The project was well-researched, and resulted in buildings which on the whole were attractive and humane for those who used them – though even here there were the initial problems inherent in many new systems, in this case the dangerous spread of flame through the cavities of the lightweight walls.

On the whole, technology offered some hope for the future and some social progress was being made. Nevertheless, it would have been unrealistic to feel euphoric about the post-War world. Fascism had been stopped, but the wartime alliances had been restructured. Now the tensions lay between the First and Second Worlds – living under international capitalism or Stalin's version of communism. The world war continued without a break into a political 'cold war', just as de-humanising in its effects. The great powers now relied on a 'permanent arms economy', dominated by what the commentator Paul Goodman called the 'military-industrial complex'. The supposed threat of nuclear war stimulated an arms race, the profitable arms economy produced the weapons, and these were tried in an unending round of neo-colonial wars, bringing real violence to the underprivileged Third World – to Korea, Israel and Palestine, South America, black Africa, Cambodia, Vietnam.

The corporate world created by these conditions, a symbiotic alliance of governments, bureaucracies and multi-national corporations, was difficult to challenge. Many writers, artists, designers, musicians simply profited by associating themselves with all this wealth and power, but there were others who rose to the challenge. Mid-20th-century culture reflected the continuous struggle of individuals to be heard, from Kafka to Solzhenitsin, from existentialism to rock music, from the Theatre of the Absurd to Francis Bacon. Most architects, however, accepted the corporate world for the opportunities it offered – to design fine buildings and to achieve fame and fortune. From the 1950s onwards, many buildings were spectacular personal statements, in a brilliant variety of colours, textures and forms. The great modern buildings, each apparently a monument to its architect's individuality, are permanent reminders of his and our dependence on the patronage of the corporate world.

## ORGANISATION MAN

Lever House in New York (1952) was designed by Gordon Bunshaft of Skidmore, Owings and Merrill, and the nearby Seagram Building (1956) by Mies van der Rohe in association with Philip Johnson. Both were variations on a theme: simple, rectangular skyscrapers whose main difference was the treatment of the metal-framed glass curtain-walling. If the Seagram Building, with its applied I-section mullions, was more interesting, Lever House was probably more influential, encouraging hundreds of imitators to whom the flat, graph-paper façade was the easiest and simplest way to clothe an office block. The proliferation of the glass-clad office tower has tended to obscure the originality of these two buildings. In their time, contrasting as they did with the stone-faced Art Deco skyscrapers of New York, their simple elegance and technical excellence helped to create a modern corporate identity for their clients, a whisky firm and a manufacturer of soap.

A similar job was done for the Pirelli rubber firm by Gio Ponti and Pier Luigi Nervi. The Pirelli tower in Milan (1957), an office-block of over thirty storeys, was elegant and visually satisfying. Nervi's structure was based on two full-width reinforced concrete diaphragm walls, which reduced in thickness towards the top. Around them, Ponti's façade was designed with classical completeness and symmetry. Nervi's present fame rests mainly on this building, on his Palazzetto dello Sport for the Rome Olympics (1958), his Olympic Stadium (1960) and his fine Palazzo del Lavoro in Turin (1961), all of them brilliant *tours-de-force* in reinforced concrete.

The affluent and cultured elegance of Milanese and Roman society was expressed in the late 1950s by an outburst of luxurious and formalistic architecture, of which the Pirelli building was an immediate precursor. The promotion of the movement by the design magazine *Casabella* earned it wide recognition and its apparently perverse resemblance to the 'Liberty' style of Italian Art Nouveau – named after the shop in London which sold many of its goods – earned it the epithet 'neo-Liberty'. Various office-blocks in Milan, the Rinascente department store in Rome by Franco Albini and Franca Helg (1961) and Ignazio Gardella's house on the Zattere, Venice, were all part of the same movement, away from the sterility of much of the current corporate architecture towards something more interesting and humane. The archetypal building was the Torre Velasca skyscraper in Milan (1958) by Banfi, Belgiojoso, Peressuti and Rogers, a rectangular block whose top six storeys projected out on brackets, giving a silhouette distinctly of the 20th century but which yet referred obliquely to the towers of the Florentine renaissance.

Profits were high in the private sector, but the general wealth also allowed the support of the public sector through high taxation. The fifties and sixties saw a great deal of public investment, by governments, city councils, public trusts, airport authorities, universities and colleges. Louis Kahn's Richards Medical Centre laboratories in Philadelphia (1957) used the vocabulary of the modern movement but in a rich, expressive way which departed from the understatement of Gropius and Mies. The complexity of the duct-work serving the laboratories became the starting-point for a display of bold rectangular forms, projecting and recessing, and for a skyline of almost romantic irregularity. Even more romantic were the silhouettes of the Sydney Opera House by Jørn Utzon and Ove Arup (1957–73), with its cluster of sail-like roofs dominating the harbour area, and of Eero Saarinen's TWA terminal at Kennedy Airport, New York (1962), the sweeping bird-like roof of which was, consciously or not, a metaphor for flight.

Wright's last great work, the Guggenheim Museum in New York (1959), was a dramatic, spiral drum-like form placed above a cluster of ancillary accommodation. The concept was anything but self-effacing. Instead of providing a building which took second place to the exhibits, Wright devised a design which dominated everything within it. The same could perhaps be said of Hans Scharoun's Berlin Philharmonic Hall (1963), specially built for Karajan's orchestra, unique among concert halls in its

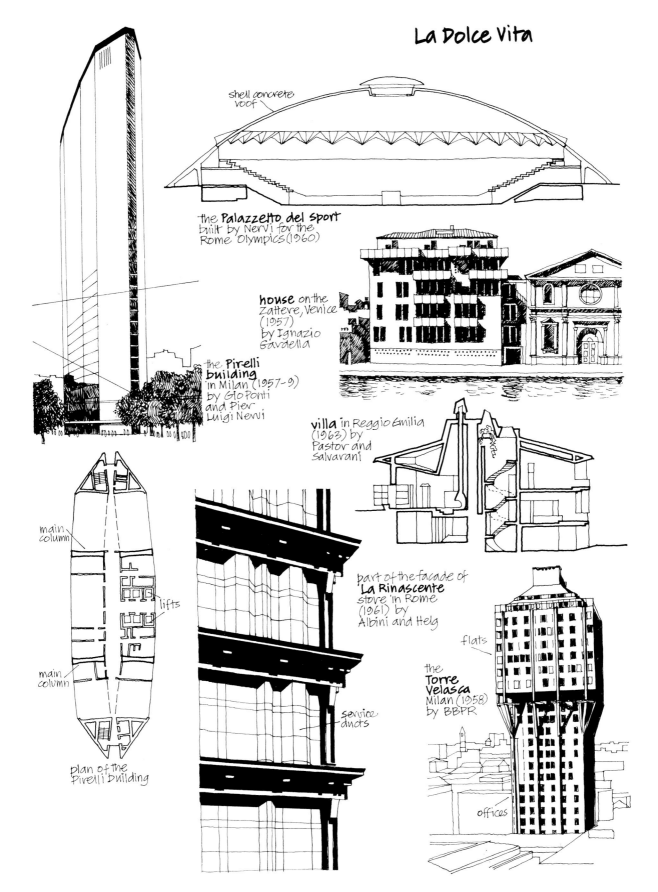

# La Dolce Vita

shell concrete roof

the **Palazzetto del Sport**
built by Nervi for the
Rome Olympics (1960)

**house** on the
Zattere, Venice
(1957)
by Ignazio
Gardella

the **Pirelli
building**
in Milan (1957-9)
by Gio Ponti
and Pier
Luigi Nervi

**villa** in Reggio Emilia
(1963) by
Pastor and
Salvarani

main
column

lifts

main
column

part of the facade of
**La Rinascente**
store in Rome
(1961) by
Albini and Helg

service
ducts

flats

the
**Torre
Velasca**
Milan (1958)
by BBPR

offices

plan of the
Pirelli building

almost centrally placed platform. The auditorium was divided into small, self-contained sections as if to emphasise the intimate relationship between any one group of listeners and the musicians.

Among the major examples of public investment was the city of Brasilia, a new capital for Brazil, built largely during the 1960s by Lucio Costa and Oscar Niemeyer. The conception – of a new capital city built in the uninhabited bush, with a sweeping, formal town plan – was one of great ambition. The buildings themselves had great panache – the vast, cool Presidential Palace and the *grande geste* of the geometrically pure Parliament buildings.

Another big public undertaking, in Montreal in the late 1960s, included, within a few years, the building of a Métro, two major central area redevelopments at the Place Ville Marie and at the Place Bonaventure, a major international exposition (1967) and, in 1976, the Olympic Games. The elegant, high-technology, German pavilion by the German engineer Frei Otto, a steel, tent-like structure supported on posts, reappeared later in a more developed form in the sports buildings for the Munich Olympics. The Israeli architect Moshe Safdie's 'Habitat', designed for Expo '67 as a permanent feature, was a huge cluster of pre-cast concrete boxes put together to form a block of 158 flats.

In Britain James Stirling (1926–92) with James Gowan (b.1924) built the Leicester University engineering building (1963). He also designed the History Faculty Library in Cambridge (1965) and the Florey Building at Queen's College, Oxford (1968). A predilection for bold, brutal, solid forms in machine-made brick and concrete enclosing large areas of aluminium-framed glazing gave his buildings a highly individual and mechanistic character. The structure was clearly demonstrated, and the mechanical services visibly arranged to be part of the architectural expression. Much was made of the way the components were put together. The conception was of the building as a machine, assembled out of parts. This approach was shared by the British architects Norman Foster, whose best early buildings included the Willis Faber offices in Ipswich (1973) and the Sainsbury Gallery (1978) at East Anglia University, and Richard Rogers of Piano and Rogers, architects of the Centre Pompidou in Paris (1976).

In 1966, the year that New York's Lincoln Center, an expensive monument to mainstream culture, opened its new centrepiece, the Metropolitan Opera House, a cluster of hovels appeared in the Colorado landscape. This was Drop City, an artists' and young people's settlement, with geodesic-dome-like buildings constructed from old car bodies and other detritus of the consumer civilisation which had made the Lincoln Center possible. Drop City was not unique. The writings of Paolo Soleri and of Martin Pawley had already introduced the idea of organic, informal building methods. The Bavinger House by Bruce Goff (1950), and Herb Greene's house (1961), both built at Norman, Okla. had been examples of the use of informal materials and shapes closely integrated with the landscape. Drop City also took its cue from the squatter movement, an increasing feature of city life since the War, whereby the landless poor were appropriating building sites on the edges of cities and putting up their own informal shelters. But Drop City did not reflect an urgent housing problem. This was an educated middle-class community dropping out and it had little in common, for example, with the homeless building-workers living in oil-drums in the French *bidonvilles*. But nevertheless it was a significant questioning of an affluent society which, despite all the post-War

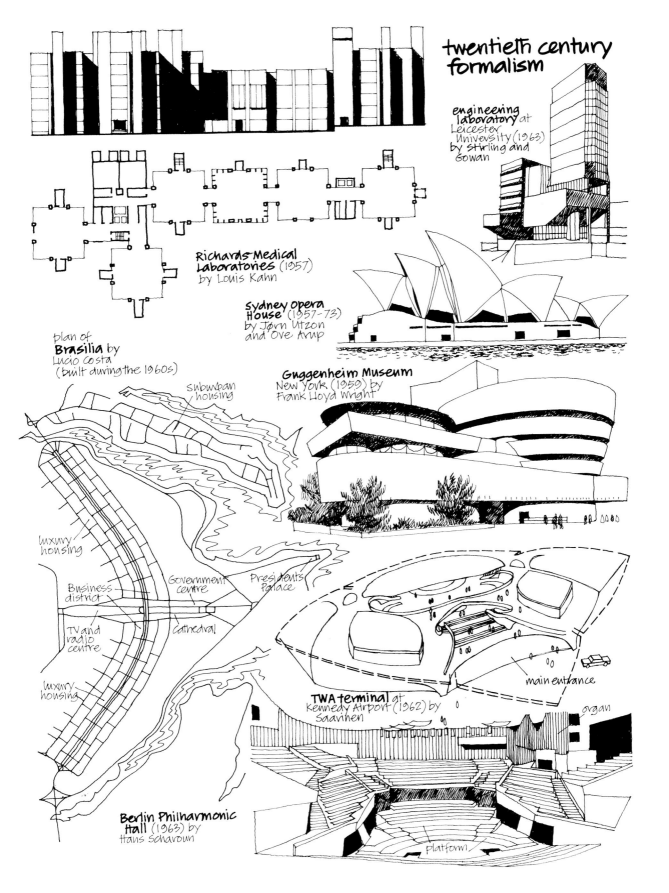

twentieth century formalism

engineering laboratory at Leicester University (1963) by Stirling and Gowan

Richards Medical Laboratories (1957) by Louis Kahn

Sydney Opera House (1957-73) by Jørn Utzon and Ove Arup

plan of Brasilia by Lucio Costa (built during the 1960s)

suburban housing

Guggenheim Museum New York (1959) by Frank Lloyd Wright

luxury housing

Business district

TV and radio centre

Government centre

Cathedral

President's Palace

luxury housing

main entrance

TWA terminal at Kennedy Airport (1962) by Saarinen

organ

Berlin Philharmonic Hall (1963) by Hans Scharoun

platform

investment, was still desperately unequal. The Lincoln Center development itself had involved the demolition of several blocks of low-cost housing and the displacement of thousands of poor families.

All over the western world, the record of post-War governments was beginning to be challenged. Many protesters saw the Cold War and the arms race as central to the problem, for their waste both of lives and of resources. In Europe, which recognised itself as a future nuclear battlefield, an active disarmament movement had been in existence since the fifties. Then, from the sixties, criticism and protest focussed on American foreign policy in Vietnam. There were protests about domestic affairs too, both in America and Europe. The linked problems of racialism and poverty in a supposedly humane and affluent society, gave rise to race riots and the civil rights movement. The inner cities, starved of resources and drained of manpower by the affluent suburbs and new towns, were the focus of a 'community action' movement in which activists tried to take back control of the city environment.

Bad housing persisted, despite years of slum-clearance. And even much of the new housing was manifestly inadequate, poorly maintained, a prey to vandalism. City streets were choked with traffic, and public services were poor. And there was growing recognition of the capitalist system's profligate use of the world's resources and its pollution of the natural environment. The protest movement reached a climax in 1968, in both America and Europe. In the USA there were campus riots against the War, in Czechoslovakia the liberalising 'Prague Spring' was heavily crushed by Russian tanks, and in the May *évènements* in Paris, an alliance of workers and students sought to overthrow the Gaullist government. It undoubtedly helped to end the war in Vietnam – though there were other, more compelling, reasons too, such as the enormous strain it placed on America's resources.

Politicians, under pressure, began to look more closely at urban problems, at the inner city, racism, pollution, the energy crisis, and at the growing demand for local autonomy. It was publicly admitted that environmental mistakes had been made in the past. Tower blocks, which in any case had been rather expensive to build, were now agreed to be socially undesirable. In recognition of their extreme unpopularity with tenants and the high incidence of vandalism, the decision was taken in 1972 to demolish some of the Pruitt-Igoe flats in St Louis, built only 17 years earlier. This event was seen by some, particularly the critic Charles Jencks, to signify the 'failure' of Modernism, and its timely, unlamented end. This was a doubtful claim.

In their different ways, the greatest modernists – Darwin, Marx, Freud, Brecht, Picasso, Joyce – were revolutionaries, who rejected the conventional wisdom of bourgeois society and created an alternative world view. Only if conventional theory and practice were transcended could the world be changed for the better. At its most dynamic, for example in Russia in the 1920s, Modernism had been assisting in a real social revolution, in which real alternatives to capitalism were being rehearsed. As Modernism had taken hold in western Europe during the twenties and thirties, it had become a symbol of the social change so many wanted but could not yet achieve. Then, with the creation of the post-war Welfare State, social change seemed to have arrived, and modern architecture had given it physical form.

But there was a basic difference between the worlds of the Constructivist architects

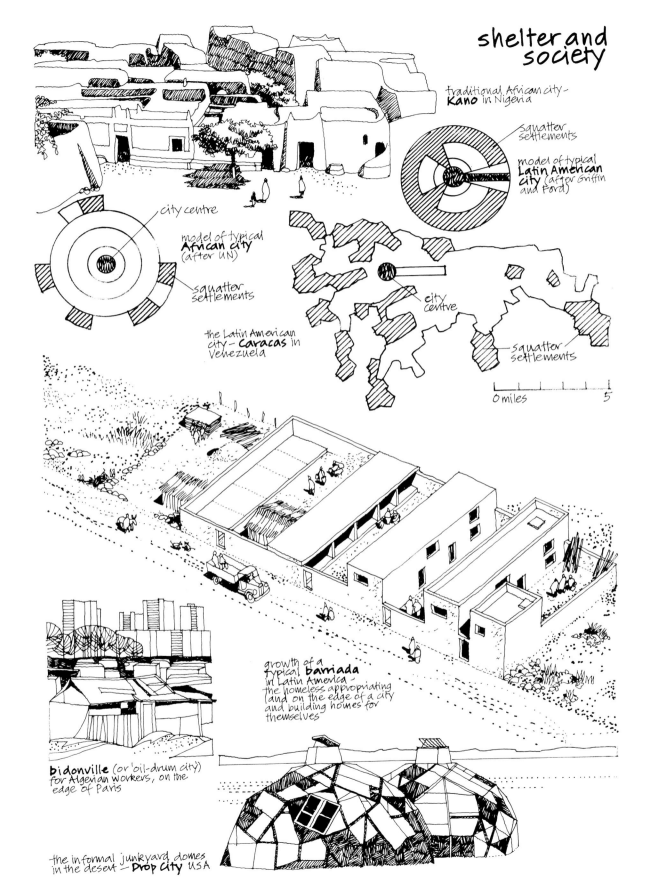

# shelter and society

traditional African city – **Kano** in Nigeria

squatter settlements

model of typical **Latin American city** (after Griffin and Ford)

city centre

model of typical **African city** (after UN)

squatter settlements

city centre

the Latin American city – **Caracas** in Venezuela

squatter settlements

0 miles                    5

growth of a typical **barriada** in Latin America – the homeless appropriating land on the edge of a city and building homes for themselves

**bidonville** (or 'oil-drum city') for Algerian workers, on the edge of Paris

the informal junkyard domes in the desert – **Drop City** USA and of their post-War counterparts. For the latter, the context was anything but revolutionary. The purpose of the Keynesian economics on which the Welfare State was based was to revitalise capitalism. The post-War boom was based not so much on social revolution as on the permanent arms economy, the military-industrial complex and the Cold War. Inevitably, the use-value of architecture was subordinated to its exchange-value. Profit rather than need, continued to dictate what was built, and how. The outward forms of Modernism – though not its substance – had become the property of the market system. The failure of Pruitt-Igoe was not that of 'modernism' but of capitalism itself.

## COMMUNITY ACTION

Modernism, in any case, was continually adapting to changing needs. The reductivist, squared-off building designs which its critics associated with Modernism in order more easily to attack it, had been largely superseded. During the years both before and after 1968 many architects and planners in the West were responding to public demand, and their own sensibilities, by humanising their approach. Efforts were made to be more respectful both to the physical and to the social fabric of existing cities. Through social studies by Wilmott and Young in London's Bethnal Green and Jane Jacobs in Boston, planners were rediscovering the traditional inner city street. The retention and refurbishment of existing buildings and of whole districts was increasingly preferred to redevelopment. Where development did take place, it was frequently phased to help keep the existing communities together. British examples included the pioneering Shelter Neighbourhood Action Plan (SNAP) in Liverpool 8, and various housing developments in the Swinbrook and Murchison areas of London's North Kensington, by the Notting Hill Housing Trust, the Kensington Housing Trust, and the Greater London Council.

In Britain, low-rise housing began to replace high towers, and brick, timber and other so-called 'natural' materials to replace the less popular concrete. Ralph Erskine's housing for Clare Hall in Cambridge (1969) and Darbourne and Darke's Lillington Gardens housing in Westminster (1970) were good examples. Public buildings too, took on an informal aspect, as in Alan Reiach's Kildrum Parish Church in Cumbernauld (1965), Arup Associates' conversion of the Snape Maltings into a concert hall for Benjamin Britten (1967) and the Minster Lovell conference centre by Ted Cullinan (1969). As a reaction against the universality of the international style, which made all cities look the same, 'regionalism' became an important European architectural theme of the early 1970s. Architects were beginning to rediscover their cultural roots and to design buildings, often quite artfully, to refer to the older, artless traditions of their locality. This could be seen in the work of Giancarlo de Carlo in Urbino – for example in his Faculty of Education (1975). It found a particular response in Catalunya, following Franco's death in 1975, with local architects leading a resurgence of local culture. In Barcelona, José-Luis Sert's arts centre, the Fundación Miró, on Montjuic, was first of a line of distinguished new Catalan buildings.

This increased respect for the physical and social fabric was given extra relevance by wider acceptance that the Earth's resources were not infinite. Individual economists like John Kenneth Galbraith and Edward Mishan were already criticising

family housing block

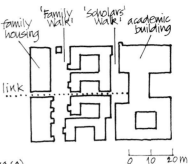

family housing — 'Family Walk' — 'Scholars' Walk' — academic building

link

0   10   20 m

At **Clare Hall** in Cambridge (1969)
Ralph Erskine rejected **academic** grandeur
in favour of domesticity, reflecting the
family lives of the College's mature graduate students

Giancarlo de Carlo's **Faculty of Education**
in Urbino (1975) respected the topography
and the intricate urban texture of the old town

The modernism of
Darbourne and Darke in their
**Lillington Gardens** housing in
Westminster (1970)
respected the materials
and urban 'grain' of
the traditional street

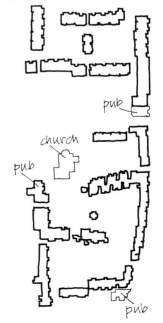

a high-density medium-rise scheme
provides 780 dwellings for 2000 people

pub

church

pub

pub

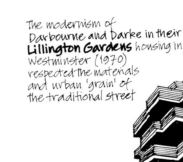

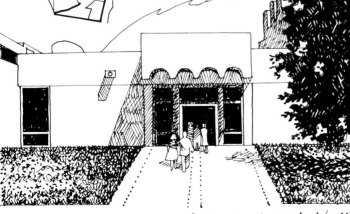

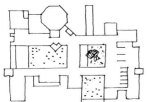

José-Luis Sert's **Fundación Miró**
in Barcelona (1975) was both modernist
and respectful of Catalan tradition

modernism
revisited

the workings of the industrial state and questioning the validity of unrestrained economic growth. Their arguments were reinforced in 1972, when the business interests represented by the influential Club of Rome published *The Limits to Growth*. In 1973, Fritz Schumacher's *Small is Beautiful*, sub-titled 'a study of economics as if people mattered', introduced the idea of 'appropriate' or 'alternative' technology. This continued to have a profound effect on architectural thought, stimulating an experimental approach to energy conservation, alternative sources of power, and eco-friendly building techniques – though the dominance of the market slowed widespread practical application of the ideas.

This was ironic, given that 1973 was an economic turning point which further emphasised the need for alternatives to the market system. The Arab-Israeli War of that year, and the associated oil crisis, marked the beginning of another major crisis of world capitalism. Once again, politicians and economists were taken by surprise. The post-war boom had seemed likely to continue, and Marx's theories of the inevitability of crisis had long since been discounted. Keynes, it was thought, had solved the problem of production. All that remained was the problem of a more equitable distribution. Now came just such a crisis as Marx had predicted. Worldwide over-production led to falling rates of profit and the cutting of investment. Unemployment began to rise; increased poverty and lower spending power reduced demand, further intensified the problem of over-production, and led to a spiral of decline.

# 13 AFTER MODERNISM
## 1973 to now

Capitalism has no other answer to a crisis of overproduction than to allow large areas of capital to be destroyed, so that production will fall sufficiently to match the reduced demand. If this creates privation and social disruption, the bourgeois argument goes, it is regrettable but unavoidable. By the end of the 1970s the political circumstances allowed such policies to be pursued. The Margaret Thatcher government in Britain, and that of Ronald Reagan in the USA, were the most prominent examples, but almost everywhere politics shifted to the right. The aim was the selective management of the process of capital destruction, leading to the protection of finance capital at the expense of industrial, and of the private sector at the expense of the public. This required anti-Welfare, anti-working class policies, and acceptance of poverty and widespread unemployment as facts of life. The effects were global: unemployment in the advanced industrial countries, privation in the Eastern Bloc, lower wages and poorer working conditions in the newly industrialising countries, increased famine and starvation in the Third World.

Where it existed, mainly in the advanced industrial countries, the Welfare State was greatly diminished through cuts in public spending and the privatisation of its services. Housing programmes were particularly affected. Britain's annual house completions, from 300,000 houses throughout the 1960s, half of them in the public sector, and a peak of 400,000 around 1970, fell by the late 1980s to 180,000, most of them in the private sector. If the big public sector housing estate had typified the 1960s, in both Europe and America, the symbol of the 1980s was the enclave of private housing protected by electric gates, video cameras and security guards. Meanwhile, in London, homelessness doubled. Any night, hundreds of people were sleeping on the streets, with thousands more living in crowded hostels or cheap hotels, sharing with other families or squatting in empty houses. A Salvation Army report in 1989 concluded that London now had a hidden shanty town 'as large as might be expected in a Latin American city'.

Such a shift in social values was not to be made overnight. The Welfare State as an institution was popular, and it was necessary to persuade people otherwise. During the 1980s the so-called New Right emerged, and right-wing ideas were expressed with increasing confidence. Anti-union, anti-socialist, anti-modernist, occasionally xenophobic to the point of racism, yet populist in style, the New Right helped create the mental climate in which such divisive policies were possible.

Architectural theory was affected too. In countries where the new Thatcherite economics took root, and particularly in Britain, there emerged critics who combined political conservatism with outright opposition – on the grounds of its socialist pretensions – to modern architecture. During the 1970s an influential conservationist movement had grown up, dedicated to saving historic buildings and old city centres from the kind of redevelopment which had so characterised the 1960s. Now, books like David Watkin's *Morality and Architecture* (1977) and Roger Scruton's *The Aesthetics of Architecture* (1979) put the case for anti-Marxist views of architectural history, and for building in the Classical style. The magazine *Country Life*, its editor Mark Girouard and his book *Life in the English Country House* (1978), as well as the producers of numerous television costume dramas, celebrated the great English country house as an architectural form and a social institution. Most influential of all, the Prince of Wales became an outspoken critic of modern architecture and an enthusiast for Classicism.

As theory affected practice, it became more fashionable to design in the styles of the past. During the 1960s, historicist architects like Raymond Erith had been submerged by the tide of Modernism. Now his successors, Quinlan Terry and Robert Adam, obtained important institutional and commercial commissions, like Queens College in Cambridge, the Richmond Riverside office development near London and an extension to the Amdahl computer headquarters – later a hotel – at Dogmersfield Park in Hampshire, all designed in a reproduction Classical style.

Classical revivals were a small part of a much bigger shift towards historicism in architecture, in the movement which became known as 'Postmodernism'. Paradoxically, the main theoretical source was not the political Right, but the disillusioned European Left, whose politics had also shifted rightwards since 1968. Postmodernism began with the failed aspirations of the Prague Spring and the Paris 'events', compounded by the economic crisis of 1973. Revolution no longer seemed to be a way forward, and even gradual social change seemed more difficult to achieve, given the retrenchment of the bourgeois state and its withdrawal from welfare capitalism. It seemed that some kind of accommodation with capitalism was needed and, intellectually, this made more sense if it could be shown that things were now, regrettably but unavoidably, different.

Postmodernism began, mainly in France, in the field of literary theory, with the structuralism of Barthes, from which emerged the post-structuralism of Foucault, and Derrida's deconstructionism. The general aim was still to pose some kind of challenge to bourgeois society, but nevertheless the modernist agenda, with its roots in the certainties of the Enlightenment and of 19th-century Positivism, was now said to be at an end. In its place was a shifting world of uncertainty, of relativity, of irony, of hidden meanings. Postmodernism began to affect all branches of culture with, for example, the novels of Burroughs, Vonnegut, Pynchon, Murakami and others, and the cinema of David Lynch and Quentin Tarantino.

Postmodernism became architectural in 1977 with the publication of Charles Jencks' *The Language of Postmodern Architecture* in which, like the literary theorists, he argued that there had now been a structural break with the modernist past. A

**Richmond Riverside** — modern commercial development in the Georgian style, by Quinlan Terry

**Dogmersfield Park**, a computer firm's headquarters, in Hampshire, England, by the contemporary architect Robert Adam

plan and detail of the housing development at Marne La Vallée in France, the **Palace of Abraxas Theatre and Arch**, by Ricardo Bofill and Taller Arquitectura

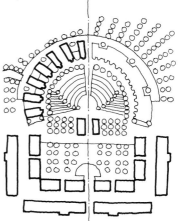

plan of the **Piazza d'Italia** in New Orleans, Louisiana, by Charles Moore

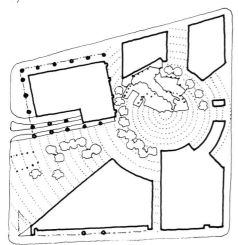

the growth of historicism

whole new group of styles, with names like Vernacular-Popular, Metaphorical, Adhocist and Historicist-Regionalist-Pluralist, were said to have emerged, to enrich the architectural vocabulary. What united them all, in the words of Jencks' colleague Paul Goldberger, was that they represented 'a reaction against everything that modern architecture has come to represent'. In his early Guild House apartments (1960), or his house for Vanna Venturi (1962), both in Philadelphia, and in his book *Complexity and Contradiction in Architecture* (1966), Robert Venturi had reacted against the single-minded, serious purpose of Modernism, advocating a kind of tongue-in-cheek sophistication through a deliberately eclectic and unashamedly banal stylism. The same could be said of a growing number of buildings, including Charles Moore's light-hearted neoclassical design for the Piazza d'Italia (1975) in New Orleans, Louisiana, and Michael Graves' 'giftwrapped' Portland Building in Portland, Oregon (1983). The AT&T office building in New York (1982) was a skyscraper designed by Philip Johnson, the former modernist and collaborator with Mies van der Rohe, to resemble a giant piece of Chippendale furniture.

In Britain, the former modernist James Stirling, moved into historicism with his Clore Gallery, an extension to the Tate in London (1987). The new gallery makes reference to the old by reproducing the proportions of its entrance portico, but as a void, rather than as a solid form. In central London, Venturi and Denise Scott-Brown were brought in to design a postmodern addition to the National Gallery after the Prince of Wales had intervened against a modernist British design, calling it a 'monstrous carbuncle on the face of a much-loved and elegant friend'. Their Sainsbury Wing uses the materials and the details of Wilkins' original building but in a more frivolous and satirical way. In France, the Spanish architect Ricardo Bofill built Les Arcades du Lac at St Quentin-en-Yvelines (1981), a public housing scheme designed in a massive, neo-classical style, the theatricality of which turns its residents into bit-part players in the architect's grand *mise-en-scène*. In Italy, Aldo Rossi used equally uncompromising neo-classical imagery, appropriately for its subject, in his sober San Cataldo cemetery at Modena (1971). In Yamagushi, Japan, Takefumi Aida made a sophisticated joke out of unsophisticated material by designing his Toy Block House (1979), a medical centre with housing above, as a pile of children's building blocks.

In rejecting Modernism, the postmodern architects rejected more than a style. They rejected the serious commitment of modern architecture, and its concern with progressive social change. The world had not changed as the postmodernists said it had. Capitalism survived, and its contradictions were more apparent than ever. The architectural tasks – the growing homelessness, the collapse of the housing programmes, the waste of resources, the worsening urban environment – were more urgent than ever, but architects were less and less confident of achieving any change for the better. They took refuge in stylistic exercises, in historical references, in tongue-in-cheek irony, rather than confront the social tasks, consciously or unconsciously reflecting the prevailing political drift to the right. It was no accident that postmodern architecture came to prominence at a time when welfare building was on the decline; it became the natural style of the phase of commercial building which took its place.

During the mid-1980s it became apparent that government policies of capital protection were taking effect. Working-class unemployment and poverty were increasing in cities everywhere. The rich were getting richer, and the gap between the two groups

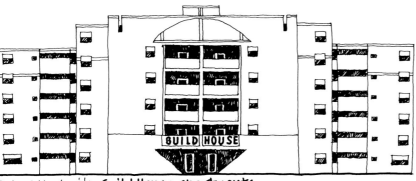

Robert Venturi's **Guild House apartments**

James Stirling's **Clore Gallery**, an extension to the Tate Gallery in London to house the work of Turner

Michael Graves' 'gift-wrapped' **Public Services building** in Portland, Oregon

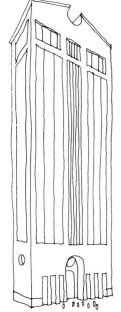

Philip Johnson's 'Chippendale' **AT and T**

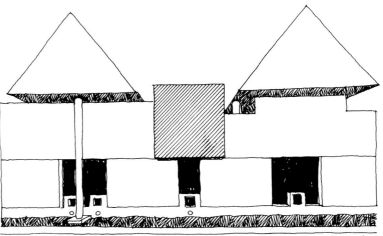

Takefumi Aida's **Yamagushi Dental Clinic**, or 'Toy Block House'

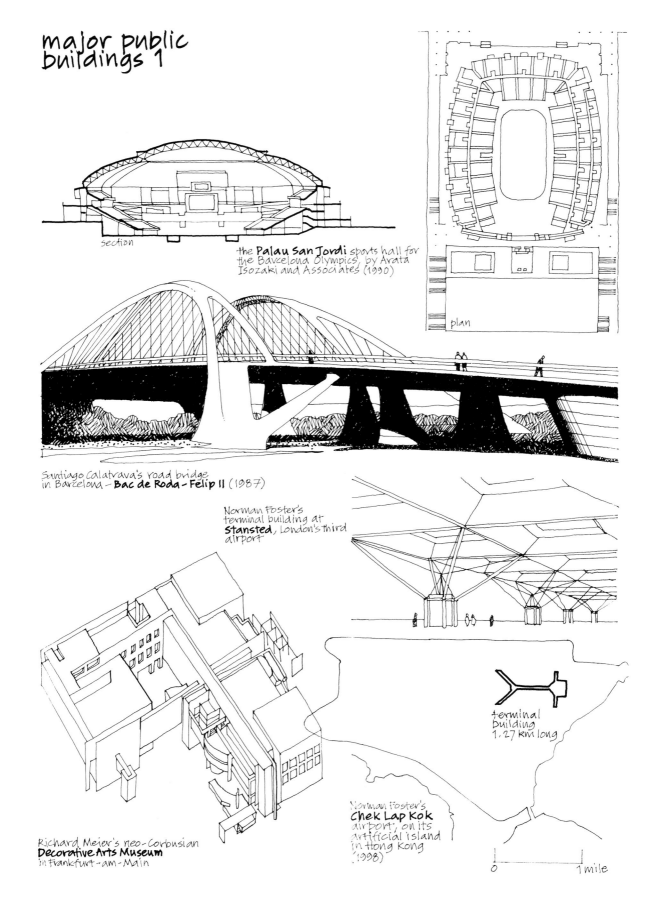

# major public
# buildings 1

section

the **Palau San Jordi** sports hall for
the Barcelona Olympics, by Arata
Isozaki and Associates (1990)

plan

Santiago Calatrava's road bridge
in Barcelona — **Bac de Roda – Felip II** (1987)

Norman Foster's
terminal building at
**Stansted**, London's third
airport

terminal
building
1.27 km long

Richard Meier's neo-Corbusian
**Decorative Arts Museum**
in Frankfurt-am-Main

Norman Foster's
**Chek Lap Kok**
airport, on its
artificial island
in Hong Kong
(1998)

0                    1 mile

I.M.Pei's **Glass Pyramid** providing a new underground entrance hall to the Palais du Louvre, Paris (1987)

detail of daylight diffusers

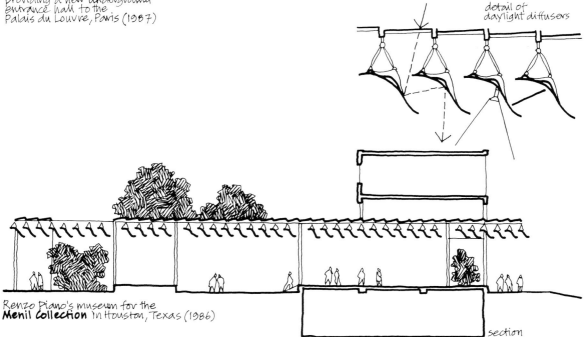

section

Renzo Piano's museum for the **Menil Collection** in Houston, Texas (1986)

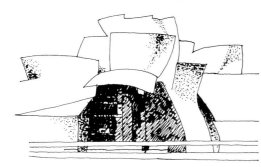

part of Frank Gehry's **Guggenheim Museum** in Bilbao, Spain (2000)

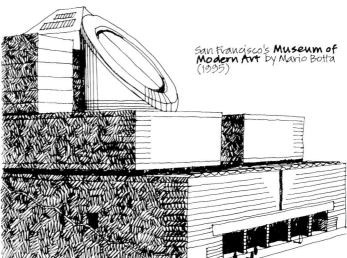

San Francisco's **Museum of Modern Art** by Mario Botta (1995)

getting wider. This was reflected in an outburst of commercial building: glossy new city-centre office developments, shopping malls and superstores contrasted with the shabby inner cities all around. A well-known example was the powerful and distinctive building designed by Richard Rogers for Lloyd's, the London insurance brokers (1986). With its apocalyptic *Bladerunner* aesthetic, all metallic surfaces and exposed pipes and ducts, the Lloyd's building became the archetypal 'high-tech' building of the late twentieth century, in which the imagery of Modernism was apparent, though without any of its social purpose.

On a much larger scale was the redevelopment of the former docks in London's East End, which began in 1980. Once London's main industry, the old docks had been declining over 20 years, and by the early eighties tens of thousands of local people were badly housed and out of work. When the opportunity came to redevelop the area it would have been possible to provide local homes and jobs. Instead, through a special agency, the government opened the area to property speculation, creating a huge surplus of profitable commercial floorspace. The most prominent feature of the development was Canary Wharf, over a million square metres of office blocks, plazas and malls, the centrepiece of which was One Canada Square, London's tallest office tower, designed by the Argentine architect César Pelli.

In many post-industrial cities, as capital shifted into the commercial sector, and developers exploited a temporary credit boom, declining working class areas were being reshaped into 'lifestyle' neighbourhoods for those profiting from the financial markets. At La Défense in Paris, at the end of the 'historic axis' from the Louvre to the Champs-Elysées, the former shanty-towns and local markets were replaced by a new office and residential city. The old Poble Nou industrial area of Barcelona, near the city centre, became the up-market district of Nova Icaria. In New York's riverside Battery Park City, a huge office and luxury residential development with a long esplanade facing the Hudson River, replaced low-rent housing. And at Bunker Hill in downtown Los Angeles a run-down residential neighbourhood became a high-rise city of offices and loft apartments.

Even more spectacular were the city-centre developments in Southeast Asia. Huge, high-density clusters of office towers grew up in the Central District of Hong Kong, in the Esplanade area of Singapore, and many other cities from Tokyo to Kuala Lumpur. Sometimes, the architectural style was international 'high-tech', as in Norman Foster's office building in Hong Kong for the Hong Kong and Shanghai Bank (1986). But increasingly, though the aim was still largely commercial, architects began to refer back to local building traditions. In the competition for investors, it was now important for cities to project a distinctive identity, through a regional image – though this apparent 'regionalism' was sometimes only a mask for the international capital which lay behind it. The Malaysian architect Ken Yeang, beginning with his 'Roof-Roof' house in Kuala Lumpur (1985) and in his later buildings, notably his Menara Mesiniaga Tower in Selangor (1992), made a big contribution to the theory and practice of regionalised modernism.

In the eighties the term 'globalisation' became popular to describe a world-wide economic system which far transcended national or regional boundaries. This was not a new concept. In 1848 Marx and Engels had described a 'constantly expanding market... over the whole surface of the globe'.

It must nestle everywhere, settle everywhere, establish connections everywhere. The bourgeoisie has through its exploitation of the world market given a cosmopolitan character to production and consumption in every country ... In place of the old local and national seclusion and self-sufficiency, we have intercourse in every direction, universal inter-dependence of nations.

As with economic connections, so it is with knowledge and creativity, and so with the work of the world's most famous architects. Money moves around the world in search of projects to invest in, and architects follow where it leads. As a result, the late 20th century and early 21st were characterized by some of the most spectacular buildings the world had ever seen, their strong imagery reflecting the wealth and political power of the clients who commissioned them, and the professional acumen of their designers. The famous public buildings of the seventies, such as the Sydney Opera House and the Centre Pompidou, which for a while, to many people, seemed the ultimate in contemporary architecture, were only the beginning of an ever more ambitious programme of city-centre building. Increasingly, city politicians made direct appeals, over their governments' heads, to international capital. The aspiring city would develop a 'cultural policy', which identified it as suitable place for businesses to locate, and for upwardly mobile business people to live. So as well as tax-breaks, cheap labour and low levels of unionisation, cities could offer glossy shopping centres, luxury housing, new cultural, sports and leisure facilities.

## URBAN 'REGENERATION'

Cities able to attract the Olympic Games, or the football World Cup, or to mount successful international expositions, might find that this provided a catalyst for the inward investment they sought, both financial and professional. In Barcelona, which hosted the Olympics in 1992, many new sports facilities were built, including Arata Isozaki's Palau Sant Jordi sports hall, and the Velodromo Horta by Bonell and Rius. The old Olympic stadium on Montjuic was reconstructed by Vittorio Gregotti. The new Villa Olímpica at Nova Icaria provided accommodation for the athletes and in the longer term, housing for sale. Numerous engineering works included a new road bridge by Santiago Calatrava, Norman Foster's Collserola telecom tower, slightly higher by intent than the Tour Eiffel – and the Cinturón, a high speed ring-road round the whole city centre. The reclamation of the waterfront for pedestrians, a new beach, a marina, a waterside shopping centre, and luxury hotels, were all offshoots of the Olympic project, and provided a basis for the physical improvement of the city.

Of course, the improvement process does not rely on one-off international events, however important, but on long-term investment. Barcelona was now part of 'the north of the south of Europe', a band of high-tech industry stretching from northern Spain through Montpellier to Provence, where the historic Catalan-Languedoc identity gave a cultural independence from both France and Spain. Here the cities tried to maintain a strong local economy, to diversify their economic base and to attract new types of industry. Barcelona was able to maintain a public sector, to continue to build low-cost housing, and to improve the city for its population as a whole. More than 100 new

# the new urbanism 1

Bernard Tschumi's remodelling of the
**Parc de la Villette** in Paris, based on
three overlaid geometries

**1** 'lines'

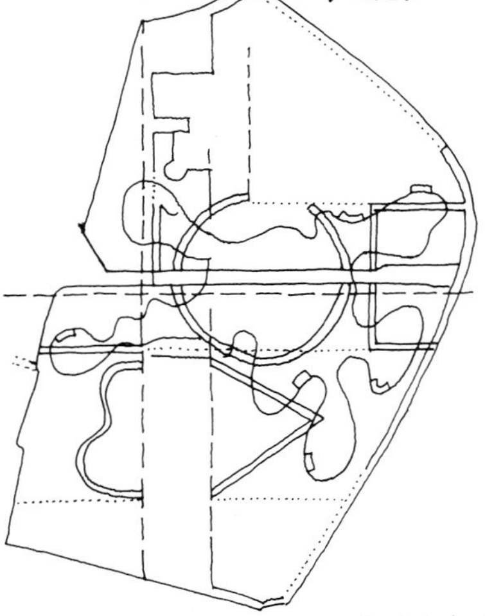

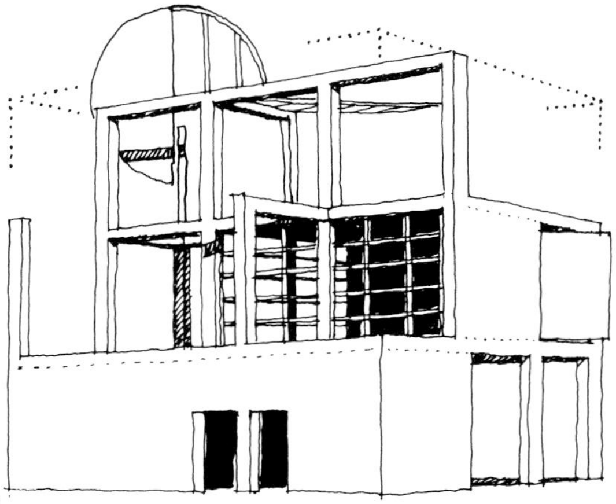

numerous small buildings
of different uses occupy the points
of the grid, each constructed
within a 10 metre cube

**2** 'points'

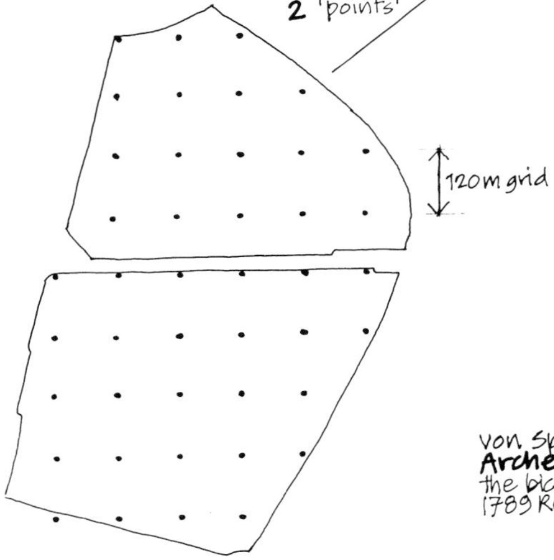

120m grid

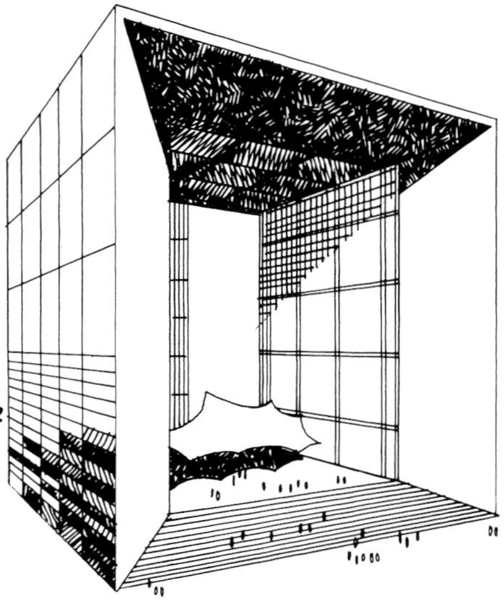

von Spreckelsen's **Grande
Arche** of offices, marking
the bicentennial of the
1789 Revolution (1989)

**3** 'surfaces'

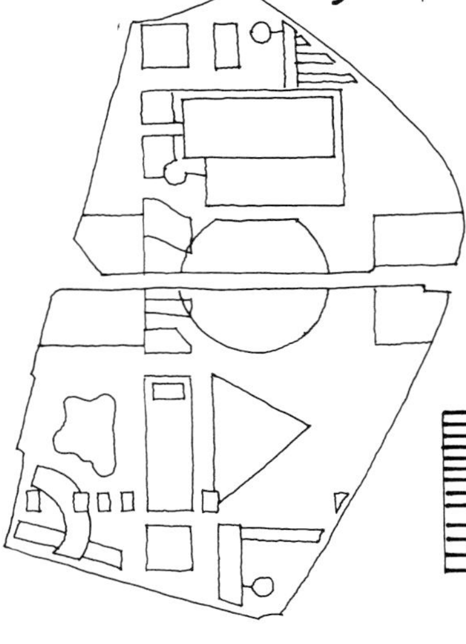

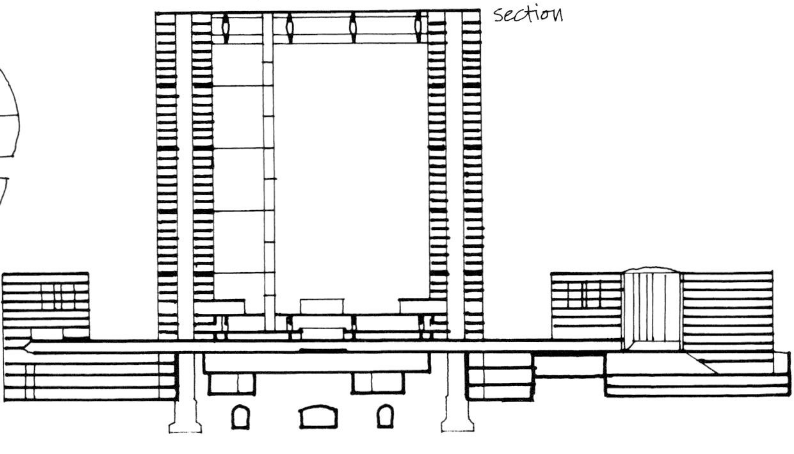

section

# the new urbanism 2

solar screens in the **Plaça dels Països Catalans** (1983) in Barcelona, by Piñón and Viaplana, with Enric Miralles

the **Moll de la Fusta** in Barcelona (1987) a pedestrian promenade on top of the city's inner ring road, designed by Manuel de Solà-Morales

the **Parc de la Trinitat** (1992) laid out inside Barcelona's biggest road junction

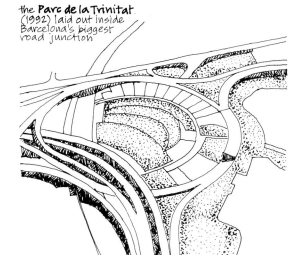

the large-scale geometry of the Parc de la Trinitat derives from the curvature of the roads

urban spaces, many of them incorporating public sculptures by Mariscal, Lichtenstein, Oldenburg and others, were built, some enormous, some tiny, but all contributing in some way to community life.

A virtue was made of the necessity of the inner ring-road by using it to improve the townscape. Where it passed by the harbour it was partly concealed under a new pedestrian promenade, the Moll de la Fusta. Its biggest road junction became the site of the huge Parc de la Trinitat, constructed in and around the flyovers. Near the old bullring came the Parc Joan Miró, with lakes, shady walkways, a library and a huge Miró-inspired obelisk. Outside Sants railway station the Plaça dels Països Catalans was built, with its curving steel sunshades and nearby, the Parque Industrial, with its Gaudí-esque towers. To the slopes of Montjuic, in an old quarry, came the beautiful Fossar de la Pedrera; a memorial to the Catalan war dead. Under the new paving of the Plaça del Sol, an underground car-park was dug, which returned the streets of the Gracia district to pedestrians. Even in the closely-packed Ciutat Vella, the old city centre, numerous tiny spaces were inserted, like the Plaça George Orwell with its playful metal sculpture, and the Fossar de les Moreres with its sober granite monument to Catalunya's historic martyrs.

The improvement of Barcelona was hailed by some as a model for other cities to follow. In 1999 the Royal Institute of British Architects awarded the city its annual Royal Gold Medal, normally given to individual celebrities. Yet Barcelona's plans also had their vociferous critics. Speaking in 2004 as the Assemblea de Resistències al Forùm, a group of local activists opposed Barcelona's much-heralded event of that year, the Universal Forum of Cultures. Criticising the Forum as being too market-orientated, they described their city as one in which decisions were taken to favour speculators and sponsors rather than local people, where over-reliance on tourism had commodified city life, where ecological sustainability was undervalued, and where there was a lack of democratic debate about future directions. They contrasted the huge sums put into the commercial redevelopment sites with the under-funding of the dilapidated working class areas nearby.

But overseas capital continued to flow into Barcelona and other aspiring cities, and the architects followed. An efficient international airport became an essential tool in the process. Barcelona's was reconstructed in 1992 by the local architect Ricardo Bofill. Norman Foster designed London's third airport at Stansted (1990), and the huge Chek Lap Kok airport for Hong Kong (1996) which, covering an area of more than half-a-million square metres, was the largest covered space ever built. Both this and Renzo Piano's Kansai airport at Osaka in Japan (1994) posed the added problem of having to be built on land reclaimed from the adjacent sea. Foster's and Piano's buildings were international in style, but the new airport at Kuala Lumpur (1998), by the Japanese architect Kisho Kurokawa, was designed in a regional style, to give visitors an immediate impression of Malaysian culture. Stansted was perhaps the first modem airport in which the roof was a lightweight structure of lattice-work and glass, to allow the light to filter through and to give an impression of airiness and space. Foster used the same principle at Hong Kong. Meinhard von Gerken's Stuttgart airport (1992), with its tree-like roof structure, and the complex lattice-work of the TGV interchange building at Charles de Gaulle airport, Paris (1994), by Paul Andreu and Jean-Marie Duthilleul, were developments of this theme.

The buildings which best define the cultural identity of a city are perhaps its 'cultural' buildings themselves. In the late twentieth century the economic battles between cities were fought through museums, art galleries and cultural centres. The building forms were as various as the locations demanded and as the celebrated architects dictated. The American architect Richard Meier developed his elegant neo-Corbusian style of building, notably in his Museum für Kunsthandwerk in Frankfurt (1985) and at MACBA, the Museu d'Art Contemporani de Barcelona (1995). Domus: the Home of Man, in A Coruña (1995), by Isozaki and Portela, was a bold and powerful response to a fine waterfront site, while Erik von Egerat's Rotterdam Natural History Museum (1991) was a more restrained addition to the city's historic museum area. In France, I.M. Pei designed his famous glass pyramid (1987) as an entrance hall to the historic Palais du Louvre. The same year, Jean Nouvel built the Musée du Monde Arabe, also in Paris, whose intricate high-tech design reinterpreted the forms and patterns of Islamic tradition, and Mario Botta designed the André Malraux Cultural Centre in Chambéry as a series of powerful geometric forms.

The US-based architect Frank Gehry first made his name with the Vitra Design Museum at Weil-am-Rhein in Germany (1988). His powerful expressionist architecture achieved a world-wide fame with the opening (1990) of the Guggenheim Museum in Bilbao. This audacious building was intended to bring new investment into the declining industrial city, as well as to emphasise the cultural identity of the Basque country itself. Soon it became common to refer to the 'Bilbao effect' and to promote similar 'flagship' schemes in other cities, in the hope of reviving them too. By 2001 the Guggenheim Foundation had received scores of requests for more museums, from city authorities ranging from Rio de Janeiro to New York.

The USA itself, with its plethora of private collections, had for long been at the forefront of museum design, Wright's original Guggenheim Museum in New York still being the most famous modern example. In 1986 Renzo Piano housed the Menil collection at Houston, in a beautifully restrained little building whose roof was designed to create the ideal lighting conditions for one of the world's best collections of surrealist art. In strong contrast, Mario Botta's San Francisco Museum of Modern Art (1995) was a composition of powerful postmodernist forms in brick and stone.

In Japan, the modernist architect Tadao Ando built the Historical Museum at Osaka (1993) in a form which reflected the burial grounds and tumuli of medieval times, and Kisho Kurokawa's Museum of Modern Art at Wakayama (1991) was a modern concrete building which used traditional Japanese architectural forms. The Museum of Photography of Tottoi (1995), by Shin Takamatsu, was also an essay in modernist reinforced concrete.

Britain had seemed slower to build or improve its museums than almost any other capitalist country, but a number of projects were set up to celebrate the so-called Millennium in the year 2000. These included the Tate Modern in London, a conversion by the Swiss partnership of Jacques Herzog and Pierre de Meuron of a former power station into a modern art gallery, and the reconstruction by Norman Foster of the Great Court of Smirke's British Museum, in which an elegant, computer-designed glass roof created a new interior space around the historic Reading Room. In the old industrial town of Walsall, Caruso St John's New Art Gallery, with its sheer terra-cotta walls, created a local Bilbao effect.

# monuments and public art

obelisks and a huge abstract Barcelona dragon, in the **Parque de la España Industrial** (1985) by Luis Peña and Francesc Rius

Eduardo Paolozzi's sculpture of **Newton** in the courtyard of the British Library in London, redolent both of Blake, and of the imagery of the early industrial revolution

Mariscal's giant crustacean on top of a sea-food restaurant on the Moll de la Fusta, Barcelona

Christo and Jean-Claude's **Wrapped Reichstag** — the German Parliament building done up like a parcel, June and July 1995

**Capsa de Mistos**, a giant book of matches by Claes Oldenburg in Barcelona (1992)

Back in 1958, on the outskirts of Copenhagen, a series of extensions were begun to the traditional Danish country house 'Louisiana', by the local architects, Jørgen Bo and Vilhelm Wohlert. The result was one of the best of all modern museums, whose almost anonymous architecture provided a perfect background for the art works and a perfect complement to the landscape, a fine wooded site on the shore of the Baltic – the essence of what modern architecture should be. By the end of the twentieth century, with a few honourable exceptions, museums and galleries had become the exact opposite: architectural tours de force, in which the buildings were more important than the collections, many of which were unconvincingly small – the essence, in fact, of postmodernism, in which form vied with substance.

Nevertheless, it was hoped that all these marvellous buildings, as in Bilbao, would stimulate the improvement of much larger areas of the city. Architects have often aspired to be controllers of the whole urban environment, Le Corbusier perhaps being the best-known modern example. For many architects, city planning was no more than architecture on a grand scale. The Centre Pompidou and the Louvre pyramid were only two of a number of *grands projets* constructed in Paris as part of a wholesale reworking of the old Haussmann city centre. To the east of the centre came the Opéra Bastille, designed by the Uruguayan architect Carlos Ott (1983), a building whose transparency and accessibility emphasised its difference from the more bourgeois institution housed in Garnier's famous old building. In the north, on the site of the former cattle yards and abattoirs, the Swiss architect Bernard Tschumi laid out the Parc de la Villette, a huge open space containing a multiplicity of small buildings for leisure and educational use, arranged according to his 'deconstructionist' principles. To the west, the city's huge business district of La Défense was further enlarged with numerous new buildings, including the Danish architect Johan Otto von Spreckelsen's 'Grande Arche' (1989), part office block, part piazza and part monument, located at the end of the 'historic axis' of Paris, to celebrate the bicentennial of the first French Revolution.

Larger and larger areas of cities were becoming available for development. As the old heavy industries declined, factory areas, railway yards and dockyards were knocked down and rebuilt, and architects found they were being entrusted with the design of entire districts. The term 'master-plan', discredited during the 1960s for its authoritarian overtones, came back into the architect's vocabulary. At first sight, it was easy to imagine that cities were being greatly improved, but many of these new areas were far from being real cross-sections of traditional urban life. Certain public benefits were on offer – an open space here, a block of low-cost housing there – but many of them were based unashamedly on commercial office developments, lively during the day, dead at night and exclusive in character. The Broadgate development in London, built on and around two old railway stations, was designed in the mid-1980s by the Chicago architects Skidmore, Owings and Merrill. Though it included 'public' squares, fountains and an ice rink, it was essentially four million square feet of office floorspace. As with Canary Wharf, Nova Icaria, Battery Park City and Bunker Hill, large areas of the old working-class city were becoming wealthy private enclaves. Their high land-values were helping to push local industry and low-cost housing out of the inner city.

It became common to refer to this process as 'urban regeneration', which from the mid-1980s, seemed to have replaced 'planning' as the accepted way of improving a city.

Implicit in it was the idea that the municipality should no longer be the main agent of change. Regeneration depended instead, it was said, on a 'partnership' between the public and private sector. In practice, this meant the former providing much of the finance and the latter using its powers to acquire the land, to smooth the path to planning permission and, where necessary, to step in with subsidies when the financial calculations went wrong. The Canary Wharf project and Richard Rogers' tent-like Dome (1999) for the hastily conceived 'Millennium Experience' in south-east London, were 'urban regeneration' projects of this kind. The private finance, the corporate sponsorship, and the revenues themselves, proved inadequate; both projects were extensively subsidised, by the public, through generous grants.

They were also subsidised indirectly by the construction of a £2 billion extension to London Underground's Jubilee Line, on which Britain's most famous designers were employed. The cathedral-like proportions of its magnificent new stations, such as Canary Wharf by Norman Foster, and North Greenwich by Richard Rogers, contrasted strangely with the shabby old stations on the rest of the network, many badly in need of repair. Both Canary Wharf and the Dome raised questions, not only about the methods, but also about the results. The limitation was that, as always, the private sector was interested only in developing for profit, not for social need. What – after the expenditure of all this money – had really been regenerated? Could not public money have been better spent elsewhere, where the needs were increasingly apparent – on local employment, housing or schools, on health services, or on transport for local people – not just to benefit the developers of flagship projects?

Architecture, it is often said, holds a mirror up to society. The ideology of architecture reflects the ideologies dominant in society as a whole. Thus, the kind of buildings that get built indicate a society's social priorities. During the 1980s and 1990s, capital was shifting from the public sector to the private, and from industrial to finance capital, and the fine public buildings of this period have to be seen in the context of a much larger mass of commercial building: not only office developments but also shopping malls, suburban retail warehouses, chain hotels, luxury housing developments and the conversion of formerly useful industrial buildings into residential pieds-à-terre. The New Right and postmodernist thinking of the 1980s had the lasting effect of disengaging architectural theory from practice. The problems of the city and its environment were becoming ever more acute, its glossy developments standing like islands among the general dilapidation and decline, but for the most part there was little reference to these realities by architectural writers and theorists.

## ALTERNATIVE CITIES

The new Thatcherite city did have its critics, like David Widgery, in *Some Lives! A GP's East End* (1991), and Patrick Wright in *A Journey through Ruins* (1992). It also had its poets, with writers like Iain Sinclair, in *Lights out for the Territory* (1997) and his books of poetry, and Peter Ackroyd, in his novels with London themes, fascinated by the decrepit, informal urban landscapes of the post-industrial city. A term was coined for such landscapes – *terrain vague* – providing one of the main themes of the Congress of the *Union Internationale des Architectes* in Barcelona in 1996, where it was used to

# the commercial city

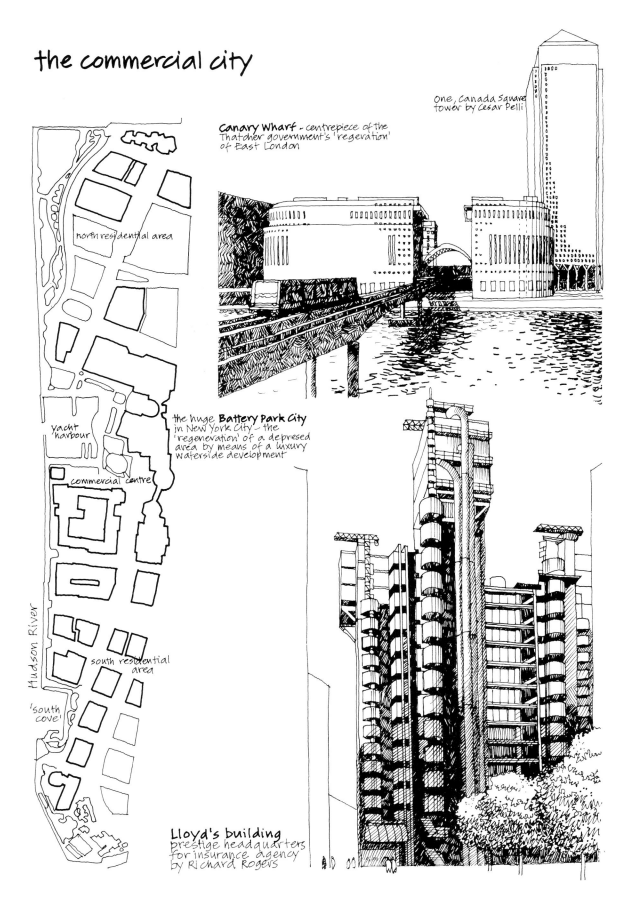

**Canary Wharf** - centrepiece of the Thatcher government's 'regeration' of East London

One, Canada Square tower by Cesar Pelli

north residential area

yacht harbour

commercial centre

Hudson River

south residential area

'south cove'

the huge **Battery Park City** in New York City - the 'regeneration' of a depresed area by means of a luxury waterside development

**Lloyd's building** prestige headquarters for insurance agency by Richard Rogers

describe, among others, the strange marginal lands in the declining industrial areas of the Besos valley.

The modernist architects had advocated architecture which was understandable. Le Corbusier in *Vers une Architecture* and Gropius in *The New Architecture and the Bauhaus*, had proposed sweeping away congested streets and dark, unhealthy homes. In their place would come clear, unambiguous environments full of sun, space and greenery. For them, theory and practice went closely together. When they came to design buildings or plan cities, they produced models of organisation and clarity.

For the postmodern urban theorists, however, the city was not necessarily to be understood. During the Eighties, there began a celebration of the complex, mysterious, unknowable aspects of buildings and cities. The French philosopher Gaston Bachelard's book *La Poétique de l'Espace* (1958) was rediscovered, and told how our perceptions of the traditional house evoke memories and dreams. In Italo Calvino's *Le Citte Invisibili* (1972), imaginary conversations between Marco Polo and Kublai Khan described a range of beautiful, illusory, mythical cities. Around such texts, a school of postmodern urban theory grew up. Now that theory was divorced from practice, the actual, physical city was left to the politicians, the developers and their architects, while the theorists talked of the mythical past and the enigmatic, unknowable present. And when postmodern urban designers, like Leon Krier or Oswald Matthias Ungers, put pen to paper they depicted strangely historicist cities with wind-blown, echoing plazas, recalling the dreamlike landscapes of the Surrealist painters.

This shift was also seen in the schools of architecture, in both Europe and the USA. The sixties had been a time of technocracy, when architecture was considered as much a science as an art. The social task of rebuilding cities and maximising housing production required organisation, management and the harnessing of modern technology. Architectural education was seen as a necessary preparation for this. But during the eighties, the shift from housing production as the main task, and from the public sector as the main agency for change, helped to change architectural education too. Courses became less concerned with the technology than with the pure aesthetics of design, and many students became more familiar with Bachelard than with bending-moments. The teaching of 'design' in schools of architecture became less a preparation for a real social task, than an end in itself. It resulted in a lot of stunning 'deconstructivist' imagery, of spiky, fragmented buildings, but its only real currency was on the walls of the studios, and on the pages of the magazines and monographs where, among the elite, it made a reputation for the school and its celebrity teachers, but had little contact with the real world outside. This was unfortunate, because the social tasks were more urgent than ever, and needed the skills of talented designers.

After 1968, when ordinary people's control over their environment became a major issue in the west, many individual architects and designers had sought to break down elitism and alienation. One of their early heroes was the eccentric Simon Rodia, whose junkyard towers in his own backyard in Watts, Los Angeles, painstakingly constructed during the 1950s out of scraps of found material, had been testimony to ordinary people's power to express themselves, no matter what the difficulties. This was also in the minds of the young people of Drop City – making your own buildings was the ultimate emancipation from the capitalist building process.

This was explored more formally in the early 1970s by the Belgian architect Lucien Kroll, in his medical faculty housing for the Université Catholique de Louvain. Kroll rejected the role of master designer and acted instead as 'orchestrator' of other people's ideas, as students, staff and building workers improvised and built sections of the building themselves. Walter Segal, an Austrian architect working in Britain, made self-build his life's work. From small beginnings in 1965, when he built himself a temporary house in south London, he developed a sophisticated, yet simple system of timber construction, suitable for two-storey houses and capable of being put together by groups of relatively unskilled self-builders. The architectural practice Architype, and the Walter Segal Trust, continued his work after his death, and hundreds of self-build buildings resulted.

But the number of people able to build for themselves is relatively few. More usually, community-minded architects have used the normal building process, but have involved potential users in the design of their buildings, or have designed them so that users can later adapt them to their needs. Le Corbusier's carefully-designed cubist housing schemes at Lège and Pessac, near Bordeaux, told a cautionary tale, having been extensively adapted by their occupiers with pitched roofs, screens, verandahs and other needs, to the detriment, no doubt, of the architectural conception but to the greater satisfaction of the users.

So Hermann Hertzberger's Centraal Beheer, a complex of offices at Appeldoorn (1973) provided a basic framework of repetitive spaces, each capable of being used in a number of different ways, as the occupiers' needs changed. At Byker, Newcastle-on-Tyne, Ralph Erskine designed The Wall (1978), a high density residential estate, where a wide range of variables – from the mix of different dwelling-types, to the details of the balconies and windows – were discussed among the potential tenants at design stage. Similar research went into Aldo van Eyck's design for the Mothers' House (1980), a refuge for women and children in Amsterdam. In 1985 Henri Ciriani completed a kitchen block at the St-Antoine Hospital in Paris, providing a pleasant and dignified environment for hospital kitchen staff, typically an undervalued group of workers.

One of Ted Cullinan's best-known early projects was his sympathetically-designed Community Care Centre in south London (1984). The next year, in London's Whitechapel, Florian Beigel built the first phase of his extension to the Half Moon Theatre, technically an ingenious solution to the problem of building next to a busy main road, and socially an attempt to create a community space in which the local people could express themselves. The design of the nearby Jagonari centre (1987), a community centre for local Bengali women and children, was based on lengthy consultations with the users by the women's architectural co-operative Matrix. The Catalan architect Franc Fernández, designer of a number of community buildings, including the Bernat Picornell swimming pool in Barcelona (1992) summed up by saying that 'people are more important than buildings'.

In the industrialised world, our alienated building process involves the heavy use of materials and energy. Obtaining raw materials on a large scale, from mines, quarries and forests, affects the environment, through resource depletion and through the pollution and scarring of the landscape. Their processing into useable form expends further amounts of energy. Their transport uses more energy and damages the

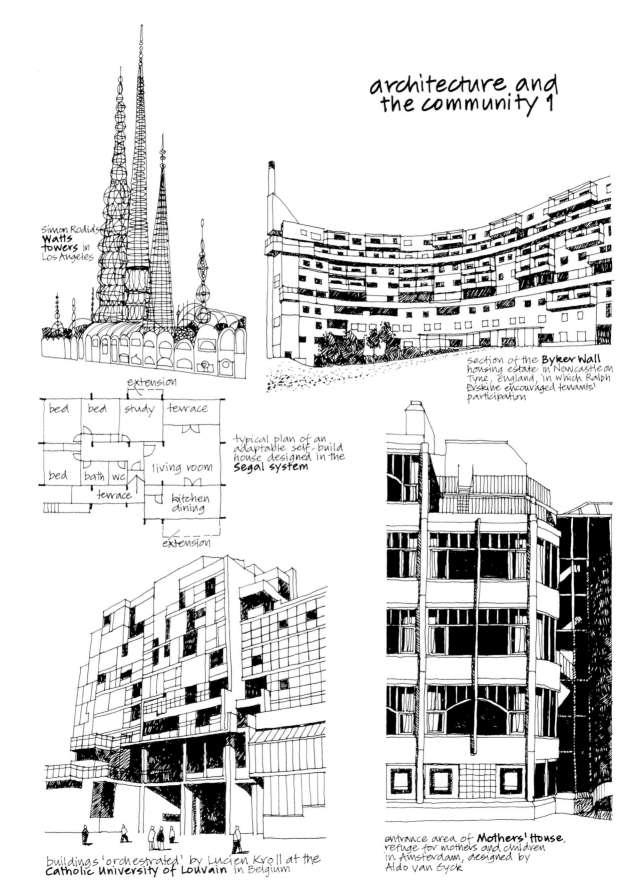

Simon Rodia's **Watts towers** in Los Angeles

section of the **Byker Wall** housing estate in Newcastle on Tyne, England, in which Ralph Erskine encouraged tenants' participation

extension

| bed | bed | study | terrace |
|-----|-----|-------|---------|
| bed | bath | wc | living room |
| | terrace | | kitchen dining |

extension

typical plan of an adaptable self-build house designed in the **Segal system**

buildings 'orchestrated' by Lucien Kroll at the **Catholic University of Louvain** in Belgium

entrance area of **Mothers' House**, refuge for mothers and children in Amsterdam, designed by Aldo van Eyck

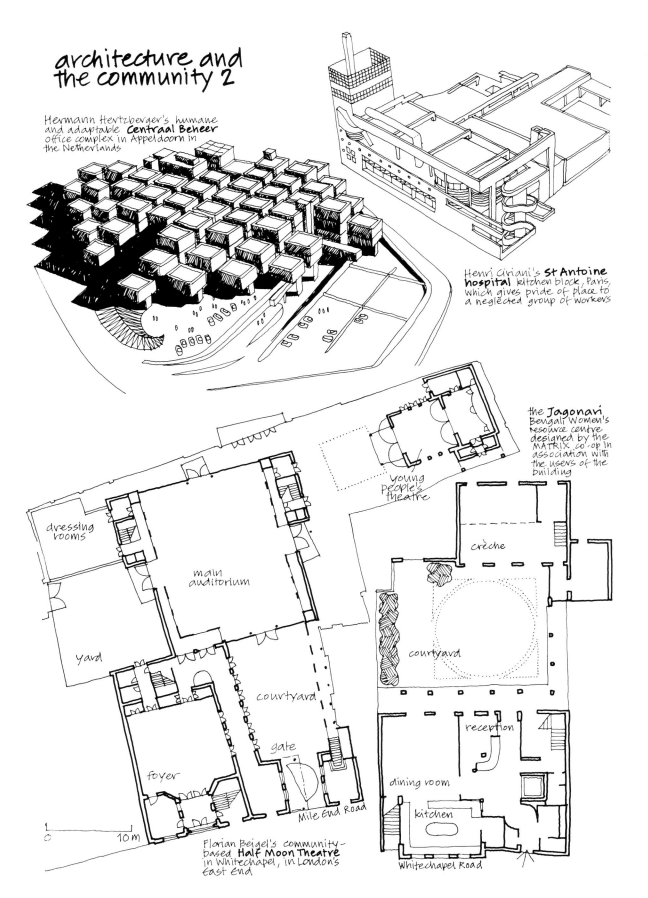

# architecture and the community 2

Hermann Hertzberger's humane and adaptable **Centraal Beheer** office complex in Appeldoorn in the Netherlands

Henri Ciriani's **St Antoine hospital** kitchen block, Paris, which gives pride of place to a neglected group of workers

the **Jagonari** Bengali Women's resource centre designed by the MATRIX .co-op in association with the users of the building

young people's theatre

dressing rooms

main auditorium

yard

courtyard

gate

foyer

Mile End Road

0    10 m

Florian Beigel's community-based **Half Moon Theatre** in Whitechapel, in London's East End

crèche

courtyard

reception

dining room

kitchen

Whitechapel Road

environment. More energy is used during the building process itself, still more by the finished buildings, for the whole of their useful life, and more again by their eventual demolition and disposal. This huge energy demand contributes significantly to global warming and the depletion of the ozone layer. This is not, it should be stressed, an argument against industrial society, still less against up-to-date building technology, both of which are very necessary, but against the way production is organised, and buildings are conceived, as functions of the process of capital accumulation.

## ENVIRONMENTAL DESIGN

From the 1960s onwards, many people in the older capitalist countries began to get concerned about 'the environment'. As a result, governments and corporations began to recognise the problems. Many early analyses of the environmental problem, such as the Club of Rome's report *The Limits to Growth* (1972) and the report of the Brandt Commission (1980), took it as axiomatic that a better environmental future was synonymous with the more efficient working of capitalism. Capitalism, however, depends on continuous expansion and exploitation, and can itself offer no real solutions. The process of 'development' encourages Newly Industrialising Countries to exploit their environment to the limit. So-called 'green' initiatives are more easily accepted in the richer countries, with their long history of exploitation already comfortably behind them, but even here progress is slow. Governments may attempt to pass laws to achieve higher environmental standards, but powerful interest groups stand in the way, ready to oppose or subvert the legislation, or to look for ways of turning the environmental measures themselves into profits. Capitalists can persuade sympathetic governments to drag their feet, so that even the most basic of controls are delayed again and again. The Kyoto protocol to limit greenhouse gas emissions, acclaimed as a breakthrough in 1997, is still not fully ratified.

However, despite the problems, some theorists and practitioners offered ways out of the straitjacket of the market system. The scientist James Lovelock's 'Gaia' hypothesis (1979) suggested a new way of looking at the earth as a complete organism. Fritz Schumacher proposed a practical course of action. His concept of intermediate technology was founded on communality, local workplaces and small production units. Instead of people serving the needs of capital, capital would begin to serve the needs of people.

Architects began to pick up on these themes, in demonstration buildings which used materials from renewable sources, conserved energy, recycled waste, and respected the natural landscape. Arthur Quarmby built Underhill, an earth-sheltered house in Yorkshire, England, as early as 1974, and in the late 1970s Thomas Herzog was building small houses with high levels of thermal performance in rural Germany. A house by Malcolm Wells at Brewster, Mass., (1980), and one by Obie Bowman at the Sea Ranch development in California (1987), showed how successfully buildings could be integrated with the local landscape. During the early 1980s the Australian architect Richard Leplastrier, in houses in and around Sydney, demonstrated his poetic use of cheap, humble materials, like galvanised iron, corrugated plastic, wood and hardboard, which seemed to draw on the informal housing tradition of the native Australians. The same tradition was developed by the American architect Kimberly Ackert in her 'Australian house of the future' (1992) in Western Australia. Postmodernism met environmental architecture in the so-called 'Soft and Hairy House' (1994), a mixture of playful architectural forms and serious environmental purpose designed by the Findlay-Ushida Partnership, at Tsukuba, Japan. At the open-air Museum of Welsh Life, near Cardiff, Jestico and Whiles built the House for the Future (2001), a combination of traditional Welsh building and up-to-date technology. The 'Buried House' (2009), built mostly underground in a sensitive rural landscape at Vals in Switzerland by SeArch and Christian Müller, achieved a remarkable affinity with the landscape. Not only was it visually reticent, but it also reduced the need for cooling in summer and heating in winter to the minimum.

Large environmentally-friendly housing developments were comparatively rare, but one of the best was Bill Dunster's Beddington Zero Energy Development, or 'BedZed' (2000), a cluster of 99 dwellings in south London. As its name suggests, the energy it used was generated on-site, from solar panels, and from its south-facing orientation, making use of passive solar heat gain. Much of its water supply was recycled rainwater, and it was made of materials that were themselves recycled or from renewable sources, obtained locally to avoid the 'embodied' energy costs of long-distance transport. The development itself was car-free, and accessed by public transport.

From the 1970s environmental principles were applied to non-residential buildings too. Public sector and community buildings were an obvious choice. Numerous schools were built in Hampshire, England, between 1974 and 1992, under the direction of the County Architect, Colin Stansfield-Smith. The best known was perhaps the Queen's Inclosure Middle School at Cowplain, the design of which maximised natural lighting and controlled solar heat gain. Many of the more recent projects of Ted Cullinan, in England, did the same, and also used renewable materials. These included the Renewable Energy Centre at Delabole in Cornwall (1999), and his building at the Weald and Downland Open Air Museum (2001), the first British use of the semi-natural 'grid-shell' timber construction.

Gradually the commercial sector too began to accept that environmental design could be good business. The later tower blocks of Ken Yeang in Malaysia, from his Menara Mesiniaga onwards, were examples of his 'bioclimatic' design, bringing up-to-date building technology and ecological principles together. At his research workshops near Genoa (1991) Renzo Piano and his collaborators investigated the use of plant fibres in architecture. His reworking of the Schlumberger Corporation's site at Montrouge near Paris (1981), turned a utilitarian industrial complex into a humane, naturalist landscape. The same was done on a larger scale by the American architect William McDonough, at the Ford Corporation's huge Rouge River site at Dearborn, Mich. He dealt with the problems of a polluted river and a badly drained site by the use grassy landscapes and the world's largest 'sedum' roof. His later Lewis Center at Oberlin College, Ohio (2000) and his headquarters building for YouTube at San Bruno, Calif. were key examples of environmentally friendly design, in which solar power and recycling played a major part. McDonough, mainly through his and Michael Braungart's book *Cradle to Cradle* (2009), argued the possibility of a rapprochement between industry and the environment. This seemed to be borne out by McDonough's own buildings and a growing number of others, including the Sonnenschiff Solar City in Freiburg (2009), a complex of commercial buildings with a big array of solar roofs which generated four times the energy that they consumed.

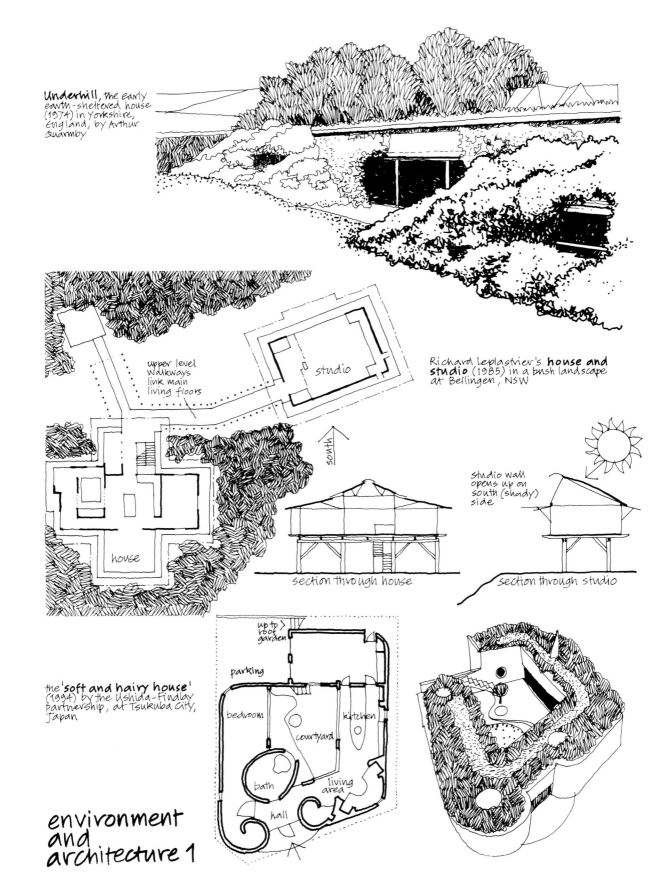

**Underhill**, the early earth-sheltered house (1974) in Yorkshire, England, by Arthur Quarmby

upper level walkways link main living floors

studio

Richard Leplastrier's **house and studio** (1985) in a bush landscape at Bellingen, NSW

south

house

studio wall opens up on south (shady) side

section through house

section through studio

the 'soft and hairy house' (1994) by the Ushida-Findlay Partnership, at Tsukuba City, Japan

up to roof garden

parking

bedroom

courtyard

kitchen

bath

living area

hall

environment and architecture 1

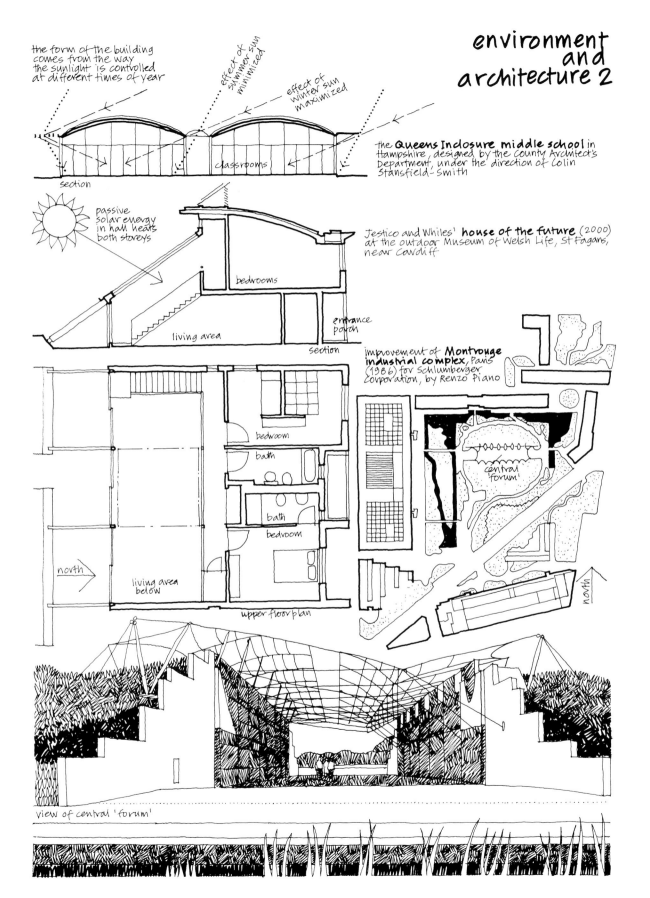

the form of the building comes from the way the sunlight is controlled at different times of year

effect of summer sun minimized

effect of winter sun maximized

classrooms

section

the **Queens Inclosure middle school** in Hampshire, designed by the County Architect's Department, under the direction of Colin Stansfield-Smith

passive solar energy in hall heats both storeys

bedrooms

living area

entrance porch

section

Jestico and Whiles' **house of the future** (2000) at the outdoor Museum of Welsh Life, St Fagans, near Cardiff

improvement of **Montrouge industrial complex**, Paris (1986) for Schlumberger Corporation, by Renzo Piano

central forum

bedroom

bath

bath

bedroom

north

living area below

upper floor plan

north

view of central 'forum'

# environment and architecture 3

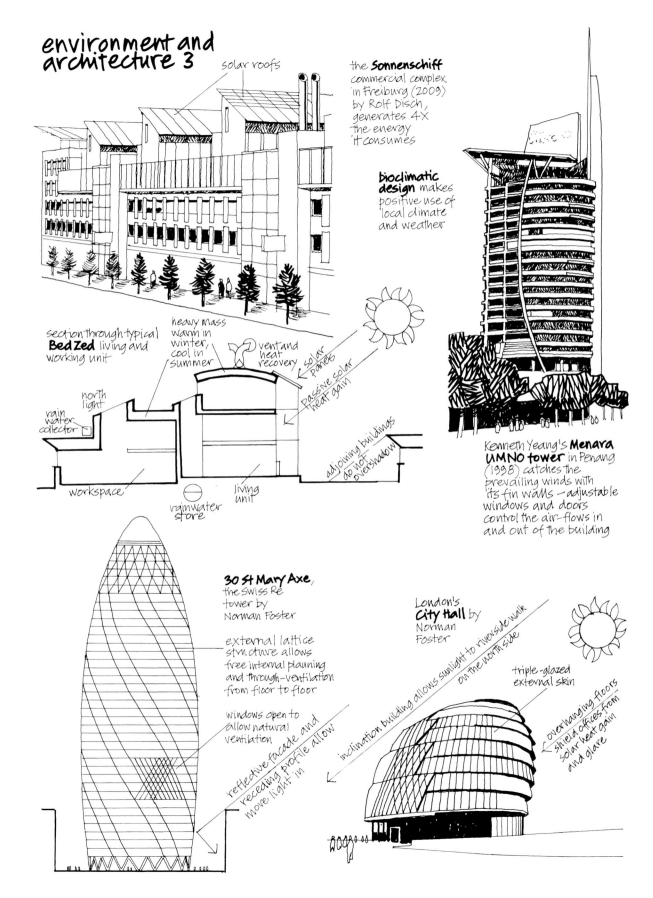

solar roofs

the **Sonnenschiff** commercial complex in Freiburg (2009) by Rolf Disch, generates 4x the energy it consumes

**bioclimatic design** makes positive use of local climate and weather

section through typical **BedZed** living and working unit

heavy mass warm in winter, cool in summer

vent and heat recovery

solar panels

passive solar heat gain

north light

rain water collector

workspace

rainwater store

living unit

adjoining buildings do not overshadow

Kenneth Yeang's **Menara UMNO tower** in Penang (1998) catches the prevailing winds with its fin walls – adjustable windows and doors control the air-flows in and out of the building

**30 St Mary Axe**, the Swiss Re tower by Norman Foster

external lattice structure allows free internal planning and through-ventilation from floor to floor

windows open to allow natural ventilation

reflective facade and receding profile allow more light in

London's **City Hall** by Norman Foster

inclination building allows sunlight to riverside walk on the north side

triple-glazed external skin

overhanging floors shield offices from solar heat gain and glare

Commercial architects like Norman Foster made forays into environmental design. Two of his buildings stand out from the remainder of his work for their serious environmental purpose. His office tower in the City of London for Swiss Re had an external lattice structure incorporating a light, efficient outside skin which provided both natural daylight and natural ventilation. Its elegant shape, earning the sobriquet 'The Gherkin', was designed to reflect light to the surrounding buildings and to the public space below. It soon displaced its neighbour, the Lloyd's building, as the symbol of a modernised City of London. Equally symbolic was his City Hall, an office on the south side of the Thames to house the new Greater London Authority. Faced largely in glass for its notional 'transparency' as a public building, it was also heavily insulated. Shaped like a distorted egg, it was angled south towards the sun, to reduce solar heat gain and to allow more light to reach a public walkway on the north side. Its cooling system made use of a natural spring far below the ground.

Sometimes, environmental ideas were embraced by whole communities. The rural community of the Centre for Alternative Technology, near Machynlleth in Wales, was one of the best-known groups researching into alternative energy sources and energy conservation. The town of Davis in California developed a programme of recycling and energy conservation. Curitiba in southern Brazil became well-known for its many environmental initiatives, including its well-run bus system and its environmental educational programmes.

During the last two decades of the 20th century, mainstream politics had moved further to the right. The repressive regimes of Eastern Europe had been a long way from real socialism, but their collapse in the late 1980s provided reactionaries everywhere with the opportunity to declare that socialism was now dead. The over-riding architectural symbol of the times was not a building but the demolition of one – the fall in 1989 of the Berlin Wall, which had been a reminder of a sorely divided Europe since the early sixties. In the newly united Berlin, Leonard Bernstein conducted a performance of Beethoven's Choral Symphony in which Schiller's reference to *Freude* (Joy) was replaced with *Freiheit* (Freedom). It seemed possible to say, with Francis Fukuyama, author of *The End of History and the Last Man* (1992), that there were no more great ideological battles to be fought, and that history itself was 'at an end'. This was the final justification for politicians everywhere – if justification were needed in an increasingly cynical political climate – to recast their policies in the mould of capitalism, as if it, with all its contradictions, were the only possible way forward.

AN UNEQUAL WORLD

But with the start of the 21st century, this view became ever more difficult to justify. December 31st 1999, or 'Y2K' as it was apprehensively known, passed without the world coming to an end. This was a relief, but there could be little cause for optimism. The first decade was dominated by the politics of President George W. Bush, his advisors and the heads of friendly states. Elected to the White House in 2000, he inherited the Reaganite plan for a 'New American Century', based on a strong arms economy, and an ideology of military intervention, with the aim of spreading market capitalism to the rest of the world.

There followed a series of destructive wars, in Afghanistan, Iraq, Darfur, Pakistan, Lebanon, Chad, Somalia, Georgia and Gaza, and also their corollary, a wave of guerrilla counter-attacks, in New York, Bali, Moscow, Madrid, Beslan, London, East Timor and Mumbai. There was also an over-reliance on the financial markets. The 'dot-com' boom of the 1990s proved to be a bubble. Yet uninhibited speculation on the markets continued, fully encouraged by western governments, and brought more crisis. The US mortgage crash of 2007 caused a sharp drop in share prices. The following year the world entered a further, deeper recession, affecting both the de-industrialising First World and the Newly Industrialising Countries.

This latter term, in common use since the 1970s to describe the southeast Asian 'tiger' economies, now described a world-wide phenomenon. The fastest growing economies were, in order, those of China, India, Brazil, Mexico, Turkey, Thailand, South Africa, Malaysia and the Philippines. Their growth was based on the industrial production which the First World countries were rapidly losing. They increasingly espoused free market economies, with all the exploitation which this implied. To attract inward investment, wages were kept low and employment rights weak, and the great cities were the focus of this process.

In the late 20th century the IT revolution encouraged theories that the city was now at an end. Financial transactions could now be carried out on-line, rather than face-to-face, so the virtual office, it was thought, would replace the physical one. This however, underestimated the office building as an exchange-value, that is, as a piece of valuable real-estate and indeed as a visual symbol of power. In 1973, New York and Chicago, like the primitive capitalist cities of the Italian Renaissance, had competed to build the world's tallest building, the former with the twin towers of Yamasaki's World Trade Center, and the latter with the Sears Tower, now the Willis Tower, by the Chicago architects Skidmore Owings and Merrill (SOM). Such architectural hubris did not diminish. The twin Petronas Towers in Kuala Lumpur (1998), by César Pelli, then became the highest buildings in the world, but were overtaken in 2004 by Li Zuyuan's Taipei 101 in Taiwan and in turn by SOM's Burj Khalifa in Dubai (2010), with its unprecedented height of 828 metres. Dubai has the largest number of high buildings in the world.

A more subtle kind of prestige could be obtained by using private capital to sponsor public buildings. Here, developers could claim to be socially responsible, and the architectural drama could come not from the buildings' great height but from their spectacular imagery. Many designers were also academics, teachers at the most fashionable schools of architecture, like Harvard, Yale and the Architectural Association. Conceived in discourses with students, artists and theorists, the angular shapes of deconstructivism moved out of the studios onto the building sites. Sometimes, when they came to build, designers whose background was more theoretical than practical, needed to learn fast.

In 2005, Herzog and de Meuron built an extension to the Walker Art Center in Minneapolis and the De Young Museum in San Francisco. They were architects of the celebrated 'bird's nest' Stadium in Beijing, for the 2004 Olympics, and of the Forum building in Barcelona the same year. Local criticism of the Forum event itself was intensified by the fact that this building went considerably over budget. This problem has often occurred in contemporary architecture. This is partly because aspiring clients,

# the highest buildings

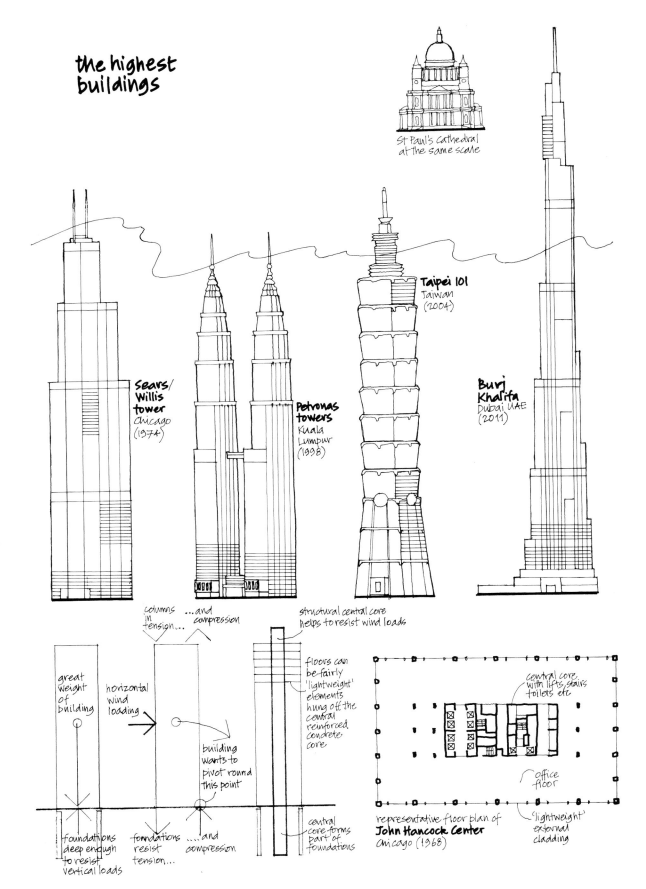

St Paul's Cathedral at the same scale

**Sears/ Willis tower**
Chicago (1974)

**Petronas towers**
Kuala Lumpur (1998)

**Taipei 101**
Taiwan (2004)

**Burj Khalifa**
Dubai UAE (2011)

columns in tension...

...and compression

structural central core helps to resist wind loads

great weight of building

horizontal wind loading

building wants to pivot round this point

floors can be fairly 'lightweight' elements hung off the central reinforced concrete core

foundations deep enough to resist vertical loads

foundations resist tension...

....and compression

central core forms part of foundations

central core with lifts, stairs, toilets etc

office floor

'lightweight' external cladding

representative floor plan of
**John Hancock Center**
Chicago (1968)

when they engage celebrity architects, are looking for unique, innovative buildings. There is always the danger that the excitement of innovation may come to take precedence over strict financial control. The sail-like roofs of the Sydney Opera House became a potent symbol of the city and of Australia, though the symbol was bought at considerable cost. The Scottish Parliament building at Holyrood in Edinburgh, by Enric Miralles, (2004) was similar. Its complex spaces, rich colours and textures and, above all, its open, democratic feeling gave it an equally strong, symbolic character, though its final cost exceeded its original budget by a factor of ten.

The later work of the influential Dutch architect Rem Koolhaas, and his prolific Office for Metropolitan Architecture (OMA), included the Seattle Central Library (2004), the Casa de Música in Porto (2005) and the headquarters for Chinese Television in Beijing (2009). Equally influential was the work of the Polish-born, American-based, Daniel Libeskind, with his Jewish Museum in Berlin (1999), his Imperial War Museum building in Manchester (2001) and his extension to the Denver Art Museum in Colorado (2006). Jean Nouvel, who had made his name with the Musée du Monde Arabe, later built the tall Torre Agbar in Barcelona (2003) and the modernist Guthrie Theater in Minneapolis (2006). The early reputation of the Iraqi-born Zaha Hadid was as a well-known teacher and a talented, but largely theoretical designer. But one of her designs was built, the Vitra fire station at Weil am Rhein, in 1994. Visually stunning and difficult to build, relying on the skills of a project architect to bring it into being, it was followed from about 2005 by a more rapid flow of practical commissions, many of which became widely admired for their powerful formalism. These included the BMW Central building in Leipzig (2005) and the MAXXI building (2010), Rome's museum of 21st century art.

Many of these architects, and their spectacular buildings, have won international prizes, like the Pritzker, or the RIBA Royal Gold Medal. Yet it would be difficult to claim that many of these buildings were serious contributions to environmental practice. With their expensive materials like steel, concrete and glass, full of embodied energy, and with their many heat-losing outside surfaces, they were buildings in which powerful sculptural expression seemed to be at least as important as environmental performance. Given the existence of BedZed and many other environmentally responsible projects, it is relevant to ask why prize-winning schemes cannot be zero-energy, as well.

For sheer architectural assertiveness it would be difficult to surpass Antilia House in Mumbai (2010). A tower block of some 27 storeys, it was designed by the US-based architects Perkins and Will, with Hirsch Bedner, for India's wealthiest industrialist. Though looking something like an office block, it was actually a single family house with 37000 square metres of floor-space, including a health spa, swimming pools, ballroom, helipad and multiple car parking – reputedly the world's most expensive house, in the world's most expensive area of real estate.

## THE POOR OF THE EARTH

The contrast between rich and poor is as apparent in Mumbai as anywhere. Of the city's 20 million population, over a million people are street-homeless, the highest number of any city in the world. Others have roofs over their heads, but these are the roofs of informal shanty towns, the largest, Dharavi, sheltering another million people. Over

# Deconstructionism

the building is clad mostly in copper

the **De Young Museum** in San Francisco by Herzog and de Meuron (2005)

the fragmented forms of the **Scottish Parliament** building in Edinburgh by Enric Miralles (2004)

Zaha Hadid's **Fire Station** for the Vitra Company in Weil-am-Rhein (1999) was later turned into a furniture museum

Daniel Libeskind's **Jewish Museum** in Berlin (1999) – its jagged forms are clad in zinc sheeting and are intended to convey a feeling of disorientation and windowless claustrophobia

half of Mumbai's population live in slums, crowded onto no more than 6% of the city's land. One of the biggest problems is health. Avoidable parasitic diseases caused by pollution, inadequate water supply and drainage cause 40% of the deaths among the poor population.

Altogether, in both the Third World and in the rapidly growing economies of the Newly Industrialising Countries, a billion people live in slums, in *bustees*, *favelas* and *barrios* on the edges of great cities which have capitalist economies at their heart. Mumbai's slum dwellers, like many others in the world, strive to take part in this economy, manufacturing goods from recycled rubbish, or working in the service sector, often through child labour. In the sixties and seventies it used to be common to talk of 'slums of hope' – how they were self-reliant and resourceful places, with strong community ties. But as cities grow hope diminishes, and slum communities increasingly get uprooted and displaced by ambitious landlords and developers anxious to join in the building boom. More and more, the slum dwellers of the world are pushed onto peripheral land which developers have no use for – the margins of polluted rivers or toxic lakes, rubbish mountains, slide areas and flood-plains, earthquake and tsunami regions. 'Natural' disasters may well be natural, but their human tragedies are generally man-made.

In class-society, great cities are divided spatially, so that extremes of wealth and poverty can co-exist in their appointed economic roles, but physically separate from each other. Engels described the lighted boulevards of 19th century Manchester, which took the wealthy from home to work, without their having to see or smell the poverty-stricken districts behind, on which their wealth nevertheless depended. It has long been the practice to separate the unfortunate from the privileged, whether in Haussmann's Paris or the Warsaw Ghetto, or Stalinist Berlin.

In the 21st century, such separation reached a new level. The barriers between Israel and the West Bank and Gaza, begun in 2003, are a complex of concrete walls, electric fences, movement sensors, cameras, road blocks and checkpoints. They are supported by patrols in the sky above and strategic roads underground – the three-dimensional architecture of control. The woods, olive groves and farmland valued by the writers of the Book of Leviticus are increasingly covered with concrete. The destruction of both the social and the environmental fabric go together.

Cities reflect the nature of class-society and of modern capitalism, which depends on a comparatively small group owning the means of production and appropriating its wealth to themselves. Of the world's population of 7 billion, the richest 10% own 85% of its wealth. The poorest 50% own no more than 1%. The hegemony of the global North over the South is secured in numerous ways, from the subversion of independence movements, the fomenting of local wars, and the appointment of friendly puppet rulers, to the restructuring of local economies to fit the demands of the market, and the burden of insupportable debt repayments. The high quality of the some people's living conditions can only be achieved *because* of the poor quality of the remainder.

At the beginning of this story of western architecture, building was a way of meeting people's needs, not only for shelter but also for fulfilment and self-development. At the end of the 18th century, in the first years of the Industrial Revolution, Schiller described man as becoming 'little more than a fragment' of the Whole:

# architecture of separation

the closely-packed streets of the **Warsaw Ghetto** during the Second World War, severed and contained by the Wall

the Wall

400,000 people were confined in about eight square kilometres

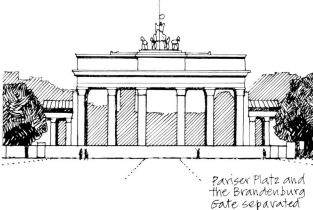

Pariser Platz and the Brandenburg Gate separated from West Berlin

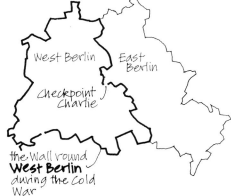

West Berlin

East Berlin

Checkpoint Charlie

the Wall round **West Berlin** during the Cold War

the Green Line

the Wall

Mediterranean

Jenin

Q Nablus

Israel

West Bank

Ramallah

Jordan

Jerusalem

Beth lehem

Dead Sea

Q Hebron

**the Wall** separating Aida Camp in Bethlehem from Jerusalem

the key is the symbol of the camp, and represents return to the land

Many refugees still hold the keys of their old houses, long since demolished

the Wall

He never develops the harmony of his being, and instead of putting the stamp of humanity on his own nature, he becomes nothing more than the imprint of his occupation or his specialized knowledge.

By the beginning of the 21st century, the complex, fragmentary nature of the building process reflected this alienation ever more deeply. Our society encourages schools of architecture to compete in the pursuit of academic recognition; professional bodies aim to protect the income and status of their members; the heads of architectural practices pursue profitability; their employees' main concern, inevitably, is job protection. The architectural profession as a whole is separated from the building industry by its different education, outlook and interests; the industry itself is polarised, as are all capitalist institutions, between capital and labour. All of these participants are separated, through the alienation of the development process, from the anonymous users for whom they are designing or building. And dominating all this is the economic logic of capitalism itself, and its treatment of buildings as marketable commodities rather than social needs.

The market does not meet, nor does it aim to meet, the needs of most of the people of the world. Though our alienated system has resulted in many fine buildings which continue to arouse the senses and uplift the spirit, it has not helped to create a better overall environment. Still less does it enable the mass of the people to be involved in the creation and control of that environment, and bring them any sense of fulfilment. Great buildings do not exist *despite* the fact that so many people live in privation, but *because* they do.

Through history, there have always been those who have sought something better for humanity. Socrates, Plato and the builders of the Acropolis aspired to the Ideal, which would transcend ordinary life. St Augustine, the gothic master-masons and the Byzantine iconographers tried to open people's eyes to the heavenly glory which lay above and beyond the earthly world. The Renaissance artists and architects focussed attention on humankind, and the greatness it was capable of. The thinkers of the Enlightenment and of the French Revolution of 1789 sought to create a new world of universal freedom and brotherhood. In the 19th century, both the reformists and the revolutionaries had their strategies for moving society on, beyond the exploitative capitalist system. The October Revolution of 1917 encouraged the Constructivists and other early modernists to use their work to help create a new socialist society. The architects who built the modern Welfare State tried to re-cast this hoped-for socialist society in the image of a benign sort of capitalism.

The current hegemony of the free market closes down formal avenues for seeking a more equitable world and a more balanced environment. There is little formal opposition. But outside formal politics, political and environmental activists at all levels, all over the world, are seeking change, sometimes violently, sometimes by just getting on with things that improve people's lives. To their credit, many architects participate in this process, and make a real *qualitative* difference to the way some people live. The *quantitative* problem remains – how to extend such benefits to the greater part of the world population. It is difficult to escape Rosa Luxemburg's conclusion that a more equal society can only be built on the ruins of the bourgeois state.

# FURTHER READING

Our story of western architecture, covering 5000 years or more, is well documented. Here are some of the books I found most useful and informative.

## HISTORY

As a primer on historical thought, Edward Hallet Carr's *What is History?* is justly popular. Less popular today, but nonetheless fundamental, are the first part of *The German Ideology* by Marx and Engels, and Volume One of the latter's *Capital*, rich and exciting reading which places the study of history at the heart of human society. Colin McEvedy's *Penguin Atlases of Ancient, Medieval and Modern History* provide a good basic introduction to the political and economic history of the West.

## ARCHITECTURAL AND URBAN HISTORY

Like 'the Bible and Shakespeare' to the notional castaway, Banister Fletcher's huge *History of Architecture* is a 'given' for the architectural historian. Nikolaus Pevsner's *Outline of European Architecture* is less compendious, but imbued with the liberal values of a great art historian. Patrick Nuttgens' *The Story of Architecture* is an approachable primer, covering the whole world and placing architecture firmly in a social context. For those to whom Lewis Mumford's great *The City in History* is too daunting, Arthur Korn's *History Builds the Town* is more friendly. Both have been around for some time, but can be brought up to date with Peter Hall's fine account of modern city building, *Cities of Tomorrow*.

## ANCIENT TIMES

Gordon Childe's classic work, *What Happened in History*, established the concept of the 'urban revolution'. James Henry Breasted's *History of Egypt*, dating from 1905, is still the touchstone for all who write on the subject. Dieter Arnold's recent *Encyclopedia of Ancient Egyptian Architecture* is both learned and approachable. I have found A.R. and Mary Burn's *The Living Past of Greece* useful both as a primer and a site-specific guidebook. Mortimer Wheeler's *Roman Art and Architecture* is still one of the best accounts available. And, of course, the ancients wrote their own history, those of Herodotus and Plutarch being entertaining, if not always factual, and Vitruvius' *Ten Books on Architecture* have had a lasting influence.

## THE CHRISTIAN ERA

The historical background is provided by Hugh Trevor-Roper's *The Rise of Christian Europe* and by Gerald Hodgett's *Social and Economic History of Medieval Europe*. Henri Pirenne's famous old study *Medieval Cities* describes the rise of the urban bourgeoisie. Richard Krautheimer's *Early Christian and Byzantine Architecture* is a classic work, as are many of the writings of Tamara and David Talbot-Rice, whose joint expertise on Byzantine and early Russian art and architecture is unrivalled. The same can be said of Kenneth Conant in the field of Romanesque architecture and of John Harvey in the Gothic. The former's *Carolingian and Romanesque Architecture* and the latter's *The Master Builders* are seminal works. The Middle Ages were chronicled by monks like Bede, laymen like Froissart, and there are also the architectural notebooks of Villard de Honnecourt.

THE EARLY MODERN WORLD

The classic background work is Jacob Burckhardt's *Civilization of the Renaissance in Italy*. Key architectural studies include Rudolf Wittkover's *Architectural Principles in the Age of Humanism*, John Summerson's *The Classical Language of Architecture* and Leonardo Benevolo's two-volume *The Architecture of the Renaissance*. The rise of the Renaissance artist is described in Peter Burke's *Tradition and Innovation in Renaissance Italy*. In their day, Alberti, Serlio, Palladio and De l'Orme all wrote post-Vitruvian architectural manuals. The exciting life of a contemporary artist is graphically described in the *Autobiography* of the goldsmith Benvenuto Cellini, and a great artist's intellectual development is charted in the *Notebooks* of Leonardo da Vinci.

THE INDUSTRIAL AGE

The historical background is nowhere better described than in Eric Hobsbawm's *The Age of Revolution 1789–1848* and his *Industry and Empire*, the latter dealing with the 19th and early 20th centuries. The rise of class divisions in the Victorian city was observed by many contemporaries, notably Friedrich Engels, whose *Condition of the Working Class in England* described 19th century Manchester. Later historians of capitalism and its effects have included Edward Thompson in *The Making of the English Working Class*, John Kasson, whose *Civilizing the Machine* charts the rise of Republican America, and Peter Carroll and David Noble in their radical history of the United States, *The Free and the Unfree*. *Victorian Architecture*, by Robert Furneaux Jordan, is a good basic introduction. Utopianism in architecture is the theme of Helen Rosenau's *Social Purpose in Architecture*, and gothic stylism is that of Kenneth Clark's early *The Gothic Revival*. The transition from the 19th to the 20th centuries is charted in Nikolaus Pevsner's famous *Pioneers of Modern Design*: from William Morris to Walter Gropius – though he mistakes Morris for an impossible dreamer, when in fact Morris's own late writings, like 'The Beauty of Life', or 'Useful Work versus Useless Toil', are unique in the 19th century for their perceptiveness of the nature of capitalism.

THE CONTEMPORARY WORLD

For me, the best account of the historical background is Eric Hobsbawm's *Age of Anxiety: the short twentieth century*. Modern architecture gave rise to many vaunting manifestoes, two of the most significant being Le Corbusier's *Vers une Architecture* and El Lissitzky's *Russia: an Architecture for World Revolution*. J M (Jim) Richards was an eloquent advocate of modernism, and his short *Modern Architecture* expressed the excitement of the time it was written. Two good, compendious accounts of the development of modern architecture, both in two volumes, and neither from an Anglo-Saxon point of view, are Leonardo Benevolo's *The History of Modern Architecture*, and Manfredo Tafuri and Francesco Dal Co's *Modern Architecture*. My own *Modern Architecture and Design: an alternative history* is a one-volume survey. Modernism was challenged in Robert Venturi's influential *Complexity and Contradiction in Architecture*, and the challenge was codified by Charles Jencks in *The Language of Postmodern Architecture* and later surveyed in Diane Ghirardo's *Architecture after Modernism*. Malcolm Millais' *Exploding the Myths of Modern Architecture* is the forthright view of a structural engineer. Postmodernisn itself was criticised, in a scholarly way by David Harvey in *The Condition of Postmodernity*, and more polemically by me in *Fantastic Form; Architecture and Planning today*. Two of the best books on eco-design are slightly peripheral to architecture: E.F. Schumacher's classic *Small is Beautiful* and Victor Papanek's *Design for the Real World*. There are many – perhaps too many – glossy books on the more spectacular examples of contemporary architecture, but against them one must set two major works on the pathology of today's city, Eyal Weizman's *Hollow Land* and Mike Davis's *Planet of Slums*, both essential reading. In some respects, books, including this one, go out of date. Magazines, and their websites, are essential for keeping in touch. For me, two of the most useful are *Building Design* and *Architecture Today*.

# Index